Building the Army's Backbone

STUDIES IN CANADIAN MILITARY HISTORY
Series editor: Andrew Burtch, Canadian War Museum

The Canadian War Museum, Canada's national museum of military history, has a threefold mandate: to remember, to preserve, and to educate. Studies in Canadian Military History, published by UBC Press in association with the Museum, extends this mandate by presenting the best of contemporary scholarship to provide new insights into all aspects of Canadian military history, from earliest times to recent events. The work of a new generation of scholars is especially encouraged, and the books employ a variety of approaches – cultural, social, intellectual, economic, political, and comparative – to investigate gaps in the existing historiography. The books in the series feed immediately into future exhibitions, programs, and outreach efforts by the Canadian War Museum. A list of the titles in the series appears at the end of the book.

CANADIAN WAR MUSEUM
MUSÉE CANADIEN DE LA GUERRE

Building the Army's Backbone
Canadian Non-Commissioned Officers in the Second World War

Andrew L. Brown

31 30 29 28 27 26 25 24 23 22   5 4 3 2 1

Printed in Canada on FSC-certified ancient-forest-free paper (100% post-consumer recycled) that is processed chlorine- and acid-free.

Library and Archives Canada Cataloguing in Publication

Title: Building the army's backbone : Canadian non-commissioned officers in the Second World War / Andrew L. Brown.

Names: Brown, Andrew L. (Andrew Lawrence), author.

Series: Studies in Canadian military history.

Description: Series statement: Studies in Canadian military history | Includes bibliographical references and index.

Identifiers: Canadiana (print) 20210313706 | Canadiana (ebook) 20210313846 | ISBN 9780774866965 (hardcover) | ISBN 9780774866972 (softcover) | ISBN 9780774866989 (PDF) | ISBN 9780774866996 (EPUB)

Subjects: LCSH: Canada. Canadian Army – Non-commissioned officers – History – 20th century. | LCSH: Canada. Canadian Army – Non-commissioned officers – Training of – History – 20th century. | LCSH: Canada. Canadian Army – Non-commissioned officers – Recruiting, enlistment, etc. – History – 20th century. | LCSH: World War, 1939–1945 – Canada.

Classification: LCC UB409.C3 B76 2021 | DDC 355.3/38 – dc23

Canadä

UBC Press gratefully acknowledges the financial support for our publishing program of the Government of Canada (through the Canada Book Fund), the Canada Council for the Arts, and the British Columbia Arts Council.

This book has been published with the help of a grant from the Canadian Federation for the Humanities and Social Sciences, through the Awards to Scholarly Publications Program, using funds provided by the Social Sciences and Humanities Research Council of Canada.

Publication of this book has been financially supported by the Canadian War Museum.

Printed and bound in Canada by Friesens
Set in Helvetica Condensed and Minion by Artegraphica Design Co.
Copy editor: Camilla Blakeley
Proofreader: Caitlin Gordon-Walker
Indexer: Cheryl Lemmens
Cover designer: George Kirkpatrick

UBC Press
The University of British Columbia
2029 West Mall
Vancouver, BC V6T 1Z2
www.ubcpress.ca

In memory of Colin Newman Brown

Contents

List of Figures and Tables / ix

Acknowledgments / xi

Abbreviations / xiii

Introduction / 3

1 Profile of the Infantry Senior NCOs / 19

2 NCO Development before the War / 45

3 The Wartime Army's Expectations of Its NCOs / 59

4 Wartime Drivers of NCO Development / 80

5 Unit and Formation Programs / 99

6 The Mass Army's Programs in Canada / 121

7 The Mass Army's Programs in the United Kingdom / 151

8 Managing the Talent / 172

Conclusion / 208

Notes / 217

Bibliography / 261

Index / 267

Figures and Tables

Figures

I.1 Strategic milestones and key NCO development programs / 16

1.1 Regimental Sergeant Major Wendell Clark / 38

2.1 Sergeant's Qualification Certificate / 48

3.1 Company Sergeant Major James A. Smith / 78

4.1 General Harry Crerar inspecting troops / 93

4.2 Sergeant Wilson training privates to use the PIAT / 96

5.1 Brigadier Howard D. Graham addressing a class of Royal Canadian Regiment NCOs / 111

6.1 No. 2 Infantry Training Centre, Borden, Ontario / 123

6.2 NCO parachute instructors / 134

7.1 Training at No. 5 Battle Wing, Canadian Training School / 153

7.2 Canadian Reinforcement Units training path / 162

8.1 Reinforcement soldiers disembarking from troopship / 179

8.2 Sergeant William MacLeod, veteran of North Africa / 192

8.3 Lieutenant-General Guy Simonds inspecting troops / 202

Tables

I.1 Canadian non-commissioned ranks and associated positions in infantry units / 7

I.2 Growth of the NCO corps / 10

1.1 Infantry senior NCO education levels / 21

1.2 Infantry senior NCO religious affiliation / 22

1.3 Infantry senior NCO pre-service employment or trade / 23

1.4 Infantry senior NCO provinces/jurisdictions of origin / 23

1.5 Average progression rate to the rank of sergeant / 24

1.6 Average time from joining the active army to becoming sergeant / 25

1.7 Soldiers skipping ranks/appointments in NCO advancement / 26

1.8 NCOs reverting in rank / 28

1.9 Canadian army NCO training programs / 29

1.10 Wartime NCOs with experience in the NPAM or Reserve Army/ 40

1.11 Length of service in the NPAM or Reserve Army / 41

1.12 Period when active duty soldiers served in the NPAM or Reserve Army / 42

1.13 Warrant officers with previous military experience / 43

6.1 Three-week syllabus, Junior Leaders School, Mégantic, September 1941 / 126

6.2 Six-week syllabus, Junior Leaders School, Mégantic, March 1943 / 127

6.3 Syllabus for A29 Instructor/NCO course, May 1942 / 130

6.4 Syllabus for Assistant Instructor Course, A15 Shilo, May 1945 / 137

7.1 Syllabus for CMHQ Course 804 (NCO Qualification) / 154

7.2 Syllabus for Canadian reinforcement units two-week refresher course / 161

7.3 Syllabus for two-week NCO conversion course (infantry) / 168

Acknowledgments

I owe gratitude to many. The non-commissioned officers who are the subject of this book must be front and centre. These soldiers gave so much in helping to destroy the dreadful regime that started the Second World War. I hope that this book promotes the recognition they deserve.

I wish to thank those who made it possible for me to pursue this project. I extend deep gratitude to Douglas Delaney for his mentorship and for helping me bring coherence and focus to this undertaking. James Kenny has been a valued teacher and an inspiration. Howard Coombs, Jane Boulden, and Kevin Brushett generously tutored and shared their wisdom. Over many years, Brigadier-General (retired) Robert Williams encouraged my aspirations to be a soldier-scholar – and demonstrated how to do it. Thank you, all. I am also grateful for having colleagues whose passion and drive have inspired me to pursue the excellence they model. Mark Frost, Meghan Fitzpatrick, Andy Belyea, Arthur Gullachsen, John Keess, and Nick Wheeler, all real pros, make the workplace stimulating and gratifying. I am deeply indebted to Randy Schmidt, Megan Brand, and Carmen Tiampo at UBC Press for their counsel and support in bringing this project to fruition. I am also in debt to Camilla Blakely whose copy editing strengthened the text and saved me from several blunders.

I must also give thanks to many anonymous people who rendered invaluable assistance. I could not have investigated how the army built its NCO corps without the help of those who safeguard the nation's archived materials. Staff at the Library and Archives of Canada, the Directorate of History and Heritage at the Department of National Defence, and the Military History Research Centre at the Canadian War Museum, gave efficient, courteous support, for which I am grateful. So did the staff at the Royal Military College's Massey Library, whose small but superb collection proved invaluable. I am tremendously grateful for access to the repositories of interviews and personal accounts of the nation's veterans. The Canadian War Museum's Oral History Project, Historica Canada's The Memory Project, and the University of Victoria's Military Oral History Collection have rendered an irreplaceable service by capturing and preserving the voices of a generation that is receding from living memory. I thank also the anonymous manuscript reviewers for their important role in making this book possible.

While serving in the army, I have had the privilege of working for and with many outstanding NCOs, who remain unnamed here, too. These exceptional soldiers gave me a foundational appreciation of their role, which proved indispensable in contextualizing the archived records that informed the analysis in the pages that follow. Canadians are fortunate indeed to have in their service such soldiers.

The errors that remain in this work are mine alone.

I could not possibly have written this book without my family's assistance. My mother and father gave me a lifetime of unconditional love and support. My daughters, Amelia and Lindsay, have always been deeply patient with my professional obligations. Special recognition goes to my wife, Mari, who has supported me selflessly for three decades. She is my stalwart, lifelong fire-team partner and a tremendous source of strength for our daughters and me.

This book is dedicated to the memory of my father, who taught me how I ought to live and whose wisdom I continue to discover.

Abbreviations

AHQ	Army Headquarters
AITC	Advanced Infantry Training Centre
ALC	Assault landing craft
ATC	Advanced Training Centre
AWL	Absent without leave
bde	Brigade
BGS	brigadier general staff
bn	Battalion
BTC	Basic Training Centre
CASF	Canadian Active Service Force
CASF RO	Canadian Active Service Force Routine Orders
CBRG	Canadian Base Reinforcement Group
CCRA	Commander Corps Royal Artillery
CGS	chief of the general staff
CIB	Canadian Infantry Brigade
CIRU	Canadian Infantry Reinforcement Unit
CITB	Canadian Infantry Training Brigade
CITC	Canadian Infantry Training Centre
CITR	Canadian Infantry Training Regiment
CMHQ	Canadian Military Headquarters
Comd	Command/Commander
CRU	Canadian Reinforcement Unit
CSATC	Canadian Small Arms Training Centre
CSM	Company sergeant major
CTS	Canadian Training School
DCGH	Deputy Chief of the General Staff
DCM	Distinguished Conduct Medal
DCO	Directorate of Combined Operations
DHH	Directorate of History and Heritage
DIRU	Division Infantry Reinforcement Unit
DMO&I	director of military operations and intelligence
DMT	director/directorate of military training

DND	Department of National Defence
DOC	district officer commanding
GHQ	General Headquarters
GOC	general officer commanding
GOC-in-C	general officer commanding in chief
Inf	Infantry
Instr	Instructor
KR&O	King's Regulations and Orders
L/Cpl	lance corporal
LOB	Left out of battle
MND	minister of national defence
NDHQ	National Defence Headquarters
NCO	Non-commissioned officer
NS(NB)R	North Shore (New Brunswick) Regiment
OCTU	Officer Cadet Training Unit
OIC	officer in charge
ORs	Other ranks
OTC	Officers Training Centre
NPAM	Non-Permanent Active Militia
NRMA	National Resources Mobilization Act
PAM	Permanent Active Militia
PIAT	Projector, Infantry, Anti-Tank
PPCLI	Princess Patricia's Canadian Light Infantry
Pte	Private
QOR	Queen's Own Rifles
RAF	Royal Air Force
RCR	Royal Canadian Regiment
R22R	Royal 22nd Regiment
RSM	regimental sergeant major
SD&T	Staff Duties and Training
Sgt	Sergeant
SSM	squadron sergeant major
TEWT	Tactical exercise without troops
TOET	Tests of elementary training
trg	Training
VE	Victory in Europe
WD	War Diary
WNSR	West Nova Scotia Regiment
WO	warrant officer

Building the Army's Backbone

Introduction

Success in war comes as the result of effective leadership at many levels. The lowest is that of the non-commissioned officer who carries half-a-dozen men forward to take out an enemy position ... Both the NCO and the statesman-general play essential parts, and it is perhaps a little hard that Corporal Jones should be forgotten, while Marlborough's name is in every textbook ... without the Joneses there could be no Marlboroughs.

C.P. Stacey

Long-accepted wisdom maintains that non-commissioned officers (NCOs) form the backbone of any modern Western army. The logic underpinning this notion recognizes that, while commissioned officers tend to rotate regularly through unit and extra-unit postings, NCOs spend most of their careers on regimental duty, focused on training and operations. Within the unit, long-serving, veteran NCOs therefore safeguard tactical expertise, corporate memory, and general efficiency. These practised soldiers draw on their years of experience to maintain discipline among the rank and file, to serve as experts in the employment and maintenance of weaponry, to act as instructors, and, as tactical leaders in the field, to execute battle plans by leading the junior ranks in combat. But the well-reasoned notion that an effective army requires a corps of strong NCOs raises questions about how Canada built its Second World War army, because when the nation began to mobilize in 1939, a corps of long-serving NCOs with a bedrock of hard-won military expertise barely existed.[1] The wartime NCO corps had to grow out of the nation's tiny and badly equipped standing forces. In July 1939, Canada's regular force, known as the Permanent Active Militia, or permanent force, had only 4,261 soldiers of all ranks, nowhere near enough to supply all the NCOs needed for the wartime army.[2] A part-time force, the Non-Permanent Active Militia (NPAM), had NCOs who could be mobilized, but it had only 51,400 poorly trained, amateur soldiers of all ranks to draw from. Furthermore, when Canada declared war, its ground forces sorely lacked modern equipment, possessing only small stocks of mostly First World War–vintage weaponry. Even uniforms were in short supply.[3] Despite whatever enthusiasm they maintained, NCOs from Canada's peacetime military had little or no expertise in fighting with modern weapons, let alone in teaching new soldiers how to use them.

Yet out of such humble beginnings grew a large and capable Canadian army. By March 1944, the active army had reached a peak strength of 495,804, which included an expeditionary contingent of five divisions and two independent armoured brigades for service in Europe, plus substantial home defence forces.[4] Historians have done a good job of counting the soldiers and formations that Canada put into the field, and of analyzing what they did in battle.[5] But they have yet to explain how Canada developed a corps of NCOs to train the rank and file and help the army win on the battlefield.

Prewar mobilization plans did account for the requirement to raise NCOs, as encapsulated in two key documents: Defence Scheme No. 3, a closely guarded blueprint that few saw; and the complementary but less specific *Mobilization Instructions for the Canadian Militia*, a document issued widely across the army in 1937. But historians have not scrutinized the NCO-related sections of these documents, nor investigated how NCO mobilization schemes were actually implemented. In fact, the literature does not even indicate whether or not a plan for raising an NCO corps existed before 1939, let alone how the army built its backbone after Canada joined the war. This book seeks to fill the historiographical gap by answering the question: how did the Canadian army develop its NCO corps during the Second World War? It argues that the wartime force used a two-track system consisting of *decentralized* training and development programs (run by units and their parent formations, the brigades and divisions) and *centralized* programs (overseen by the army) – a hybrid of regimental- and mass-army approaches. Decentralized training occurred as units and formations designed and ran programs for their own troops as schedules or operations allowed. These programs, intended to meet local needs, occurred in unit or formation lines and were temporary. Often only a single class, or serial, of a course ran, and seldom more than a few. Unsurprisingly, training and operational schedules often consumed unit and formation capacity to train their junior leaders, and decentralized programs alone could not produce the numbers required. Besides, someone needed to produce NCOs for the massive training and reinforcement systems the army raised. Therefore, the army operated centralized programs continuously at static training institutions, both in Canada and in Britain. Trainees had to leave their units temporarily and travel to these schools. The programs tended to be long-running, with schools conducting numerous serials of a course over months or years, and had high-level oversight from National Defence Headquarters (NDHQ) in Canada or Canadian Military Headquarters (CMHQ) in Britain. The centralized schools also played an important role in providing advanced training to NCOs to give them additional specialist and instructional skills.

While the two-track system allowed the army to maximize NCO production, it had one notable downside: NCO training was anything but standardized across the force, and each junior leader's professional development path was unique. The senior leadership mitigated this weakness and fostered uniform development across the corps as a whole by circulating NCOs between the field units, where expertise grew fastest, and the reinforcement and training systems. While doing so was essential to ensure that well-trained reinforcements were ready to step up once the army started taking casualties, moving good NCOs out of field units for duty elsewhere sometimes caused tension within the system. After all, what was good for the NCO corps as a whole was not good for the field unit that saw some of its best NCO talent drain away. This tension flared when units had to give up strong NCOs for instructional duty in the training system, sometimes for longer than an agreed-on period and sometimes even without consent. Conversely, training authorities periodically protested that field units were withholding their good men. Complaints from both sides ultimately resulted from the reality that the rapidly growing army had only so many good NCOs to spread around.

In short, then, the army ran a wide range of NCO qualification courses and professional development initiatives that put individual soldiers on unique paths to professional growth, yet also formed a backbone of NCOs who collectively possessed the necessary leadership skills, tactical acumen, and instructional ability.

To be sure, the two-track approach was a clear departure from the army's usual method for producing NCOs. Before the war, the army had used a unit-based approach whereby commanding officers selected, trained, and promoted their NCOs while adhering to training standards laid down by NDHQ – not unlike the contemporary system of producing new NCOs with a standardized qualification course run at various locations. To advance up the NCO rank structure in today's professional force, junior NCOs must meet time-in-rank criteria and developmental milestones, and they must obtain certain advanced qualifications. But when the army went to war in 1939, such an ordered and rigid approach could not possibly generate all the NCOs needed for all the field units, reinforcement holding units, training schools, and administrative organizations that soon stood up. The two-track approach also differed from the centralized approach the wartime army eventually adopted for producing new officers, with an Officer Cadet Training Unit (OCTU) established in Britain by August 1940 and two centralized Officers Training Centres (OTCs) up and running in Canada by the spring of 1941.[6] Centralized officer production worked because the army did not need to produce as many junior officers as it did NCOs.

Researching the development of the NCO corps has the potential to add new material and fresh insights to the history of Canada's Second World War army, and particularly, the people who served in it. This book follows recent scholarship that has made important contributions in the area of manpower. Thanks to Geoffrey Hayes's structural and cultural study of junior officers, *Crerar's Lieutenants: Inventing the Canadian Junior Army Officer, 1939–45,* we now know a great deal about how the army selected and trained its junior officers.[7] In *Strangers in Arms: Combat Motivation in the Canadian Army, 1943–1945,* Robert Engen reveals just what drove Canadian troops to fight so hard while they served in a volunteer army that did not coerce its men as the German and Russian armies did.[8] Importantly, he also establishes that infantry training below battalion level was indeed effective, despite impressions to the contrary. And Caroline D'Amours, whose research is the closest work to this inquiry, contributes an important evaluation of how the army trained junior NCOs for the infantry.[9] But to date, scholars have focused very little attention on the wartime NCO corps as a distinct entity. John English raises the point in *The Canadian Army and the Normandy Campaign* and identifies the requirement for "investigation into the entire area of Canadian NCO training and employment."[10] This matters because, as historian Charles Stacey reminds us in the epigraph that opens this work, good NCOs form a vital part of any effective army. They lead men in battle, provide the direct day-to-day oversight of junior soldiers, maintain discipline, and champion the interests of the rank and file. They serve as the army's experts in the use and maintenance of weapons and technology. They provide the instructors who train soldiers in basic and specialist skills. They render mentorship and seasoned advice to junior officers, and replace them when they fall in battle. Simply put, understanding an army requires an appreciation of its NCOs, and yet, seven plus decades since the war ended, we still know little about how Canada produced its NCO corps for the Second World War. What is more, there are very few hints to take from the British model because no literature exists on how the British army developed its wartime NCO corps. In exploring this subject, then, this book aims to generate new knowledge in the field of Canadian army history and enrich our understanding of how the nation built a field force capable of fighting alongside, and against, some of the world's most formidable armies.

Any discussion of the wartime NCO corps requires an appreciation for the army's rank structure for non-commissioned soldiers. The Canadian structure for NCOs conformed to the British model. Table I.1 shows the army's non-commissioned ranks and their typical associated positions in an infantry battalion.[11] Corporals commanded ten-man sections. With higher rank came more subordinates and greater responsibility.[12] A sergeant was responsible for all non-commissioned soldiers, or "other ranks," in a platoon, which was formed of up to thirty-five men (that is, three sections plus a platoon headquarters element).[13] A company sergeant major (CSM) oversaw all other ranks in a company (generically comprising three platoons), which included about 117 soldiers. And a regimental sergeant major (RSM), the senior non-commissioned officer in a battalion (generically comprising four rifle companies, a support company, and several specialist platoons), had about 740 subordinates. Only a corporal had full command over his troops, however, because officers commanded all elements from the level of platoon and above. A sergeant took command of his platoon only when the platoon commander was absent or fell in battle, and less often, a CSM took command of a company when its commissioned leadership was absent or fallen. An RSM very rarely, if ever, took command of a battalion.

Table I.1

Canadian non-commissioned ranks and associated positions in infantry units

Rank	Associated position
Private	Section member
Private (appointed lance corporal)	Section second-in-command
Corporal	Section commander
Corporal (appointed lance sergeant)	Performed duties of a sergeant
Sergeant	Platoon second-in-command
Staff sergeant	Company quartermaster sergeant (CQMS)
Warrant officer class 3*	Platoon sergeant major (PSM)
Warrant officer class 2	Company sergeant major (CSM)
Warrant officer class 1	Regimental sergeant major (RSM)

Source: Data from Canada, Department of National Defence, *The King's Regulations and Orders for the Canadian Militia, 1939.* For a detailed list of the positions associated with each rank, in units of all type, see pp. 47–49.
* Shortly before the war, the Canadian army followed British practice and introduced the rank of warrant officer (WO) class 3 to allow non-commissioned ranks to command a proportion of the platoons in each infantry battalion. The practice quickly proved undesirable, and by 1940 both the British and Canadian forces stopped appointing WO Class 3s to command platoons. Many who held the rank went on to earn commissions, but others continued to hold it for several years. C.P. Stacey, *Six Years of War: The Army in Canada, Britain and the Pacific,* 128 and 237.

Before proceeding further, a comment on terminology is necessary. In the Second World War Canadian army, as in the British and other dominion forces, the term *non-commissioned officer* officially referred to corporals, sergeants, and staff sergeants, and the *appointments* of lance corporal and lance sergeant. Technically, warrant officers constituted a distinct non-commissioned class, higher than NCOs.[14] However, people frequently referred to the two groups collectively, albeit colloquially, as NCOs, partly because they made up a single structure for non-commissioned ranks, and partly because they had the same overarching responsibilities: maintaining discipline, administering the rank and file, advising the officer corps on morale and other soldiers' issues, providing tactical leadership in battle, mentoring junior officers, and so on. This book uses the term *NCO* in its broader form to include all grades from lance corporal to warrant officer class 1. This inclusiveness hardly offends convention. Second World War soldiers at all levels very often used the term to describe personnel from lance corporal to warrant officer class 1, just as soldiers today commonly use the term to describe all ranks from corporal to chief warrant officer. Also, where appropriate, this book uses the terms *junior NCO* (for lance corporals and corporals), *senior NCO* (for sergeants to warrant officers class 1), and *warrant officer* (for warrant officers class 3 to 1).

The NCO Production Problem

The problem of raising NCOs became increasingly burdensome and complex as a result of shifts in the strategic situation as the war progressed. When Canada first mobilized, the army raised two divisions, which necessitated generating about 16,000 NCOs for a force of about 64,000. Many came from the prewar permanent force and NPAM already trained, or at least partially trained, which reduced the burden of producing NCOs out of new soldiers. In the late spring of 1940, when, in the wake of the disastrous Anglo-French campaign in France and Belgium, Ottawa authorized the formation of two more divisions and the assembly of a corps in Britain, the army grew to about 178,000. This necessitated increasing the NCO cadre to about 43,000. In January 1941, the government added an armoured division. And when Japan entered the war and home defence seemed urgent, NDHQ organized three additional divisions, the 6th, 7th, and 8th, each comprising three brigades.[15] In fact, every year from 1940 to 1943, the government authorized increases to the army. And as the NCO corps grew, fewer men from the prewar army were available to help fill out the numbers, which meant having to produce NCOs out of soldiers who were new to the military. Furthermore, a bigger army needed a bigger training system, which in turn increased the NCO requirement as training units clamoured for more instructors. For instance, in the fiscal year 1942–43, the number of basic training camps alone rose from twenty-eight to forty, creating an NCO shortage.[16] In March 1944, the First Canadian Army of two corps (comprising three infantry and two armoured divisions, plus two independent armoured brigades), plus the home defence force in Canada, had reached nearly half a million men. The whole army required an estimated 110,660 NCOs – a sevenfold expansion since the original two-division force was raised in 1939. The NCO production issue continued after the Normandy invasion, as high infantry casualties brought challenges when it came to furnishing replacements. Table I.2 summarizes how strategic milestones over the course of the war progressively increased the problem.

Throughout the war, the army's senior leadership understood the problem and responded appropriately by taking the two-track approach to creating NCOs just described. Decentralized programs were the default choice, given the army's regimental traditions and peacetime promotion policies. In fact, from the war's outset, commanding officers were responsible for developing and promoting their own NCOs.[17] Units ran their own NCO training when they could, and formations helped occasionally by running NCO programs for their units.[18] Brigades ran courses, and eventually, so did all five overseas divisions. A few courses even ran at the corps level. The decentralized approach was practical in that it allowed units and formations to tailor NCO training to local needs, especially in the theatres of operations. However, the NCO production problem – one of volume and standardization – was too big to be resolved by decentralized training alone. Thus, the military leadership gradually introduced several centralized NCO training programs. In Canada, training centres ran NCO courses using syllabuses that NDHQ controlled, while a school dedicated to NCO qualification training ran at Mégantic, Quebec. In Britain, the Canadian Training School (CTS), an institution that provided different types of training for soldiers from across the overseas army, ran NCO qualification and refresher courses. NCOs who trained at these army-run schools brought army-standard ways of doing things back to their units and to the decentralized training programs. Neither decentralized nor centralized approaches dominated across the NCO corps. The army expanded much too quickly to allow for any standard professional development path.

The two-track approach had its flaws. Training programs varied from place to place. After all, a unit in Italy taking advantage of a pause in the fighting to train replacement NCOs provided instruction that looked markedly different from that at a well-established training centre back in Canada that had the time to run longer courses. However, while individual NCOs followed different

Table I.2

Growth of the NCO corps

Army*	Estimated NCO corps**	Date	Milestone
63,476	15,710	End-December 1939	First stage of mobilization complete, with two divisions raised
		May 1940	Government decides to raise two more divisions and form a corps in Britain
177,810	42,910	End-December 1940	
		28 January 1941	Government approves Army Program for 1941: expansion to three infantry divisions, an armoured division, and an army tank brigade
274,813	63,000	End-December 1941	
		6 January 1942	Government approves Army Program for 1942: expansion to a two-corps army
425,377	98,920	End-December 1942	
		11 March 1943	Government approves the Army Program for 1943: brings up to full strength two armoured divisions and all corps and army troops
494,545	111,710	End-December 1943	
495,073	110,660	End-June 1944	Campaigns underway in Italy and Northwest Europe

* C.P. Stacey, *Six Years of War: The Army in Canada, Britain and the Pacific*, 522, Appendix A (Strengths and Casualties). The army reached its peak strength on 22 March 1944, with 495,804 all ranks. Stacey corrects several errors to Appendix A in *Arms, Men and Governments: The War Policies of Canada, 1939–1945*, 34.

** This data is based on the calculation that the other ranks (ORs) numbered about 94 percent of all ranks in the army. This column also accounts for the growing size of the overseas army and of the total army. The data assumes that of the ORs in the Canadian Army Overseas, 18 percent were NCOs, as opposed to 27 percent of the ORs in Canada. This is based on E.L.M. Burns's statement, in *Manpower in the Canadian Army, 1939–1945*, that these proportions existed by January 1944 (p. 99). The proportion in Canada was higher because administration and training establishments required more clerical and technical staff, and more instructors.

developmental paths, the senior leadership cultivated even development of the NCO corps as a whole by implementing programs that spread talent and the latest expertise across the army. This meant circulating strong NCOs between the field units overseas, the reinforcement system in Britain, and the training system in Canada. Over time, authorities organized several talent-sharing programs. These included taking field unit soldiers in Britain, carefully selected for their skills and instructional aptitude, and sending them back to Canada for temporary instructional duty. As will be shown, the demand in Canada for a constant flow of excellent instructors from overseas put stress on the supply, as the army had only so much talent to spread around. Similarly, Canada-based NCOs travelled across the Atlantic to spend a few months with field units in Britain. And to ensure that the reinforcement stream had its fair share of good NCOs available to replace casualties, the army overseas also rotated NCOs between field and reinforcement units. Finally, once the army started fighting, it sent NCOs from Italy, and later Northwest Europe, back to Britain to share their battle experience with those in the reinforcement stream. Doing all this necessitated convincing field unit commanders that it was in their long-term interests to accept the short-term pain of giving up some of their best NCOs to instruct in the reinforcement and training systems, but the cross-pollination project for distributing NCO expertise generally worked.

Filling the Knowledge Gap

Taking stock of the main deficiencies in our understanding of NCO development brings into relief how little we actually know about the topic and delineates the size and shape of the knowledge gap. For one thing, the role of the prewar forces in building the wartime NCO corps requires investigation. Many soldiers from the permanent force and the NPAM certainly volunteered for active duty. Particularly in the war's opening weeks, the peacetime army provided thousands of soldiers for service overseas. These peacetime forces maintained a nucleus of NCOs that proved invaluable for building a big wartime field army of five-plus divisions. The army's official historian for the Second World War, C.P. Stacey, certainly believed so. In *Six Years of War*, he recognizes that even if the prewar permanent force was too small to provide an expeditionary force (let alone a counter-assault force to protect Canada from raids), and even if the NPAM reservists lacked the training and equipment of the most modern military forces, the two elements at least "constituted a useful and indeed essential foundation upon which, over a period of months, an army could be built."[19] In fact, he explains, almost half of the 58,337 personnel who joined the active army in September 1939 were either already serving in the permanent force or NPAM, or had done so in the past.[20] He also states that all the officers and warrant officers in the units mobilized in 1939 came from the prewar military forces. Furthermore, over the course of the war, soldiers from the permanent force and the NPAM made up a significant portion of the army's commissioned and non-commissioned leaders. However, Stacey does not indicate what that portion was, and no historian since has investigated just how many of the war-time army's NCOs came from the permanent force and NPAM.[21] What is more, given the prewar military's small size and the scale of the expansion, the proportion of soldiers coming from the permanent force and the NPAM grad-ually declined in the years that it took to build the army. In short, the extent to which these prewar forces furnished NCOs for active service abroad remains unclear.

Furthermore, given the limited supply of potential active-duty NCOs from the permanent force and the NPAM, the army clearly had to turn some of its civilian volunteers into NCOs quickly. Much of the wartime NCO corps must have comprised citizen-soldiers who had no military experience when they enlisted. In fact, by the end of 1941, the NCO corps was probably larger than the entire prewar permanent force and NPAM combined.[22] The extent to which raw civilians eventually filled out the NCO corps requires explanation. So, too, does how the army turned factory workers and farmers into junior leaders and the "backbone" of the army.

Except for Caroline D'Amours's work on infantry junior NCO reinforce-ments, the secondary literature says almost nothing about NCO training. What kind of qualification training did NCOs receive? Who conducted it? How did it evolve? And to what extent did the army maintain uniform training standards across the force? These questions require attention, as do others about how the army prepared NCOs for the vitally important task of instructing other soldiers and how authorities handled the ongoing professional development of those who had completed formal qualification training. And how long did it take to turn a civilian into a decent NCO? After all, NCOs epitomize experience and tactical expertise, qualities that cannot be developed overnight. But the army had to form quickly, and no one knew how long they had to produce junior leaders.

While conscription is a well-studied aspect of Canadian Second World War history, the effect of the policy on the NCO corps has yet to receive much scholarly attention. In June 1940, when Canada implemented conscription for home service under the National Resources Mobilization Act (NRMA), the army suddenly needed more NCOs to train and lead the citizens compelled to serve.[23] In *Zombie Army: The Canadian Army and Conscription in the Second World War,* Daniel Byers discusses how the army dealt with the requirement.[24] He shows that authorities relied heavily on the NPAM, which had a supply of NCOs who did not meet the age or physical criteria for active service overseas but who could help train recruits.[25] Most of these reservists proved enthusiastic instructors. Byers also explains that to produce NCOs for the three home defence divisions the army eventually raised, and to free general service NCOs for duty overseas, authorities resorted to promoting many conscript privates to NCO rank. By April 1944, most of the NCOs in the 13th Canadian Infantry Brigade, a formation that sent troops overseas later that year, were conscripts.[26] These are important findings, but we still do not know how many conscripts with NCO rank, if any, ultimately served abroad. In addition, we know that many conscripts eventually "went active" – over 58,400 of the 157,841 men compelled to serve at home later volunteered for operational duty overseas.[27] How many of them became NCOs in the active army remains unknown. This work addresses these gaps by investigating whether any conscripts of NCO rank proceeded overseas for active service, and how many general service NCOs began as conscripts.

There also remains the matter of how the army maintained the NCO corps' strength once sustained operations began in July 1943. The army eventually took high casualties in both of its major theatres of operation, and 22,917 Canadian soldiers died while on active service.[28] By the early fall of 1944, high casualties left units, particularly in the infantry, seriously undermanned, with battalions, companies, and platoons often going into battle at half-strength.[29] How did the army deal with NCO losses? The existing scholarship gives us only impressions. Some replacements must have come forward in the reinforcement stream, although the secondary literature notes that units resisted taking inexperienced reinforcement NCOs.[30] But commanding officers had few options. Units could either accept NCOs from the reinforcement stream or promote from within their depleted ranks. The extent to which units exercised these options and the apparent impression that reinforcement NCOs were often lacking experience both merit investigation.

This book pursues several lines of inquiry. First, it investigates NCO promotion policies to determine how the army governed advancement in noncommissioned rank. The army required a system that ensured that the most able reached the highest rank, yet had enough flexibility to allow for rapid promotions when casualties drained NCO cadres. Prewar promotion regulations and qualification standards shed light on the quality of the permanent force and NPAM soldiers who formed the foundation of the wartime NCO corps. Of course, wartime policies regarding NCO development require examination and are considered as well. This includes investigating who controlled promotions, probationary periods for the newly promoted, and what units could do with those who failed to live up to expectations.

Additionally, NCO development *practices* deserve consideration: how the army ran its schools, and with how much throughput. NCO training was of course not static. It had to evolve as the army transformed from a tiny, outdated peacetime outfit into a modern field force designed and equipped to fight alongside British forces against Hitler's best. In other words, the training had to stay current with the army's latest weapons and tactics. Who ran NCO training mattered as well. Most military historians know that it takes NCOs to train NCOs, but how exactly the army produced instructional cadres remains poorly understood, so this book examines how authorities sourced trainers. Raising and maintaining enough trainers with the necessary expertise proved a stubborn problem, and the army faced serious challenges in reconciling the need for experienced NCOs in the field units, in the reinforcement system in Britain, in the training system back in Canada, and in the home defence forces. In fact, military authorities in Ottawa continuously beseeched the overseas army to send experienced instructors back to Canada. The overseas army did what it could, but there were never quite enough to meet demands. This tension is examined, along with the programs that were implemented to foster NCO professional development across the army and ensure that the new knowledge and skills building up in the field units disseminated all the way through the reinforcement and training systems in Britain and Canada. Eventually, spreading combat experience was part of this, and the text also looks at programs that the army implemented to send battle-hardened NCOs back to Britain to help train the soldiers still preparing to deploy.

To investigate these issues, research for this book included a survey of soldiers' service records, using a sample group large enough to identify general trends. These files reveal who had experience in the permanent force and/or the NPAM, what courses soldiers attended, how quickly men rose through the ranks, and who joined fighting units as reinforcements. The files also contain information that, when aggregated and analyzed, uncovers the social fabric of the NCO corps: the ages, provinces of origin, education, prewar employment, first languages spoken, rural or urban residency, and religions of the men. Individual service records also reveal the proportion of NCOs who attended particular courses, how long soldiers spent at each rank, whether or not some bypassed certain ranks, and the proportion receiving rank reductions.

By necessity, the scope of the study must be limited. NCO development practices varied somewhat by corps of arms. For example, learning how to instruct on the 25-pounder gun (for artillerymen) was different from learning how to teach marksmanship for the Lee-Enfield No.4 rifle (for infantrymen). Examining particular practices across all military occupations would be a massive undertaking, with separate investigations for each of the fighting arms (infantry, artillery, armour, engineer) and each of the supporting corps (intelligence, signals, service, ordnance, medical, dental, pay, postal, forestry, provost). To attempt to do so within a single volume would necessitate narrow examinations of each military occupation, only to produce conclusions with limited relevance to the greater question of how the wartime army produced the NCO corps. Research therefore focused on the army's largest corps of arms, the infantry. Fundamental to combat power on land, the infantry served as the army's "sledgehammer," and no battle could be won if infantrymen did not secure their objectives.[31] Of course other corps played essential roles, but they ultimately acted in a supporting capacity for the infantry, which was the only arm that decided battles by holding ground. Moreover, the infantry suffered, overwhelmingly, the highest casualties, and consequently experienced the most stress in maintaining a corps of NCOs. Looking closely at the infantry corps – as the only arm to be instrumental in every important army battle and the one that experienced the most stress in keeping its ranks filled as the reinforcement pool shrank – thus has the advantage of producing strong conclusions. The disadvantage is that these conclusions do not account for training idiosyncrasies in other arms of service. To some extent, this book pertains more to the infantry than to the army as a whole, but the army's wartime NCO development policies, and many of the related courses and practices examined here, nevertheless applied to all arms of service. Policies on promotion, for example, were army wide, and the centralized NCO courses trained soldiers from across the arms and services. Only some parts of this text are particular to the infantry: the profile of the army's infantry senior NCOs in Chapter 1; explanations of the army's expectations of its infantry NCOs in Chapter 3; and descriptions of NCO training run by infantry units and brigades in Chapter 5.

The sample group of individual service files examined for this book consists of the records of infantry senior NCOs – sergeants to warrant officers class 1 – who died on active service in the 1st and 3rd Canadian Infantry Divisions and the 4th Canadian Armoured Division, and in one specialized unit, the 1st Canadian Parachute Battalion. This group includes 388 individual service records, enough to form a good representation of the infantry corps, with soldiers from both major theatres (the Mediterranean and Northwest Europe) and both

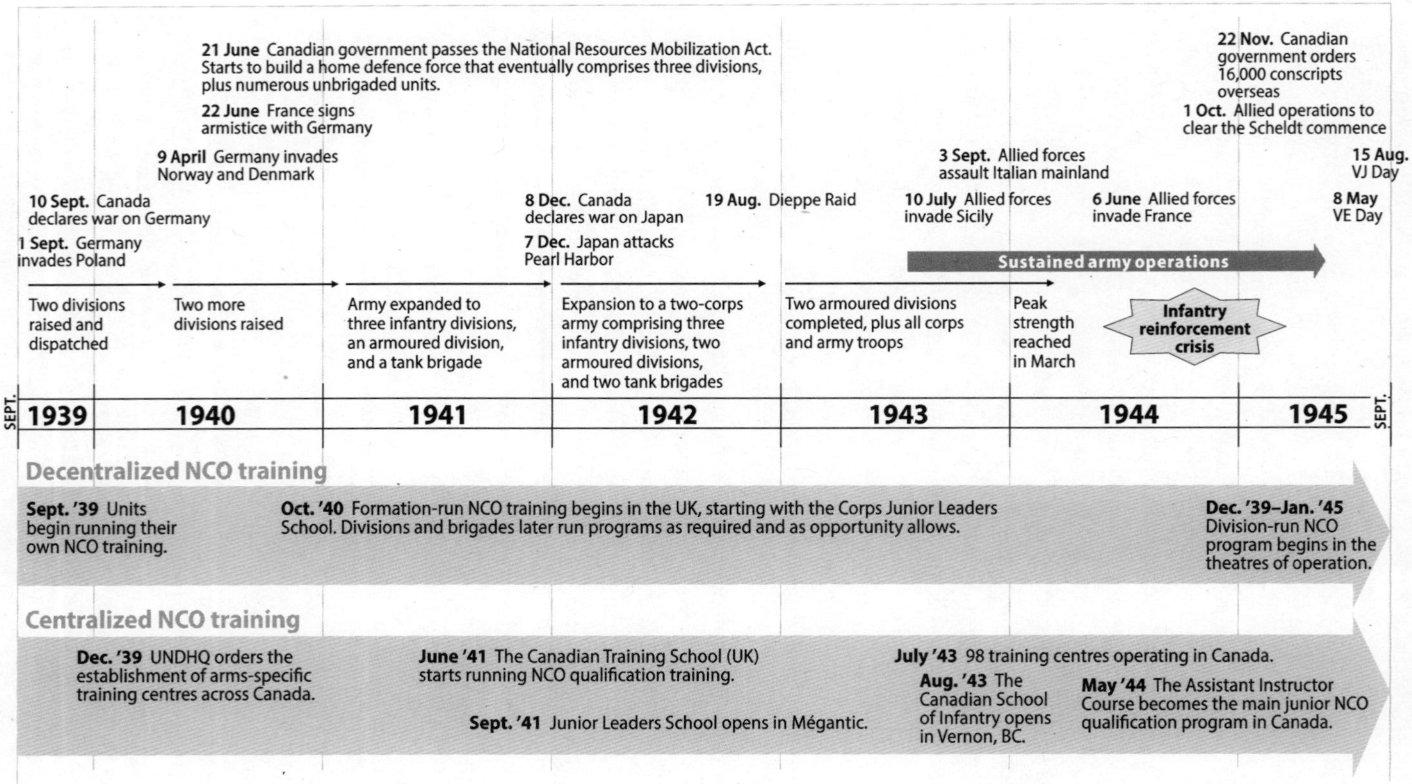

1939

1 Sept. Germany invades Poland

10 Sept. Canada declares war on Germany

Two divisions raised and dispatched

1940

9 April Germany invades Norway and Denmark

21 June Canadian government passes the National Resources Mobilization Act. Starts to build a home defence force that eventually comprises three divisions, plus numerous unbrigaded units.

22 June France signs armistice with Germany

Two more divisions raised

1941

Army expanded to three infantry divisions, an armoured division, and a tank brigade

1942

7 Dec. Japan attacks Pearl Harbor

8 Dec. Canada declares war on Japan

19 Aug. Dieppe Raid

Expansion to a two-corps army comprising three infantry divisions, two armoured divisions, and two tank brigades

1943

10 July Allied forces invade Sicily

3 Sept. Allied forces assault Italian mainland

Two armoured divisions completed, plus all corps and army troops

Sustained army operations

Peak strength reached in March

1944

6 June Allied forces invade France

Infantry reinforcement crisis

1 Oct. Allied operations to clear the Scheldt commence

22 Nov. Canadian government orders 16,000 conscripts overseas

1945

8 May VE Day

15 Aug. VJ Day

SEPT.

Decentralized NCO training

Sept. '39 Units begin running their own NCO training.

Oct. '40 Formation-run NCO training begins in the UK, starting with the Corps Junior Leaders School. Divisions and brigades later run programs as required and as opportunity allows.

Dec. '39–Jan. '45 Division-run NCO program begins in the theatres of operation.

Centralized NCO training

Dec. '39 UNDHQ orders the establishment of arms-specific training centres across Canada.

June '41 The Canadian Training School (UK) starts running NCO qualification training.

Sept. '41 Junior Leaders School opens in Mégantic.

July '43 98 training centres operating in Canada.

Aug. '43 The Canadian School of Infantry opens in Vernon, BC.

May '44 The Assistant Instructor Course becomes the main junior NCO qualification program in Canada.

SEPT.

Figure I.1 Strategic milestones and key NCO-development programs.

division types (infantry and armoured). In short, statistics compiled from these files provide empirical evidence to buttress a wider explanation of how the army developed NCOs.

Finally, in answering *how* the NCO corps was developed, this book does not assess *how well* the programs worked. It makes the assumption that the NCO corps was capable in battle, based on the army's overall good performance, which historians in the last two decades or so have demonstrated thoroughly.[32] Surely, the creditable battlefield performance of Canadian ground forces in Italy and Northwest Europe owed much to a sturdy backbone of NCOs.[33] Besides, evaluating any NCO training program's effectiveness would require the selection of assessment criteria, a dubious undertaking at best, plus a great deal of subjective judgment.

To INVESTIGATE THE two-track approach to NCO development and the programs that spread NCO expertise across the force, the text is organized thematically. Chapter 1 profiles the wartime corps of infantry senior NCOs, based on information gathered from individual service records, to establish the composition of the corps empirically. It assesses demographic characteristics, the proportion of soldiers from the permanent force and NPAM, the training that NCOs received, and how long the army took to turn a civilian into an infantry sergeant. Chapter 2 builds on this picture by describing the demands the army placed on its NCOs, a necessary exposition for demonstrating the high degree of skill infantry NCOs required, which in turn complicated the NCO production problem. Chapter 3 examines NCO development in the prewar army to assess the quality of the peacetime soldiers who became the foundation of the wartime NCO corps. This chapter also investigates the mobilization plans that affected NCO development when war came. Chapter 4 analyzes the wartime policies that governed NCO development. Then, to describe how the army implemented these policies, Chapter 5 discusses the decentralized NCO training programs that infantry units and formations ran. Chapters 6 and 7 examine the centralized programs that operated in Canada and Britain, respectively, for NCOs from across the arms and services. Finally, Chapter 8 explains the army's efforts to disseminate continuously developing NCO expertise, which grew fastest in the field units, across the entire force, so that the training and reinforcement systems could turn out sufficiently prepared soldiers to replace casualties.

This thematic approach to describing NCO development programs necessitates returning to the same periods in different chapters, but the alternative, a chronological approach, would have involved revisiting certain themes in various chapters and repeatedly picking up the story for each theme where it left off previously. Even then, each chapter would still move up and down the timeline in describing the different NCO development programs. Nevertheless, chronology is important. Figure I.1 maps out the strategic milestones affecting the army's growth and the major developments in the army's NCO production system.

This book intends to demonstrate how the army's two-track approach for training NCOs, coupled with programs that distributed NCO expertise across the force, made for a flexible system that authorities used to build and sustain a corps of NCOs for Canada's ambitiously large army. The system had to be adaptable. When the war began, no one knew how soon Canadian troops would start fighting, or how much time the army had to produce all the corporals and sergeants who would lead the rank and file in battle, and who would teach the troops passing through the training system. And as the war progressed, with new weapons arriving and new tactics evolving, NCO training grew increasingly complex and had to adapt continuously. The two-track approach had the flexibility to deal with these challenges, allowing units and formations to train NCOs to local conditions and requirements, while the centralized courses used carefully controlled syllabuses to turn out a steady stream of NCOs for units and for the training and reinforcement systems.

1
Profile of the Infantry Senior NCOs

The battle of Normandy was over ... Now [in late August 1944] we had a very different A Company from those 120 or so who had landed on the beaches June 6 ... Joe Meagher, on D-Day a rifleman but now a sergeant, headed up 7 Platoon ... Bill Lenox, a corporal on D-Day and now a sergeant, had 8 Platoon ... Jackie Bland ... was another D-Day rifleman who had moved up to sergeant.

CHARLES CROMWELL MARTIN, QUEEN'S OWN RIFLES

KNOWING WHO INDIVIDUAL NCOs were and what they did is an important first step in understanding how the army created them. To this end, several questions come to mind. What were the basic social characteristics of the NCO corps, such as age on enlistment, education level, and work skills? How long did it take for raw recruits to become seasoned NCOs? What training did they undergo? Did soldiers rise in rank gradually, or did the army, in its rush to raise forces, have to promote men quickly? Did NCOs in the reinforcement stream lack training and experience, as some have implied? And to what extent did men from the permanent force and the Non-Permanent Active Militia (NPAM) form the wartime NCO corps?

The individual service records in our sample group of 388 senior NCOs reveal one particularly important fact: no typical path existed for professional development. Some soldiers attended centrally run courses at army schools. A roughly equal number trained at temporary decentralized schools run by units and formations. Unlike in today's professional army, which demands that soldiers follow prescribed courses and particular types of employment, soldiers in the wartime army took whatever NCO training was available to them, attended whatever specialist courses their units could send them on, and served wherever suitable – from field units to the training and reinforcement system, and to the administrative posts that kept the army functioning.

Infantry Senior NCO Demographics
Company Sergeant Major (CSM) Alexander Connolly was a typical Canadian NCO of the Second World War.[1] A resident of Toronto, Ontario, he spoke

English and attended the Anglican Church. Connolly came to the army with a partial secondary education, having left school after Grade 10, and he had some skill as an apprentice steam fitter. He also had a little experience in the NPAM, having served in a local infantry unit from 1933 to 1934. Connolly enlisted in the active army in July 1940 at twenty-four years of age and he joined an infantry unit, the Lincoln and Welland Regiment, known as the Lincs. He spent two years as a private before earning a promotion to corporal in July 1942. A week later, he reported to the Junior Leaders School at Mégantic, Quebec, to learn how to be an NCO. Later, he attended several training programs that gave him specialist and instructional skills, including courses in driving, platoon weapons, and urban combat. In March 1943, and with thirty-three months in the army, Connolly earned his sergeant's stripes, having skipped over the appointment of lance sergeant. In July 1944, he deployed to France with his unit and started fighting. In mid-August, he suffered a gunshot wound to the chest and was evacuated back to Britain. After two months in hospital, he returned to the continent, where he rejoined his unit in November. The Lincs were probably happy to receive him as a reinforcement, because they knew him and he had battle experience. In fact, they promoted him to warrant officer class 2 (CSM) within a month. On 1 March 1945, at twenty-nine years old, Connolly died of wounds received in action.

Like Connolly, the soldiers in the sample group generally joined the wartime army as fairly mature individuals, probably older than most might think. On average, they enlisted for active service at twenty-five years of age. About one-third had previous military experience and therefore tended to be well-established adults. In fact, 4 percent came from the permanent force, 32 percent came from the NPAM, and another 4 percent had served in the First World War. Even if one filters out those who joined the active army with some form of prior service, however, the average age on enlistment was still twenty-four. On reflection, this finding makes sense. Most enlistees with NCO potential were likely to arrive in the army with a developed sense of maturity. Also, regulations allowed men up to forty-five to enlist. Twelve soldiers in the sample group, or 3 percent, were thirty-five or older and without previous military experience when they enlisted for active service.

Education levels varied quite a bit. Allowing for the different education systems across the country, Table 1.1 – which, like all tables in this chapter, derives from analysis of the 388 service files – indicates that somewhat less than 80 percent of senior NCOs joined the active army without having completed high school.[2] Just over 10 percent had a full high school education, and less than 6 percent had some postsecondary education. Roughly 35 percent had only

Table 1.1

Infantry senior NCO education levels

	Proportion of NCOs (%)
Partial elementary (up to Grade 7)	9.75
Elementary (completed Grade 8)	26.50
Partial high school (Grades 9 to 11)	42.00
Completed high school (Grade 12)	10.75
Partial college or university	5.50
Completed college or university	0.25
Army education certificate	1.50
Unknown (records not clear)	3.75
Total	100.00

elementary or partial elementary schooling. Even fewer, under 2 percent, possessed army education certificates, which testified that a soldier had achieved a degree of knowledge in certain elementary subjects.

The vast majority of Canadian infantry NCOs in the sample group spoke English and prayed in Protestant churches. Some 89 percent spoke English only, compared to 67 percent of the national population.[3] Just over 2 percent spoke only French (versus 19 percent of the population), and about 9 percent spoke both languages (versus 13 percent of all Canadians). Furthermore, almost all senior NCOs declared Christianity as their religion when they attested. Only one individual in the sample declared a non-Christian faith (Judaism). As indicated in Table 1.2, about three out of four declared themselves to belong to some form of Protestantism, and 22 percent were Roman Catholic. The remainder claimed affiliation with other denominations, in very small numbers, such as Greek Catholic, Latter Day Saints, or simply "Christian." That Anglicans made for the largest proportion is puzzling. As the third-largest denomination in Canada, they formed just over 15 percent of the population, behind the United Church (with more than 19 percent) and the Roman Catholic Church (with over 43 percent).[4] Perhaps the Anglican Church actively encouraged its members to support the war effort, as it had during the First World War, when Anglican men volunteered for the army in disproportionately high numbers.[5] More research is required to explain this peculiarity. Nonetheless, it echoes Robert Engen's finding that Anglicans constituted one-third of recruits in 1939 and half of the officers appointed that September, which he postulates was due to high volunteerism among those with ties to Britain.[6]

Table 1.2

Infantry senior NCO religious affiliation

	Proportion of NCOs (%)
Anglican	27.0
Roman Catholic	22.0
United Church	22.0
Presbyterian	18.0
Baptist	4.5
Methodist	2.0
Lutheran	1.5
Other	3.0
Total	100.0

Canada's wartime senior NCOs came to the army with a wide variety of job skills. Unfortunately, it is impossible to ascertain from personnel records precisely how many men left jobs to enlist and how many were unemployed.[7] Still, attestation forms allow us to form a good picture of the type of skills – or in some cases, work – volunteers held before joining the active army. As Table 1.3 indicates, the largest proportion came as skilled workers, such as tradesmen and trained workmen. The next largest group, almost one in five, comprised unskilled labourers. Only one in ten came from the farming sector – a finding that undercuts the oft-heard supposition that many soldiers were hardy men who came from the country's farms – and a similar number were drivers. Beyond that, volunteers came in relatively small numbers from a wide range of employment sectors. Relatively few, roughly 15 percent, declared white-collar skills or employment.

The typical Canadian NCO came from central Canada. As Table 1.4 shows, the greatest proportion, just over 40 percent, lived in Ontario when they joined the active army, while almost 9 percent came from Quebec. The conspicuously high proportion of Ontarians reflects the province's much larger population of military-age males (aged eighteen to forty-five).[8]

A second, somewhat less important factor may have been related to education levels. From a national perspective, citizens of Ontario had the second-highest numbers of years in school and therefore had slightly better potential to rise to senior NCO rank.[9] British Columbia was at the top of the education scale, and with Manitoba, Saskatchewan, and Alberta made Western Canada home to the second-largest proportion of infantry senior NCOs, almost 38 percent of them.

Table 1.3

Infantry senior NCO pre-service employment or trade

	Proportion of NCOs (%)
Skilled worker	32.25
Unskilled worker/labourer	18.25
Farmer	9.75
Driver	9.00
Clerk	6.75
Unemployed	4.50
Retail (e.g., department store, groceries)	4.25
Permanent force	3.75
Salesman	3.75
Civil servant	2.00
Hospitality (e.g., waiter, bartender, hotel)	1.50
Skilled white collar (e.g., accountant)	1.25
Student	1.00
Emergency services (e.g., police and fire)	0.75
Fisherman	0.75
Business (e.g., manager, advertising)	0.50
Total	100.00

Table 1.4

Infantry senior NCO provinces/jurisdictions of origin

	Proportion of NCOs (%)
Ontario	41.00
British Columbia	11.00
Saskatchewan	10.25
Manitoba	10.00
Quebec	8.50
Alberta	6.50
New Brunswick	5.75
Nova Scotia	5.25
Prince Edward Island	0.50
United States	1.00
Britain	0.25
Total	100.00

Just over 11 percent came from the Maritimes, although the proportion of Maritimers who volunteered for the armed forces was slightly higher than the proportion of Ontarians.[10] A handful (five individuals in the sample, or just 1.25 percent) resided in the United States or Britain when they joined. Furthermore, an urban–rural split existed among senior NCOs. About 59 percent lived in cities when they enlisted, while 41 percent lived in rural areas.[11]

How Long It Took to Produce a Sergeant

The rate at which individual soldiers rose to senior NCO rank varied considerably. Several factors explain this: over one-third of all NCOs came with previous military experience and climbed more rapidly than those who did not; overall promotion rates increased as army expansion accelerated; some soldiers rose quickly in the field when units had to replace casualties; and individuals came with different levels of leadership ability, intelligence, and motivation. It is thus not possible to describe how long it *typically* took to turn an enlistee into an experienced NCO. That said, we can determine how quickly personnel progressed through the ranks *on average* to reach sergeant, the first senior NCO rank. Table 1.5 shows the average amount of time soldiers in the sample spent at each rank or appointment below sergeant, and how long they took to reach sergeant after enlisting for active service

These data should be read with a few caveats. First, they include those who went straight to NCO rank on joining the active army. So, for example, a soldier from the permanent force who joined the active army at the rank of corporal would probably have reached sergeant much more quickly than an inexperienced recruit. A sergeant in the NPAM who volunteered for active service and

Table 1.5

Average progression rate to the rank of sergeant

	Months
Time as lance corporal	6.0
Time as corporal	11.0
Time as lance sergeant	5.0
Time as private	8.5
Total time to reach sergeant	30.5

Note: To reach the rank of sergeant, soldiers in the sample group took between 0 months (those appointed to sergeant on enlisting for active service) and 61.5 months. Some soldiers skipped over the first three ranks/appointments listed in the table.

kept his rank counts as having taken zero months to reach sergeant. Second, many soldiers skipped over the appointments of lance corporal or lance sergeant, and a smaller number did not progress through the rank of corporal. Third, progression did not always occur in a continuously upward direction. Many soldiers in fact dropped in rank at least once. And finally, the time a soldier spent at each rank or appointment varied a great deal, based on personal ability. Nonetheless, Table 1.5 does depict the cumulative time soldiers spent, on average, at each rank or appointment before sergeant, even if they held a given rank more than once. Producing sergeants took on average just over two and a half years in wartime. If one excludes those who put up sergeant's stripes when they joined the active army (within one month of enlisting), it took on average thirty-three and a half months to reach sergeant. And, if one excludes all those who came to the active army with military experience, it took on average thirty-five months.[12] That is, it generally took raw recruits almost three years to become a senior NCOs. This seems at first glance a rather short period in which to turn a civilian who might not know the difference between a hobnail and a howitzer into a platoon sergeant responsible for the leadership and discipline of over thirty men, and for commanding them in battle. But of course the army had no choice.

Rates of progression varied depending on the year and what the army was doing at the time. Table 1.6 shows how long it took soldiers to reach senior NCO rank, by half years, from the time they joined. Generally speaking, between 1939 and mid-1942, the later one joined the active army, the faster one rose to

Table 1.6

Average time from joining the active army to becoming a sergeant

		Months
1939	September–December	31.5
1940	January–June	35.5
	July–December	30.5
1941	January–June	21.5
	July–December	22.5
1942	January–June	15.5
	July–December	17.0
1943	January–June	18.0
	July–December	17.0

Note: No soldiers in the sample group enlisted after 1943.

sergeant. As the army expanded, the urgency to produce NCOs increased. The trend for greater speed coincided with the pace of the army's growth. Thus, those who joined in 1942 rose to sergeant most quickly, which makes sense given that this was when the government ordered expansion of the overseas force into a two-corps army. Demand outstripped supply for a time. Interestingly, the rate of advancement pretty much plateaued after 1942 despite combat losses from July 1943, when major operations began. By then, ramped-up NCO production lines prevented progression rates from accelerating even further (see Chapters 5 to 7).

Growing a large army from a small base necessitated placing capable individuals into whatever jobs they could handle, and sometimes this meant rapid promotion. On rare occasions, the army even fast-tracked promising new recruits who had no military experience. This occurred when mobilizing units that were rushing to fill their war establishments (the level of equipment and manning authorized in wartime) promoted men who had more education than most recruits (such as a bit of university) or several years of work experience. These men received a promotion within weeks or even day to lance corporal or corporal. Burton Harper's experience exemplifies this process. As he explained during an interview about his wartime service, when undergoing recruit training in the summer of 1940 with the North Shore (New Brunswick) Regiment, he stood out from his fellow recruits: "My platoon commander realized that I was ... one of the two or three in the platoon who had high school education. The rest, I must say, were perhaps a little less and so I got to be a Lance Corporal."[13] Harper must have done well, because by December he was a full corporal. On the whole, such rapid promotions occurred infrequently. The

Table 1.7

Soldiers skipping ranks/appointments in NCO advancement

Rank/appointment skipped	Proportion skipping (%)
Lance corporal	27.5
Corporal	14.00
Lance sergeant	50.50
Sergeant	6.00
Staff sergeant	10.50
Warrant officer class 2	0.25

Note: Some soldiers skipped over more than one rank or appointment.

sample group contains about ten cases, or 2.6 percent of the total. Plainly, turning raw recruits into instant junior NCOs was not sound practice, but in the haste to assemble units, a small proportion of the wartime NCO corps was raised this way and went on to render good service. Also, while regulations allowed units to give more authority to a certain proportion of their capable privates and corporals by appointing them to lance corporal or lance sergeant, soldiers often skipped over the lance appointments.[14] And soldiers who held NCO rank in the permanent force or NPAM typically kept that rank on enlisting in the active army, technically passing over the subordinate ranks and appointments. Table 1.7 shows the considerable extent to which soldiers in the sample group skipped various ranks and appointments.

Reverting in Rank

Many NCOs did not advance but only slid backward in rank, or "reverted," at least once. Reversions occurred for many reasons. Soldiers who held acting rank to fill a particular position reverted to their permanent rank when no longer filling that position.[15] This occurred often in fighting units. For example, if a soldier with the rank of acting sergeant was evacuated from his unit because of wounds or illness, he reverted to his permanent rank, usually corporal. An NCO could also petition his commanding officer for a voluntary reversion, and soldiers had many reasons for doing so. Sometimes an individual wanted a posting to another unit but no vacancy existed for his current rank. Edward George Evans, a sergeant in the Royal Hamilton Light Infantry, voluntarily reverted to private to join the 1st Canadian Parachute Battalion.[16] Some in Canada chose to revert to proceed overseas. In other cases, the chain of command ordered a reversion in rank for disciplinary reasons, inefficiency, or unsuitability.[17] For example, Paul Eugene Dugas rose to sergeant quickly in Les Fusiliers du St-Laurent but reverted to private after refusing to obey an order.[18] Dugas, who had already been in trouble as a sergeant for drunkenness and for failing to obey standing orders, gave cause for reversion on both disciplinary and suitability grounds. In fact, reversions occurred frequently enough that a soldier might revert more than once during his wartime career. Table 1.8 shows that a significant proportion of NCOs in the sample group, almost one-half, reverted to a lower rank at some point during the war. About 16 percent reverted more than once, but very few reverted more than twice.

Reversion policy and acting ranks built much-needed flexibility into the process by which authorities matched personnel to war establishments. In the rapidly expanding army, the chain of command could revert or demote soldiers who could not fulfill their duties or who, for disciplinary reasons, no longer

Table 1.8

NCOs reverting in rank

Number of reversions	Proportion reverting (%)
1	28.6
2	12.4
3	2.8
4	0.5
5	0.3
Total	44.6

merited a given rank. Furthermore, formations and units had to respect their authorized strengths, and they could not just promote soldiers arbitrarily. Reversion policies allowed the army to move personnel around to meet requirements while respecting fixed war establishments. Acting ranks also helped in the other direction. A custom of making all new promotions conditional on ability to perform came into effect as soon as the force mobilized. As the army's mobilization instructions declared: "All promotions ... will be to acting rank. They will be confirmed, or otherwise, at the end of a period of three months."[19] This policy lasted the duration of the war with few changes. Overseas, unit commanders authorized all NCO promotions up to warrant officer class 2 on the basis of acting rank for three months and then confirmed the rank if appropriate. Division commanders authorized promotions to acting warrant officer class 1 and the subsequent confirmations.[20] In Canada, corporals and sergeants had to serve for three months in an acting capacity before receiving consideration for confirmation. Staff sergeants and warrant officers class 2 had to serve for eight months in acting rank, warrant officers class 1 nine months.[21] With so many promotions occurring across the army, first to fill out war establishments while the army expanded and later to replace casualties, a sizable proportion of NCOs held acting rank at any given time. In fact, of the soldiers in the sample group, one-third were holding acting rank when they died.

Forms of Training

The army used a wide variety of courses to teach soldiers how to be NCOs. Centralized NCO programs – qualification courses, instructor courses, and specialist skills courses at permanent schools – were implemented as needed and adjusted over time in response to the latest developments in weapons and tactics. For example, several thousand soldiers from across Canada passed through the centralized NCO qualification program at the Junior Leaders School in Mégantic, Quebec, while scores of soldiers in Britain passed through the NCO qualification program at the Canadian Training School (CTS). Meanwhile, decentralized training across the army played a major role. Units and formations periodically ran their own courses, which varied considerably in length and content, to fill identified gaps in training. Table 1.9, which is based mostly on data extracted from service records, reveals the army's two-track approach to training NCOs, with a good but incomplete sample of the many agencies involved.

As mentioned above, NCOs followed no typical training path. None of the centralized courses listed in Table 1.9 – even the big programs, such as the Junior

Table 1.9

Canadian army NCO training programs

Location	Centralized programs	Decentralized programs
Theatres of operations		Various brigades All five divisions
Canada	Basic training centres	Field units
	Infantry training centres	Brigades
	Canadian Small Arms Training Centres	4th Canadian Division (1941)
Mégantic, Quebec	No. 52 (later S6) Junior Leaders School	
Vernon, British Columbia	S17 Canadian School of Infantry	
Sussex, New Brunswick	A34 Special Training Centre	
Britain	Canadian Training School	Field units
	13th Canadian Infantry Brigade	Brigades
	13th Canadian Infantry Training Brigade	1st Canadian Division Infantry Reinforcement Unit
		7th Corps (later Canadian Corps) Junior Leaders School

Note: Because many personnel records are incomplete, and because the sample group does not include soldiers from all units and formations, this list shows only some of the formal NCO training that ran across the army.

Leaders School at Mégantic – trained more than a small proportion of the NCOs in the sample group. But this is consistent with a centralized "train the trainer" approach. At least 14 percent of the sample attended centralized NCO qualification training, and they, in turn, trained others. At least 15 percent underwent decentralized NCO qualification courses at the unit, brigade, division, or corps level. And because all units developed their NCOs when they could, one can assume that most of the remainder attended some form of unit-level training. Finally, nearly all NCOs received some type of specialist training. A few such courses focused purely on skills, such as parachuting. But many focused both on skills and on how to teach those skills to others, as with small arms, urban fighting, and assault landing courses.

Various battle drill programs, usually run as instructor courses, also contributed to NCO corps development. Derived from information in the service files, the following list depicts the wide range of specialist courses that NCOs attended:

SPECIALIST COURSES (INFANTRY NCOs)

Advanced Infantry Assault
Anti-aircraft Defence
Anti-aircraft: 20mm gun
Anti-gas
Anti-tank: 2-pounder
Anti-tank: 6-pounder
Assault Landing
Battle First Aid
Bomb Recognition
Camouflage
Chemical Warfare
Company Quartermaster Sergeant
Defence against Gas
Drill Instructor School
Driver and Maintenance
Driver Mechanic
Driver Motorcycle
Driver Wheeled
Equipment Repairer
Field Sketching and Camouflage
Field Works

Flame-thrower
Infantry Warrant Officer Field
   Engineering
Instructor Refresher
Intelligence
Map Reading
Mine Clearing
Mine Laying
Movement Control
NCO Assault Engineer
Parachutist – British
Parachutist – Canadian
Patrol School
Paymaster
Personnel Selection Clerk
Physical Training
Pioneer
Range Finding
Recognition of Enemy Aircraft
Regimental Butcher
Regimental Signaller

Regimental Stretcher Bearer
Sanitary Duties
Small Arms: 3-inch mortar
Small Arms: 4.2-inch heavy mortar
Small Arms: battalion weapons
Small Arms: medium machine gun
Small Arms: platoon weapons
Small Arms: spigot mortar
Small Arms Instructor (general)
Sniper
Sniper (brigade-run)
Storeman
Street Fighting
Tank Destruction
Unarmed Combat
Unit Chiropodist
Universal (Bren) Carrier
Waterproofing Vehicles
Welding
Winter Training

Battle drill

Battle Drill (A31 Training Centre)
Battle Drill (Airborne)
Battle Drill (brigade run)
Battle Drill (Canadian Training
    School)
Battle Drill (Mortars)
Battle Drill (unit run)
Battle Drill (Universal Carrier)

British Brigade of Guards courses

Brigade of Guards (Windsor)
Drill (Welsh Guards Depot)
Guard Depot (unspecified)
Guards Depot Drill (Caterham)

The majority of these courses ran at centralized schools, although specialist training was certainly conducted by units and formations as well. Records reveal that individual NCOs typically took as many as five specialist courses. In conjunction with the individual service files, the list demonstrates that developing the NCO corps entailed seeding it with a very wide range of specialist skills by sending individuals to qualify as regimental instructors who could pass particular skills on to their units.

Some courses were more important than others and so were administered to large numbers of candidates. For instance, variations of small arms, driver, and physical training courses were run across the army for many troops. Programs less relevant to the core activities of fighting and moving saw far fewer students because units only required one or two experts, as with sanitary duties or unit chiropodist courses.

Replacing NCO Losses

Units often replaced NCO casualties by promoting from within. Some soldiers therefore received rapid and successive promotions, especially after proving themselves in action. For instance, Joseph Downey, who joined the army in

June 1942, was still a private when he went to France with the Algonquin Regiment in July 1944.[22] After suffering a wound, Downey left the battalion from August to mid-October but on rejoining it, he shot up to lance sergeant in under two weeks, skipping over corporal, and made sergeant three months later. He rose from private to sergeant in just over three months.

Sometimes a soldier who had demonstrated poor potential before going into battle suddenly rose conspicuously quickly after performing well in combat. William Steele enlisted in the Algonquin Regiment in July 1941 and stalled at private, notwithstanding a short stint as a lance corporal in 1943. Steele hardly proved a model soldier, racking up multiple charges for absenting himself without leave, quitting a guard duty without permission, abusing alcohol, and earning a civil conviction for larceny while stationed in Newfoundland.[23] He deployed to France in July 1944, still a private. But he rose to corporal in late September, to sergeant eighteen days later, and to company quartermaster sergeant (CQMS) in mid-November. In other words Steele, for years the most undisciplined of men, went from private to CQMS (staff sergeant) in just under two months.

Sometimes soldiers who joined the army relatively late in the war, and who presumably had much to learn about soldiering before becoming an NCO, shot up in rank after joining a unit fighting in the field. Glen Miller was one. He enlisted in March 1943 and, after completing basic training, went overseas in the reinforcement stream. In April 1944, he joined the Loyal Edmonton Regiment in Italy as a private. Just twenty-two days later, he rose to lance corporal, and in less than three weeks skipped over the rank of corporal to sergeant. So, after little more than a year in the army, he went from private to sergeant.[24]

Clearly, unit commanding officers believed that the Downeys and the Millers of the army did not necessarily need to attend centralized training to show them how to be NCOs. In fact, these men were not outliers. About 7 percent of the soldiers in the sample group vaulted forward in rank after proving themselves in action. Their cases also suggest a lingering regimental mindset that preferred promotion from within (when possible), as opposed to accepting unknowns or outsiders from the reinforcement stream.

But reinforcement NCOs were not necessarily greenhorns. Sometimes units even knew the men they received as NCO reinforcements. The Royal Canadian Regiment (RCR) took on Corporal John Gray in late December 1943.[25] Gray, who had reverted from sergeant to corporal to join the battalion in Italy, was well known to the Royals as a good soldier, having first joined the regiment when he enlisted in September 1939. But he had not deployed to Italy with the unit because, in January 1943, the army sent him back to Canada to teach officer candidates at the Officers Training Centre in Brockville, Ontario, where he proved a solid instructor at the rank of sergeant. Before that, he had taken a regimental NCO course with the RCR and performed very well. His Personnel Selection Record describes him as "an aggressive soldier of above-average ability, alert [and] co-operative. Eager to get back overseas with his unit in combatant work." Gray was an enthusiastic and competent NCO, which was why the RCR had sent him back to Canada to train officers, and the unit was lucky to receive him as a reinforcement.

At other times units did not know who they were receiving as reinforcement NCOs, but that did not mean the incoming men were of low quality. Some had been in the army a long time. For example, in mid-January 1944, Company Sergeant Major (CSM) Robert Joyes joined the Loyal Edmonton Regiment in Italy.[26] The unit probably did not know him, as he had no previous association with the Loyal Eddies, but Joyes was not new to soldiering. He had volunteered for active service in September 1939 with the Essex Scottish Regiment, a unit he had served with as a reservist since 1935. In Britain, Joyes moved between his unit and the reinforcement system, like so many other soldiers did, as the army tried to keep expertise circulating through the field force and the system that provided it with replacements. In November 1943, he went to Italy as a reinforcement, which is how he ended up with the Loyal Edmonton Regiment, new to the unit but no newer to the army than most.

Reinforcement NCOs often proved excellent soldiers. William Johnston had to revert to private from sergeant when he joined the Saskatoon Light Infantry in Italy in October 1943.[27] But the unit recognized his leadership ability at once and promoted him to corporal in just ten days. He was holding that rank when killed in action a few weeks later. In August 1944, the Queen's Own Rifles (QOR) took on Corporal Aubrey Cosens. He had been with the Argyll and Sutherland Highlanders since enlisting in November 1940 and had gone into a reinforcement unit just one month before joining the QOR.[28] Cosens worked out well. The unit promoted him to sergeant in October, and in February 1945, the twenty-three-year-old demonstrated exceptional bravery and effectiveness under fire, for which he won the Victoria Cross. These different reinforcement profiles demonstrate that such soldiers were not necessarily novices, even if they lacked combat experience. What is more, many actually came *with* experience in battle.

Reinforcement NCOs were often veteran soldiers returning to frontline duty after convalescing from injury or illness. Units in action frequently lost wounded and sick soldiers to the medical system. After the men healed, the army returned as many as possible to the reinforcement stream and, at least for the infantry, these veterans (including many NCOs) often constituted a large proportion of the reinforcement drafts proceeding to the theatres of operation. In late August 1944, Canadian Military Headquarters (CMHQ) emphasized to commander Canadian Reinforcement Units (CRU), the officer responsible for confirming the readiness of soldiers released from hospital, that all reinforcement drafts proceeding to Italy or Northwest Europe should include a large proportion of soldiers with combat experience: "Wherever the number of available rfts [reinforcements] permits, 50% of drafts should be composed of battle experienced pers[onnel]."[29] When it came to infantry senior NCOs, the army just might have succeeded in attaining or even exceeding that proportion over the course of the war. Of the soldiers in the sample group who went through the reinforcement stream to units in Italy or Northwest Europe, a surprising 61 percent returned to operational duty as veterans after recuperating from illness or injury, and a few of these men returned to units two or three times.

In his 1956 book *Manpower in the Canadian Army, 1939–1945*, E.L.M. Burns, who had commanded the 1st Canadian Corps in Italy, wrote that units balked at taking reinforcements in the ranks of corporal and sergeant, and particularly disliked taking warrant officers.[30] The insinuation was, and has continued to be, that this attitude was caused primarily by the poor quality of reinforcement NCOs.[31] But a survey of NCO records does not support the negative appraisals that supposedly underpin this point of view. Units may very well have preferred to promote their own men as replacements for NCO casualties, and they may have "objected strongly" to absorbing NCOs from the reinforcement stream, as Burns states. But these attitudes probably had more to do with enduring regimentalism than with the alleged inadequacies of reinforcement NCOs.

Making the Best Use of Available Manpower

The army made good use of its manpower, wringing whatever it could from the material available to man its two-corps expeditionary force, home defence formations, and training systems. For instance, it found ways to use the older men who volunteered.[32] Arthur McIlvena, for example, joined the Edmonton Regiment at thirty-seven years old.[33] While he might have lacked the youth and vigour needed to keep up in a field unit, he came with two decades of valuable work experience. He had worked for the city of Edmonton as an administrative clerk and a relief worker, and he had been a police officer for five years. The army recognized his experience and skills, promoted him to sergeant within a month, and employed him in positions appropriate to his age, for example, as a quartermaster sergeant and eventually as a clerk. A March 1944 Personnel Selection Report assessed him as "a perfectionist who drives himself and others hard" and noted that he had "held positions of responsibility and trust requiring organizing and executive ability."[34] When the army released him in August 1944 for health reasons, he had given nearly five years of valuable service as a senior NCO. Some older men even made good soldiers in field units. Charles Nelson enlisted in the Regina Rifle Regiment at thirty-seven years of age with no previous military experience, and spent practically his whole military career with the unit. He rose relatively quickly in rank, becoming a sergeant after just twenty-one months, and a company sergeant major (warrant officer class 2) in three years. Nelson was holding the latter appointment when he was killed two days after going ashore at Normandy on D-Day.[35] In fact, 3 percent of the NCOs in the sample enlisted at thirty-five years of age or older, and with no previous military experience, and all rendered valuable service. This constituted but one way the army sought to make the best use of its available manpower. (First World War veterans were another group of older Canadians with something to offer, as discussed below.)

Units also kept poorly disciplined but able soldiers who would not have lasted long in any peacetime force, but who eventually smartened up and became NCOs. John Elliott was one such soldier.[36] He enlisted in January 1940 and over the next two years proved to be a chronic absentee without leave. Even a sentence of sixty days in detention failed to change his ways. But in the fall of 1942, he turned a proverbial corner and began to rise in rank. In July 1943, Elliott made it to sergeant. And in October 1943, he went to Italy as a reinforcement for his regiment, the 48th Highlanders of Canada, with whom he served until his death in January 1944. After two-plus years of disobedience, Elliott got himself together in time to become a senior NCO in a frontline unit.

Sometimes a recalcitrant soldier not only smartened up but excelled in battle. Such was the case with William Howard, who enlisted in December 1939 with the Canadian Scottish Regiment.[37] Over the next three and a half years, he amassed about sixteen absent without leave (AWL) charges, plus a few more charges for other offences. But Howard, if not very disciplined, was quite bright, having scored very high on the army intelligence test (putting him in the category of "superior ability"), and he clearly had latent potential. He spent most of his un-incarcerated time with reinforcement units until he went to the Mediterranean theatre to join the Princess Patricia's Canadian Light Infantry (PPCLI) in July 1943. He earned a promotion to acting lance corporal in January 1944, after which time he began to advance steadily in rank. On 22 September 1944, by then a corporal, he demonstrated exceptional leadership when it counted most. That day, when a German blocking position held up a PPCLI advance at the Marecchia River, Corporal Howard, then in command of a badly understrength platoon, led his men across a hundred yards (91 m) of open ground swept by machine-gun fire.[38] After placing his men under cover, he assaulted the enemy position, killing three and forcing the rest to withdraw. He then gathered his men and pursued the enemy as they fled to a nearby house. Once at the building, he forced five more to surrender before coming under yet more machine-gun fire. Howard next led a withdrawal, taking the prisoners with him and ensuring the evacuation of a wounded comrade. His leadership, determination, and bravery were key to overwhelming the enemy blocking position, and his efforts allowed the unit to continue its advance. Howard won the Military Medal for his actions, and he soon earned a promotion to sergeant. It had taken him sixty months to earn his sergeant's stripes, a very long time by Second World War standards, especially for one so intelligent. It was a good thing the army kept him, and the likes of him.

The story of Albert Laprade reinforces the theme of disobedient soldiers sometimes becoming ferocious NCOs in battle. In June 1940, Laprade enlisted in the Lake Superior Regiment.[39] He rose to corporal in just ten weeks but reverted to private six months later, probably because of an all-too-common tendency to absent himself without leave. He remained a private for three and a half years, piling up at least nine AWL charges, some for incidents lasting several days. In July 1944, by which time he had finally kicked his habit of shirking duty that did not interest him, he deployed to France with his regiment, and finally earned a promotion to lance corporal in October. In mid-March 1945, after fifty-seven months in the army, he finally earned his sergeant stripes. Three weeks later, he demonstrated extraordinary courage and leadership under fire.[40] On 5 April, as his unit advanced to capture the Dutch town of Coeverden, Laprade, in command of a carrier-based section of the unit's scout platoon, moved forward until coming under intense small arms fire. Deciding that the situation called for speed rather than carefully considered action, he rushed his section forward, killing and wounding many of the enemy. Just before he reached a key bridge, more German troops opened fire at close range, killing all the men in one of his vehicles. Laprade led his remaining men forward, all the while under heavy fire, and caught a German sapper party preparing to destroy the bridge. He killed the engineers, established a hasty defence, and fought off German counter-attacks until the rest of his company moved forward to finish clearing the town. Laprade's capture of the bridge allowed the 4th Canadian Armoured Division to continue its advance. His ability to read the situation and lead aggressively earned him the Military Medal – quite a good showing for a soldier who for four years had been a model of non-compliance.

The army benefited in battle by keeping early offenders like Elliott, Howard, and Laprade around. They were not alone. About 3.5 percent of the senior NCOs in the sample group took much time to develop into junior leaders, due to poor disciplinary behaviour. Five even won Military Medals. Despite their slow acceptance of discipline, these soldiers possessed uncommon steadiness under fire and a fierce determination to win. While their numbers represented a relatively small portion of the total NCO corps, the army did well to retain them.

The Contributions of Soldiers with Prior Military Experience

According to the official history, the permanent force and the NPAM supplied much of the active army's leadership. C.P. Stacey explains that the officers and men of the permanent force made important contributions, even if they formed only a tiny proportion of the wartime army.[41] As for the NPAM, he states,

> it would be difficult, indeed, to over-estimate the debt of the wartime Army to the Non-Permanent Active Militia [that] provided the foundation upon which the great new structure was built. It produced, to no small extent, the leaders who built and developed that structure. And it gave the Army a group of personnel, officers and men, who continued to play dominant parts in it even when the great majority of the Army's members had come to be volunteers of no militia experience recruited from civil life.[42]

But to what extent did permanent force and NPAM soldiers populate the wartime NCO corps? For that matter, to what extent did the wartime army draw on those with other forms of military experience to produce more NCOs?

Permanent force soldiers played a significant part. Sixteen (more than 4 percent) of the soldiers in the sample came from the permanent force. While this might seem a small share, it actually indicates that the permanent force played a role out of proportion to its size, considering that it was just 0.85 percent of the wartime army's peak strength of approximately 495,000. What is more, these men joined the active army as soon as the country mobilized, so their numbers were proportionally much higher in the initial force of about 60,000, in which their role as professionals shepherding the citizen-soldiers was most important.[43] Also, as service records show, permanent force soldiers helped develop the NCO corps in several ways. Many of them came to the wartime army as privates, with only a few years of service or less.[44] Yet these young professionals did well, often rising quickly to sergeant or higher.

Wendell Clark, who had served with the RCR since 1936, is a good example. Clark was still a private when he joined the active army in September 1939,

Figure 1.1 Regimental Sergeant Major Wendell Clark, the highest-ranking NCO in the 1st Canadian Parachute Battalion on D-Day, was a talented private in the permanent force when the war started and shot up in rank quickly as the army expanded. | Library and Archives Canada/Department of National Defence fonds/a179716.

although he received an immediate promotion to lance corporal.[45] An intelligent and driven soldier with excellent leadership ability, he rose quickly in rank, making sergeant in just five months. Thirteen months after going active, he rose to company sergeant major (warrant officer class 2). In November 1942, Clark became the regimental sergeant major (RSM) of the newly formed 1st Canadian Parachute Battalion. The growing army had to build its backbone quickly, and competent permanent force professionals like Clark were important to filling vacancies as required. He remained the RSM of the high-performance airborne unit until Operation Overlord, but he died in action hours after parachuting into France.

Of course, longer-serving permanent force NCOs joined the wartime army as well. For example, Lewis Pengelley of the RCR was a sergeant instructor (a member of the permanent force's elite Instructional Cadre) with over ten years of service when the war started.[46] He remained in Canada as a trainer, gradually ascending to the rank of warrant officer class 1. Pengelley never deployed overseas – he received a serious wound during training when a smoke bomb detonated in his hand, and he suffered kidney disease that killed him before the war ended – but he played an important part in training the wartime force. Pengelley spent his whole war as an instructor, initially in Borden for two years, and then in Toronto, from where he travelled around the province to various training camps. Many soldiers, probably thousands, trained under his watch. Another long-serving professional, Victor Cahill, had been in the PPCLI since 1919.[47] Cahill was a sergeant in 1939, but within a week of mobilizing received a promotion to CSM (warrant officer class 2). Although thirty-eight years old when he went to war, Cahill served overseas with the PPCLI until September 1942, after which time he moved on to training reinforcements, a role he played until the end of the war.[48] (As discussed in Chapter 4, at around that time, field units shed some of their older men, like Cahill.) These professional soldiers provided invaluable service in helping raise and lead the wartime force, especially in the first nine months of war, when the army was cobbling together the first two divisions.

Soldiers from the NPAM (called the army reserve after November 1940) made up a much larger percentage of the NCO corps. Of the soldiers in the sample group, 32 percent had NPAM or army reserve experience. Again, this was disproportionately high, given that the NPAM in 1939 was about one-tenth the size of the army at its wartime peak. Moreover, the full NPAM did not simply roll into the active army, and the government did not compel NPAM troops to serve anywhere during the war.[49] So the NPAM provided the wartime NCO corps with a significant proportion of its talent, including many men who filled NCO positions immediately upon enlisting for active service.

Table 1.10 shows the ranks held by NPAM or army reserve soldiers on enlistment in the active service force, and the proportion of each rank within this group of men with prior military experience. About one-third of the infantry senior NCOs in the wartime army had previous experience in the NPAM: 123 out of 388 in the sample group.[50] Of these, one-third filled NCO positions as soon as they enlisted for active service; the rest began their wartime careers as privates. And some of these NPAM men came with high ranks. For instance, the NPAM provided some regimental sergeants major, the most senior non-commissioned soldiers. When forty-two-year-old Andrew Currie attested for active duty in September 1939 with the Cameron Highlanders, he had been serving with the unit since 1920, and as its RSM since 1931.[51] Naturally, he became RSM of the active unit when it mobilized. Currie not only had almost two decades of experience with the Camerons but also had operational experience, having served with the British Expeditionary Force during the First World War. Between 1915 and 1920, Currie had served with the Royal Scots Fusiliers

Table 1.10

Wartime NCOs with experience in the NPAM or Reserve Army

	Experienced men enlisted at given rank (N)	NCOs as proportion of experienced group (%)
Private	83	n/a
Lance corporal	2	1.6
Corporal	13	10.6
Lance sergeant	0	0.0
Sergeant	17	13.8
CQMS (staff sergeant)	3	2.4
CSM (warrant officer 2)	3	2.4
RSM (warrant officer 1)	2	1.6
Total	123	32.4

Note: Ranks are those given on enlistment for wartime service.

in France, Belgium, Egypt, and Palestine. The Camerons were thus fortunate to have had an experienced RSM in place when they mobilized a wartime battalion.

Some former NPAM soldiers rose quickly to senior NCO rank in the active army, thanks in part to the head start of their prewar service. For example, in January 1940, John Daly enlisted in the active army after having spent seven years in the Elgin Regiment.[52] The wartime force accepted him as a corporal and made him a sergeant two months later, then CSM (warrant officer class 2) by November 1941. Just weeks later, he voluntarily reverted to private so that he could proceed overseas as a reinforcement. In March 1942, he joined the RCR and began to climb the ranks again. He reached sergeant for the second time in May 1943, just in time for Operation Husky, the Allied invasion of Sicily, and reclaimed his CSM appointment in July 1944. He died six weeks later from wounds received in battle. So, in four and a half years, Daly served as a sergeant for thirty-four months, and climbed to CSM twice. Similarly, when Austin Murray joined the active army in June 1942, he had served since 1937 in the 2nd/10th Dragoons, a militia unit in southern Ontario.[53] The army took him on as a sergeant. He served in Canada until June 1943, when he joined the Algonquin Regiment in Britain. Murray proved a strong soldier. The Algonquins accepted him as a CSM, and appointed him RSM the following November. Murray went to France with his unit in July 1944, and as RSM performed in battle with remarkable skill and bravery, taking grave personal risks to ensure ammunition resupply of isolated companies, inspiring soldiers when conditions threatened to break their fighting spirit, and personally leading clearing parties to rout out enemy soldiers around the battalion headquarters. In November 1944, he received the Military Cross for his outstanding performance in combat.[54] He died in action just six days before VE Day.

While such success stories highlight how the NPAM provided the NCO corps with some strong performers, several factors should temper any sentimental notions of the NPAM's overall contribution (as might flow from the old "militia myth," according to which Canada's reserve soldiers had innate soldiering talents that flourished whenever the country went to war). First, and most obvious, before the war the NPAM suffered from equipment shortages and poor training because of severely inadequate budgets, so NPAM NCOs joining the active army lacked knowledge of modern weapons and probably had limited experience exercising leadership in the field. Much of that had to be made up on wartime service. And just because a man had served in the NPAM did not mean that he was a good soldier. Furthermore, as personnel records reveal, men who came to the active army with NPAM or army reserve service arrived with widely varying degrees of experience, some with decades in uniform, others with months. Table 1.11 shows the degree to which experience varied.

Finally, these soldiers did not necessarily come to the active army straight from the NPAM. Many had been released before the war started, and in some

Table 1.11

Length of service in the NPAM or Reserve Army

Length of service	Experienced men (N)	Proportion of those with experience (%)
<6 months	18	15
6–12 months	11	9
1–2 years	27	22
2–3 years	7	6
3–4 years	12	10
4–5 years	9	7
5–10 years	20	16
>10 years	14	11
Unknown	5	4
Total	123	100

Table 1.12

Period when active duty soldiers served in the NPAM or Reserve Army

Time in NPAM	Number	Proportion (%)
In NPAM when war broke out	55	45
Released from NPAM *before* the war	38	31
Served in NPAM/Army Reserve *after* war broke out	25	20
Records unclear	8	7
Total	126*	103*

* Although 123 soldiers in the sample group had NPAM or Reserve Army experience, three with interrupted service fit into two of the categories in this table.

cases they had not worn a uniform in over ten years, so skills had often atrophied by 1939. Others did not join the NPAM until after the war broke out. Table 1.12 illustrates how these soldiers served as reservists in different periods.

Nonetheless, training reservists in Canada before and even during the war started the professional development of many who later served as NCOs in the wartime army. Almost a third of those who went on to be wartime NCOs had over five years of service as reservists. Unfortunately, ascertaining just what they did in the NPAM is difficult because wartime personnel files contain very little information in this regard. Realistically, soldiers who first became NCOs as reservists, most in the peacetime army, probably learned just the basics about leadership, administration, and tactics – the sorts of knowledge that peacetime promotion examinations tested for – which at least helped start these men down the path to professional development. In short, the NPAM was a source of un-evenly developed talent for NCOs.

First World War veterans constituted another element of the nation's man-power with military experience, and therefore military potential. Of course, almost all were too old to do any actual fighting. A man who had been in his early twenties in 1918 was in his early forties when the Second World War began. Still, faced with the challenge of mobilizing a large army from only a tiny peace-time foundation, the nation needed to marshal all its military experience. So the army found ways to employ veterans who volunteered, using them mainly in a home defence capacity.[55] Four percent of the soldiers in the sample group had First World War experience, enlisting in the active army at an average forty-four years of age. Most filled NCO positions on enlisting, with just under one in five joining as privates and becoming NCOs later. In rare cases, First World War veterans with long NPAM service to boot provided units with their first RSMs. Few of these veterans served their entire Second World War careers with operational units and only one in the sample group actually saw action. Most served in non-operational capacities – as trainers, military police, personnel selection staff, district depot storesmen, and so on. Thus, First World War veterans helped develop the NCO corps mostly by filling leadership positions that did not require the stamina needed by soldiers in combat.

Finally, a small proportion of the active army's senior NCOs, 6 percent of the sample group, started out as conscripts. Most of these men volunteered for active service within four months of call-up, and all but a very small handful went active within a year of entering the army. Only 0.8 percent of the sample group rose to NCO rank while still serving as conscripts, an interesting finding given that the proportion of conscripts serving as NCOs in Canada was likely to have been much higher before the autumn of 1944.[56] Regardless, some of the men the nation compelled to serve at home volunteered for service overseas and became NCOs. In fact, service records suggest that overall these men made for good soldiers.[57] The sample group did not include any conscripts who deployed abroad as NCOs after the government's November 1944 decision to order 16,000 "zombies" – the derisory term that volunteers used for conscripts – overseas.

Warrant Officer Origins

Those who came to the active army with previous military experience formed the largest part of the upper NCO ranks, as one would expect and the sample group demonstrates. Table 1.13 shows the extent to which those in the sample who had previous military experience made up the warrant officer cadre. Almost three-quarters of the warrant officers in the infantry had prior service, most in the permanent force or NPAM. These findings indicate that the prewar army was the principal source of NCOs who would become wartime warrant officers.

Table 1.13

Warrant officers (seventy in the sample group) with previous military experience

Experience	Number out of 70	Proportion of WOs with experience (%)
Permanent force	16	23
NPAM	30	43
First World War	5	7
None	25	36

Note: Several soldiers appear in more than one row.

An astonishing 23 percent came from the tiny permanent force alone – perhaps one of this study's most surprising findings.

Conclusion

The army produced NCOs relatively quickly. It took *on average* thirty-three and a half months for a soldier to reach sergeant, often with one or two ups and downs in rank. Those who had no prewar military experience took only slightly longer, at thirty-five months. This was a short period in which to transform a raw civilian into a skilled platoon sergeant, responsible for the leadership, discipline, and administration of thirty-plus soldiers. But Canada had to raise the army quickly, and those building it did not know how much time they had. Only in hindsight do we know that Canada would not commit troops to sustained combat until July 1943. The army was fortunate to have had the time it did to develop its NCOs.

Service records reveal that the army relied heavily on men with experience in the permanent force or the NPAM to populate the NCO corps, especially its senior ranks. Permanent force soldiers constituted 4 percent of the wartime infantry senior NCOs, and men from the NPAM made up 32 percent, both disproportionately large contributions given the enormous disparity in size between the wartime army and the prewar forces. Furthermore, permanent force soldiers formed a remarkable 23 percent of the active army's warrant officers, and NPAM soldiers made up another 43 percent. So, men from Canada's tiny prewar army made up a surprising two-thirds of the wartime warrant officers.

The service records also give some indication of how the army made good use of available manpower. It found suitable work for NCOs who were either too old or medically unfit for field units. Men up to forty or forty-five could join the infantry (depending on when they enlisted), which allowed the army to draw on their skills and experience even if they were unsuited for the rigours of service in a field unit. On rare occasions, the army also fast-tracked raw recruits to NCO rank if they had talent, valuable work experience, or higher education. And the army even retained soldiers who possessed leadership potential despite poor disciplinary records. Some of these soldiers eventually smartened up and made good, sometimes even exceptional, combat leaders. Together, these three groups formed about 9 percent of the infantry's senior NCOs, demonstrating that efforts to cast a wide net paid off. Of course, given the nature of the sample group, all these findings are biased toward the infantry in the overseas army. More research is necessary to determine the extent to which they apply to the other arms and services.

NCO Development before the War

When the QOR mobilized for overseas service, most of the militiamen like myself automatically enlisted ... I was promoted to Warrant Officer Second Class the next day ... Peacetime service in the Non Permanent Active Militia (NPAM) stood us in good stead for the basics of Army service: how to teach drill, saluting, rifle handling, and so on.

HARRY FOX, QUEEN'S OWN RIFLES

IN THE YEARS LEADING up to the Second World War, the Canadian army did what it could with meagre resources to maintain the basis for a much larger force that could stand up on order. But depression-era budgets precluded doing more than keeping the bare scaffolding intact. Equipment was old, much of it from the First World War. And units received few funds for routine training, or even for paying part-time soldiers to parade.

Still, the army had a few strengths that could be maintained at little cost. A tiny professional component, the permanent force, kept up a cadre of carefully selected instructors who ran training for the country's part-time soldiers who would form the bulk of any fighting formations that took the field during wartime. Soldiers aspiring to rise in rank, professionals and part-timers alike, had to meet set promotion standards for advancement. Instructional schools ran courses that gave NCOs and officers the fundamental skills they required as leaders and specialists. And throughout the 1930s, National Defence Headquarters (NDHQ) maintained detailed mobilization plans for raising any forces needed to defend national territory or deploy abroad.

Canada's prewar military was starved of resources, no doubt, but it kept alive the vital structures needed for raising an army in time of crisis. The force maintained units that would serve as basic building blocks when the time came to assemble formations, all in accordance with reasonably well conceived mobilization plans. And the basic apparatus for producing NCOs – promotion standards and training institutions – ensured that the tiny force sustained at least a rudimentary backbone of trained non-commissioned leaders, many of whom helped form the wartime NCO corps.

The Prewar Army and Its NCO Corps

The prewar army maintained a network of professional and part-time forces across the nation. The Permanent Active Militia (PAM), as the professional component, included the permanent force (the name most often used for Canada's peacetime regular force), plus some officers permanently employed but not carried on any regimental or headquarters establishment. The PAM served two functions: it maintained standing forces that remained available for general service; and it trained the part-time soldiers of the Non-Permanent Active Militia (NPAM). For the latter role, the permanent force maintained the Instructional Cadre, an organization composed of soldiers who, with special teaching qualifications, ran training wherever the army required.[1] NDHQ in Ottawa exercised overall command, control, and administration. Under NDHQ sat eleven military districts, each headed by a district officer commanding who held responsibility for the command and administration of all units within his geographical boundaries. These military districts conformed to provincial, intra-provincial, or extra-provincial boundaries. For example, Military District 7 covered New Brunswick. Military Districts 1, 2, and 3 existed within Ontario. Military District 6 included Nova Scotia and Prince Edward Island.

To keep the peacetime force filled with soldiers the government could employ as needed, NDHQ maintained fairly straightforward entrance requirements and terms of service. The army was not very particular about the age or size of men it enlisted. Anyone wishing to join had to be between eighteen and forty-five years of age and capable of passing a medical examination. One's chest had to measure at least thirty-four inches (86 cm), although an eighteen- or nineteen-year-old could have a thirty-two-inch (81 cm) chest if a reasonable chance existed that he would grow during training. One had to stand at least five feet, four inches tall (162 cm), while artillerymen had to be two or three inches (5–7.6 cm) taller, depending on unit type. And applicants had to weigh at least 140 pounds (63.5 kg), or 135 pounds (61 kg) for cavalry. The medical examination also verified whether a prospective recruit had sufficient mental capacity, as well as good vision, good hearing, well-developed limbs, and no serious illnesses or physical impediments.[2] Those who met the physical standards could be attested into the army for a three-year period. Serving soldiers, in either the permanent force or the NPAM, who wished to continue their service after their contracts expired signed on for additional three-year engagements.[3] All soldiers were subject to call-out for active service anywhere in Canada or, if necessary, abroad to ensure the direct defence of Canada. However, the government could only compel NPAM soldiers to serve continuously for up to one year, or in cases of "unavoidable necessity," for up to eighteen months. Permanent force soldiers were liable for permanent service when called out.[4]

Training and Development before the War

The army demanded that soldiers qualify for promotion by passing qualification examinations, a practice that dated back to at least 1911. That was when Major-General William Otter, then inspector general of the militia, found to his dismay that no clear standard of qualification for NCOs of either the permanent force or non-permanent units existed and therefore that "various degrees of efficiency" prevailed in both.[5] To redress the problem, Otter recommended that the army establish uniform NCO qualification standards by producing a training syllabus for each arm of service. Shortly after, the chief of the general staff, Major-General Sir Colin Mackenzie, directed the commandant of each arm's School of Instruction to draft a standardized syllabus that all schools of that arm would use.[6] The commandants provided their input, and before long the army had standardized NCO qualification criteria. Non-commissioned soldiers now had to earn qualification certificates at Schools of Military Instruction, a regulation the army codified in the next version of the *King's Regulations and Orders for the Canadian Militia* (KR&Os), published in 1917.[7]

Non-commissioned soldiers already serving when the Second World War broke out had earned their ranks according to rules that for the most part had been in place since at least 1926, when the army published a new version of the KR&Os.[8] For example, the 1926 regulations stipulated that promotion to the rank of sergeant in both permanent force and NPAM combatant units required a sergeant's qualification certificate in the relevant arm of service (Figure 2.1).[9] The army ran the qualification training at royal and permanent Schools of Instruction and at local camp schools. Soldiers nominated to attend these schools had to pass an entrance exam to demonstrate elementary knowledge of subjects outlined in a "common to all arms" syllabus.[10] The course curriculum for promotion to sergeant focused on platoon-level (or equivalent) leadership, and included the same subjects as those studied by officer cadets and second lieutenants for qualification to lieutenant, although instruction and the final examination were limited to the knowledge a sergeant required. The final examination consisted of practical tests in drill, the use of arms and equipment, and NCO duties in the field, plus written tests in organization, regimental duties, military law, tactics, administration of troops in the field, map reading, and field works.[11]

The regulations governing promotion to NCO ranks other than sergeant varied by component. For example, NPAM soldiers had to earn certificates of

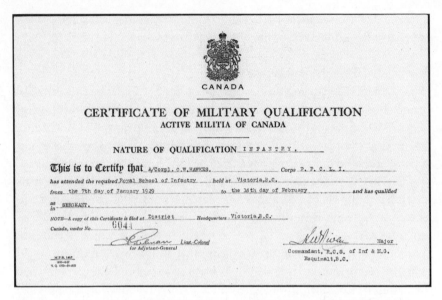

Figure 2.1   Acting Corporal G.W. Hawkes, a permanent force junior NCO, earned his Sergeant's Qualification Certificate in 1929 at a Royal School of Instruction. | Qualification Certificate of Acting Corporal G.W. Hawkes, Service Number P21152 © Government of Canada. Reproduced with the permission of Library and Archives Canada (2020). Library and Archives Canada/Department of National Defence fonds/RG24 vol. 26079.

qualification for the ranks of corporal and warrant officer class 2. A soldier earned a corporal's certificate by attending the same sergeant's qualification course outlined above. If, on the final examination, he failed to meet the standard required of a sergeant but demonstrated enough proficiency for employment as a corporal, he could be awarded a certificate of qualification for that rank. To qualify for promotion to warrant officer class 2, a soldier attended a course similar to that for qualification to sergeant, but with additional instruction in the subject of command and in the administrative duties of a sub-unit sergeant major (company-, battery-, or squadron-level) or a unit quartermaster sergeant.[12] Meanwhile, eligibility for promotion to warrant officer class 1 varied by component and arm of service. All infantry and cavalry soldiers, plus permanent force members of the Royal Canadian Army Service Corps, had to possess a small arms instructor certificate of qualification from a Canadian small arms school. Artillerymen seeking appointment as second- or first-class gunners (at the rank of warrant officer class 1) had to graduate from a master gunner's course in Canada or Britain.[13]

Earning the requisite certificate was only the first step, as the chain of command decided who among those qualified merited promotion into a unit's vacant positions. The army carefully controlled promotions to warrant officer class 1. Only NDHQ promoted soldiers to this rank, based on recommendations that flowed up through the districts. For promotions up to warrant officer class 2, generally speaking, unit commanders decided whom to promote, although some exceptions existed. For example, sub-unit commanders could promote soldiers to corporal in some permanent force arms of service (cavalry and artillery) and in some NPAM arms of service (the Corps of Guides, independent signals companies, and machine-gun squadrons). For certain permanent force supporting corps (service, medical, veterinary, ordnance, pay, and staff clerk), the officer administering the corps decided on all promotions up to warrant officer class 2.[14] Furthermore, all non-commissioned soldiers in the permanent force required good instructional skills for advancement. Therefore, before a man could receive a promotion, his sub-unit commander had to certify not only that the candidate possessed the requisite general military knowledge and that his general character suited him for the next rank but also that he was a capable instructor.[15]

Authorities placed a premium on teaching soldiers, permanent force and NPAM alike, how to teach. The army ran courses to qualify soldiers as regimental instructors in a wide range of fields: small arms handling, drill, protection against gas, gunnery, and so on. NDHQ demanded that only candidates who demonstrated an aptitude for instruction and who already possessed good knowledge of the subject in question be selected for instructor training. By at least 1938, and in some cases much earlier, instructor courses began with an entrance examination to weed out those lacking instructional ability or sufficient baseline knowledge.[16] Meanwhile, the training schools ran these courses to national standards. The Canadian Small Arms School, for example, trained NCOs and officers to serve as small arms instructors. Located at the Connaught Ranges in Ottawa and with a branch in Sarcee, Alberta, the school designed its courses to ensure that small arms training across the force adhered to a uniform and up-to-date program of instruction.[17]

The Instructional Cadre was a particularly important group of instructors. It consisted of select permanent force soldiers who taught particular subjects and ran physical training across the army. Cadre members belonged to operational units on a supernumerary basis, over and above authorized establishments. As required, NDHQ dispatched these soldiers to military districts for instructional duty. Members of the Instructional Cadre constituted a sort of elite and therefore held special appointments: warrant officers class 1 were appointed sergeant major instructor; quartermasters sergeant (warrant officers class 2) were appointed quartermaster sergeant instructor; sub-unit sergeants major (warrant officer class 2) were appointed squadron, company, or battery sergeant major instructor; and sergeants were appointed sergeant instructor.[18] Because the army considered the Instructor Cadre's role so important, the chain of command carefully controlled the group's membership. To join the cadre, a soldier required a commanding officer's recommendation. The aspiring soldier also had to have a sergeant's certificate in his arm or branch of service, and he had to pass an examination set by NDHQ and administered locally. He also needed certain qualifications particular to his arm or branch of service. For example, infantrymen required a qualification certificate from the Canadian Small Arms School, and engineers needed a 2nd Class Instructor's Certificate from the Canadian School of Military Engineering.[19] Earning one's way into the Instructional Cadre took a great deal of effort. As John Clifford Cave, who served before the war with the Princess Patricia's Canadian Light Infantry (PPCLI), explained: "You had to work like spit to become a sergeant major, and [in] particular an instructional sergeant major. You have to work like spit and you've got to study like hell. And a lot of it. And you've got to be better than anybody else at it or you're not going to make it."[20] Upon posting to the cadre, a soldier had to perform well as an instructor or he would not keep his job. New members were on probation for a full year, in fact. But soldiers had good reasons for joining the group and meeting its high standards.

The army enticed quality candidates to the Instructional Cadre with several incentives. For example, even during his probationary period, a corporal held the rank of acting sergeant and received the pay and allowances of a sergeant instructor. On completion of the probation he earned confirmation in the rank of sergeant. Soldiers higher than sergeant joining the Instructional Cadre received the associated appointment, with its enhanced pay and allowances. Furthermore, the cadre offered good prospects for future promotion. So long as a soldier performed as expected, earned the qualification for the next rank, and received a recommendation, he earned promotion after three years.[21]

Before the war, NCOs benefited from a reasonably good individual training system for leadership.[22] The army might not have enjoyed anything close to adequate funding in the lean years of the 1930s, but NDHQ directed much of its limited capital to the foundationally important business of training junior leaders. Non-commissioned soldiers in the prewar army trained to national standards and passed promotion examinations to ensure they had the necessary skills to perform at the next rank. It had to be that way. The army's senior leaders knew that good NCOs would be crucial for raising, training, and operating an expeditionary force if ever the nation mobilized.

Prewar Mobilization Plans

Throughout the 1930s, NDHQ developed and continuously updated mobilization plans to defend national territory or deploy expeditionary forces abroad in the event of war. In fact, work on the plan Canada eventually used began in 1927, when the chief of the general staff, Major-General James MacBrien, ordered staff to draft a contingency plan for the expansion of military forces. The plan soon focused on raising a two-division corps, plus a cavalry division and the necessary supporting elements, based on establishments for a British expeditionary force.[23] The carefully guarded plan became Defence Scheme No. 3.[24] Several years passed before the general staff finalized matters down to the last details, but by the fall of 1932, planners had most of the nuts and bolts worked out in a series of classified appendices that laid out arrangements for the composition of the force, appointments to command and staff positions, the provision of personnel to unit and formation headquarters, and how permanent force personnel would provide instructional services to the deploying forces.[25] In fact, the plan dictated that permanent force units would form part of the second group to deploy, not the first.[26] This would allow Canada's professional soldiers to train the NPAM units forming the bulk of any expeditionary commitment.

Appendix 4 of the plan included a standing list of instructional positions the permanent force would fill upon mobilization, with NCOs and officers identified by name. NDHQ set the requirements and tasked each military district to fill particular positions that were key to training the contingent. The districts, in turn, submitted nominations to NDHQ, which authorized and published the confirmed list as Appendix 4.[27] These instructors, mostly NCOs from corporal to warrant officer class 1, included many soldiers from the Instructional Cadre plus some officers up to the rank of major. On mobilization, soldiers listed in the appendix would move quickly to their assigned "first flight" NPAM units, where they would start the work of preparing the men for early deployment.[28] Providing instructors to mobilizing NPAM units became a priority task for the permanent force, and NDHQ designed Appendix 4 to ensure that the dispatch of instructors occurred quickly and without confusion.[29] Planners in Ottawa periodically worked with the districts to update the list and keep it current. By 1937, NDHQ renewed the appendix of names annually.

In the spring of 1937, Defence Scheme No. 3 took the form of the mobilization plan with which Canada eventually went to war. That March, the chief of the general staff, Major-General Ernest Ashton, requested that Minister of National Defence, Ian Mackenzie, review and authorize an updated version because the evolving security situation abroad had necessitated amendments. Ashton explained that since 1930 Defence Scheme No. 3 had focused on the most likely requirement for mobilization: dispatching forces "in co-operation with other Governments of the British Empire ... to fulfil our possible obligations under the Covenant of the League of Nations."[30] Direct threats to Canadian territory had not been a serious concern. But, Ashton warned, the international security environment had changed. Germany and Japan had left the League, and Italy had snubbed its covenant obligations. All three powers were building formidable armed forces. Furthermore, if war broke out between the great powers, Canadian territory could be at risk, with Japan's navy perhaps menacing the West Coast and the range and power of modern bombers potentially putting Canada within range of air threats from overseas. Consequently, military planners had revised Defence Scheme No. 3 to include a plan for defending the homeland, in addition to raising expeditionary forces.[31] The scheme prepared for three potential scenarios: war in the Far East between Britain and Japan, war in Europe between Britain and Germany, and a world war involving a German–Japanese coalition. Mackenzie reviewed the proposal and, just two days after receiving it, indicated his support for both the home defence and expeditionary measures:

> I am glad to observe that the dominant motif of the plan is the defence of Canada and internal security; but I realize that whereas Government policy is at the moment concerned with the defence of Canada and the protection of Canadian neutrality it is the duty of the staff to prepare for every possible contingency. I therefore approve the plan in principle and detail.[32]

The revised plan focused primarily on raising forces to defend Canadian territory, but also considered the process of sending them abroad if the government wished.[33] Measures detailed the mobilization of units to defend coastal areas and to conduct internal security tasks for protection against sabotage or other minor enemy operations. In addition, the plan called for raising a "Mobile Force of all arms capable of independent action."[34] This force could operate in Canada or overseas. If employed at home, its purpose was to deal with enemy landings in Canada that local forces could not handle. If sent overseas, it would operate with other British Commonwealth forces. In any scenario, the Mobile Force would consist of a corps headquarters, a cavalry division, two standard divisions, line of communications troops, and the resources to run camps and bases in Canada and, if necessary, overseas. Formed units would come from the NPAM and the permanent force. The plan recognized that mobilizing these forces would necessitate a great deal of assistance by the nation's scarce professional soldiers. This was why permanent force units would not be part of Force A, the first group to mobilize, although individual permanent force soldiers would join Force A in key command and staff appointments or as instructors.[35] Thus, military authorities planned to raise a wartime NCO corps partly by mobilizing existing militia units and stiffening them with intense and targeted training by permanent force instructors.

The military districts played a crucial role in the development and evolution of Defence Scheme No. 3. At the end of each year, NDHQ solicited from the districts lists of resources that could be committed in support of specific mobilization requirements. For example, each district nominated units to perform local defence and internal security tasks. Selecting units in advance enabled the cabinet to place them on active service immediately during an emergency, a strict legal requirement under the Militia Act. Similarly, districts proposed which of their units should be designated for the Mobile Force. In making recommendations, district staff considered a unit's efficiency as judged by its annual training and inspection results, the qualifications of the unit officers, the capacity of the unit to mobilize to its war establishment, and the potential demands of local defence. NDHQ made the final selections, which appeared in Appendix 2 of the Defence Scheme, but only the affected district officers commanding and certain staff knew which units had made the cut. The units themselves were not to be informed until mobilization was imminent. Similar arrangements existed for nominating and approving officers for command and staff positions in the Mobile Force (which appeared in Appendix 3) and, of course, for permanent force instructors to whip designated units into shape (Appendix 4).

Because authorities kept Defence Scheme No. 3 secret, NDHQ published a pamphlet called *Mobilization Instructions for the Canadian Militia, 1937*, which informed the army at large how to mobilize.[36] The process would start when NDHQ issued mobilization orders by telegram to the district officers commanding. Units ordered to mobilize would immediately recruit to their war establishments. Volunteers had to be between eighteen and forty-five years of age to join. And, owing to the Militia Act's stipulation that NPAM soldiers could not be compelled to serve overseas or for more than eighteen months straight, anyone wanting to serve in the mobilizing force had to sign duration-of-war engagements for general service. When war establishments were complete – supposedly within seven days – units for the first contingent would gather at a concentration area for dispatch to a theatre of operations or to an intermediate base overseas.[37]

Meanwhile, the army would raise the institutional architecture needed to produce a continuous stream of reinforcements for replacing casualties. New recruiting centres would open.[38] Depots to receive, clothe, and equip enlistees and post them to training units would expand to accommodate the rush of recruits. NPAM infantry and cavalry units would bring their depots up to war establishment, as would the district depots, which supported the other arms and services. Mobilizing permanent force units would establish depots as well. On top of that, training units would stand up across the country to prepare the reinforcements. Each district would form one or more infantry training centres, while NDHQ would organize training centres for all other corps and services. All these depots and training camps were to be manned with NCOs and officers from the units they supported.

Authorities knew that mobilization would place huge demands on Canada's limited supply of trained NCOs. Permanent force personnel would have to continue running qualification courses for the army while also raising reinforcements for deployed permanent force units. NDHQ therefore intended to establish new depots, training units, and royal schools at permanent force stations.[39] Clearly, this would increase demand for NCO instructors. In fact, the *Mobilization Instructions* warned that the permanent force alone would post at least 20 percent of its total strength to training institutions. More than that, permanent force units would also expand to their war establishments, which would in turn require yet more NCOs. Meanwhile, the army's new recruiting centres would need NCOs in recruiting and administrative roles.[40] The district and corps-of-arms depots and training centres standing up across the country would spike demand for NCOs as well. If the Mobile Force deployed overseas, a Canadian overseas headquarters would establish new training units to prepare both reinforcements from Canada and personnel discharged from hospitals and convalescent depots. Army authorities planned several measures to meet high demand with scarce NCO resources. Some measures were small. To staff overseas training units, the army planned to employ Mobile Force personnel who had proven physically unfit for combat duty after deploying abroad. Additional staff would be drawn from Canada as needed. But the biggest measure to make up shortfalls was the early and rapid promotion of suitable soldiers to NCO rank. Qualification examinations would be out of the window, so to speak.

The *Mobilization Instructions* catered to this requirement, specifying how promotion would occur swiftly across the NCO corps on mobilization. NCOs proceeding on active service would either keep their ranks or receive a promotion. The instructions even guaranteed that NPAM soldiers would keep confirmed ranks when they joined their permanent force colleagues in the Canadian Field Force, the name to be given to the entire force mobilized for general service.[41] No NPAM NCO could be required to serve in the Field Force at a rank lower than his confirmed rank in the NPAM. Not that there would be much need to demote soldiers, given the many newly established NCO positions. To fill their war establishments, the officers in command of field units, headquarters, depots, and training units were responsible for making necessary promotions up to the rank of warrant officer class 2, but to acting rank only with confirmation possible after three months. For promotions to warrant officer class 1, unit commanders submitted nominations through their district headquarters to NDHQ for approval. The *Mobilization Instructions* accounted for *where* the NCOs would come from for the expanding Field Force, but with so many newly promoted NCOs – many of whom were bound to lack the qualifications or essential knowledge for their new ranks – the force would contain scores of junior leaders who needed time, if not training, to develop the expertise they needed. On this issue, the *Mobilization Instructions* were mute, aside from plans for the permanent force to continue running qualification courses, or at least as many as possible. Presumably, authorities expected mobilizing units to train their own newly promoted personnel, but the *Mobilization Instructions* did not explicitly say so.

Shortly before the war broke out, NDHQ amended parts of the mobilization plan that seemed impractical. Raising a division of horsed cavalry made little sense, for example, and the idea was soon jettisoned. Similarly, the plan for units to fill their war establishments within a week of receiving mobilization orders was unrealistic. NDHQ calculated that they needed three weeks to do so, to allow recruiting staff to do a proper job of conducting medical examinations, enlisting volunteers, and filling out the paperwork for each new soldier. Finally, the 1937 plan to place permanent force units in the Mobile Force's second division required reconsideration. The chief of the general staff, Major-General Thomas Anderson, pointed out to the minister that the permanent force would be left behind if the government decided to dispatch only one division, causing it to lose prestige. Anderson made a strong argument. How could the permanent force fulfill its vital instructional role over time if its members gained no operational experience? He therefore recommended that permanent force units form part of the first division instead of the second. The minister agreed with Anderson's reasoning and approved the changes.[42]

Other shortfalls complicated matters. Two decades of austere defence budgets had left the force poorly prepared for high-intensity warfare. The 1930s were especially lean years. Spending bottomed out in the fiscal year 1932–33, when the total defence budget amounted to just under $14.15 million, shared across the services.[43] The army's slice was a mere $8.7 million, for a force of about 3,200 permanent force and 42,500 NPAM soldiers.[44] Despite slowly increasing funding, the army had little choice but to focus on individual training for NCOs, officers, and specialists. There was barely any money for anything else, including collective training. In 1935–36, so few funds were available that NPAM units received authority to pay soldiers to train for a mere twelve days of the year. Many units actually conducted additional training but without paying their men.[45] Although defence spending continued to tick up a bit, for the fiscal year 1938–39 the average NPAM unit trained for only about nine days locally and about eight days in camp.[46] That year, the last before spending increased dramatically with mobilization, the total defence budget was still just $34.8 million. Of this, the army received only $15.77 million, a $1.45 million *decrease* from the previous year, as air and naval forces started to garner greater proportions of defence estimates.[47] The army's paltry sums did not permit even moderately strong field forces to be maintained, let alone starting a sorely needed rearmament program. By then, collective skills had degraded badly. From 1930 to 1938, tiny budgets precluded the permanent force and the NPAM from conducting any substantial collective training.[48] When the permanent force finally ran a brigade-sized field exercise in 1938, the first since 1929, sloppy overall performance demonstrated a lack of unit-level skill in executing tactical doctrine.

Just days before the war broke out, the service chiefs of staffs briefed the government on the readiness of Canada's armed forces. In short, the chiefs advised that the nation possessed sufficient manpower to defend Canadian territory, execute standing air force and naval plans, and send overseas a 60,000-man Mobile Force consisting of a two-division corps with supporting troops. They also emphasized the essential problem undermining the army: a lack of equipment. They were candid about where much of the scanty prewar resources had been expended: "The policy for training for years has concentrated on the training of officers, N.C.O.s and specialists so as to facilitate expansion of units to a war footing on mobilization."[49] But, as the chiefs remarked, equipment was in terribly short supply and stocks could barely facilitate training in Canada:

It is true that, apart from a small number obtained for training purposes, we are completely deficient in such essential items as armoured vehicles of all descriptions, anti-tank guns and the anti-aircraft guns and equipment needed for the force. Moreover, our field artillery, though adequate for training purposes is obsolescent insofar as its use in active operations is concerned.[50]

Nevertheless, the chiefs indicated that the Mobile Force could be dispatched overseas, albeit only partly equipped and trained, within three months of receiving the order to mobilize. With far too much optimism, they also suggested that if the British could finish equipping Canadian formations shortly after they arrived in Britain, the Mobile Force could "take the field as a powerful fighting force, about six months after mobilization." But simply acquiring sufficient quantities of good equipment hardly made for an effective army. The force required doctrine to employ different weapon types in concert with one another as part of a greater fighting system, and it needed to master applying that doctrine in the field. At lower levels, individual soldiers and crews had to learn how to operate, move, and maintain the newly acquired armaments. This demanded NCOs who were both expert weapons handlers and competent instructors. All this would, and later did, take time and effort.

On 1 September 1939, Canada started mobilizing for war and Defence Scheme No. 3 went into effect. The district officers commanding received their mobilization telegrams, ordering the establishment of a two-division corps with ancillary troops, plus units for coastal and air defence.[51] In passing various orders-in-council to initiate mobilizing the three services, Cabinet replaced the name Canadian Field Force with Canadian Active Service Force.[52] And the army began its long preparations for war.

Conclusion

The wartime army built its corps of NCOs on the prewar army, but that foundation was neither large enough nor very sturdy. The system for training NCOs had a few strong points. The permanent force focused much of its effort on training the NPAM, in part by maintaining the Instructional Cadre, whose purpose was to train the rest of the army. Permanent force–run schools provided standardized leadership training and NCO qualification courses. Soldier-students had to pass demanding examinations. And the army at least gave NCOs an environment that kept alive regimental traditions, military culture, and even some hard-won lessons of the First World War. Yet there was only so much Canada's little military could do to prepare for a major conflict.

Five months before the war started, the Department of National Defence reported that the permanent force numbered 4,169 men, including 3,714 other ranks, of whom roughly 600 were NCOs. The NPAM comprised about 51,400 men, including 45,045 other ranks, among them roughly 7,600 NCOs, not all of whom could be counted on to volunteer for active service.[53] From a purely quantitative perspective, these were small numbers compared to the half-million-strong force that Canada eventually raised, with its NCO corps of over 110,000.[54] The prewar army – permanent force and NPAM combined – could thus have provided only a fraction of the NCOs needed for the wartime force. The rest had to be built from scratch. Additionally, many NCOs lacked sufficient professional development opportunities, especially when it came to collective training. Tiny defence budgets meant that money for field exercises was always short, so soldiers had limited opportunities to hone their skills in tactics and leadership. Worse still, the army possessed few arms, and nothing modern, so NCOs had no way of becoming experts in operating and maintaining modern weapons, let alone instructing in their use. At least the army had a fairly well conceived mobilization plan that allowed for assembling forces with an efficiency that contrasted sharply with the chaos of 1914. But the NCOs who proceeded overseas still needed much training and time to develop before they became proficient in their new roles.

The Wartime Army's Expectations of Its NCOs

Most of us had become battle-wise through experience in Normandy and during several years of training in England before D-Day. We had endured the toughest sort of training – tougher, in many instances, than conditions encountered in actual battle. Even in training we were blooded; live ammunition was used, and there were casualties ... And we were fit. Part of our training on the Isle of Wight for the Dieppe raid included frequent fifteen-mile march-and-runs in full battle order ... One man who was badly wounded in the Dieppe raid was told in hospital that there would have been many more deaths if the men had not been in such excellent physical condition. Shock alone, he was informed, would have finished off a lot more of them.

DENIS WHITAKER, ROYAL HAMILTON LIGHT INFANTRY

WHEN THE WAR STARTED, military authorities knew perfectly well what they needed in the NCO corps. After all, NCO roles had never changed much.[1] NCOs ensured that the rank and file executed higher orders. They maintained discipline in the ranks by enforcing rules, modelling appropriate behaviour, and demonstrating calm under fire. They advised officers on morale. They looked after their soldiers' well-being and ensured that the men were prepared for the extreme challenges ahead. As technical experts, they possessed comprehensive knowledge of how to employ weapons and equipment. As instructors, they ran the army's training programs. And they served as able tacticians who led soldiers in combat and assumed command when junior officers became casualties.

As the war continued, the list of essential NCO competencies grew, complicating the NCO development problem. As units and formations learned how to assemble the elements of modern combat power and fight as coordinated teams, the army needed its NCOs to elevate their abilities in two domains: physical fitness and knowledge of tactics. Canada's citizen-soldiers had to be fit and tough if they were to defeat veteran German forces, so formation and unit commanders used physical training to harden their men for battle. Forced marches featured prominently and over time, Canadian troops developed a capacity to cover long distances – sometimes two dozen miles (about

40 km) or more in a day – at a surprisingly fast pace and repeated over several consecutive days. NCOs had to possess the vigour not only to keep up but to lead, motivate, and coerce as necessary. Consequently, youth and stamina became key NCO characteristics, particularly in field units. While training in Britain, units therefore gradually posted out their older NCOs who had played an important part during the early mobilization period but who could not keep up with the growing physical demands.[2] Meanwhile, cooperation between arms improved, so infantry NCOs had to learn more about operating with tanks, artillery, and engineers. In units that had to become proficient at combined operations in preparation for an eventual forced entry onto the continent through amphibious assault, NCOs learned how to work with the navy.[3] And, as units readied themselves for assaulting towns and villages on the continent, NCOs had to master the tactics of town fighting, because house-to-house combat necessitated operating in small NCO-led teams. In all these endeavours, NCOs trained and led the rank and file. All of these new requirements brought new challenges to how the army developed it non-commissioned leadership. They meant that NCO training programs had to evolve over time in anticipation of how the army expected to fight. Investigating how the army developed the NCO corps to meet these new requirements therefore requires an appreciation of the wartime demands that NCOs had to meet.

Rising Fitness Standards

In early 1941, long forced marches, conducted to make soldiers harder and fitter, became a regular feature of army collective training. For instance, the 2nd Canadian Division training instructions for the first two and a half months of the year declared that physical fitness in the newly assembled formation required improvement and that "particular attention should, therefore, be paid to route marches and various forms of physical training. Units must be able to march 20–25 miles [32–45 km] in a day and 50–60 miles [80–97 km] in three successive days and yet be fit to fight at the end of the march."[4] Commanding officers wasted no time in readying troops to meet the challenging standard. The division's battalions started conducting intensive route marches about once per week and, by late February, were covering distances of twenty to twenty-five miles.[5] Units in the 1st Canadian Division trained to a similar standard. For example, in May, the 2nd Canadian Infantry Brigade ran a three-day exercise during which units conducted a twenty-mile route march on the first day, a twenty-five mile march (followed by an attack) on the second day, and a twenty-mile march to barracks on the third and final day.[6]

Units continued to build up their marching capacity well into 1942. During Exercise Tiger, which ran that spring from 19 to 30 May, Canadian units across the overseas army demonstrated an impressive capacity for endurance. Lieutenant-General Sir Bernard Montgomery, as General Officer Commanding-in-Chief South Eastern Command, planned and ran the exercise, which pitted the 12th British Corps against the 1st Canadian Corps (less most of 2nd Canadian Division, then preparing for the Dieppe raid).[7] Montgomery had designed the training to put soldiers through an exceptionally arduous test of endurance. He imposed hard ration scales, with no supplements allowed, and prohibited the use of motor transport for the infantry. Moving forces from one location to another therefore meant marching long distances. Things went well. After the exercise, Montgomery commented approvingly that most infantry units had marched over 150 miles (240 km) and that many infantrymen had finished with no soles left on their boots. He did not exaggerate. Records show that the infantry units in the 3rd Canadian Division covered, on average, 149 miles each.[8] On the low end, the Royal Winnipeg Rifles marched 104 miles (167 km), while the Régiment de la Chaudière clocked the most at 183 (294 km). Units typically moved considerable distances each day. The Queen's Own Rifles came close to the average, marching in consecutive days 9, 14, 18, 14, 5.5, 31, 17.5, and 19.5 miles (14, 22.5, 29, 22.5, 9, 50, 28, and 32 km), followed by three days with no marching, and then a final 31 miles (50 km) – and covering 159.5 miles (257 km) during the course of the exercise. The Chaudières put in the longest distance in a single day at 42 miles (68 km). Units must have put in much work in the previous months to be capable of such feats. Some might have succeeded Montgomery's test in part because they had shed older NCOs before the exercise. For instance, the Queen's Own Rifles had just posted out RSM Gordon Alexander because he was fifty.[9] Earlier in the year, the Cape Breton Highlanders had posted out their aged RSM as well.[10]

After Exercise Tiger, units continued to march long distances at fast paces to keep their men hard and fit. In mid-July, the Royal Canadian Regiment (RCR) compiled data on how long it took platoons to march from a range to the battalion camp at Arundel, a distance, depending on a company's bivouac area, of thirty to thirty-two miles (48–51.5 km). Platoons covered the distance in times ranging from six hours, fifteen minutes to seven hours thirty-six minutes, not including breaks.[11] On average, this amounted to marching between four and five miles (6.5–8 km) per hour, an impressive pace to maintain over that distance. Similarly, in the 3rd Canadian Infantry Brigade, the Royal 22nd Regiment (R22R) conducted an exercise that required the unit to march to a ship embarkation point and back. The unit war diary recorded the exploit: "We have marched some forty odd miles in 27 hrs. In a few instances we have walked 3½ miles and once 4 miles in 50 minutes."[12] Marching for forty miles (64 km) took stamina at even moderate speeds, and doing so at the R22R's pace demonstrated considerable hardiness. NCOs played an important role in such demonstrations of fitness. Corporals and sergeants were responsible for maintaining discipline on the march, motivating the tired, and ensuring that everyone worked together as a team. No NCO could have done so without high levels of fitness and drive. And none could have his men's respect if he struggled to keep up with them.

The army senior leadership did not let up on fitness standards. In the fall of 1942, Lieutenant-General H.D.G. Crerar, then commanding the 1st Canadian Corps, imposed a new training regimen to prepare his divisions for combined operations, especially amphibious assaults.[13] He told his formation commanders to expect that after conducting beach landings, forces would immediately have to seize any high ground that dominated the beaches and approach routes. This, he emphasized, had implications on fitness training: "Troops will be made physically fit to climb steep slopes, and press home an attack on heights held by the enemy, without the slightest needless delay. The rapid development of accurate, concentrated fire, co-ordinated with quick, decisive movement, will be stressed." Because the corps would break out of its beach head quickly, tactical training would also continue to emphasize cross-country movement. So, the army had real operational reasons for demanding high fitness standards in its fighting units. (Airborne forces maintained even higher requirements.[14]) In Canada, however, it took some time for the training system to catch up to the overseas army's high standards.

Not until May 1944, ten months after Operation Husky and only one month in advance of Operation Overlord, did National Defence Headquarters (NDHQ) take meaningful action to improve the fitness standards of reinforcement soldiers. The Directorate of Military Training (DMT) had for some time received repeated complaints from Canadian Military Headquarters (CMHQ) about the substandard fitness of soldiers arriving in Britain. Therefore, to elevate fitness levels in Canada, NDHQ implemented new British army physical efficiency tests, which assessed an individual's agility, strength, and endurance.[15] Three different tests were administered at army training centres: basic individual tests for soldiers completing recruit training; basic achievement tests for soldiers undergoing corps-of-arms training (such as infantry or artillery); and battle physical efficiency tests for trained soldiers. The battle physical efficiency test, which set high and quantifiable fitness standards, included seven tasks:

AGILITY

1   With a run, surmount a six-foot (1.8 m) wall with assistance.
2   Jump a ditch nine feet (2.7 m) across, landing on both feet.
3   Sprint 80 yards (73 m) to a 30-yard (27 m) firing point. Load with five rounds of .303. Fire five rounds on no. 3 target (200 yard size). Score to pass this test is three hits on target. Total time = 60 seconds.

STRENGTH

4   Carry a man 200 yards (182 m) by means of "fireman's lift" on the flat in 1 minute, 45 seconds. The man to be carried must be approximately the same weight as the carrier (and must be in field service marching order). The carrier will carry both rifles or other appropriate weapons.
5   Climb a vertical rope twelve feet (3.6 m) high, traverse a twenty-foot (6 m) span of horizontal rope, and come down with the aid of a rope.

ENDURANCE

6   Run two miles (3.2 km) on roads in eighteen minutes.
7   Cover ten miles (16 km) on foot and then complete a similar firing practice as for Test 3. The whole test, including the firing practice, to be completed in two hours.[16]

To pass, soldiers, including NCOs, had to complete five of the seven tasks, including one from each of the three categories of agility, strength, and endurance. For each of the tasks, soldiers dressed "as for battle," which included carrying a personal weapon (rifle for most soldiers), steel helmet, bayonet, fifty rounds of ammunition, a full water bottle, and other standard equipment for one's corps of arms. While the test did not include marching long distances for several days in a row, the individual tasks – especially the final one of marching ten miles in full battle kit and then conducting a shooting test, all within two hours – required a good deal of stamina.

As the army built up its fitness, field units in Britain posted out older NCOs who lacked the physical hardiness to keep up. Sometimes the senior leadership encouraged unit commanders to do so. In early 1942, when Montgomery inspected all of the Canadian battalions, he discovered too many old NCOs still serving with field units, and he said so to Crerar.[17] It was time for battalions to shed their older men who had helped flesh out NCO cadres when the units first mobilized. Crerar reacted by exhorting his commanding officers to send as many back to Canada as they could for instructional duty.[18] Units responded to this direction, although to what extent remains unclear.[19] Nonetheless, even the sample group in this text contains examples of units clearing out older, unfit NCOs – even though the group comprises mostly soldiers who had died in battle and who had therefore avoided the culling.[20] For instance, in October 1941, the North Shore (New Brunswick) Regiment posted out Lance Sergeant William Beattie, a forty-year-old soldier who had developed health problems.[21] Such culling made way for younger men, like William Davidson of the Princess Patricia's Canadian Light Infantry (PPCLI), who in mid-April 1942 received a promotion to warrant officer class 2 at just twenty-two.[22] In fact, the sample group suggests that the average age of infantry warrant officers class 2 dropped from thirty-two in December 1941 to twenty-eight in December 1942, coinciding with Crerar's direction for units to shed their older NCOs. In short, physical fitness was essential for NCOs in the army's field units. Brains and experience hardly mattered if a soldier could not keep up with the army's rigorous physical demands, which were designed to get soldiers through battle.

Developing Expertise in Interarm Cooperation and Combined Operations

Maturing skill in interarm and interservice operations represented another important aspect of the army's growing proficiency. Shortly after the first Canadian formations arrived in Britain, senior commanders started developing their forces' competency in interarm cooperation. Later, as the strategic situation began to shift in early 1942 with the diminishing likelihood of a German invasion and with a new focus on projecting land forces onto the continent, Canadian soldiers started preparing for combined operations. These developments had implications for the NCO corps. The soldiers responsible for leading in the field had to learn the nuts and bolts of fighting as part of larger teams.

To be sure, just how proficient soldiers became at interarm cooperation is questionable. Several historians have criticized the Canadians for neglecting interarm training. John English argues that the army failed to train adequately for all-arms cooperation, finding that formation commanders in particular did not know how to exploit each arm's strengths, which resulted in unnecessarily high casualties during the Normandy campaign.[23] More generally, C.P. Stacey argues that the army did not make good enough use of its years of training in Britain, because regimental officers had taken a casual approach to preparing for combat. Consequently, he adds, the army did not perform as well as it might have in the Normandy campaign.[24] Some criticize the larger British army. Carlo D'Este argues that lacklustre performance in Normandy stemmed from British failure to develop a culture of interarm cooperation, especially between infantry and tanks. Unlike the Germans and Americans, he states, the British quarrelled non-stop about the role of tanks and were very slow to learn the importance of interarm cooperation.[25] Similarly, Timothy Harrison Place argues that poor training in infantry–tank cooperation before June 1944 had adverse consequences during the Normandy campaign.[26] Despite these critiques, though, even if the Canadians did not train enough in interarm cooperation, the leadership at least recognized that NCOs and officers alike had to work at it, and periodically saw that they did so.

Division-level attention to interarm cooperation began in 1940. In March, the 1st Canadian Division started its first round of collective training with a six-week period of unit-level activities. Training instructions ordered the first small steps, directing that engineer units fit themselves for cooperation with infantry brigades and that machine-gun battalions prepare "to operate in co-operation with other arms."[27] Then, in late April, when the division began six weeks of unit- and formation-level collective training, division headquarters directed that exercises include "co-operation between all arms," meaning infantry, armour, artillery, and engineers.[28] Units and formations soon began to take bigger steps. In early May, the Seaforth Highlanders practised attacking with artillery support and, during an exercise run by 2nd Canadian Infantry Brigade (2 CIB) later that month on Salisbury Plain, practised it again at night and once again with tanks during the day.[29] By the late spring, brigades began training as "brigade groups," each comprising an infantry brigade matched with reconnaissance, engineer, anti-tank, and machine-gun sub-units, plus a field regiment of artillery.[30] And at least one, the 1st Canadian Infantry Brigade (1 CIB), started practising battalion-level infantry-cum-tank attacks before events on the continent re-focused attention on preparing to defend against a German invasion.[31] All this training was needed to familiarize soldiers with the tactics that the army eventually put to use. Clifford Cave, who fought with the Sherbrooke Fusiliers (27th Armoured Regiment), provides an example of how cooperation with the infantry worked in Northwest Europe:

Infantry-cum-tank was a procedure with the big Churchill tank and the slow-moving tanks to put the infantry on to an objective, and then move up and consolidate on the objective with their tanks. And they did that in many ways, sometimes with the infantry following the tank, so one troop with one company, and there'd be some [soldiers] following, sometimes riding on [tanks] if it was possible to do so without getting them all shot off. [Other support included] supporting fire, overhead fire, enfilade fire, flanking fire, and this sort of thing.

But they [Churchills] were designed for that, to work with infantry. Ours [Shermans] were faster tanks, and we had the liberty to move more quickly and we would get into position and support the infantry on to an objective and then roar forward and help them consolidate it.[32]

The 2nd Canadian Division wasted no time in ordering interarm training as soon as the formation finished assembling in Britain in late December 1940. First, the division held a series of tactical exercises without troops (TEWTs) that featured interarm cooperation. Subsequent training continued in the same vein. In late February 1941, the commander, Major-General Victor Odlum, reported to the Canadian Corps[33] headquarters that he had made some progress:

Emphasis has been continually placed upon co-operation during all forms of training and it is considered that satisfactory progress has been made in this respect. Close liaison is maintained between Inf Comds and the Comds of arms making up the Bde Gp. During Bn and Bde exercises the usual difficulties have been encountered and the importance of co-operation is realized by all concerned.[34]

Formation headquarters above the division level gradually insisted on developing proficiency in interarm cooperation as well. For the four months from December 1941 to March 1942, the Canadian Corps headquarters mandated progressive interarm training. Unit-level TEWTs forced leaders down to low levels to study tactical scenarios that demanded cooperation between arms, in preparation for full exercises that would progress from company to brigade level. These scenarios included cooperation in the attack between infantry and armour, infantry and artillery forward observation officers, and assault engineers and tanks.[35] They also included cooperation in the defence between infantry and anti-tank artillery.

Later in 1942, the newly formed First Canadian Army also ordered interarm training. In its first training instruction, army headquarters dedicated an entire section to "co-operation between arms."[36] Canadian forces had already made some progress, the instruction acknowledged, but more was necessary to make the army ready for battle. Recent experience had revealed areas for improvement. Infantry and armour needed to work together more and to foster close personal relations between junior leaders, NCOs included. The army headquarters also wanted all formations to form standing brigade groups – infantry brigades with permanently affiliated supporting arms and services – to promote "close mutual understanding and the spirit of co-operation ... between all Arms." Efforts to force the arms together naturally affected the NCO corps, as the instructions emphasized: "Trg programmes should be arranged so that junior leaders and O.R.s of all Arms can practice co-operative trg on the sub-unit level. Only in this way will they become fully conversant with the characteristics and limitations of the other Arms."

Higher formation commanders continued to stress the importance of fighting in all-arms teams, right up to the final preparations for the invasion of Normandy. In mid-May 1944, Crerar, now commanding the First Canadian Army, emphasized to his senior officers the absolute necessity for collaboration between arms: "Co-operation between tanks and infantry and artillery is not simply desirable – in the conditions of battle, intimate team-play between these three arms is a stark, staring necessity." Therefore, he concluded, "it follows that the closest personal and professional relationships between Commanders and personnel of tanks, infantry and artillery units should be regarded as an essential matter in every formation, at all times, and is something requiring the constant personal attention of higher Commanders."[37]

These corps- and army-level directives were not just lip service. In 1942 and into 1943, commanders ordered and conducted collective training to instil a culture of interarm cooperation. For example, in January 1942, a Canadian Corps training order promulgated procedures for integrating tanks into all-arms operations.[38] First, training programs were to educate soldiers on the capabilities and limitations of each arm. Then, a series of exercises would progress through combined platoon and troop training, company and squadron training, regiment and battalion training that incorporated artillery, and finally, brigade-level all-arms training. It was all designed to cultivate understanding of each arm's capabilities and limitations, while promoting interarm tactics. Units and formations conducted the training accordingly. For instance, during the first ten weeks of 1942, key staff in each brigade and unit of the 1st Canadian Infantry Division attended TEWTs, cloth model exercises, and demonstrations that focused on interarm operating procedures. This training placed particular emphasis on cooperation between infantry and tanks. The activities built up to Exercise Mickey in March, when each brigade conducted an all-arms attack.[39] The following summer, all three brigades in the 1st Canadian Infantry Division worked up to brigade-group live-fire attacks with artillery supporting infantry-tank assaults.[40] For example, on 3 August, the 3rd Canadian Infantry Brigade paired with the 14th Army Tank Battalion to conduct an attack, supported by three regiments of artillery that fired rounds over the soldiers' heads.[41] Then, in September, formations practised interarm cooperation in offensive operations by exercising all-arms battalion groups and brigade groups in establishing bridgeheads, and breaking out of them.[42] And in late 1942 and early 1943, all infantry and armoured units rotated through a three-day exercise that practised platoon/troop leaders and company/squadron commanders in interarm operations.[43] Of course, if platoon and troop leaders had to be proficient in interarm cooperation, so did their NCOs. For one thing, platoon and troop sergeants had to be ready to take command when their officers became casualties, which occurred frequently in battle. Besides, at the lowest tactical level, it was the NCOs who led the infantry sections and individual tanks that communicated, moved, and fought in concert with one another.

British experience in North Africa reinforced the importance of interarm cooperation.[44] In June 1943, British military authorities circulated "Notes on a Common Doctrine for the Employment of Infantry and Tanks," which explained the tactics the Eighth Army had developed for attacking prepared defensive positions.[45] This particular missive explained in detail how the British had combined infantry and armoured elements, with engineer and anti-tank support, to defeat enemy defences protected by minefields and forward outposts. Officers and NCOs had played an important role in galvanizing such interarm cooperation: "Every offr and NCO must make personal contact with his opposite number in the other arms. It is only by this means that proper understanding and confidence will be obtained in the battle." The Notes on a Common Doctrine, widely distributed across the Canadian army, provided guidance on how all-arms cooperation should work. And the Canadians acted on these lessons: in July 1943, for instance, infantry and armoured units of the 5th Canadian Armoured Division worked together to practise these British methods.[46]

Despite these efforts, mastering and maintaining expertise in the tricky business of cooperation between arms proved difficult. Robert Engen argues that troops in combat often proved underprepared for combined arms operations.[47] Importantly, he draws on the testimony of veteran infantry officers to demonstrate that at least part of the reason was the necessity for units to adapt tactics to each battlefield's distinct conditions. For instance, in Normandy, infantry and armour units had to devise new ways to cooperate because of how the enemy exploited the terrain.[48] Scores of well-concealed German anti-armour weapons posed a serious threat to Canadian tanks, which therefore rarely operated in front of the infantry instead of leading out front. This caused some infantrymen to complain about supposedly reluctant tank crews. Similarly, the dyke-and-polder country of Belgium and Holland affected how tanks and infantry worked together.

Sometimes, though, the Canadians adapted successfully to the situation. In Sicily in early August 1943, 1st Canadian Division commander Major-General Guy Simonds created an ad hoc battle group to take advantage of the open country and force a crossing of the Simeto River to seize important high ground.[49] Comprising the 12th Canadian Tank Regiment (Three Rivers Regiment) and the Seaforth Highlanders, plus some artillery, anti-tank, and reconnaissance support, the aggressive battle group achieved its mission, executing what a CMHQ historian called a "model infantry-cum-tank action, where both arms provided excellent mutual support."[50]

Things did not always go so well. In the official history of the Italian campaign, *The Canadians in Italy, 1943–1945*, G.W.L. Nicholson shows that training occurred periodically as units prepared to work with each other for specific operations, and that infantry–armour cooperation sometimes worked well in part because of experience.[51] But he also presents numerous examples of poor infantry–armour cooperation, often when the tanks and the infantrymen became separated, sometimes by the enemy's design.[52] What is more, because developing proficiency in interarm cooperation required collective training of different unit types, soldiers in the reinforcement system might not have received enough interarm training. This appeared to be the case in Italy during the spring of 1944, when the 1st Canadian Infantry Division was preparing to assault the Hitler Line. The Seaforth Highlanders of Canada learned that the division commander, Major-General Chris Vokes, had ordered his forces to conduct thorough "instruction in the techniques of infantry co-operation with tanks," something that units had not had the chance to practise over the winter months. The problem, as Lieutenant Robert McDougall saw it, was that the reinforcements needed the training more than anyone else:

Some Seaforths had of course had excellent schooling in co-operation with tanks under the most exacting of conditions. But by this time new members. of the battalion far outnumbered the old – and of these, it must be said, few had received anything like the intensive training which members of the original battalion had had before they left England in 1943.[53]

The unit therefore underwent three days of intensive training with the North Irish Horse of the 25th (British) Tank Brigade, with whom the Seaforths partnered for Operation Chesterfield. As always, NCOs needed the training because of their leadership responsibilities in battle. As it turned out, senior NCOs played a conspicuous role when the attack went in. McDougall relates that when two company commanders became casualties early in the battle: "Command of 'A' Company passed to C.S.M. F.D. McMullen ... Command of 'C' Company passed to C.S.M. J. McP. Duddle. C.S.M. Duddle was awarded the D.C.M. [Distinguished Conduct Medal] for his outstanding contribution to the day's action."[54]

These examples from Northwest Europe, Sicily, and Italy suggest that the persistent challenges with interarm cooperation in battle were not attributable purely to a lack of training in England. Not enough practice might have been a factor, as historians have argued, but so too were changing battlefield conditions that necessitated changes to how the different arms exploited each other's strengths. High personnel turnover in the field might have had something to do with it as well, as did the periodic regrouping of forces that meant units and sub-units sometimes executed operations with unfamiliar counterparts with whom they had not rehearsed enough. In short, the army did not neglect interarm training altogether, either in England or in the theatres of operation. More to the point, NCOs (and officers) had to learn about fighting in interarm teams, even if the army as a whole found it difficult to cultivate enduring proficiency between units.

In addition to training as part of interarm teams, Canadian soldiers also had to learn how to operate in close conjunction with the navy. In late 1941, the army began to work at combined operations, which demanded new and special expertise for the exceptionally complex business of conducting amphibious assault. Thus, the Canadian Corps began sending teams to HMS *Northney*, a shore establishment on the British southern coast, for assault landing craft (ALC) training. Every other week until at least mid-March 1942, three teams of two officers and eighteen non-commissioned soldiers underwent an elementary one-week course. Eventually, seventy-three officers and 630 other ranks completed the training.[55] The Canadian Corps then accelerated the ALC training program. Staff arranged for detachments from each infantry division to undergo training at British Directorate of Combined Operations (DCO) establishments.[56] The plan called for each detachment, consisting of 17 officers and 173 other ranks (including privates and NCOs), to take six to eight weeks of ALC training. Trainees received lessons from DCO instructors in the routine on board infantry assault ships, the preparation of orders for amphibious assault, the use of special equipment, the loading of landing craft, and the use of weapons from landing craft to cover approaches to the beach – all matters of concern for the NCOs who would lead their men in assaulting enemy-held coasts.

The sample group in this text shows that ALC instructor training for NCOs occurred fairly often relative to other specialty programs. Soldiers such as

Corporal Wilfred Grimshaw of the PPCLI and Corporal William Moore of the 48th Highlanders of Canada participated in the program and qualified as ALC instructors.[57] Shortly after the new ALC training began, the corps ordered units to employ those who had completed the program as local instructional cadres.[58] In November 1942, plans to send whole units and formations on combined operations training went into effect.[59] And as a 1st Canadian Corps training instruction emphasized: "The development of initiative on the part of junior leaders and of their capacity to take charge of situations and turn them into tactical advantage is of greatest importance."[60]

Fighting in Built-up Areas

When the army began to contemplate offensive operations on the continent, it also had to think about fighting in built-up areas. Town fighting posed particularly difficult challenges, especially for attacking forces. Well-concealed defenders enjoyed significant advantages by creating obstacles such as physical barriers, booby traps, or nasty combinations of the two. Fighting in close quarters made for exceptionally dangerous duty, and the NCOs who would lead the small teams in town fighting had a great deal to learn about it.

Canadian formations began to prepare for urban combat in the fall of 1942.[61] Town fighting in Europe was almost certain, and Crerar wanted all units and sub-units to train hard for it. Following British training guidance, he distributed a War Office military training pamphlet that explained in good detail the complexity of fighting in built-up areas.[62] Standard platoon weapons had certain strengths and weaknesses that affected how soldiers employed them for town fighting: rifles were too cumbersome for assaulting troops; light machine guns provided good support but when fired from the ground could be difficult to aim at upper windows; the machine carbine was a "splendid weapon" for close-in work; 2-inch mortars provided invaluable smoke projection but no destructive effect against buildings; and all weapons expended large quantities of ammunition, which could render replenishment difficult and uncertain. Fighting in built-up areas also required special equipment. For traction and stealth, men needed rubber-soled footwear instead of army boots. Sections always required picks and crowbars for breaching doors, walls, and floors. Each section needed four toggle ropes for scaling walls and periscopes to peer around corners. Standardized section drills for fighting inside buildings were essential. Searching houses required noise discipline, as defenders would simply shoot at attacking forces through walls, ceilings, and floors. Booby traps were a guaranteed hazard wherever defenders had time to prepare. And tanks generally proved too vulnerable to be of much use but could sometimes help by setting buildings on fire. When it came to fighting in urban areas, there was a lot to be learned – and practised.

In many ways, town fighting was a section commander's or corporal's battle. In fact, the training pamphlet emphasized that fighting in built-up areas typically entailed section-level operations. Section commanders therefore had a great deal to remember. To keep the men in a section fighting while remaining as safe as possible, a section commander had to understand and enforce myriad rules and drills: dispatching security teams to cover entrances of buildings just cleared; taking care not to expose oneself and others to fire from across the street; using sewers as safe routes for raiding or bringing up reserves and supplies; conserving ammunition and enforcing fire discipline; remaining suspicious of any object that was even slightly unusual (because it might be booby-trapped); and so on. NCOs had to master all of this knowledge. As the training pamphlet stressed, "a very high degree of leadership and initiative, cunning, courage, determination and drive are required of platoon and section commanders."[63]

Town fighting became a standard subject in all major NCO training programs, and both centralized and decentralized NCO qualification courses usually had students learning and practising how to fight in urban areas. So did the many tactics (battle drill) courses that the army conducted in various locations. In 1943 and 1944, the army even sent NCOs to a course entitled "Street Fighting" at a British-run School of Tactics. In short, fighting in built-up areas became a fundamental skill NCOs had to pick up, and NCO qualification and tactics courses that ran across the army proved important to prepare them for the vicious fighting they eventually encountered in places like Ortona, Italy, where they relied on their training while innovating new techniques. When Sydney W. Thomson, who commanded the Seaforth Highlanders of Canada at Ortona, was asked in a postwar interview if there was an army street-fighting pamphlet to help the soldiers fighting in the town, he replied,

Yes, there was; but all these things, mouseholing [breaching walls to move from room to room] and so on, had already been taught in battle-school before we left England. It's true that there were innovations that the boys thought up while they were there; but it was all done by the front-line soldier, not by the colonel or even in most cases[,] the company commander. They just ran into a problem, and they found some way of solving it.[64]

Battle Drill

Beginning in early 1942, training below the unit level intensified with the advent of battle drill, which was designed to increase collective fighting skills while making training as realistic as possible.[65] Battle drill focused on teaching practical methods for executing various battlefield tasks at the level of platoons and sections. The main elements were tactical drills (for flanking attacks, for example) based on teamwork, plus intense physical conditioning and battlefield simulation. This aggressive and demanding form of training increased morale across the army, in large part because soldiers who had grown somewhat bored with the monotonous training regimen welcomed the change. Battle drill acted as an antidote, bringing realism, excitement, and even risk to training. And it pushed the army's fighting men, NCOs included, further up the learning curve.

Battle drill began as an attempt to redress the lacklustre performance of the British infantry during the 1940 campaign in France and Belgium. Major-General Harold Alexander, who had overseen the last days of the evacuation from France, complained in a post-operation report that, while individual soldiers had performed bravely, unit chains of command down to section level often became ineffective.[66] Platoons and sections had failed to act as teams, and when the situation called for quick sub-unit action, companies had waited for orders instead of acting with initiative. Acting was better than waiting, but lack of standard action had too often led to inaction. Furthermore, Alexander claimed, soldiers across the force suffered from inadequate physical toughness. He implored the British army's training authorities to increase realism in sub-unit training. He also suggested the establishment of a school to teach battle drill, and one soon opened in South Eastern Command.

Before long, the Canadians enthusiastically adopted the new form of training. It started as a sort of grassroots movement with the Calgary Highlanders, who in October 1941 sent three officers to attend the British program.[67] Thoroughly impressed with the training, these three convinced their commanding officer, Lieutenant-Colonel J.F. Scott, to open a battalion battle drill school. Scott and his Calgary Highlanders became passionate battle drill advocates and they gradually encouraged, perhaps even hastened, its adoption in the Canadian army.[68] On 30 December, the unit demonstrated battle drill to all battalion and company commanders in the 2nd Canadian Division.[69] Everyone was impressed. CMHQ soon established a battle drill wing at the Canadian Training School (CTS), for the production of battle drill instructors. (CTS was the overseas army's principal centralized training institution, as described in Chapter 7.) The first month-long course ran with ninety-six NCOs and ninety-six officers in the spring of 1942.[70] Those who passed earned qualifications to train others in battle drill. The course officially became CMHQ Course 801 (Battle Drill), and CTS eventually offered variants focusing on rifles, carriers, and mortars.[71] Battle drill also became part of the curriculum for CMHQ's NCO qualification course, to teach students how to handle common battlefield situations.[72] And in early 1942, Canadian divisions, brigades, and units began to build their own battle drill programs.[73]

Battle drill made low-level collective training more demanding and realistic while teaching students how to react in a broad range of tactical scenarios. According to a CTS précis, battle drill aimed to instill battle discipline and team spirit, teaching team "plays" that would be understood by all troops.[74] The training included battle inoculation to accustom soldiers to the noise of combat, for example, by firing live ammunition over trainees' heads and detonating explosives nearby. The drills themselves prescribed the actions to be taken for a wide variety of tasks or tactical situations that sections and platoons could encounter in battle: the platoon in the attack, patrolling at night, the section and the platoon in the defence, infantry procedures for dealing with enemy tanks, clearing streets and villages, clearing woods of parachutists, defence of a river line, platoon crossing of a water obstacle, and defence of a vulnerable point. Clearly, NCOs had much to learn and practise, but the training was useful for them. Ernest MacGregor, who as a junior officer in the Loyal Edmonton Regiment taught battle drill in Britain, described its value from the perspective of an instructor:

> One had the opportunity to see somebody come in who was uncertain of themself and who didn't really know what tactics were at the lower level, for an infantry battalion. And after a month's course where he was drilled in how to do many things, and drilled in what to say, and drilled in how to give orders, he became a very confident and competent individual. Under all sorts of pressures – bursting thunder flashes and battle noises, and smoke and tear gas, chemical grenades and everything of that nature that were designed to throw him off his stride – by the end of the course he was able to concentrate through this kind of distraction and still command a platoon quite competently.[75]

Battle drill quickly spread to Canada. In late April 1942, just as CTS was about to start running formal battle drill courses in Britain, NDHQ decided to establish a battle drill training centre at Vernon, British Columbia. The plan called for the centre to run a three-week course that would train instructors who could organize brigade or unit battle drill schools.[76] At first, candidates at the A31 Canadian Battle Drill Training Centre came only from operational units, but NDHQ eventually opened the course to instructional staff from training centres across the country.[77] By December, 825 candidates had completed the training.

By the spring of 1943, the high command believed that battle drill had given soldiers a solid grounding for the challenges of combat. Around that time, First Canadian Army circulated a note that a British infantry NCO in the Middle East had sent to the commanding officer of a training battalion in Britain.[78] The corporal expressed gratitude for the battle drill training that had helped him lead effectively in difficult combat situations. He described an assault during which his officer and platoon sergeant became casualties, leaving him, at that time a section commander, in command of the platoon. Under intense fire that pinned down his troops, the corporal applied his battle drill training, deploying Bren guns to engage the enemy while he led two sections around the enemy position and assaulted from the rear. His attack succeeded, killing thirteen enemy and capturing four machine guns. The biggest factor in his success? The corporal believed fervently that it was battle drill training. He even pleaded with his former commanding officer to "see that all men received such training, so that they can come and fight shoulder to shoulder to finish the job off." Clearly, British and Canadian military authorities considered that this testimony from the field validated the value of battle drill, which is why they circulated it so widely. Recent scholarship reinforces the notion that battle drill gave soldiers useful skills that they employed in combat. In Robert Engen's survey of 150 veteran infantry officers, 85 percent reported that they had applied in combat the battle drill principles they had learned in training.[79]

Battle drill became an important part of an NCO's professional development. In January 1943, NDHQ encouraged unit commanders across Canada to conduct their own battle drill programs. Ottawa established the *Instructors' Handbook on Fieldcraft and Battle Drill* as the bible on battle drill training and distributed it to promote a uniform training standard.[80] Meanwhile, the A31 battle drill school at Vernon ran monthly courses, with classes of up to a hundred soldiers at a time, the majority being NCOs.[81] Battle drill programs spread to training centres, units, and formations across the army, and eventually a high proportion of the NCO corps qualified in battle drill training. In fact, the personnel records of the sample group reveal that NCOs attended more battle drill courses than any other specialist program. At least 21 percent of the sample qualified in battle drill. Of those, almost three-quarters attended CMHQ Course 801 (Battle Drill) at the Canadian Training School in Britain, while almost one-quarter took the course in British Columbia. Even those who did not attend formal qualification courses learned battle drill. Some went to locally run courses at the unit or formation level, and most also trained in battle drill as part of routine collective training.

Leadership within the Sub-Unit

In all the endeavours discussed above, NCOs – especially senior NCOs, who personified experience and the wisdom that comes with it – were vital to leadership within sub-units (companies, squadrons, and batteries). For instance, infantry senior NCOs mentored untested platoon commanders. Young officers with little experience leaned on their platoon sergeants, particularly in the field. Memoirs are full of examples. Kenneth Smith – who fought with the Hastings and Prince Edward Regiment as a platoon commander from January 1944 until he was wounded seriously at the Hitler Line in May – describes how helpful his NCOs were when he joined the battalion in Italy. Smith's non-commissioned leaders epitomized the seasoned NCO:

> They soon taught us [reinforcements] the difference between the sound of Jerry shells and our own, and hence the right time to take cover. They were able to work out immediately just where our Bren guns should be sited ... These marvellous NCOs made the youngest rookie feel confident, not to mention what they did for a young officer's morale.[82]

And when Lieutenant Walter Keith, a reinforcement officer, reported to the Regina Rifle Regiment in March 1945 and took command of a platoon, his platoon sergeant gave invaluable help:

> When I was taken to 16 Platoon in a wrecked house somewhere in Sonsbeck I was first introduced to Sgt Tommy Tomlinson. Tommy had commanded the Platoon for probably two weeks ... I fully expected him to resent having a new and very green officer put over him ... He was with me for the next several weeks including the first two or three days of the Emmerich battle and was most helpful. He never once interfered or showed lack of trust in my limited ability, but was always there if I needed help. Whatever actions he felt he had to take he took quickly and unobtrusively. He was a great man and leader.[83]

NCOs played a crucial role in battle by rallying soldiers in the face of extreme danger, leading men forward and overpowering the survival instincts that told them to get down and stay down. This role was nothing new, as the army's training doctrine throughout the war emphasized. The 1938 training pamphlet *Infantry Section Leading* describes the responsibility of the section commander in planning and leading the section's actions in the attack.[84] A subsequent official training pamphlet warned: "Infantry once launched into the assault must keep on the move. Once they halt and lie down it may be difficult to start them again in the way intended," a phenomenon that NCOs and platoon commanders had to overcome.[85] Another observed that discipline in battle "is largely a matter of section leading. Great care should be taken in the first place to make sure that the section commander is chosen primarily because of his ability to lead men; he must be the sort of man who others will instinctively follow."[86]

Sure enough, as the following examples illustrate, NCO leadership would indeed play a key role in battle once the army started fighting. During Operation Varsity in March 1945 – the Anglo-American airborne mission to support Allied forces crossing the Rhine – strong senior NCO leadership carried the day for the 1st Canadian Parachute Battalion. The unit faced hard fighting from the battle's outset, when the paratroopers descended on a "hot" drop zone swept with heavy fire. Able company's CSM George Green organized and drove efforts to suppress the opposition, allowing the company's dispersed personnel to gather at their rendezvous site and get organized.[87] Shortly after, the company's attack on an enemy position faltered because of strong fire pouring out of a group of fortified houses. With the Germans blasting away at the Canadians, Green arranged for troops to provide covering fire, and then led an assault team that cleared each of the houses. His restoration of the company's initiative earned him the Distinguished Conduct Medal (DCM). Equally important leadership occurred in B company as it attacked an enemy position anchored by a group of fortified farmhouses. After German mortars and machine guns killed several Canadian officers, CSM John Kemp led an assault team forward and, with intense fire streaming toward him and his men, attacked the German machine-gun positions and assaulted the enemy-held buildings.[88] Thanks to Kemp's leadership in extremely dangerous circumstances and disregard for his own safety, the company captured the position and he, too, earned a DCM.

NCOs also had to be ready to assume command when junior officers became casualties. Accounts of NCOs stepping into command roles abound. For example, a history of the Queen's Own Cameron Highlanders records that when the unit was fighting in Normandy, "the temporary failure of the attack on the Verrières Ridge brought the Camerons under almost continuous fire ... So many officers were either killed or wounded that many N.C.O.'s were commanding platoons and even companies. They carried on like seasoned veterans."[89] During the advance to Falaise, when the unit was "fighting in the village of Fontenay, Major McManus was wounded. C.S.M. Arbour took over command of 'B' Company as practically every other officer in the company was already a casualty ... C.S.M. Arbour ... put in a successful attack on the right flank." And he won the Military Cross for his actions.[90] The requirement for NCOs to remain prepared to assume command had implications for training programs and career

Figure 3.1 Company Sergeant Major James A. Smith of the South Saskatchewan Highlanders receiving the Military Medal, 30 November 1944. Smith won this award for his actions in battle at the end of the Normandy campaign, when the officers of C company became casualties. Smith took command, led his company in repulsing three determined German counter-attacks, and destroyed a machine-gun post. | Library and Archives Canada/Department of National Defence fonds/a159593.

development. The army had to teach sergeants how to handle a platoon (or troop) in battle, and so sometimes they trained alongside junior officers in various battle drill and other junior leader programs.

Conclusion

Building the wartime NCO corps entailed more than training soldiers for traditional NCO roles as the army's leadership understood them at the outbreak of war. As the army steadily built proficiency in prosecuting high-intensity operations, NCOs had to keep up with developments. They had to meet higher fitness standards, which meant that age became a barrier to service in field units. By early 1942, field units began shedding older NCOs who were unsuited for the rigours of service. As the army prepared for the type of fighting it expected in Europe, keeping up with developments also necessitated mastering new tactics inherent in interarm and combined operations, town fighting, and battle drill. In essence, NCOs had to learn how to be low-level tacticians and combat leaders in an army tasked with dislodging and clearing well-prepared German defences.

In all these endeavours, NCOs had to train and lead their men. These new requirements complicated the NCO development problem, lengthening the list of competencies the army demanded of its non-commissioned leaders. The result, as Chapters 5 to 7 describe, was that NCO training programs had to evolve to impart new skills. For the senior leadership, then, training and developing enough fit, intelligent, and motivated soldiers to fill the army's expanding NCO requirements – twin problems of quantity and quality – constituted a major and continuous challenge in building the army's backbone.

4
Wartime Drivers of NCO Development

A unit with an ignorant or undependable cadre of Non-Commissioned Officers is unfit to overcome the problems of the battlefield or withstand any severe strain on its discipline or morale. It follows that the development of reliable, knowledgeable, self-respecting and loyal Non-Commissioned Officers must be a matter given prior[ity] attention by every Unit Commander.

LIEUTENANT-GENERAL H.D.G. CRERAR,
COMMANDER 1ST CANADIAN CORPS, JUNE 1943

WHILE ALL THE ALLIED forces had mobilization challenges, Canada's army faced a particularly steep incline. After two decades of meagre budgets that had left the largely amateur military undertrained and severely underequipped, the leadership needed time to assemble, arm, and train forces capable of prosecuting prolonged high-intensity operations. Developing the NCO corps was an important part of the process, but could occur only so quickly. Experienced, capable NCOs could not be generated overnight. And from the outset, no one knew when the army would have to fight, so units had to populate their NCO cadres quickly, then train them as time allowed. Canada spent the first forty-two months of the war building a modern field force before committing formations to Operation Husky, the Allied invasion of Sicily in July 1943.

Several things drove NCO development during this period. Above all, the senior military leadership, aware that the army could not win without a corps of strong NCOs, understood the imperative of building that backbone. Therefore, as soon as the government initiated mobilization, the army leadership activated policies to accelerate NCO promotions and development. Suddenly, unit commanders were responsible for training and promoting their NCOs, a break from the peacetime policy of running centrally controlled programs to certify soldiers for promotion. The new policy allowed commanding officers to fill out their war establishments quickly, and to keep them filled, by putting the men they thought most suitable into vacant NCO positions. Later, to assist units in deciding how best to employ the available manpower, the army created innovative tools for assessing each soldier's aptitude and physical and psychological health. Once the army settled in to long-term training after the Dunkirk evacuation, the senior leadership sustained top-down pressure to push development of the NCO corps, insisting over and over that formations and units prioritize the training of their non-commissioned leaders.

Wartime NCO Development Policies

The moment mobilization began, units assumed full responsibility for developing their NCOs. The peacetime practice of having soldiers qualify for higher rank by attending courses at centralized Schools of Instruction and undergoing promotion examinations controlled by National Defence Headquarters (NDHQ) would have been unmanageably cumbersome and impractical. Therefore, in accordance with the *Mobilization Instructions for the Canadian Militia, 1937,* commanding officers held authority to promote NCOs as required, up to warrant officer class 2.[1] The policy made sense because unit commanders had to fill their NCO cadres quickly, and in some cases, they even promoted new recruits to lance corporal or corporal to do so. As explained in Chapter 1, all soldiers promoted on mobilization received acting rank, with confirmation possible after three months provided the necessary skills had been acquired and proven. Several weeks after mobilization started, NDHQ reiterated that responsibility for training the newly promoted, and those yet to be promoted, remained with the unit. Canadian Active Service Force (CASF) Routine Order No. 22 declared that during the time allotted to individual training, units "should" run regimental courses to prepare leaders for their duties, using "as a guide" the syllabuses in *How to Qualify,* the army pamphlet that described the training and examinations peacetime soldiers underwent to qualify for promotion.[2] However, promotion exams were no longer necessary, even for officers above the rank of lieutenant.[3] Doing away with them no doubt constituted a lowering of peacetime standards but was necessary for filling all the NCO (and officer) billets the army needed filled right away. (Canada was hardly taking radical action on its own here. Just as the war began, the War Office authorized the granting of acting ranks for non-commissioned members in the British army so that units could fill their vacancies quickly. Shortly after, it suspended promotion examinations for officers in the British army.[4])

These practices remained in effect for forces that deployed abroad. In 1940, the overseas army issued similar promotion policy for its units. Unit commanders in the expeditionary force still held responsibility for making all promotions up to the rank of warrant officer class 2.[5] The authority to promote soldiers to fill vacancies in a unit's war establishment later became essential for units in battle, when commanding officers had to promote the best of their available men to replace fallen NCOs. Sergeant George Caya, MM, of the Algonquin Regiment explains how he became a senior NCO in the field after his unit suffered casualties:

> All the old boys got killed, or wounded or evacuated ... and I was the oldest left there ... with the experience ... I knew when to duck, I knew when to run, I knew when to hide, and they [reinforcement NCOs] don't. When they come in, they're green ... [The chain of command] said you're going to be sergeant, and I said well I'm not going to take orders from a green guy because he wouldn't know [the job of a platoon sergeant in battle], he wouldn't want it anyway, unless he was a know-it-all guy. And that's how I got to be the sergeant.[6]

Before long, NDHQ solidified wartime qualification and promotion policies with *Canadian Army Training Pamphlet No. 8: How to Qualify, 1941*. This publication, which superseded the 1939 *How to Qualify* and CASF Routine Order No. 22, confirmed the authority of commanding officers to qualify and promote their own NCOs.[7] Every unit commander held responsibility to conduct courses as he saw fit to prepare his soldiers for promotion up to staff sergeant. The new policy further recommended that an NCO up for promotion to warrant rank "should" hold Small Arms Training Centre certificates for the courses Protection against Gas and Platoon Weapons.[8] In any event, active army units controlled their own NCO promotions by running internal selection processes. To ensure that uniform standards existed within a given unit, and to verify a candidate's readiness for promotion, the new policy stated that a commanding officer "*should* arrange for practical tests to be held under a unit board."[9] In short, NDHQ devolved responsibility for the development and promotion of NCOs, and disseminated guidance on how to do it.

As the war progressed, the army developed methods for assessing a soldier's aptitude and suitability for particular work. This helped units decide how best to select, train, and employ NCOs and potential NCOs. The Canadian army was not innovating independently here. As Jonathan Fennell explains in *Combat and Morale in the North African Campaign*, the British army learned early in the war that it had allocated too many men to jobs for which they were unsuited, because of too little or too much intelligence.[10] In June 1941, British military authorities therefore established the Directorate of Selection of Personnel to help the army make the best use of its limited manpower. David French shows in *Raising Churchill's Army* that this new organization took on responsibility for assessing the physical and mental requirements of all jobs in the army.[11] It also produced aptitude and intelligence tests and administered them to recruits and to men in units that converted to other arms. This testing helped reduce training failures and identify which new recruits were suited for employment as tradesmen. By September 1942, intelligence testing of both serving personnel and new intakes rectified the problem of misallocating soldiers.[12] Jonathan Fennell also shows that similar personnel selection initiatives designed to ensure the proper allocation of manpower occurred in Australia (1942–43) and India (1943) as well.[13]

The Canadian army was not far behind the British. In September 1941, NDHQ established the Directorate of Personnel Selection to place army examiners in all basic training centres and district depots. These officers administered an aptitude test, called the M Test, to personnel entering the army.[14] The test comprised a booklet with eight sub-tests in both English and French. Three of the sub-tests required no ability to read or write, making it possible to assess the intelligence of illiterate recruits. The highest possible score was 211, but an average score on the English test was 125 to 130. The army categorized candidates into seven groups based on their test scores. Group 3 included scores of 130 to 159, or "high average" ability, and most of the soldiers who became NCOs scored here. Groups 2 (160 to 174) and 1 (175 to 211) represented "superior ability," indicating strong suitability for service as an NCO, officer, or technical specialist.[15] (Geoffrey Hayes shows that the army used the M Test as part of a suite of selection methods for officers. He argues that these methods tended to be as advanced as those used in the British, American, and German armies, but that they were not perfect – the army continued to rely heavily on the old practice of interviews as a key part of the process – and were still in their infancy. The M Test nonetheless made it possible for non-commissioned soldiers to seek a commission if they had brains but lacked higher education.[16]) Army examiners recorded a soldier's M Test score on a Personnel Selection Record form, along with a summary of educational and occupational backgrounds and interview-gleaned information regarding the man's personality and military experience. The whole process led to employment recommendations, and the Personnel Selection Record became part of a soldier's regimental documents. Thereafter, the chain of command could refer to it when considering a soldier's suitability for promotion to NCO rank, special training, or even employment.[17]

A refined system for assessing an individual's overall medical state also helped determine soldiers' abilities. Starting in 1943, the army implemented a new medical categorization model called the PULHEMS profile. It evaluated both physical and psychological factors, which helped ascertain an individual's aptitude and suitability for particular work.[18] Medical officers assigned a score to each of seven qualities denoted by the acronym PULHEMS:

Physique – General development, height and weight, capacity to acquire physical stamina during training, and capacity for work
Upper extremities – Functional use of hands, arms, shoulder girdle, and upper spine
Lower extremities – Functional use of feet, legs, pelvis, and lower spine
Hearing and Ears
Eyes and eyesight
Mental capacity – Intelligence
Stability – Emotional steadiness

The score was on a scale from 1 to 5, from normal to total disability for army service:

1 = Normal function, suitable for combat service
2 = Suitable for accessory front-line work (drivers, mechanics, sappers, signallers)
3 = Suitable for duty on lines of communication or at a base
4 = Suitable for duty in Canada, but an identified disability could be aggravated by strenuous service abroad; unable to assume duties in operational units
5 = Total disability for army work, cause for discharge.[19]

Each type of duty required a certain PULHEMS profile. For example, general service infantry required a profile of 1112121, while the Army Service Corps required a PULHEMS profile of 2222121.[20]

NDHQ officials believed that the combination of the PULHEMS profile, the M Test score, and the army examiner's report was invaluable for personnel selection and placement.[21] By and large, the system brought some science to the important business of assigning soldiers to trades and training most suited to their abilities. And it provided useful information for commanding officers who had to make the best use of the human material at hand.

The system was not perfect. Individual service records in the sample group show that, on occasion, some men with very high M Test scores made for ill-disciplined soldiers, while others with low scores climbed to high non-commissioned rank. And, as Terry Copp and Bill McAndrew show in *Battle Exhaustion: Soldiers and Psychiatrists in the Canadian Army, 1939–1945*, the army's psychological testing program had some flaws.[22] In Canada, the newly minted assistant army examiners who tested and interviewed soldiers were officers who had received their commissions based on university or partial university education. Sometimes they overstepped and rendered diagnoses without the necessary training. Meanwhile, the army's psychiatrists, or army examiners, complained that they did not have enough time to interview cases referred to them by the assistant army examiners, yet they still pronounced thousands of recruits to be neurotic, and the army then rejected them. Overseas, the army transferred too many supposedly inadequate men to pioneer (labour) companies. These had been established to employ those with psychological troubles, but later research showed that many of these men were likely to have performed well enough in field units.

The Senior Leadership's Role in NCO Development

The senior military leadership clearly understood the importance of competent junior leaders for success in battle. Throughout the three years leading up to Operation Husky, Canada's highest-ranking field commanders emphasized the need to develop the budding NCO corps. Soon after the drama surrounding the Dunkirk evacuation had subsided, high-level formation commanders pressured subordinate formations and units to cultivate their NCOs and get them to embrace their vital role as unit instructors, junior leaders, and disciplinarians.

Corps-level attention to NCO training began in the fall of 1940, shortly after the 1st Canadian Division helped form the 7th Corps, an Anglo-Canadian formation under the command of Canada's Lieutenant-General Andrew McNaughton.[23] In early October, McNaughton's training instructions directed the Canadians to focus on developing junior leaders, especially by reinforcing elementary skills: "Particular attention will be paid to the training of Junior Officers and N.C.Os., and emphasis is laid on the importance of map reading, and of practical training by means of the sand table and exercises without troops."[24] His headquarters helped by establishing a corps junior leaders school that focused on platoon sergeants and platoon commanders. The school opened in mid-October and ran three-week courses for senior NCOs and junior officers (described in Chapter 5).[25]

After the 7th Corps became the Canadian Corps in late December, formation commanders continued to emphasize NCO development. For example, the 2nd Canadian Division, which had just joined the corps, worked on improving rudimentary NCO and junior officer skills by running refresher leadership training, instruction on map and compass skills, and lessons in how to conduct basic vehicle maintenance and inspections.[26] Progress took time and the leadership stayed on top of things. In February 1942, Lieutenant-General Harry Crerar, then the General Officer Commanding (GOC) Canadian Corps, stressed to his subordinate commanders that they must grip their junior leader training, a matter too important to be left solely to centrally controlled courses and schools:

> It can not [sic] be too strongly emphasized that it is the duty of Commanders to train their officers and non-commissioned officers. The provision of numerous outside courses of instruction for such personnel in no way relieves Commanders of this primary responsibility. In this connection it is safe to assume that an officer or N.C.O. in a formation or unit who is not trained or generally equipped to assume the duties of the next higher rank is not really qualified for the rank he presently holds.[27]

Crerar was reacting to a push from Lieutenant-General Bernard Montgomery, who, as General Officer Commanding in Chief South Eastern Command, had just begun to take a critical look at the state of the Canadian NCO corps. From late January to early March 1942, Montgomery visited all Canadian infantry battalions. He assessed each unit's NCOs and other key personnel, and passed his findings to Crerar in a series of written reports. Early on, Montgomery provided some observations that applied in a general sense across the Canadian force. As discussed briefly in Chapter 3, he worried about "the great difficulty in disposing of W.O.s and N.C.O.s who are too old for service in a fighting battalion." He also commented that some commanding officers lacked the ability to train their NCOs. Too many unit commanders did very little in the way of NCO training, especially in the French Canadian battalions.[28] Montgomery also determined that too many units left it to companies to promote NCOs, when NCO development and promotion required unit-level attention. The forthright reports also provided Crerar with frank assessments of NCO quality in each unit.

According to Montgomery, many Canadian NCOs were not suitable for wartime service.[29] He found numerous old warrant officers and NCOs in the Fusiliers Mont-Royal, for example, who were "quite unfit to serve in a fighting Bn." The entire 7th Canadian Infantry Brigade had "no system for teaching privates how to be N.C.O's *before* they are promoted." He seemed to be referring to the tendency for units to promote soldiers to corporal before giving them any formal leadership training.[30] Worse, he stated: "There are too many old officers and W.O.'s in this Brigade. They are clogging up the machinery and should be removed at once." Meanwhile, NCOs in the Royal Highland Regiment of Canada (the Black Watch) were "generally very patchy; promotion is by companies, which is quite unsuitable in war." The Carleton and York Regiment might have had an excellent RSM but suffered NCOs who "generally are not very good ... There is no proper system of instruction to ensure a good foundation in the L/Corpl rank." In the 3rd Canadian Infantry Brigade, Montgomery advised: "The N.C.O. situation wants to be taken in hand seriously. The C.O.'s do not seem to realise the immense importance of having a really first class cadre of N.C.O.'s; this cannot be possible without a good battalion system for promotion, and without a good system of instruction." In many units, Montgomery judged the RSM as too old or too incompetent for active service.

Not everything Montgomery had to say was critical, however. He also made a few favourable observations. The Canadian Scottish Regiment's RSM seemed "good, and young." The Nova Scotia Highlanders' RSM was "very good," even if three of the battalion's CSMs were "of no use." The Royal Regiment of Canada had "good N.C.O.'s." The Seaforths of Canada had an RSM who was "good and tough." Montgomery judged the NCOs in the Edmonton Regiment as "generally – adequate." The Princess Patricia's Canadian Light Infantry (PPCLI) had "the best" NCOs in the 2nd Canadian Infantry Brigade, probably because this battalion was the only one in the formation that had an efficient system for NCO selection, instruction, and promotion. The Carleton and Yorks' RSM was "first class; the best I have seen in the Corps." The Royal 22nd Regiment was generally on the right track – "N.C.O. situation is handled properly" – but things required a bit of tightening at the top, "not enough grip and supervision of N.C.O.'s by R.S.M." By and large, Montgomery found a mixed bag in the quality of Canadian NCOs, with much dead wood that needed clearing and a fair amount of good potential. By this time, however, even though some battalions had been mobilized for two and a half years, unit schedules allowed only limited time for dedicated NCO training. Other obligations – especially individual training for myriad and important specialist skills, operational tasks such as coastal defence, and collective training – took up a great deal of time, complicating the rush to mass-produce NCOs. By shining a light on Crerar's NCOs, Montgomery illuminated several problem areas that the chain of command still needed to address. And it did. For instance, Crerar directed units to send their older NCOs back to Canada as instructors, which helped remove prewar army men who were now too old for combat duty.[31]

Montgomery pressed Crerar to pay closer attention to NCO training and development. For example, in early March 1942, he advised Crerar on what to look for when inspecting units. Montgomery emphasized the importance of ensuring that commanding officers took their NCO development responsibilities seriously. First, he declared, a visiting commander needed to investigate a unit's system for selecting, promoting, and instructing NCOs. "The N.C.O.'s are the backbone of the battalion," so a commanding officer had to be aware of his responsibility to build a solid foundation from lance corporals and up, and he also needed to "interest himself directly in everything concerned with his N.C.O.'s and W.O.'s."[32] He also stressed that company commanders held responsibility for training NCOs in all their field duties, both tactical and administrative. But responsibility for NCO development did not end there, he counselled:

> The Adjutant and the R.S.M. must take a very definite hand in keeping the N.C.O.'s up to the mark, in instruction in discipline matters, and generally in ensuring that the non-commissioned ranks are a credit to the battalion, are able to maintain a high standard in all matters, are not afraid of the men, and are trained on for promotion.[33]

Montgomery emphasized that the regimental sergeant major was "one of the most important people in the unit." When inspecting a unit, he told Crerar, one should always make a point of asking to meet the RSM, treating him like an officer and shaking his hand in front of the troops as a mark of respect. The RSM exercised "supreme" authority over his NCOs, Montgomery asserted, and deserved the commanding officer's support. The RSM should frequently address each of the company's NCOs to enforce unit discipline and routine. And the RSM should work with the adjutant as a team, the two frequently touring unit lines and "keeping an eye on the general show." In short, the RSM was crucial to the unit's NCO cadre: "It is very difficult, in fact practically impossible, to have a good cadre of N.C.O.'s without a good R.S.M."[34]

These views flowed down to Canadian formations through Crerar. He prohibited commanding officers from allowing their sub-units to promote NCOs, instead ordering each unit to establish an NCO selection board consisting of the sub-unit (company/squadron/battery) commanders with the unit commander in charge. A board was to review all NCO promotion recommendations and advise the commanding officer which ones to accept.[35] But when it came to developing NCOs, responsibility was shared across the unit. Crerar echoed Montgomery:

> The training of the N.C.Os. in all duties in the field, tactical and administrative, must be carried out by the company, etc., commanders. On the other hand, the battalion or regimental commander must supervise the arrangements made to this end. The adjutant and the R.S.M. have also a definite responsibility in instruction of N.C.Os. on matters of discipline, in maintaining the proper relations with

their men, and to see that they are trained for promotion and are generally a credit to the unit.[36]

Some of the faults that Montgomery and Crerar found with the NCO corps pointed to the greater challenge of cultivating professionalism among junior leaders – NCOs and officers alike – across the new citizen-soldier army. Qualification courses alone did not automatically transform men into the seasoned leaders and disciplinarians the army needed. Formal leadership training was a crucial step, but the professional development of tactical leaders did not end on a course graduation parade. Forging a strong culture of leadership in unit lines took time and effort.

Throughout the rest of 1942, Crerar periodically saw indications that the army's low-level leadership was still developing. Despite 1st Canadian Corps direction in late March that units were responsible for preventing pilfering during exercises and for punishing soldiers guilty of theft and damage, such incidents increased in April and May.[37] During exercises Beaver III and Beaver IV, troops engaged in petty thievery by stealing poultry, eggs, and game from civilians, particularly odious crimes given that Canadian troops enjoyed higher ration scales than the civilian population. It had to stop. As the Corps prepared for its next big event, Montgomery's army-level Exercise Tiger, Crerar wanted all unit commanders to understand their responsibility for discipline. Inadequate efforts to impose it at low levels soon embarrassed him.

During the high-profile Exercise Tiger in late May, a platoon of marching Canadians booed the chief of the imperial general staff (CIGS), General Sir Alan Brooke, and Montgomery himself, as they passed by in Brooke's official car.[38] An investigation revealed that twenty-eight members of a platoon in the Edmonton Regiment had perpetrated the act. At the time, a corporal had been leading the platoon, as the platoon commander and platoon sergeant were on duty elsewhere.[39] Of course, the incident troubled Crerar considerably as a potential and very visible symptom of weak discipline and lack of control over the rank and file. He ordered disciplinary action against the unit commanding officer and the company and platoon commanders, even though none had been present at the time, because all bore responsibility for their men's discipline.[40] And, of course, Crerar singled out the on-scene NCOs for punishment: "The fact that no action was taken on the initiative of the N.C.Os. of the Section raises doubt as to their suitability for non-commissioned rank." Justice followed swiftly. The commanding officer and the platoon commander paraded for dressing-down before the division and brigade commanders, respectively, although no charges followed because they had not been present during the incident.[41] The platoon sergeant, who also had not been present, received a demotion to private, as did the four on-scene junior NCOs who had neglected to act. Seventeen privates lost seven days' pay, and four also received twenty-eight-day sentences. That the booing had occurred in the first place was terrible and humiliating enough, but that the on-scene NCOs had failed to react swiftly and decisively reflected a troubling complacency or lack of control, or both, in the unit's lowest echelons of leadership. An embarrassed Crerar, and later McNaughton, surely thought as much as they wrote apologies to the CIGS.[42]

Further signs of inadequate leadership within units came to Crerar's attention in the weeks after Exercise Tiger. In late June, the chief constable of West Sussex complained about the Royal 22nd Regiment to provost marshal staff in South Eastern Command.[43] Over the previous seven months or so, the unit had troubled the area with criminal activity, including fifty-three proven offences by thirty-nine men, and probably many more incidents that had gone unpunished – not to mention stabbings and even a shooting in incidents with other units. The complaint made its way to Montgomery, who asked Crerar to move the battalion.[44] Days later, Montgomery rebuked Crerar again, this time after having received from the chief constables of East and West Sussex reports of theft – mostly poultry and fowl but also money, cigarettes, and tea – during Exercise Tiger.[45] In fact, he stated, such reports had been arriving with increasing frequency from several sources, and he wanted Crerar to "stop this petty pilfering" and get his commanding officers to exercise the necessary discipline. An embarrassed Crerar took up the matter with his formation commanders.[46] Despite previous orders to stop stealing, he vented, soldiers continued to pilfer food from civilians. He dished out a bit of motherhood on leadership: "Prevention of this type of offence is a matter of unit discipline and administration. Every officer and N.C.O. must be brought to realize that he is personally responsible for eliminating such behaviour." Frustrated, Crerar directed his subordinate commanders to ensure that their NCOs and officers understood and fulfilled their responsibilities.

With such periodic indications that leadership culture was still maturing within his units, Crerar repeatedly emphasized the importance of junior leader development. A July 1942 1st Canadian Corps instruction on sub-unit training directed that all potential NCOs receive opportunities to develop leadership skills.[47] And in the early autumn, Crerar felt compelled to remind his junior leaders, officers and NCOs, of their fundamental responsibilities. On 28 September, 1st Canadian Corps issued an order regarding the "Responsibilities of Officers, Commissioned, Warrant and Non-Commissioned."[48] The order contended that these leaders were failing to appreciate their responsibility to exercise their powers and ensure discipline across the army, not just in their units. Leaders were duty bound to correct misbehaviour at all times and in all situations, on duty or off. And Crerar wanted the message passed directly to all junior leaders: "The general responsibility of all officers, commissioned, warrant and non-commissioned, for the maintenance of discipline and the good name of the Canadian Army will be brought to the attention of all concerned." Another corps-level order issued the same day addressed the matter of "considerable slackness with regard to the dress of Canadian soldiers."[49] Corps headquarters became concerned that soldiers too often violated dress regulations with unauthorized, slovenly, dirty, and improperly worn uniforms.

That the corps commander felt the need to publish such orders and take the extraordinary measure of explaining to low-level leaders their most basic responsibilities in enforcing discipline reflected a still-maturing culture of leadership. Two weeks later, Crerar issued updated training direction in which he emphasized that "the first consideration of a C.O." must be the training of officers and NCOs.[50] And for the month of November 1942, when the corps focused on individual training, Crerar directed that section commanders receive careful guidance and instruction to improve their initiative and control.[51] Units responded to all this top-down pressure. As discussed in Chapter 5, in 1942, battalions ran in-house NCO training throughout the year.

In spite of all this guidance and practice, by the end of 1942, Crerar was still not satisfied with NCO performance in the corps. Inspections in December and his observations of training led him to believe that the NCOs continued to lack leadership, a sense of responsibility, and command skills. He warned subordinate commanders that "a unit which does not possess a cadre of strong, self-respecting and thoroughly dependable Non-Commissioned Officers is not in a healthy condition. The Warrant and Non-Commissioned Officer is the backbone of any military organization."[52] Crerar insisted that brigade and division commanders take a more direct hand in NCO development plans: "The Warrant and Non-Commissioned Officers in the Canadian Corps must be made to appreciate and fulfill their important responsibilities and to take pride in loyally carrying them out ... Action to increase the efficiency of all N.C.Os must be thoughtfully planned, on a high level. Arrangements to this end must be thorough and continuous." These were not empty talking points. Three weeks later, Crerar ordered his formation commanders to report back on the measures they had taken.[53]

All responded quickly. Major-General Harry Salmon, GOC 1st Canadian Division, reported having ordered his units to conduct an "NCOs week with the object of developing the knowledge, power of leadership and sense of responsibility of all NCOs."[54] Salmon also stated his intention to address personally all NCOs in his division. Major-General John Roberts, GOC 2nd Canadian Division, reported that he continuously stressed to his unit commanders the necessity for strong junior leadership.[55] He acknowledged that some NCOs and junior officers had at times let discipline slide, but he attributed this to junior leaders not wanting to be judged by their men for "throwing their weight about" without cause, especially during "this trying time of waiting." Nevertheless, he assured Crerar: "We are doing our best to stamp this out." He also provided Crerar with a copy of a letter he had sent to his commanding officers stating that they were to "do everything possible" to cultivate in their NCOs "a keen sense of responsibility, of leadership and of command." It contained verbatim passages of Crerar's discourse (itself based on Montgomery's) on NCO roles in the unit.[56] Major-General Rodney Keller, GOC 3rd Canadian Division, reported having addressed in turn all NCOs in each of his formations, each time speaking for an hour and forty minutes.[57] His addresses emphasized that NCOs were responsible for enforcing discipline on and off duty, that they had particular responsibilities in the field, and that they played a part in maintaining the Canadian soldier's prestige. Keller also directed his formation commanders to emphasize to their NCOs and officers the necessity to exercise leadership "both on and off parade." He had personally questioned each of his immediate subordinate commanders to confirm that they had carried out his orders. Finally, Brigadier Robert Wyman, Commander 1st Canadian Tank Brigade, reported having discussed Crerar's direction at a brigade commanders' conference, during which he had insisted that his commanding officers demand the highest standards from their NCOs and junior officers.[58] Wyman had also ordered commanding officers to reduce in rank those who did not meet expectations.

While Crerar's formation commanders had certainly acted on his direction, how much their responses raised the NCO corps' proficiency is another question. More needed to be done, at least from Crerar's perspective. On 22 March 1943, he counselled his division commanders that they should personally imbue NCOs and junior officers with a greater sense of responsibility and understanding of "man-management."[59] Later that week, he distributed an extract from 1st Canadian Infantry Division's training instructions, as an example of the type of NCO training he thought appropriate. Salmon had ordered his unit commanders to conduct an "NCOs day" once per month, during which commanding officers personally led tactical exercises without troops (TEWTs) similar to those attended by officers. Furthermore, all unit commanders were to hold monthly discussions with all their NCOs in an ongoing effort to develop responsibility and pride.[60]

Figure 4.1 The army's highest field commanders, such as General Harry Crerar (as he was in this photo), constantly stressed the importance of developing a strong NCO corps. Here, Crerar inspects soldiers of the Lord Strathcona's Horse (Royal Canadians). Date and location unknown, but probably Northwest Europe, 1945. | Library and Archives Canada/Department of National Defence fonds/e010932989.

In the final months before Operation Husky, the direction to focus on NCO development continued to flow from Canada's highest formation commanders. McNaughton's First Canadian Army training instruction for the months of May and June 1943 included several points on junior leader development: "The conditions of modern mob[ile] war involve an increasing measure of decentralization of comd down to junior offrs and NCOs. Success in ops therefore demands the highest qualities of leadership and tech[nical] and tactical efficiency on the part of all junior leaders. The responsibility for the trg of junior leaders rests upon the CO."[61] A section of the instructions on "man management" emphasized the importance of junior leaders down to sections, or even detachments of just a few men, continuously exercising responsibility. Formations were therefore to avoid, to the extent possible, separating junior leaders from the men they commanded, whether for taskings or for discretionary courses. First Canadian Army also ordered fundamental leadership and discipline training through weekly periods of close order drill, which consisted of practice in marching in formation and reacting as a group to verbal commands, usually on a parade square. NCOs and subaltern officers (2nd lieutenants and lieutenants) were to be given "ample opportunity to exercise command on parade." Corps and divisional headquarters passed on the guidance, practically verbatim.[62] And, as unit war diaries show, units held professional development events, such as briefings and discussions on particular subjects of interest or demonstrations of tactics, as opportunity arose.[63] They also sent their NCOs to various formal courses, and in units that had strong senior NCOs and a good RSM, informal and ongoing professional development occurred through mentoring. Units and formations were taking the business of NCO development seriously.

Even so, fostering a culture of professionalism underwritten by extensive knowledge and experience took more time than the senior leadership would have liked, one of the prices to be paid for the nation's long neglect of its army before 1939. After all, as the sample group shows, at least for the infantry, about 60 percent of the senior NCOs had no military service before the war.[64] It should not come as a surprise that in the long period leading up to the commitment of Canadian formations to sustained combat, the senior leadership constantly felt the need to nudge NCO professionalization along, pushing formation and unit commanders to prioritize the cultivation of NCO competence. Fortunately, as the 1st Canadian Division's sound performance in Sicily suggests, the army managed to get it right, or at least right enough, by mid-1943.

The Evolving Nature of Training

NCO training evolved continuously throughout the war because of the army's growing demands on its junior leaders. The essential problem was that the army was racing to catch up to an enemy that had been preparing for war for years, and that by the summer of 1940 possessed not only modern weapons and sound doctrine but also combat experience. For Canadian troops, the roots of the problem grew deep. The British army, on which the Canadian army modelled itself and on which it depended for everything from equipment choices to doctrine and training manuals, was playing catch-up, too. As David French relates, for the first half of the war British combat capability was poor relative to the German army.[65] This was because in the interwar period, the British army spent most of its time, and was equipped mostly for, garrisoning the empire, although it also provided air defence for the United Kingdom. When the war began, London's strategy focused on the Royal Navy, the Royal Air Force (RAF), and the French army. Relatively few resources went to the British army, whose role was only to help French forces defeat Germany after it had been weakened by naval blockade and strategic bombing. The British army's poor state worsened when the resources it had managed to build up for fighting on the continent were lost at Dunkirk. Even after, the Royal Navy and the RAF continued to receive priority while the army struggled for resources. Its capability did not improve significantly until late 1942, when sufficient quantities of good equipment were finally available.[66] If the British army was for several years ill prepared for fighting a major war, so too was the Canadian army.

Over the course of the war, NCOs played an important role in mastering, teaching, and leading troops in the latest tactical procedures. There were many. David French describes some of the techniques that the British army developed as it prepared to fight the Germans – new techniques that the Canadians had to master as well.[67] These included things like procedures for crossing man-made obstacles (such as minefields) and natural obstacles (such as rivers), conducting night attacks, and launching an opposed amphibious landing, the most complex type of operation. As French recounts, over time even the Germans grew impressed with their enemy's ability to execute interarm cooperation at night to breach German defences at Alamein and, later, to fight skilfully at Normandy. But these things had to be learned, taught, and practised, with NCOs leading the rank and file at the platoon and company levels, which explains why Canadian NCO qualification and specialist training evolved so much as the war continued. Of course, tactics were not the only element that evolved. Courses developed and expanded to accommodate the latest in fitness training, instructional technique, recognition of armoured vehicles, and many other subjects.

Wartime changes in the family of infantry weapons alone illustrate well why Canadian NCO training changed so much over time. As the war progressed Canadian troops adopted new weapons, and it was the NCOs who had to master them first and teach them to everyone else. The Canadians started the war with almost no modern weapons but adopted new ones as the British brought them into service, often assisted by Canadian manufacturers.[68] Canadian infantrymen used the Lee-Enfield No.1 (Marks III and IV), a First World War rifle, until November 1942, when the modernized No.4 finally became available. Early in the war, the Canadian army, like its Commonwealth counterparts, adopted the

Figure 4.2   Sergeant D. Wilson of the Highland Light Infantry of Canada training two privates to use the PIAT during an exercise in England, 13 April 1944. | Library and Archives Canada/Department of National Defence fonds/a132894.

aging but effective .45 calibre American-made Thompson sub-machine gun.[69] In January 1941, impressed by the ability of the German MP38 sub-machine gun to spew 500 rounds per minute, the British decided to build a sub-machine gun of their own.[70] By June, the first 9mm Sten guns rolled off the assembly line. The simple and cheap new weapon proved effective at ranges below 300 yards (274 m) but required skilled hands, meaning that training and practice, shepherded by NCOs, were essential. Sten guns made their way into Canadian units by 1942, and by June 1943 Canadian-made versions had become standard issue across the army (although Canadian troops in Italy followed the British practice of using the Thompson until they moved to Northwest Europe, where they adopted the Sten).[71] As for larger automatic weapons, the army went to war with First World War Lewis machine guns, but gradually swapped them out for the much better Bren guns in 1940–41. Anti-tank weapons also evolved during the war. Early on, infantrymen carried the heavy, awkward, magazine-fed .55-inch Boys anti-tank rifle, but troops lost confidence in it after it proved effective only against armoured cars and light tanks.[72] It was useless against newer German tanks. In fact, after the British Eighth Army's Operation Crusader in the Western desert in late 1941, staff found no evidence of the weapon's effectiveness against German armour. It had to be replaced. In 1942, the British finally adopted a new anti-tank weapon, the Projector, Infantry, Anti-Tank (PIAT), which launched a powerful anti-tank bomb.[73] Canadian units started receiving this shoulder-fired weapon in early 1943.[74] Over the course of the war, the Canadian army also adopted three types of mortars: the 4.2-inch, the 3-inch, and the 2-inch. Finally, flame weapons made their way into Canadian units. In late 1942, Canadian troops took delivery of the Ronson flame-thrower. Later, the army replaced it with the Wasp, which had a greater range. Every time the army adopted a new weapon, NCOs had to be trained to master it and to instruct other soldiers in how to use and maintain it.

Conclusion

Before July 1943, the Canadian army faced a tremendous challenge in building its corps of NCOs. The sheer speed and scale of the army's growth, and the rickety foundation on which it had to build, meant that most NCOs had to learn how to be leaders from scratch. Even the ones with prior military experience, especially those who had received promotions on volunteering for the wartime force, required much training.

The senior leadership understood the challenge and implemented several measures to drive NCO development as quickly as possible. Responsibility for NCO training, promotion, and development was devolved to unit commanding officers. The peacetime policies of running qualification courses at royal and permanent Schools of Instruction, and subjecting soldiers to nationally controlled promotion examinations, would not have worked for a mobilizing army that had to expand so quickly. Units knew what they needed and the new policy gave them flexibility to make the best use of their manpower. It also gave unit commanders a stake in the NCO development process. Eventually, new and innovative processes for assessing a soldier's intelligence, aptitude, and physical and psychological constitution gave unit commanders better tools for deciding how best to employ their personnel. Meanwhile, the senior leadership beat a constant drum on the importance of growing junior leaders and cultivating their sense of responsibility. In early 1942, Montgomery gave the Canadians a jolt when he scrutinized their NCOs and pointed out the faults. His counsel flowed downward through subordinate formations and into units.

Despite all this emphasis, NCO development occurred more slowly than Crerar wanted, and as late as June 1943 he felt compelled to push his subordinate commanders to stay on top of it. While Crerar's frustration was understandable, so too was the time it took to build a strong NCO corps. Given the little cadre Canada had at the start of the war, developing competent NCOs with the knowledge and experience they needed to beat German forces that had a significant head start in their development was bound to take longer than anyone wanted. Good NCOs could not be produced with a snap of the fingers. It took a combination of attention and expertise – and time.

5
Unit and Formation Programs

*Another Regt. N.C.O.'s school is history ... These schools have done much
for the Bn. It is from them that we look to for our new N.C.O.'s. It is from the
school records that N.C.O.'s receive promotion.*

CALGARY HIGHLANDERS WAR DIARY, 29 NOVEMBER 1941

AS THE ARMY EXPANDED at a frantic pace, commanding officers had a daunt-
ing challenge in raising and developing their NCO cadres. They had to train
privates to be junior NCOs, provide catch-up training to junior NCOs who had
not yet received any leadership instruction, prepare strong corporals for promotion to sergeant, and provide supplementary training to fast-tracked senior NCOs.
This was a lot for units concerned with countless other matters while preparing
for operations. What is more, these same NCO training requirements continued
once units went into battle, when war establishment vacancies resulted from
casualties and not just rapid expansion.

Units ran NCO training when they could, but none had the capacity to meet
requirements, so parent formations (brigades and divisions) helped by running
courses, in most cases to train soldiers to be corporals or sergeants. Formation-
run NCO courses were particularly important for units in the operational
theatres, where battalions were too busy fighting to conduct much individual
training. Not far behind the forward lines, brigades and divisions ran short programs that taught just the essential skills. From the outset, decentralized NCO
training occurred in an ad hoc fashion, as units and formations put whatever
training time was available to best use.

Forming Unit Backbones: Training before July 1943

Shortly after mobilization began, units began to whip their fledgling NCO cadres
into shape. At Fort Osborne Barracks in Winnipeg, the Princess Patricia's Canadian Light Infantry (PPCLI) typified how units raised and trained their NCOs
in these early days. Soon after receiving orders to mobilize, the unit gave eighty-
two men acting NCO rank.[1] Training for them quickly followed with an NCOs
"regimental qualifying course," which began on 21 September. The students also

included many privates. The unit was so busy preparing for war that the last part of the course had to run during evenings, however, and it finally ended on 18 November. But with the rush to fill the war establishment and provide instructors to various military districts – after all, the PPCLI was a permanent force unit – even more NCOs were needed. So on 22 November, a second qualifying course began. This time, seventy-six candidates took the training, most of them privates. Of these, about thirty were from the permanent force; the remainder were brand new troops. The unit had less time to run this course but managed at least to train and examine the men in small arms instruction and drill before the unit ceased all training in mid-December for the move overseas.

Other units similarly fit NCO training into their frenzied schedules as they could. The Royal Canadian Regiment (RCR), another permanent force regiment, whose companies were scattered across eastern Canada when war broke out, did not start a formal NCO course until 30 October. Most of the sixty-two candidates had just joined the army.[2] In Quebec City, the Royal 22nd Regiment (R22R), the last of the army's three permanent force regiments, began a six-week NCO qualification course on 18 September, and started a second course a month later.[3]

Meanwhile, activated Non-Permanent Active Militia (NPAM) units took similar action. In Vancouver, the Seaforth Highlanders promoted a batch of soldiers to NCO rank at the end of September and started their development with mentoring from the unit's permanent force Instructional Cadre representative.[4] Similarly, around the same time, the 48th Highlanders in Toronto had its Instructional Cadre personnel grip the unit's NCOs too.[5] The Edmonton Regiment even ran training for some of its higher-ranking NCOs, launching a regimental Warrant Officers School of Qualification in late November.[6]

The Queen's Own Rifles (QOR) demonstrated how newly mobilized battalions struggled with immature NCO cadres early in the war. The unit's initial crop of NCOs was weak, partly because the regiment did not mobilize until 5 June 1940, and much of its talent had already left to join battalions that had mobilized earlier.[7] Three months after the unit stood up, the commanding officer, Lieutenant-Colonel Harry MacKendrick, expressed concern to his company commanders that the battalion had little opportunity to work on NCO teaching skills, which was adversely affecting training overall:

> While considerable time is being spent on training, it is felt that in some cases, not much is being learned. This is partly due to lack of time and opportunity for turning N.C.O.'s into instructors. It has been noticed, for instance, that while

demonstration and description of a [drill] movement is properly given, no check is made of incorrectness of the men in the squad. Similarly instruction is being given without the essential stores being used.[8]

At the time, the unit was deployed to Newfoundland, where security tasks reduced the opportunities for training, so improving the NCO cadre took a while. A month later, D company's officer commanding, Major Ralph Hudson, expressed his own frustrations. As part of his company standing orders, Hudson reminded his junior leaders of their basic responsibilities:

> The section leader is directly responsible to the Platoon Commander for the men under his command. He must see that the men in his section are ready to go on parade, five minutes before parade time and that at all times, they are properly dressed and that they are properly equipped ... He must see that his men are up at Reveille, shaved and rifles cleaned before breakfast, at Last Post that they are in their lines and in their bed[s] at Light Out ... He must see that all his men are fed and that if for any good reason a man misses or is late for a meal, arrangements are made for him to get his meal ... He should see that his section is properly instructed in all things that a soldier should know ... He must insist on immediate and implicit obedience to all his orders, on the instant.[9]

And, Hudson emphasized: "HE MUST, AT ALL TIMES, BE AN EXAMPLE TO HIS MEN." He must have felt exasperated at having to tell NCOs how to do their jobs. The company, in his opinion, did not have a sturdy backbone of experienced junior leaders. These were the sorts of NCO problems that had to be addressed in a rapidly expanding army with a limited pool of experienced junior leaders.

At least one QOR company ran training to improve NCO performance. During a week of sub-unit training in early November 1940, C company supplemented the daily routine with a "refresher course" to improve the standard of instruction by NCOs. All company NCOs gathered daily in the late afternoon for a forty-minute refresher on the next day's rifle training, and they gathered again in the early evening for another forty-minute refresher on the next day's light-machine-gun training.[10] The same company ran leadership and instruction courses a few months later, by which time the unit had moved to Camp Sussex, New Brunswick. One of the courses lasted five and a half days.[11] Major topics included methods of instruction, squad handling, discipline, tactics, and map reading. Specific classes included lectures on discipline, developing and encouraging esprit de corps, and the duties of a section leader. Several periods focused on how to teach, demonstrate, and practise particular subjects. And staff put students through several periods of mutual instruction in small arms training and drill. The courses might not have been long, but they allowed the company commander to redress identified areas of weakness. They also complemented longer NCO training programs conducted at the battalion level.

Canada-based units preparing for deployment overseas ran different types of courses to build their NCO cadres. Some courses forged rank-and-file soldiers into junior NCOs. For instance, shortly after the Canadian Scottish Regiment mobilized, it ran a course to train men to be corporals. One of the candidates, Raymond Gray, recalls that in the fall of 1939, "we had an NCOs course ... I had the full course for corporal ... so I qualified." The course included "a bit of everything: drill, compass reading, map reading, and trained [us] to teach other people because we were still just a nucleus of what was to come."[12] Starting in mid-January 1941, the QOR ran a similar in-house program, a seven-week Regimental NCO School. The students included almost all of the unit's lance corporals, corporals, and lance sergeants.[13] Training occurred five and a half days per week and included several evening lectures.[14] The program involved instruction on fundamental subjects, such as the section in battle, small arms training, fieldcraft, map reading, protection against gas, military law, and discipline. Apparently, it yielded some quick results. After the first week, the commanding officer commented that the school had "effected a noticeable smartening up of all personnel attending."[15] His battalion's backbone might not have been strong in the months immediately following mobilization, but it grew sturdier with time, helped along by unit-level training.

Meanwhile, units in the overseas army conducted courses to build up the strength and quality of their NCO cadres as unit and formation training schedules allowed. Just like in Canada, programs varied a great deal from unit to unit. Naturally enough, unit commanders took different approaches, based on local needs and the time available. Generally, unit-run courses lasted anywhere from one week to two months. Sometimes a battalion conducted only a single serial of a given course, and sometimes several in succession. Some courses gave catch-up training to soldiers who had received promotion to junior NCO rank before undergoing leadership training, while others refreshed and updated the skills of sergeants. Some units ran structured courses with graded performance examinations leading to particular qualifications. For example, in January 1943, Lance Corporal L.J. McMurray of the Calgary Highlanders – one of the soldiers in the sample group – attended the unit's month-long NCO school and "qualified" for the rank of sergeant.[16] Of course, this was not a national qualification but a unit one, which is what counted in an army that left NCO promotions to the discretion of unit commanding officers.

Sometimes schedules allowed for only a little NCO training, but units did what they could. In early 1942, when units of the Canadian Corps (called the 1st Canadian Corps as of 6 April) started a phase of collective training that progressed from platoon to division level by May – and included the Canadians' first large-scale offensive exercises – some units squeezed short courses into their packed schedules.[17] The R22R ran a short course in March and another in May.[18] The Regina Rifles ran two eight-day NCO schools but had to pause them when students and instructors participated in battalion training.[19] The ambitious RCR tried to run an eight-week course but had to stop it after five weeks, probably due to other unit commitments.[20] The PPCLI ran a short but intensive twelve-day course, into which it squeezed instruction on the essential knowledge and skills candidates required as section commanders.[21] Most days began with a one-hour period of close order drill during which the candidates took turns giving commands to the group on parade. Delivering drill helped set students in their roles as leaders and disciplinarians who could bark out confident orders, demand obedience, and instinctively correct faults as they spotted them. This was vital for conditioning young soldiers to be leaders and disciplinarians – not friends – with the men. Russell Smith, who rose to warrant officer rank during the war, explained the distance that sergeants had to keep from men under their training:

When you're doing certain drills, you have to get them mad. You have to make them put a lot more force into it ... You yell a lot. You keep them running, you keep on chasing them all the time. But in the evenings, you leave them alone, you don't go near them, you stay away from them ... You go to the same shows and that sort of thing but you don't eat with them as a sergeant. As a lance corporal and a corporal, you do, but as a sergeant and up, you have your own quarters. So you leave them alone and let them get over their mad ... You find fault a lot. You find a button undone or a badge dirty or a dirty rifle or pants not pressed or boots not shined properly or a bit of rust on the bayonet or a bed not made properly. Every day, they're inspected for everything.[22]

So things like drill acclimatized students to the leadership roles they would eventually assume. After the morning drill period, students attended classes on such topics as tactics and battle drill, military law, and man management. Classes for "instructing the soldier" in small arms took up much of the time, as candidates practised their teaching skills for weapons handling, aiming and firing, and care and cleaning of various armaments. And course staff administered tests and examinations to confirm each man's learning. For instance, on the sixth day, staff ran students through tests on close order drill, weapons training, and controlling a section in battle. For the whole of the tenth day, students underwent examinations on the platoon and the section in the attack. And on the twelfth day, staff examined students on drill, weapons training, and military law. In March, the PPCLI managed to cram in at least two similar serials, although one of these lasted only six training days.[23]

In the second half of the year, when the 1st Canadian Corps gave units more time to conduct individual training, battalions ran longer, more comprehensive courses. Such was the case with the West Nova Scotia Regiment (WNSR), which from the late summer of 1942 to December ran four consecutive month-long section commander courses.[24] When the last one ended, the West Novas had trained about a hundred soldiers to be junior NCOs. Even the four-week course may not have been quite long enough to give a man all the knowledge and skill he needed to command a section – at the time, centralized and more formal junior NCO qualification courses in Canada and in Britain ran for six weeks or so – but the WNSR clearly made a serious effort to make the best use of the time available to start growing future leaders in the unit's rank and file.

The example of the North Shore (New Brunswick) Regiment typifies how units sometimes trained their NCOs after they had been promoted. This unit designed and implemented a reasonably thorough program of leadership training for soldiers already holding junior NCO rank. In mid-October 1942, the battalion conducted a six-week course for lance corporals and corporals, running six days per week.[25] For the first three weeks, the regimental sergeant major (RSM) started each day with a period of drill. These drill classes tapered off in subsequent weeks, but throughout the course the RSM stayed involved, delivering lectures on NCO duties. The students also learned the skills to command sections in the field, with lessons on fieldcraft, navigation, and defence against gas. Pioneer officers and NCOs taught classes in field engineering, which included lessons on booby traps and digging various defensive works. Unit officers lectured on administration, the evacuation of casualties, and hygiene and sanitation in the field. Small arms training, taught by senior NCOs, reinforced students' expertise in the use and maintenance of all platoon weapons. Tactics lessons gave students a basic understanding of woods clearing, village clearing, and the section in the attack. Twenty-one candidates finished the course, with a graded ranking of *distinguished* (85 percent), Q1+ (75–85 percent), Q1 (60–75 percent), or Q2 (50–60 percent). Most students finished with a Q1. The unit ran the course again beginning in early December for nineteen soldiers, who again consisted mostly of lance corporals and corporals.

Thus, the North Shore (New Brunswick) Regiment made a strong investment in junior NCO training for a total of forty soldiers, almost all of whom had already received NCO rank or appointments. That the commanding officer believed such an effort was necessary suggests many of his junior NCOs had attained their ranks or appointments *before* undergoing leadership training. Edward Joseph Rigley, serves as an example.[26] Rigley, who attended the first course, had been confirmed as a corporal several months earlier, without any formal NCO training. He was one of the many men that units promoted to fill an NCO vacancy and worried about training later.

Sometimes units ran courses to keep skills sharp among the senior NCOs. In late October 1942, the West Novas ran a one-week refresher course for twenty-two of the unit's sergeants, which was most of them. A junior officer, Lieutenant J.K. Rhodes, ran the course, which probably says something about the unit's senior NCOs at the time.[27] In a professional army, long-serving senior NCOs with years of experience under their belts would have balked at receiving mentorship and refresher training from a subaltern officer, but this was 1942 and many of the unit's senior NCOs probably did not have much more time in uniform than the battalion's lieutenants. That the unit even felt the need to provide a refresher course for sergeants suggests as much. Indeed, the syllabus reviewed the fundamental leadership skills all NCOs required. Small arms training, for example, refreshed students on platoon weapons.[28] And students reviewed basic field skills, such as compass use, locating targets, issuing fire control orders, message writing, and field signals. However, the course also provided lectures designed specifically for senior NCOs. For example, the commanding officer addressed the students on NCO duties, the adjutant presented a class on military law, and the RSM gave another on discipline. The unit war diarist recorded that the program had been worth the effort: "It is felt that this course proved highly beneficial to all ... Gatherings of this nature also promote a feeling of fellowship that is invaluable to the esprit-de-corps of the unit."[29] While such courses were not very long, they were useful and they typified how units periodically conducted in-house NCO training to suit their own particular needs.

In the period leading up to Operation Husky in July 1943, field formations also conducted NCO training from time to time. Units busy with defensive tasks and collective training simply did not have the capacity to run all the qualification, refresher, and specialist training needed to build up and sustain their NCO cadres. (The overseas army eventually helped by running NCO training at a centralized location, but that did not start until the spring of 1941.) Something had to be done to boost NCO training locally, and in the autumn of 1940, the British came up with a solution. At the time, when Canadian formations formed part of the multinational 7th Corps, the War Office planned to establish several formation-level junior leaders schools.[30] Thus, in October, Canadian authorities began running a corps-level junior leaders program. The 7th Corps (which soon became the Canadian Corps) developed a three-week course for twenty NCOs and twenty officers at a time.[31] The NCOs trained in one wing, the second lieutenants and lieutenants in another.[32] The former group ranged in rank from lance corporal up to warrant officer class 2 (company sergeant major, or CSM), with the heaviest representation at the rank of sergeant.[33] In addition to providing instruction in essential NCO skills such as map reading, fire control orders, and anti-aircraft drills, the course emphasized that all members of a platoon should understand the tactical situation at all times. That way, subordinates would be able to take over when leaders became casualties.[34]

NCOs found the course quite worthwhile, particularly for how it encouraged sharing tactical awareness among all platoon members.[35] School staff learned that platoon sergeants were used to having a poor understanding of the current tactical situation because, back in their units, they too often remained in the rear or with the platoon truck. Therefore, many NCOs reported that the training was an eye opener. Of course, these were early days in the war for the Canadian army, and the NCO corps – if not the greater army itself – still had a way to go in its development. The inexperienced candidates badly needed the training to prepare them for the extreme leadership challenges that lay ahead. Charles Martin, who served as a CSM in the Queen's Own Rifles, describes a company assault in Northwest Europe that exemplified the intense circumstances in which these fledgling NCOs would eventually find themselves:

> The Boss [company commander] had sent two platoons of about fifteen men each down the forward slope and through the trees [to assault a pair of farmhouses]. These woods were full of anti-tank mines and booby traps. Before long they were pinned down by terrific machine-gun fire and were badly exposed to sniper activity ... Things were now looking grim. The enemy snipers were having a field day. If our two platoons stayed where they were in the woods, they'd be picked off one by one. If they tried dropping back, they'd get the same fate ... I was working my way forward, still with the pack on my back, when I caught a flash and saw a nest of snipers on a platform high in a tree ... I moved up and took out one ... But now we were identified and caught in an ambush ... We fixed swords [bayonets], the

thirty or forty of us who were left in A Company, and made ready for a head-on straight-ahead charge ... It really was a do-or-die affair. We couldn't stay and we couldn't go back, so we went forward. For a time the enemy kept up a steady fire. Then they broke. We got the two farmhouses. [36]

Prevailing under these sorts of conditions required aggressive, competent, and well-trained NCOs who could assume command when needed. Some 220 NCOs and 220 subalterns passed through the Corps Junior Leaders School before it closed in September 1941, seven months after it had been scheduled to cease operating.

Meanwhile, every addition of new units and formations to the army's growing order of battle increased demand for qualified regimental instructors. This is exactly what happened when the 4th Canadian Infantry Division mobilized in mid-1941.[37] NCOs and officers in the division's newly raised units had to be taught how to teach before they could conduct basic training themselves.[38] Most of them had only served for the previous year or so as reservists. This was why National Defence Headquarters (NDHQ) gathered as many of the division's NCOs and officers as possible in Manitoba and Quebec for a five-week instructional cadre course. The trainers came from established training centres and from division units that had already mobilized. It was a big project, with NDHQ demanding a top-notch training staff of 125 NCOs and 31 officers.[39]

The division's authorities did what they could with what they had, as the instructional cadre course run at Saint-Hyacinthe, Quebec, demonstrates. Course planners designed the program so that over five weeks the student-instructors reviewed the army's eight-week basic training syllabus while also learning how to teach it.[40] The training plan included classes in how to instruct and as much mutual teaching as possible. Squeezing eight weeks of material into five, and learning how to teach it all, necessitated scheduling long hours that stretched into most evenings. Anticipating different levels of experience among students, both NCOs and officers, training companies prepared to group candidates into squads of soldiers with roughly equal expertise. And because planners appreciated that no student could possibly retain all the subject matter, the course taught students to make good use of reference materials – textbooks, orders, memoranda, instructions, and their own notes – whenever preparing to instruct.

The program in Saint-Hyacinthe became the large operation that NDHQ had hoped for, with training proceeding as planned. By the end of June, the camp hosted 169 administrative staff, 73 instructors, and 181 students.[41] A month later, the student population grew to 274.[42] Because students arrived over several weeks, staff staggered the training, with squads in each company following different schedules. As expected, the students reported with widely varying degrees of skill and expertise. A training report stated that trainees ranged from raw recruits to already well trained NCOs and officers.[43] Students included all ranks from private to lieutenant and represented all arms and corps, such as infantry, artillery, engineers, the Veteran Guards, and even the medical and dental corps.[44] The school placed students into three groups: an Officers Wing plus two NCO companies, A and B. The least-experienced students went to B company, which became practically a recruit company, with men in small squads for close instructional attention. To deliver a common standard of instruction, staff met each afternoon to coordinate demonstrations and teaching methods, all based on official publications.

The syllabus mirrored the army's eight-week basic training program as closely as possible. Staff designed the cadre course to include five-eighths of the basic training content, including all the fundamental skills taught to recruits.[45] Staff also supplemented the program with methods-of-instruction training, including six periods on "how to instruct." A lesson on how to teach drill conveyed the "seven stages of instruction," the rigid sequence the army used to instruct drill movements.[46] Staff also allotted several periods to teaching the duties of an RSM, platoon sergeant, corporal, and orderly sergeant.[47]

The course was a formation-level response to a critical and sudden need for NCO instructors, run with support from centralized training centres and NDHQ. Running a crash program suited the circumstances, given that the division had only so much time to train its trainers and very few experienced and qualified trainers with whom to work. The program probably did not produce an ideal instructional workforce – few of the inexperienced candidates became stellar instructors in just five weeks – but the division had little choice but to make the best use of the time and human capital available. In early September, the school closed and the new trainers took their places as instructors in the division.[48]

NCO training periodically occurred at the brigade level as well. Brigade-run courses were yet another means of increasing NCO production and development, allowing units to pool the resources needed to run a decent training program. For example, in August 1942, the 2nd Canadian Infantry Brigade (2 CIB) opened an NCO school at Jevington Place, East Sussex. It ran several serials of a month-long course designed to provide elementary leadership training to prospective junior NCOs. Like the Canadian Corps Junior Leaders School, the 2 CIB program was temporary, so the brigade drew on its three infantry units for instructional staff and equipment.[49] The Seaforth Highlanders of Canada provided the course commander and four sergeant instructors. The Edmonton Regiment provided the company quartermaster sergeant and four more sergeant instructors. And the PPCLI provided the RSM and another four sergeant instructors. The units also provided the school's administrative staff, while the instructors drew from their battalions the required training pamphlets and weapons. The first time the course was offered, each of the three units sent twenty candidates and brigade headquarters sent six – not a bad return for what each unit had committed to running the program.

The four-week course took a progressive approach, starting with basic subjects and increasing in complexity as the days and weeks wore on. During the first week, students worked at discipline, drill, leadership, and morale. Small arms training also began in the first week, with instruction on the Sten gun.[50] During the second week, small arms training proceeded in full swing, with classes on the rifle, Thompson sub-machine gun, anti-tank rifle, and grenades. Other classes focused on map reading, military law, protection against gas, and battalion organization. The course also spent a full day on controlling a section during the different phases of an amphibious assault landing.[51] During the third week, students practised teaching during classes of mutual instruction. They also practised leading sections and rehearsed more assault landings. Small arms training proceeded apace, as did practice in map reading and anti-gas drills.[52] In the fourth week, the brigade commander, Brigadier Chris Vokes, delivered a lecture on Canada's place in the war effort. Finally, students handled and fired small arms for four days, and practised combined operations (including yet more assault landings) for two evenings and one full day. The course graduation on 12 September featured a demonstration of the assault landing tactics the students had learned. Vokes attended the ceremony and, according to the 2 CIB War Diary, "was more than impressed with the results."[53] In fact, the course proved useful enough to run several more serials, the second starting just two days after the completion of the first.[54]

Additional serials followed in quick succession, with moderate adjustments to the syllabus as the weeks went by. The second serial included closing exercises and an intersection fire control competition, while the third provided training to platoon sergeants and NCOs holding the rank of acting sergeant.[55] The chain of command was so impressed with the training that the fourth and final serial, which began on 23 November, included NCOs from supporting elements (such as medical and transport sergeants, and sanitary corporals).[56] By the time the 2 CIB NCO School closed on 30 December, it had trained some 280 NCOs and potential NCOs, and in so doing had given the brigade's junior leadership establishment a healthy shot in the arm. The program allowed each of the three infantry battalions to go into 1943 with about eighty soldiers who had passed through the school – almost equivalent to a unit's entire complement of sergeants and corporals.[57] This decentralized yet structured training exemplified how formations bolstered their NCO cadres.

Within Sound of the Guns: Training in the Theatres of War

On deploying to the theatre of operations, forces only paused their NCO development programs, rather than stopping them. When commanders had the opportunity, they ran courses to sharpen proficiency and to develop the next generation of junior leaders. Understandably, in-theatre NCO training was not as elaborate as some of the programs conducted in Britain or Canada. Still, commanders thought they needed to conduct training tailored to local requirements, as circumstances allowed.[58] For instance, in November 1943, the Hastings and Prince Edward Regiment in Italy had RSM Angus Duffy run a course. According to a regimental history,

> he was ordered to prepare an intensive course of training for a number of corporals and a few sergeants who had been promoted in action. These NCOs were going to have to prove that they could show leadership and good judgement ... [The RSM] could see that not all the candidates were really NCO material, in spite of having done well in action. Three or four failed to qualify.[59]

In fact, units across 1 CIB ran NCO training that month, just after the formation came out of the line.[60] However, such unit-run courses in operational theatres were rare. But formations had more capacity to run training. For example, after the campaign in Italy slowed down for the winter in early 1944, brigade-level NCO courses began and ran well into the following summer.

That February, 2 CIB took advantage of a pause in major operations to run an NCO school in Ortona. At the time, the Canadian forces in Italy were recovering from intensive operations at the end of 1943 that had taken a heavy toll on manpower. When General Bernard Montgomery's Eighth Army ran out of steam in late December and had to stop its offensive, the 1st Canadian Division was in rough shape.[61] It had taken heavy casualties from the hard fighting that month, and had also suffered an abnormally high illness rate. An influx of reinforcements helped repair the personnel losses, but the division still had a deficit of 1,050 soldiers when the year ended. These losses hit the sharp end particularly hard, the division commander Major-General Chris Vokes reported, with battalions suffering about 50 percent casualties in their rifle companies.[62] He needed to restore his formation's offensive power and a pause in major

Figure 5.1 Brigadier Howard D. Graham, commander of the 1st Canadian Infantry Brigade, addresses a class of NCOs from the Royal Canadian Regiment. This photo was probably taken in November 1943, just days after the unit came out of the line for rest. | Library and Archives Canada/Department of National Defence fonds/ e002505412.

operations allowed him to do so. From about 10 February, the Canadians experienced twelve weeks or so of relative quiet, as the belligerents settled in for a period of static warfare.[63] As the Canadians occupied defensive lines, conducted reconnaissance and fighting patrols, and attempted to snatch prisoners, units periodically rotated out of the line to rest and undergo refresher training. In these conditions, staff began operating a brigade NCO school under Major C.M. McDougall, a PPCLI officer appointed commandant.[64] The program had a focused aim: to train NCOs in the duties of a platoon commander.[65] Candidates therefore consisted of platoon sergeants and corporals who had potential to serve as platoon sergeants. Staff kept class sizes small, giving each of the brigade's units just eight vacancies for serials that ran for ten training days. The brigade commander, Brigadier Bert Hoffmeister, took a close interest in the school, visiting regularly and sometimes bringing Vokes with him.[66]

The program covered the basic skills required for commanding a platoon in the brigade's area of operations.[67] The curriculum covered tactics, patrolling, and working with other arms, with lectures on artillery support and cooperation with tanks. Classes on the enemy covered German organization and weapons. Students learned about leadership, morale, and discipline. And they brushed up on the things they needed to know as platoon commanders-in-waiting, such as company and battalion weapons, radio procedure, and map reading. The program compressed a lot of material into a ten day schedule.

The course must have been useful because the brigade ran it for several months. A few weeks after opening, the school moved from Ortona to better accommodations at San Vito Marina, about five kilometres south, which the British and Canadians had built up as an administration and rest area.[68] Thereafter, even as the brigade rotated into and out of the line, the NCO school continued running about two serials per month. The brigade headquarters kept a close eye on the training, with the commander and the brigade major (the senior staff officer in the headquarters) making regular inspections. By the end of April, five serials had run, and each unit had put about forty soldiers through the program, easily enough for every infantry company in the brigade to have several NCOs freshly trained to take over as platoon commander when necessary. The program helped prepare men like Corporal Leslie McMurray. He was one of those in the sample group who earned his double chevrons after a minimum of leadership training. With only a three-week regimental NCO course under his belt, he had become a corporal in June 1943, five months before deploying to Italy as a reinforcement.[69] In late January 1944, McMurray joined the Loyal Edmonton Regiment as a green junior NCO. He attended the 2 CIB course in April, which must have been of some use to him when he became a sergeant in early September. It was the only sergeant-level training he received.

Around the end of April 1944, the school introduced a second course, this one designed to keep up the strength of unit NCO cadres by developing future junior NCOs. The units of 1st Canadian Division had just come out of the line (as had 5th Canadian Division units the month before), and 1st Canadian Corps was preparing for its role in the Allied spring offensive, including the Eighth Army's advance in the Liri Valley that would start on 11 May.[70] In the fierce fighting to come, someone had to replace NCOs as they fell in battle, so the training focused on privates likely to receive appointments to lance corporal.[71] The "2 Brigade Junior NCOs course" lasted seven training days and gave troops just the basics. Each morning began with a thirty-minute warm-up period for inspections and drill, followed by eight periods of instruction, with the training ending at 4:30 p.m. – probably a long enough day for soldiers recently out of the line.[72] The program placed particular emphasis on small arms training but also included other fundamental NCO skills, such as navigation, knowledge of basic platoon tactics, and man management. Although the training gave privates only the essential knowledge they needed to start serving as junior NCOs, the brigade considered the course important enough to keep it running even after offensive operations resumed. Again, someone had to replace NCO casualties.

In fact, the school remained open well into the summer, regardless of the brigade's high operational tempo. By mid-May, preparations for assaulting the Hitler Line consumed unit and staff attention. Yet the brigade ordered the school to follow behind the formation – and continue running courses.[73] It did. On 23 May, the 1st Canadian Corps assaulted and cracked the Hitler Line, a great victory but a costly one. In just twenty-four hours, 1st Canadian Corps casualties included 20 officers and 538 other ranks, with 2 CIB taking particularly heavy losses after assaulting the line's strongest sector.[74] While the corps fought, courses continued. Just five days after the battle, each unit sent ten candidates to a new one. The school continued running until 15 July, when the brigade commander finally closed it.[75]

Running the NCO school from mid-February to mid-July 1944 was a sensible investment. Reduced brigade activity in the three months before the Liri Valley operation afforded an opportunity to prepare small and successive groups of unit soldiers for the higher duties that inevitably came. Casualties were unavoidable and would leave vacancies to be filled. Section commanders, in particular, frequently became casualties. As PPCLI NCO Felix Carriere recalled, platoon commanders and corporals "were people who got hit first, because they're leaders. An officer is supposed to lead his men and he did. A corporal leads a section, he's number two. So the officer's number one, he gets it first, followed by the next guy who was going to be the leader. And so corporals and officers had a very short lifespan."[76]

Although the reinforcement system existed to replenish such losses, units required their soldiers to be capable of stepping up in the middle of a battle. By running its own NCO training and gradually building a surplus of men with some fundamental leadership knowledge and skill, 2 CIB increased platoon-level capacity to handle losses. Furthermore, by continuing to run the NCO school during the Liri Valley offensive, the brigade commander – by now, Brigadier Thomas Gibson – demonstrated that he considered it essential to keep investing in NCO training while his forces fought. It helped build resilience in the brigade's backbone.

With high infantry casualties draining unit NCO cadres in the fall of 1944 – the army suffered unexpectedly high infantry casualties in the Normandy campaign and after, leading to an infantry reinforcement crisis that lasted well into the fall – all five Canadian divisions had to start NCO training programs in the field. Before then, no division-run programs had existed in the theatres of operation, and their creation resulted from the high command's resolve to replace NCO casualties with competent successors. In Northwest Europe, Headquarters First Canadian Army directed its divisions in November to organize battle schools for NCO training and various other types of instruction.[77] Both divisions in Italy ran NCO training too, starting in January 1945. And when the 1st Canadian Corps moved to Northwest Europe the commander, Lieutenant-General Charles Foulkes, ordered that "Div schools will be opened earliest and the trg of NCOs and junior offrs will continue."[78]

Even 21st Army Group, the British formation comprising the First Canadian and Second British armies, concerned itself with division-level NCO training, suggesting that the Canadians were hardly alone in their need for more NCOs. In mid-January 1945, army group training staff asked First Canadian Army if an army-level school for field unit NCOs should be formed, perhaps even an army group school to serve both field armies under its command, or if the divisional schools sufficed. Having consulted its two corps (1st British and 2nd Canadian), First Canadian Army responded that the divisional schools met requirements.[79]

Each division took a different approach, tailoring instruction to local conditions and requirements. Yet all five programs worked toward the same goal: keeping unit NCO cadres strong. Too often, junior NCOs badly needed the instruction because they had received promotions in the field but had little or no leadership training, so the divisions ran courses when possible, often in Spartan field conditions and well within earshot of the fighting.

In early January 1945, for example, the 1st Canadian Infantry Division started operating an austere training school in Riccione, Italy. The school operated for just over six weeks and ran only three serials of a leadership course, but it provided refresher training in fundamental skills for approximately 150 sergeants, lance sergeants, and lieutenants. Students came directly from units in the line, dirty and tired, for the short but intense program.[80] The first serial ran for just eight days, but students reviewed a wide range of subjects that dealt with local fighting conditions. These included patrolling, German defensive methods, platoon morale, bridging expedients, house clearing, infantry–tank cooperation, preparing for a counter-attack, and set-piece attacks.[81] Tactical exercises without troops (TEWTs) gave students practice in river crossings, attacking an enemy outpost, and defence against a counter-attack. Night training included lifting mines in the dark, reconnaissance patrols, and tank hunting. And short exercises ran students through infantry–tank operations, house clearing, the set-piece attack, tank hunting, and ambushes. The second and third serials ran for a full two weeks each, with an expanded curriculum including lectures on appreciations (tactical situation assessments) and operations orders, TEWTs for the defence of platoon and company positions, and practice periods in field formations, lines of advance, street fighting, and night occupation of company positions.[82]

The course might have been short but it was much needed. Students arrived with widely differing degrees of knowledge, much of it insufficient. When staff ran candidates through weapons tests on the second serial, the weak results surprised the instructors, who feared that platoon sergeants and platoon commanders were not as familiar with their weapons as they should have been.[83] Similarly, varying overall performance indicated a mixed bag of competence. Most students in the first two serials finished with an "average" rating, but eight or nine (a mix of NCOs and officers) required additional training before returning to the field.[84] After the third serial, the school's commandant commented that the standard of NCOs passing through the school varied considerably, ranging from experienced platoon sergeants to recently appointed lance sergeants who, with no formal NCO training, demonstrated difficulty with basic skills such as map reading and issuing verbal orders.[85] He believed that the course should be lengthened even further – to eighteen days, to allow for additional instruction in these problem areas. The school ceased operating before staff could implement his recommendation, however, because the division received orders to move to Northwest Europe.[86] Still, the school gave about seventy-five NCOs and an equal number of officers valuable – and for some newly promoted men, badly needed – refresher training.

While the other division-run NCO schools designed their own curricula, most focused on training junior NCOs with intense two- or three-week programs that were just long enough to teach the essentials. The 2nd Canadian Infantry Division school used a fourteen-day syllabus that provided elementary NCO training to promising privates and to junior NCOs who required some instruction in leadership.[87] Lectures covered subjects these soldiers had to master to command sections in Northwest Europe: German tactics, booby traps, patrols, battle procedure, and junior NCO responsibilities. Short exercises allowed students to rehearse practical skills such as obstacle crossing, handling a section in the attack and in the defence, patrolling, house clearing, village and woods clearing, and attacking a pillbox.[88] The 3rd Canadian Division school taught similar material but over a three-week course. Tactics took up one-third of the classes, while weapons training and map reading also took up a fair amount of time. Beyond that, the syllabus allotted smaller numbers of classes to a variety of essential skills and knowledge, such as radio procedure, information handling and reports, and mines and booby traps. The course concluded with examinations that lasted half a day.[89] Elsewhere, the 5th Canadian Armoured Division designed a two-week junior NCO course that looked much like the others.[90]

The more ambitious program of the 4th Canadian Armoured Division's school stood out from the others. While it, too, focused on training junior NCOs, the school was designed to generate "a steady flow" of infantry and armoured NCOs who were trained as section and crew commanders respectively, but who were also partially trained as platoon and troop sergeants.[91] The school ran a four-week program, and every two weeks a new course began with forty-two students drawn from the division's infantry and armoured units (five students from each unit, plus two from the independent machine-gun company). Candidates received instruction for the first two weeks and then, under close supervision, helped staff instruct for the first two weeks of the next course. The program covered all the bread-and-butter skills an NCO required, with periods for weapons training, fieldcraft, and navigation.[92] Physical training helped keep students fit with bayonet fighting classes, an assault course, a hardening march, and unarmed combat. Staff used lectures and demonstrations to teach the duties of an NCO, enemy tactics, infantry-tank cooperation, methods of instruction, and appreciations and orders. Short exercises allowed students to practise stalking, working with tanks, and navigating at night. And TEWTs helped students learn about the platoon in the attack and the defence, and how to form a bridgehead after crossing a river or an anti-tank obstacle.

For all five divisions, running NCO schools in the field meant that students and staff could never completely turn their focus away from the war. Sometimes this was a positive, as the nearby presence of enemy troops allowed for good training opportunities. At the 2nd Canadian Infantry Division school in Cuijk, the Netherlands, students practised observation skills on real German soldiers who were in winter camouflage just a thousand yards away (914 m). They also monitored enemy troops as they moved about in their lines.[93] When the school moved to Rindern, just inside Germany, students practised village fighting in a real war-ravaged town and rehearsed drills for assaulting a pillbox on the real thing.[94] Sometimes the enemy posed real hazards. Shortly after the school opened, Captain T.D. Murray, one of the instructors, was wounded when his quarters were hit in a German barrage of "Moaning Minnie" rockets.[95] Meanwhile, at the

3rd Canadian Infantry Division school in Ravenstein, the Netherlands, the Germans periodically sent reminders that they could still pose a menace. V-1 rockets frequently cruised overhead or nearby, sometimes many in a single day, and sometimes they struck in the vicinity of the training.[96] Fortunately, no one at the school was killed, but local civilians were not always so lucky.

Division-run NCO schools were important and commanders took a direct interest in them. Major-General A. Bruce Matthews visited 2nd Canadian Infantry Division courses when he could, often addressing students to empha-size the program's importance.[97] As the school's war diarist recorded: "The students realize that their course is important when even the General comes down to talk to them."[98] The division headquarters even sent a "brains trust" of staff officers to hold lectures and discussions on operations, tactics, the German army, artillery challenges, machine guns, heavy mortars, field engineering, and signals.[99] Occasionally, brigade commanders delivered lectures on the "respon-sibilities of the NCO."[100] Likewise, at the 3rd Canadian Infantry Division, Major-General Daniel Spry visited the school, as did his brigade commanders, to address students and staff. Unit commanders visited periodically as well.[101] In the 4th Canadian Armoured Division, Major-General Chris Vokes inspected the first five graduating classes and gave closing addresses. On two of these occasions, he brought along the commander 1st British Corps, Lieutenant-General John Crocker. Brigadiers reviewed the six and seventh graduating classes. Even at the 5th Canadian Armoured Division school, which ran most of its courses just after Germany's surrender, Bert Hoffmeister, now a major-general, visited periodically and reassured students that the army still needed fresh NCOs, which it did. As he told students and staff, the school was still "playing a very vital part ... in producing N.C.O.'s to fill the vacancies that are being created by return to Canada of long service personnel."[102]

Despite different levels of production, most division-run schools managed to train enough NCOs to produce discernible benefits at the unit level. The 2nd Canadian Infantry Division's school eventually provided elementary junior NCO training to about 630 soldiers, or roughly 70 from each infantry battalion, before Victory in Europe (VE) Day.[103] Similarly, the 3rd Canadian Infantry Division's program churned out about 675 soldiers, or roughly 75 per battalion. This meant that about 15 soldiers in every company underwent focused junior NCO training – probably enough to ease the degenerative effect that casualties had on NCO cadres. The 4th Canadian Armoured Division turned out fewer NCOs, but its course was longer and trained soldiers as platoon or troop ser-geants. And as an armoured division, smaller than its infantry counterpart, it had a smaller NCO complement to maintain. Nine course serials had run by the time Germany surrendered, producing about 380 graduates. This amounted to about 45 well-trained junior NCOs for each of the division's manoeuvre units, plus 18 for the independent machine-gun company. Even the 5th Canadian Armoured Division managed to train 150 students before moving from Italy to Northwest Europe (plus another 180 in the weeks immediately after VE Day).

Finally, division-run NCO courses allowed unit chains of command to determine who was good enough to promote when the time came to fill vacancies. School staff came from the units themselves, which meant they saw first-hand how their men performed. More formal feedback helped as well, as assessments of candidates at the 2nd Canadian Infantry Division school illustrate. At the end of each course, the brigades received a list of students, every name annotated with brief and frank commentary on performance and an overall rating of *poor, average, fair, good,* or *very good*.[104] Private Sanderson of the Black Watch had performed quite well: "This Pte is very keen, dependable and quick to take initiative when occasion demands it, is quite confident and did extremely good work during [the] course. By his work he warrants promotion and more responsibility. (Very Good)." Lance Corporal Peelar of the Essex Scottish Regiment had not performed quite as well: "Steady, reliable and apparently knows field work but is too self-concious [sic] to be able to express himself – a good L/Cpl and no more. (Average)." And Corporal Cousins of the same unit had not impressed his instructors at all: "Is not in our opinion fit to hold any rank – he's untidy and irresponsible and can't take care of himself, let alone a section. (Poor)." Such reports were no doubt useful for units deciding whom they should promote in the field to keep their NCO cadres up to strength.

The division-level NCO training programs helped sustain unit NCO establishments in the last five months or so of the war against Germany. These programs necessitated investments of people and resources, taking soldiers out of busy combat units to run or undergo the training. The soldiers involved sometimes found that going straight from the line to a divisional NCO school entailed a significant mental shift. But the training was important for keeping NCO cadres strong, and even as the divisions fought on in the final big push against Germany, they found it necessary to spend some of their valuable energy running NCO development programs in the background.

Conclusion

The army's decentralized approach to NCO training and development made sense. For one thing, when the nation went to war, a large system of schools for NCO training did not exist. In fact, the wartime network of advanced training centres in Canada that taught specialist skills did not appear until early 1941.

Dedicated NCO schools did not open in Britain until the spring of 1941 and in Canada until the following September.[105] For another, for the first three years of war, no one knew how soon the army would have to fight. In Britain, units had to be ready to repel an invasion at short notice and therefore could not send away large numbers of junior leaders to Schools of Instruction, even after centralized training had been put in place.

Quite practically, decentralized NCO training took many forms as units ran qualification and refresher courses when schedules allowed. This approach allowed units to tailor NCO training to local requirements – for example, correcting observed weak areas or introducing new tactics or weapons – and to build a thorough appreciation of talent in ranks. Decentralized training was also in the regimental tradition of the Anglo-Canadian armies.

Despite both practical and traditional underpinnings, the system was nonetheless far from perfect. Competing demands cramped the time battalions could allot to NCO training. Furthermore, a unit's NCO cadre could fail to thrive if the commanding officer lacked the competence to train his men. In any event, during the army's years in England, guarding against a German invasion and training for offensive operations on the continent meant that busy units did not have the time or the resources to run enough NCO training, so formations helped out by periodically running programs for their units. From an army-wide perspective, no single solution existed for making more NCOs. Instead, units and formations took an ad hoc approach, doing what they could, when they could.

Once formations were in action, the decentralized approach proved quite useful to units that could not send their men back to Britain for formal NCO training. No centralized programs existed in the theatres of operation, but formations ran programs close to the forward areas, helping keep unit backbones strong and allowing commanding officers to replace casualties with trusted and proven unit members instead of having to accept unknown men from the reinforcement pool. In-theatre NCO training allowed privates who had demonstrated leadership in battle to prepare for promotion, and provided catch-up instruction to NCOs who had received promotions in the field. What is more, it made it possible to teach locally developed tactical expertise. The two CIB NCO courses in Italy, for example, included instruction in street fighting and prisoner snatching, no doubt allowing students to learn from instructors who had recent experience of what worked in battle.

Nonetheless, the decentralized approach to NCO development had one serious problem: it could never train enough soldiers. Even with units and formations both running courses when they could, operational forces were just too busy to train the numbers required. The sample group gives an indication of the extent to which this was true: just over half of the NCO qualification and refresher courses attended by soldiers in this text's sample group were unit or formation programs.[106] Centralized programs were therefore crucial to making up the difference.

6

The Mass Army's Programs in Canada

The contribution of this camp to Canada's fighting divisions has been no small one ... There are men all over Canada who at one time or another spent some time here at Aldershot ... A14 [Infantry Training Centre] certainly played a very important part in getting Canada's [F]irst Army ready for action. It could be estimated that approximately one division passed through the Centre.

A14 WAR DIARY, 29–30 APRIL 1946

FROM THE MOMENT UNITS mobilized, they were exceptionally busy dealing with countless requirements. In the early days, units were consumed with recruiting, training, acquiring new equipment, learning how to use it, and so on. After units arrived in Britain, collective training, guarding against a German invasion, and unending administrative tasks eroded every commanding officer's capacity to run NCO training. It became even more difficult once units starting fighting. Formations helped from time to time but they were no less busy, and in any event, any training they ran required instructors and administrative support from their constituent units. Moreover, training schools and the reinforcement system needed a steady input of trained NCOs as well. Consequently, on both sides of the Atlantic, the army had to raise machinery dedicated to helping train and develop non-commissioned leaders.

In Canada, National Defence Headquarters (NDHQ) established and controlled a network of training centres to which both field and training units sent their soldiers. These centralized schools ran two main types of program: courses that qualified the rank and file as junior NCOs, and courses that trained NCOs to be instructors. Some of the latter taught NCOs to be regimental instructors for particular subjects, such as small arms and battle drill, while other programs taught NCOs general teaching skills. The tremendous growth of the army in Canada created a huge demand for NCOs. Many were needed as leaders in the home defence force (much of it conscripted), which by April 1943 had grown to three divisions plus numerous unbrigaded coastal defence, anti-aircraft, and other combat arms units that guarded cities across the country.[1] Many more NCOs were needed as instructors in the massive training enterprise that developed, comprising ninety-eight training centres and schools by July 1943.[2] Around the time the army reached its peak strength in March 1944, about 240,000 troops remained in the North American Zone, almost all in Canada.[3] This force needed an estimated 60,900 NCOs.[4] The centralized programs in Canada not only generated the NCOs needed but also brought a measure of standardization to a system that had pushed responsibility for NCO training and development down to the unit level.

Centralized NCO training in Canada began in early 1941 and remained essential to the NCO corps' development for the rest of the war. After the army began major operations with the invasion of Sicily in July 1943, the training machinery continued to operate and refine a variety of NCO development programs. Even though the active army had just finished building all of its formations and filling them with personnel, the force still needed a large reinforcement pool of properly trained soldiers to replace casualties.[5] As training camps across Canada helped keep the army's backbone strong, they had two fundamental challenges: producing an adequate quantity of NCOs for an army that kept growing until March 1944, and ensuring that training kept up with developments overseas. After all, armies never stop learning and training authorities had to ensure that their programs integrated the latest lessons of battle.

Various measures implemented to meet these challenges included increasing the number of training centres across Canada; gradually adding new material to courses based on official doctrine and training pamphlets for the latest methods developed overseas; preparing NCOs for their roles as trainers by running instructor courses in subjects such as platoon weapons, drill, or methods of instruction; opening a School of Infantry that operated as a sort of graduate-level skills program for experienced NCOs and junior officers; and, starting in the fall of 1944, screening NCOs to ensure their suitability for operational duty before they shipped overseas.

Dedicated Training Centres

Like everything else, most wartime centralized training centres had to be built from scratch. As soon as Canada joined the war, NDHQ started planning to train reinforcements, and it took about a year and a half to form a network of training centres. In January–February 1940, fourteen new reinforcement training centres opened.[6] Half of these trained men for infantry or machine-gun units, and the rest were allotted to the other arms and services, one for each. After Germany invaded the Low Countries and France in the spring of 1940, further army expansion required more training camps. An alarmed Canadian government decided to raise a third and fourth division for overseas service,

Figure 6.1 Training centres popped up across Canada to facilitate the army's dramatic expansion – and they all needed instructional cadres of NCOs, such as the one seen here at the No. 2 Infantry Training Centre in Borden, Ontario, in 1940 (later known as the A11 Advanced Infantry Training Centre). Nearly a third of the senior NCOs in this photo appear to be wearing ribbons from service in the First World War. | Library and Archives Canada/Andrew Audubon Merrilees fonds/e010932763.

plus eight battalions and other forces for home defence, and to implement conscription for the defence of Canada.[7] In October 1940, the training system ballooned when thirty-nine new training centres opened to accommodate conscripts raised under the National Resources Mobilization Act that Ottawa had passed on 21 June. The system evolved once more in early 1941, finally taking the form that lasted for the rest of the war, when the army decided to train conscripts and volunteers together.

Accordingly, NDHQ transformed the system into a network of basic training centres (BTCs) that gave two months of common training to all recruits, and advanced training centres (ATCs) where soldiers received training in their arm of service (infantry, artillery, armoured, service corps, and so on). The advanced centres also ran specialist courses for things like mortars and driving, plus courses that qualified officers for the rank of lieutenant, along with NCO training. By the fall of 1941, the system comprised twenty-seven basic and thirty-two advanced training centres. But it wasn't done growing yet, because the army wasn't either. After Japan entered the war in December 1941 and then seized Allied possessions in Hong Kong, Malaya, Singapore, and the Philippines –

making home defence seem much more urgent, at least to an anxious public in British Columbia – the government gradually expanded the home defence force to include the 6th, 7th, and 8th divisions, plus five unbrigaded battalions and anti-aircraft units for both coasts.[8] To facilitate this growth, many more training centres opened in 1942. Furthermore, NCO training also ran at specialized schools of instruction that the army gradually added to the system of basic and advanced training centres.

For instance, in September 1941 at Mégantic, Quebec, NDHQ opened the largest of the centralized schools that taught soldiers how to be junior NCOs. The new school of instruction, called the Number 52 Junior Leaders School, ran course serials of about 160 students each. According to the syllabus, the program aimed "to train [the] Junior Leader in daylight and at night, that by initiative, cunning, fieldcraft and skilful use of arms, he will achieve his objective with minimum delay and casualties."[9] In other words, the program focused on leadership in the field. This entailed providing students with "a thorough grounding in minor tactics" and preparing them to handle their men in combat. The straightforward three-week course gave students lectures in fieldcraft (lines of advance, stalking, observation), planning (verbal orders, supply, medical arrangements), and tactical operations (village fighting, the attack, the defence, different types of patrols, quick decision making). Short exercises lasted from a single period to a half day and examinations assessed student learning. This challenging program prepared young soldiers for the demands they would face as lance corporals and corporals.

The course grew more demanding as staff continuously improved the curriculum. In December 1941, the program was extended to four weeks to add more training in the attack and in village fighting, plus student-run "lecturettes" to practise teaching.[10] It also accommodated more review periods, four new examinations, and a half-day skills-confirmation exercise. The school followed the four-week format for the first half of 1942, although staff continued to adjust the content, gradually adding more patrol training and periods on the German army and NCO duties.[11] Starting in mid-July 1942, the four-week program began with a two-hour examination to determine students' level of knowledge. By now, battle drill had spread to Canada, so staff added it to the curriculum. Students trained in unarmed combat and received instruction in maintaining security in correspondence and in conversation. A series of two-hour written examinations tested candidates on battle drill, tactics, and map reading.[12] And staff added well-conceived exercises to practise students' patrolling skills. For example, a night patrolling exercise pitted students against each other in a force-on-force scenario that involved reconnaissance and fighting patrols, and bumping into enemy patrols in the dark.[13] The sophisticated scheme aimed to teach candidates about the orders process while they practised all the skills needed for planning and executing different types of patrols and, after each mission, writing post-patrol reports.

In mid-1942, the school's mandate changed slightly to address the army's deficiency in qualified francophone NCOs. Until then, the program had provided training to both English- and French-speaking soldiers. The school ran ten courses in one or the other language, producing about 1,680 graduates.[14] High demand for French-speaking NCOs convinced NDHQ to devote Number 52 Junior Leaders School entirely to supporting French-speaking units, while English-speaking soldiers took NCO training only at the ATCs.

After the school at Mégantic began operating under its new mandate, staff continued to enhance the training. The new course for French-speaking NCOs ran for six weeks, and incorporated up-to-date material in such subjects as anti-aircraft defence, woods clearing, village fighting, river crossing, and the administration of a rifle platoon, company, and infantry battalion.[15] Staff tested student learning with a written examination on map reading and oral examinations on military law, battle drill theory, battle procedure, field engineering, and, most important, the duties of platoon sergeants and section commanders. In March 1943, the school expanded the course's aim, which now included training "N.C.O.'s in order that, by knowledge, initiative and endurance, they will adapt and *fit themselves for the responsibilities of instructing men in their units.*"[16] So now the course sought to create NCOs with first-rate instructional skills, a logical addition to the program given that many of the graduates would end up teaching in the huge training system that now existed.

By the spring of 1943, then, NCO training at the Junior Leaders School in Mégantic had come a long way since the program had begun eighteen months earlier. The course had doubled in length, with much new subject matter to prepare soldiers as NCOs in the increasingly capable army. Indeed, the army as a whole was not just growing but modernizing as it adopted new weapons and developed new tactics (not least the battle drill program) as it prepared to fight and beat Hitler's battle-proven forces. NCO training had to keep up with this modernization, as reflected in the increasing length of qualification training at Mégantic. Moreover, centralized schools in Canada, like the one at Mégantic, may have been an ocean away from the army in England, where the modernizing and innovating occurred fastest, but they had one advantage over the decentralized NCO programs run by units and formations: they could afford to dedicate more time to training. As detailed in Chapter 5, units and formations in England ran NCO courses when operational and training schedules

Table 6.1

Three-week syllabus, Junior Leaders School, Mégantic, September 1941

Subject	Periods	Subject	Periods
Addresses	2	Gas	1
Attack	14	Loading platoon truck	1
Defence and protection	19	Map reading	14
Discipline	2	Patrols	12
Drill	12	Quick decision making	3
Examinations	3	Reconnaissance, appreciation, orders	4
Exercises	4	Rifle fire control	5
Fieldcraft	15	Supply and medical arrangements	2
Field defences	6	Village fighting	1
		Total periods	120

Source: Data from Appendix D to S6 Canadian Army Junior Leaders School War Diary for September 1941, LAC, RG24-C-3, vol. 16892.

allowed – and only rarely had the time to run courses that lasted six weeks. Tables 6.1 and 6.2, which show the curricula for September 1941 and March 1943 at Mégantic, illustrate the considerable evolution of NCO training in the period leading up to Canada's commencement of major combat operations.

By the time of Operation Husky, the Junior Leaders School at Mégantic – now called the S6 Junior Leaders School – had trained several thousand soldiers.[17] The seven courses for French-speaking soldiers alone had produced about 1,170 graduates.[18] Overall, using a progressively improving syllabus, the Junior Leaders School provided junior NCO training to about 2,850 soldiers in its first twenty-two months of operation – roughly enough to fill the platoons of thirty battalions.[19] This was an important contribution to the active army, which eventually had thirty-nine battalions in First Canadian Army overseas and another forty-eight in the North American Zone.[20]

After Operation Husky, the francophone junior NCO program operated for several more months. In the last half of 1943, the school ran three more courses for soldiers of all arms and services. In August, the course expanded from six to seven weeks to accommodate more instruction in small arms coaching skills, which reflected the aim of producing NCOs who could instruct.[21] And students now spent the last two days writing a series of examinations.[22] In the end, the school produced an impressive number of junior NCOs, with about 1,480 soldiers attending the francophone-only courses between mid-1942 and December 1943.[23] However, military authorities must have believed that Mégantic had

Table 6.2

Six-week syllabus, Junior Leaders School, Mégantic, March 1943

Subject	Periods	Subject	Periods
Addresses	2	Security	1
Administration (platoon to		Snowcraft	3
battalion)	4	Study	36
Appreciation & orders	10	Tactical exercises without	
Assault & obstacle course	18	troops	8
Battle procedure	2	Tank hunting	2
Citizenship	1	Training films	18
Drill	3	Weapons: Anti-aircraft	5
Examinations	20	Weapons: Anti-tank rifle	6
Fieldcraft	18	Weapons: Bayonet	5
Field engineering	8	Weapons: Grenades	9
Gas, protection against	15	Weapons: Light machine gun	
Map reading	26	(Bren)	21
Military law	3	Weapons: Revolver	3
Organization	6	Weapons: Rifle	18
Patrols	13	Weapons: Thompson machine	
Range course	11	carbine	5
Section leading	4	Weapons: 2-inch mortar	10
Section leading – Battle drill	45	Weapons: 3-inch mortar	7
		Total periods	366

Source: Data from Appendix E to S6 Canadian Army Junior Leaders School War Diary for March 1943, LAC, RG24, vol. 16894.

served its purpose of training enough francophone junior NCOs, because the school was closed at the end of 1943.[24] Subsequent French-language NCO training took place at an infantry training centre (probably at Farnham or Valcartier), similar to the way the army ran NCO programs for anglophone soldiers.[25]

The Mégantic school ultimately produced about 3,160 anglophone and francophone junior NCOs for an army that eventually grew to almost half a million, with an NCO corps of more than 110,000. While it offered the largest junior NCO qualification program in Canada, it was thus just one cog in a much larger army-wide system. In the sample group for this study, somewhere between 2.3 and 4.6 percent of the senior NCOs surveyed passed through the junior NCO training program at Mégantic.[26] The best that can be said, therefore, is that the school made a positive but limited contribution to NCO development.

The army also ran NCO development programs at various arm-specific training centres across the country. The NDHQ Directorate of Military Training (DMT) decided which courses ran at each camp and, importantly, controlled the syllabuses.[27] The A15 Advanced Infantry Training Centre (AITC) in Manitoba (it opened in Winnipeg and moved later to Shilo), exemplified how arm-specific training camps helped develop NCOs. This establishment conducted numerous types of training, including recruit, basic infantry, specialist, Veterans Guard, and junior leaders. The latter included a suite of courses that qualified soldiers as NCOs, refreshed NCO skills, sharpened instructional proficiency in small arms, honed drill instruction, and improved senior NCOs' instructional ability.

Like the AITCs in other military districts, A15 was assembled hastily using whatever resources and instructors were available. In late December 1939, NDHQ ordered district officers commanding (DOCs) across the country to establish training centres "with the least possible delay."[28] Military District 10 (Manitoba and Northwest Ontario) responded by establishing a school at Fort Osborne Barracks in Winnipeg. Permanent force soldiers were the bedrock of the new institution, at least in the early weeks and months. On 1 January 1940, the Princess Patricia's Canadian Light Infantry (PPCLI) regimental depot, also at Fort Osborne Barracks, sent three officers, two warrant officers class 1 (sergeant major instructors), and fifty-three other non-commissioned soldiers to the centre. Twenty-five of the non-commissioned personnel came from the permanent force, including both warrant officers class 1, one warrant officer class 2 (CSM instructor), and nine sergeants. Many of these professionals received a promotion on posting, and the two warrant officers class 1 received commissions as second lieutenants.[29] In the following days and weeks, more soldiers, including some permanent force troops, reported for duty as staff, while the centre took over several buildings at Fort Osborne Barracks and prepared them for use.

Very quickly, the centre commenced operations and eventually evolved into an elaborate teaching institution. On 16 January, 260 soldiers arrived from the PPCLI depot for training. Most required an initial recruit course, but others reported for basic infantry training, and some were trained infantrymen who required specialist courses. Meanwhile, the centre began to train its instructional staff, not all of whom came from the permanent force. On 25 January, A15 personnel started running an NCO qualifying course during the off-hours for all camp NCOs not yet on instructional duty. The course ran over four evenings per week and was conducted by permanent force soldiers.[30] Over the following months, the training centre gradually took shape, eventually forming a company for specialist training to run courses for mortars, motorcycles, signals, universal (Bren) carriers, and so on, plus regimentally affiliated training companies. By January 1941, the A15 training centre included a headquarters company, a specialist company, plus recruit and infantry training companies for each of the South Saskatchewan Regiment, the PPCLI, and the Queen's Own Cameron Highlanders.[31]

Later, the centre added a School of Instruction, which ran an NCO qualification program. This course lasted six weeks and, as the Mégantic program did, taught NCOs how to operate in the field and how to teach. Small arms training took up more of the syllabus than any other subject, about 60 percent of the training time, and included periods of mutual instruction during which students practised teaching each other how to handle and fire weapons. The second-largest subject was drill, which took up 20 percent of the training time. Beyond that, the course covered other miscellaneous subjects such as military law, map reading, and protection against gas.[32] Unlike the large courses run at Mégantic, with its cohorts of about 160 students, the NCO qualifying course at A15 trained perhaps a few dozen students at a time.[33]

The A15 School of Instruction ran several other NCO-related courses to produce what the army needed. For example, the rapidly expanding force required many NCOs to train new soldiers, so the school ran a course for soldiers tapped for employment as instructional staff. The Assistant Instructors, Instructional Cadre, and Training Staffs Refresher course put candidates through four weeks of intense training to make them expert instructors.[34] (The army often used the term *assistant instructor* to refer to NCOs employed in instructional capacities and *instructor* to refer to officers.) Also, because the army placed priority on drill to instill obedience and discipline, the school ran another course to train NCO drill instructors. This one-week program included forty periods during which students either received instruction or practised giving drill, all to the standards laid down in the *Manual of Elementary Drill*.[35] The army also needed its NCOs to serve as small arms instructors, so the School of Instruction ran an NCOs Small Arms Training School. This four-week program taught soldiers how to instruct in the basic platoon weapons: the rifle, light machine gun, anti-tank rifle, and bayonet.[36] And finally, the school ran the NCO Instructors course specifically to furnish instructors for Military District 10. This five-week course taught students instructional techniques for various common subjects, such as drill, platoon weapons, and protection against gas.[37]

Meanwhile, in southwestern Ontario, the army trained NCOs at the A29 AITC, another multipurpose training centre. In the spring of 1942, just a few months before the Junior Leaders School at Mégantic started to focus on

Table 6.3

Syllabus for A29 Instructor/NCO course, May 1942

Subject	Periods	Subject	Periods
Characteristics of unit weapons	1	Section leading	20
Defence against gas	5	Small arms: 2-inch mortar	10
Drill (elementary, foot, squad,		Small arms: Anti-tank rifle	6
and arms)	30	Small arms: Application of fire	8
Fieldcraft	40	Small arms: Bayonet	15
Field defences and wiring	5	Small arms: Bren light machine	
Field signals	1	gun	24
Firing instructions and range		Small arms: Grenades	6
duties	18	Small arms: Rifle	15
First aid	10	Small arms: Theory of small arms	
Map reading	20	fire	1
Night training	19	Small arms: Thompson sub-	
Opening lecture	1	machine gun	8
Organization, administration,		Unarmed combat and silent	
and military law	14	killing	10
Reports and messages	1	Use of ground formations	1
		Total periods	289

Source: Data from Appendix to A29 AITC War Diary for May 1942, LAC, RG24-C-3, vol. 17127.

training francophone soldiers, Military District Number 1 established an Instructor's School for the new A29 camp at Listowel, about 120 kilometres west of Toronto.[38] The school stood up on 23 April and within just a few days, it had absorbed instructional and administrative staff, prepared the school barracks, and begun receiving students. The first course, which started on 27 April, trained soldiers to be both NCOs and instructors, using a syllabus that gave candidates a solid grounding for leading troops in the field and in garrison. At first billed as an instructors' course but a few months later changing its name and focus to become an NCO course, the program ran for five weeks, six days per week, with nine periods each day plus occasional instruction at night.[39] Training included thirty periods of drill instruction, which cultivated candidates' sense of responsibility for checking faults and helped promote a "voice culture" for giving clear, aggressive orders. Naturally, small arms training featured prominently in the syllabus. Bread-and-butter subjects such as map reading, first aid, defence against gas, and constructing field defences also received due attention. A portion on "section leading" taught section tactics for flanking movements, the assault, consolidation and reorganization, street and village fighting, the defence, and the withdrawal – the sorts of things that the army overseas was by now getting better at. Night training included navigating in the dark, crossing obstacles, patrolling, and escaping from a German prisoner of war camp. The program packed a great deal of content into five weeks, as Table 6.3 demonstrates.

It should be noted that the A29 training centre, like those elsewhere, taught from the army's official training and doctrine pamphlets. Instructional staff across the army taught common standards, with explicit reference to numbered Military Training Pamphlets (such as *MTP No. 13 – Map Using* and *MTP No. 23 – Operations*), the Small Arms Training series of weapons manuals, the Infantry Training series (such as *Part VIII – Fieldcraft, Battle Drill, Section and Platoon Tactics*), the *Manual of Elementary Drill*, and the *Manual of Military Law*. (Most of these were reprints of War Office publications.) Building curricula at training centres across the country based on the army's official manuals ensured that all soldiers learned the same drills, tactics, techniques, and procedures

After just a few months of running NCO courses, the A29 training centre moved to another camp. This was part of a wider effort to meet the needs of a still-expanding army. The force still had much building to do in mid-1942. At the end of June, the army had 347,000 soldiers in its ranks, and it would add almost 150,000 more before reaching its peak strength.[40] Training that many personnel required new basic training camps, one of which displaced A29. In early October, with notification that a BTC would soon take over the camp facilities in Listowel, the A29 establishment moved 100 kilometres southwest to Camp Ipperwash, where the Department of National Defence had recently expropriated Chippewa land beside Lake Huron.[41] Staff completed the move by 11 October and then busied themselves with raising new camp infrastructure, levelling roads, clearing brush and trees to make room for a rifle range, laying pipes to Lake Huron, and building a drill hall. The new camp opened officially with a visit by Minister of National Defence James Ralston on 27 November.[42] A29 now expanded its repertoire, running several different training programs. Five companies provided elementary training, including recruit and infantry qualification courses for both general service and conscripted soldiers. A specialist company qualified soldiers in specialist skills such as mortars, motorcycles, and Bren gun carriers, and the School of Instruction provided NCO and officer training.

The School of Instruction offered an NCO course for general service recruits identified as potential junior instructors, and another to qualify basic training instructors as "advanced instructors." By July 1943, about five NCO-related courses, each with about fifty students, had run at Ipperwash. Candidates found this training demanding. Private Robert Sanderson, a bright young soldier with partial university education who found basic infantry training fairly straight-forward, described the junior NCO course as "tough as can be."[43] As he stated in a letter home to family,

> We did battle drill all day including river crossing. There is a great deal to know and it's difficult to remember the various commands for the different formations ... We will all be sent to the companies in the [A29] training centre which we left when we entered the S.[chool] of I [Instruction]. There we will be instructors ... I'll be glad when next Friday rolls around and this course is over.[44]

New soldiers like Sanderson, identified as potential NCO material, learned the NCO business at Ipperwash and then went on to serve as instructors and field unit NCOs.

Over time, the A29 AITC improved NCO qualification training so that it stayed current with developments overseas. In June 1944, the school transformed the NCOs course it had been running since the spring of 1942 into the standard-ized "assistant instructor course" that NDHQ had directed training centres to adopt.[45] Calling it an assistant instructor course did not, however, fully reflect its raison d'être. The curriculum gave students not just instructional skills but also the up-to-date tactical expertise required both for teaching students the latest techniques and for serving in a theatre of war. For instance, by Septem-ber 1944, staff at A29 had implemented an intensive four-day end-of-course "round the horn" exercise that tested students in a variety of realistic combat scenarios. On the first day, each platoon of candidates conducted a live-fire flanking attack, an assault on a bridge, two river crossings, and a navigation march through forested terrain.[46] On the second day, each platoon moved on foot to the town of Parkhill, about sixteen kilometres due east of Ipperwash and rather longer by road. While on the march, the students executed a platoon attack, skirted around a gas-contaminated area, dispatched a section to assault an isolated enemy position, and conducted yet another platoon attack. When the students finally arrived at Parkhill, they dug in and established defensive positions, from which they sent out night patrols and defended against an enemy attack.[47] On the third day, staff had students correct any mistakes made during the first forty-eight hours. And on the final day, students conducted a house-clearing exercise, assaulted an enemy position in an orchard, cleared another house, attacked a prepared defensive position, and executed a river crossing, all before finally heading back to camp.[48] Clearly, planners had designed the exercise to test students' stamina and battlefield skills in scenarios that replicated the fighting overseas. In fact, the school used its instructors with overseas experience to help make the training as realistic as possible.[49]

The pace of NCO training at A29 AITC did not slow with Germany's defeat. When the fighting in Europe ceased, military authorities had no idea that the war with Japan would end in August, but they knew that Canada intended to deploy ground forces to help achieve Japan's defeat.[50] On Victory in Europe (VE) Day, the camp declared a holiday and personnel listened to Winston Churchill's speech over the camp's loudspeakers, but the break ended quickly. The next day, training resumed and the course in progress began its round the horn exercise.[51] By the end of the month, the school had more students at one time (110) on the assistant instructors course than ever before, suggesting that efforts to address the infantry shortage of the previous year remained in effect. School staff worked as hard as ever, preparing those who had volunteered for service in the Pacific.[52] By the time Japan surrendered in mid-August, students of the twenty-fourth assistant instructor class were almost ready to graduate. A29 had completed four serials in the period between the German and Japanese defeats, generating about 220 new NCOs.

Training Instructors

Every army requires competent instructors to transform raw recruits into trained soldiers, and to teach trained soldiers various specialist skills. If the Canadian army was going to expand into a force capable of fighting and beating a formidable enemy, it had first to train its trainers – a crucial part of building the army's backbone. First, the army required a certain mass of instructors. The prewar army could not possibly have furnished enough to train all the personnel that Canada eventually put into uniform. Authorities therefore had no choice but to turn many of the new citizen-soldiers into instructional staff. Second, the army needed instructors with expertise in weapons, equipment, and tactics that Canada simply did not have when the dominion declared war. Even the most capable permanent force NCOs in 1939 would not have known about 6-pounder anti-tank guns, flame-throwers, battle drill, or the amphibious landing techniques the army eventually adopted. In short, the military had to train scores of new and relatively unskilled NCOs to provide instruction across a wide and expanding range of subject matter. Many of the NCO courses described thus far included *some* generalized instructional training. Others focused exclusively on teaching NCOs how to instruct particular subjects.

For example, the assistant instructor course was a nationwide program that taught NCOs how to be effective teachers. NDHQ implemented the course in

Figure 6.2 Possessing highly specialized instructional skills, these NCOs served as parachute instructors at Camp Shilo, Manitoba, where they trained soldiers to be parachutists. The army had no such instructors in 1939. In fact, the army did not add paratroopers to its order of battle until July 1942. | Library and Archives Canada/ Department of National Defence fonds/a179717.

May 1941 to teach the latest methods of instruction and to improve candidates' teaching abilities.[53] Direction from Ottawa emphasized that candidates were to report for the course "thoroughly up to date" in their military training, so that they could focus entirely on elevating their instructional skills. Furthermore, each training centre was to run the course "based on the actual syllabus for instruction given to reinforcements" in location. Students were to practise teaching under the supervision of a qualified instructor, either in classes of mutual instruction or, for "thoroughly good" candidates, by instructing re-inforcement soldiers. Training centres across Canada implemented the four-week program for new NCOs and aspiring privates, running courses regularly until the end of the war.

The course eventually required modernization in tandem with recruit train-ing programs that grew more complex as the war continued. In the spring of 1944, NDHQ learned that commandants and their chief instructors believed that the standard four weeks no longer sufficed because recruit and corps-specific basic training programs had grown longer.[54] Assistant instructors, the NCOs who taught the material, now had more to learn than could reasonably be taught in one month. NDHQ also grew concerned that training centres lacked a uniform approach to running the course, and unrelenting demand for instructors across Canada meant the army had to make them out of less-developed material.[55] For all these reasons, NDHQ lengthened the assistant instructor course from four to six weeks.

The change occurred in May 1944, when DMT imposed uniformity on course delivery and upgraded the content by establishing a two-part program. Part 1 lasted two weeks and focused on teaching candidates how to teach.[56] (This was in keeping with new training developments in the overseas army. As Chapter 7 outlines, by this time teaching NCOs the latest in instructional methods was receiving serious attention in both the British and Canadian armies.) Students received classes on "the theory of teaching" and on "good teaching methods," and they practised by conducting periods of mutual instruction, using material from the army's basic training curriculum, the General Military Training course. Part 2 lasted four weeks and prepared students to teach particular courses. So, students destined to instruct at recruit training centres continued with the General Military Training program, while others practised teaching material for the corps-specific programs they would join. In all cases, candidates had to be skilled soldiers at the start because the program focused entirely on teaching students how to teach particular subjects, not on learning the subject matter. To earn the assistant instructor qualification, a candidate had to demonstrate "unquestioned ability and [the] necessary enthusiasm and personality to impart that knowledge to others." To keep basic and leadership skills sharp, staff put students through daily periods of drill and rigorous fitness training, plus one period per week on NCO duties and responsibilities.[57] Finally, and significantly, NDHQ directed that the new program serve not just as an instructor course: "It has been the practice in the past at some TCs to run Junior NCO Courses in addition to A/Is Courses. It is considered that the [modernized] course outlined herewith for Part I and Part II will render any other NCOs course unnecessary."[58] By declaring the new format to be the standard junior NCO qualification program in Canada, NDHQ brought greater consistency to how the army trained NCOs and made the training system more efficient by reducing the number of programs individual training centres had to run.

The assistant instructor course became the army's vehicle for fast-tracking brand-new soldiers to NCO rank so that they could serve as instructors. DMT hoped to draw more potential instructors out of the reinforcement stream, deciding to earmark for instructional duty the best-qualified reinforcements who had just completed their basic corps-of-arms training. These newly produced troops, the cream of their crop, would attend the assistant instructor course and then serve as instructional staff for eight months before proceeding overseas as reinforcements.[59] Unfortunately for the training system, the proportion of new soldiers with the aptitude for the course was on the decline – and this became a problem as the army began to struggle with maintaining its pool of good instructors.

While the revised course was an improvement, demand soon began to outstrip the supply. By late June 1944, almost all training centres in Canada were suffering a growing shortage of non-commissioned instructors.[60] The problem had several causes. The quotient of potential instructors among new trainees fell as the average age of recruits declined. Also, the overseas army, which since late 1940 had been sending NCOs back to Canada for instructional tours of duty, now had precious few to spare. At the same time, the sheer size of the training enterprise – which required one instructor for every eight recruits plus a reserve pool to permit a continuous flow of instructors through refresher training – sustained high demand. NDHQ attempted to find more soldiers with instructional aptitude among unfit-for-duty soldiers returning from overseas, but this never made up the shortfall. In fact, a chronic shortage of NCOs for instructional duty in Canada dogged the army until the end of the war. The instructional cadre never grew as strong as it needed to be, because ultimately the nation could supply the army with only so much human talent.

Still, after the Canadian army began fighting in Northwest Europe in June 1944, the standardized assistant instructor course played a vital role in maintaining up-to-date instruction back home. With fewer trainers returning from overseas and with unremitting domestic demand for instructors, the program, with its focus on preparing NCOs for both the field and for training establishments, took on greater importance. The policy of allowing training centres to keep graduates for eight months of instructional duty before sending them into the reinforcement stream gave a much-needed boost to instructional staffs.[61]

Table 6.4

Syllabus for Assistant Instructor Course, A15 Shilo, May 1945

Subject	Periods	Subject	Periods
2-inch mortar	12	Military law	11
Armoured fighting vehicle		Mines & booby traps	15
recognition	4	Organization and administration	11
Bayonet	5	Projector Infantry Anti-Tank	
Drill	35	(PIAT)	12
Fieldcraft	14	Protection against gas	18
Field works	19	Ranges	9
Final weapons examinations	5	Rifle	12
First aid	12	Sten and Thompson	12
Grenades	12	Techniques of instruction	35
Light machine gun	21	Unarmed combat	10
Map reading	22		
		Total periods	306

Source: Data from Assistant Instructor Course #196 Syllabus of Training, appended to A15 CAITC Shilo War Diary for April 1945, LAC, RG24-C-3, vol. 17060.

Meanwhile, keeping the program current required periodic revisions to the syllabus. For example, training authorities added subjects such as unarmed combat and recognition of armoured fighting vehicles. With all sides increasing the different types of tanks they used, soldiers needed to learn which vehicles to shoot at and which not to engage. Table 6.4 summarizes the assistant instructor course syllabus used at A15 Shilo in May 1945. Just like at A29 Ipperwash, training centres across the country ran the course beyond VE Day, only stopping after Japan surrendered.

Building small arms instructional expertise within the NCO corps was another important aspect of developing the army's backbone. After all, providing expert instruction in how to use small arms had long been an NCO's role – as it remains today – and over the course of the war, the army adopted many new infantry weapons. Thus, numerous soldiers were sent to small arms courses at four schools in Canada: Connaught Camp, Sarcee Camp, Long Branch, and Nanaimo.[62] Raymond Gray of the Canadian Scottish Regiment recalls attending small arms instructor training so that he could teach weapons handling in his unit: "I went on a small arms course to Sarcee ... [for] training in all form of small arms, with the idea that I would be an instructor. Everybody that went there was [a] potential instructor for the future. And then when we got back we [ran] a lot of the [unit] training."[63] The personnel service records in this text's sample group show that *at least* 16.5 percent of the men attended small arms or machine-gun courses, although the proportion of soldiers who actually attended such training was probably higher, given the incomplete nature of many files. In other words, of the infantry soldiers who rose to senior NCO rank, the army trained nearly one in five to instruct in basic small arms. And this figure does not include soldiers who attended courses for specific weapon systems, such as anti-air light machine gun, 6-pounder anti-tank gun, sniper, and various mortar programs. In the end, producing competent small arms instructors paid off where it mattered most – in battle. Historian Robert Engen, who surveyed a batch of War Office battle questionnaires completed by veteran Canadian infantry officers, ascertained that these combat leaders had "indicated their confidence in the reliability, consistency, and volume of small arms fire being generated by their troops," and that there had been "no general failure on the part of soldiers to make adequate use of their weapons."[64]

Few things demonstrated the army's investment in instruction more than its programs to teach the teachers about teaching. Whereas the assistant instructor, small arms, and other specialist instructor courses taught NCOs how to teach particular subjects, this training focused on teaching more generally. Formal courses in methods of instruction came to the army in the summer of 1941. That June, NDHQ made arrangements for a small group of education specialists to provide a short course in teaching methods for training staffs across Canada.[65] The course focused only on how to instruct, and not on any particular subject matter, as the outline shows for the Special Course in Teaching Principles and Methods:

> The Role of the Instructor
> What the Instructor Should Learn at a Training Centre
> Methods of Instruction
> > Lecture
> > Discussion
> > Demonstration
> > Induction-Deduction
> > Practice (Group and Individual)
> The Psychology of Learning
> Habit Formation and Learning a Skill
> Individual Differences and Learning Problems
> Planning Instruction
> Aids to Instruction

Motivation
Qualifications of an Instructor

A team of six civilian and military experts in education and teaching methods travelled across the country to provide the instruction. NDHQ designed the program so that at each camp, one of the educational experts provided the training over three evenings for all instructional staff, while any student instructors on course received training over two evenings. During the day, the expert observed camp training activities and provided advice or help as requested. A few weeks later, he returned for a second visit, spending two or three days to assist with any outstanding challenges that had been identified.

The army continued to enhance training in modern instruction methods by introducing a longer formal course that focused exclusively on general teaching skills. In January 1942, the Small Arms Training Centres in Canada began running a three-week Methods of Instruction course, under the control of DMT. The course educated students on how to convey material effectively and gave them plenty of opportunity to practise. The first week included lectures on how to prepare and present lessons, "the art of questioning," the presentation of "skills and drills," and the value of review.[66] Staff first presented a model lesson. Then students gave thirty-minute classes on assigned topics and, after each student-led class, the candidate's peers offered constructive criticism. The second week included more lectures on how to create and maintain student interest and how to maintain class control. The students learned about techniques for field demonstrations, differences in trainees, tips on how to study, and the "instructor's bag of tricks." Meanwhile, practice instruction and mutual criticism continued. The third week was devoted to practice lectures and it concluded with a three-hour examination. About 800 NCOs and junior officers who instructed at basic and arm-specific training centres completed the training by July 1943.

In October 1944, NDHQ paired the Methods of Instruction course with a Methods of Coaching program and made the whole package a staple of NCO development in Canada. DMT announced that *all* personnel employed as instructors in the army's training centres had to take Methods of Instruction, either at one of the small arms schools or at a locally run program that used the authorized syllabus.[67] Plus, all instructors had to take Methods of Coaching. Each training centre ran the latter for its own staff, using a syllabus NDHQ provided, but only personnel who had taken the course at one of the small arms schools could teach it. Instructors at the A15 School in Shilo certainly believed that the coaching course had value, as an article in the school paper indicated:

Men who during their service have been consistently poor shots, after being coached on the ranges by students on the methods of coaching course ... have improved 35 to 45 percent better shots. This is a course that should be taken by all NCOs ... A man is not born a good marksman; it is something that calls for patience, good nerves, and good supervision and knowledge ... To[o] many people approach this matter of shooting with the rifle indifferently; LMG's, Tommys, Stens infatuate them; what does it matter about being a good rifle shot or not? We have heard this so often and IT DOES MATTER. To quote one instance: In Sicily at a town named Agira, the Canadians were committed to considerable house to house fighting ... An officer of the Canadians crept on top of one of these houses endeavouring to spot one of these [German] snipers, momentarily exposing himself for a couple of seconds. He fell back with a bullet through the head. The sniper responsible – later killed by one of our snipers – must have been a good 200 yards away. Again, one of our men running across an exposed piece of ground was shot through the shoulder by a German rifleman at 300 yards ... Could you have done as well? Why not? Your rifle is the best in the world. What's wrong with you?[68]

Soon after, the small arms schools worked at improving *how* they delivered the training. In January 1945, the A25 Small Arms Training Centre in Long Branch, Ontario, integrated methods of instruction and methods of coaching courses into a single, more sophisticated instructor program. The new course sought to produce well-rounded instructors by running students through a three-part regime: methods of instruction (part 1), drill and duties (part 2), and methods of coaching (part 3). The school's war diarist articulated the staff's certainty in the new program's value, boasting: "This Course is the baby of them all."[69]

It was indeed a comprehensive program. The two-week methods of instruction phase taught NCOs the latest teaching methods.[70] Staff delivered lectures on instructional technique, with classes on the principles of instruction, creating interest, "the art of questioning," and how to conduct TEWTs. And half the course involved practising teaching, with students presenting lectures on assigned topics, followed by criticism by classmates and directing staff. Each week concluded with a review of that week's work and an examination. Then, the six-day drill and duties phase rounded out students' general NCO skills. Drill-related periods taught students to drill troops, with and without arms, up to the battalion level.[71] Duties-related periods included instruction on guards and sentries; care and custody of men in detention; a lecture on the roles of sergeants, company sergeants major, and regimental sergeants major; the application of military law; and the roles of company and battalion orderly rooms. The methods of coaching phase naturally complemented the others, given that small arms instruction and teaching soldiers how to shoot was a bread-and-butter role for NCOs. By the end of the war, the A25 program – just one of four that operated in Canada during the war – trained about 1,200 soldiers to be expert weapons instructors. Some were officers, but most were NCOs.[72]

Another program, called the NCOs and Warrant Officers Course, ran at training centres across Canada to enhance the instructional skills of established NCOs. Under NDHQ control, each serial was given at multiple training centres concurrently. For example, a serial that began in June 1941 ran at nine training centres, all either infantry or machine gun.[73] Another, which began in July, ran at fifteen training centres, this time for the artillery, engineer, service corps, and infantry.[74] For all serials, NDHQ controlled attendance by allotting vacancies to the military districts and operational formations. The DMT designed this course to ensure that candidates possessed instructional skills commensurate with their higher rank.[75] The training reinforced the instructional ability of the army's higher-ranking NCOs, up to the warrant officer class. Given how quickly the army expanded and NCOs rose in rank, as well as the prewar army's inability to provide adequate training, many of the wartime senior NCOs needed to elevate their instructional proficiency. The NCOs and Warrant Officers Course therefore filled an important requirement. When sustained Canadian operations began with the invasion of Sicily in July 1943, the forty-ninth serial of the course was underway at seven training centres across Canada. By then, several thousand soldiers had attended.[76]

Advanced NCO Tactical Training

In the late summer of 1943, professional development opportunities for trained NCOs in Canada leaped forward when NDHQ established in Vernon, British Columbia, the S17 Canadian School of Infantry, modelled on the British School of Infantry.[77] The latter had opened in the summer of 1942, absorbing a battle drill school located at Barnard Castle, in County Durham. The new British training centre impressed Canada's chief of the general staff, Lieutenant-General Kenneth Stuart, who visited it in early 1943. Soon after returning home, he decided to open a Canadian "Barnard Castle." Accordingly, NDHQ sent Colonel Milton F. Gregg, VC, on fact-finding missions to the British School of Infantry and to the American Infantry School at Fort Benning, Georgia. (Gregg, a First World War veteran of the Royal Canadian Regiment who had won the Victoria Cross for leading men under fire near Cambrai in September 1918, had already played an important role in the training system in

Canada. Geoffrey Hayes documents how, in April 1942, Gregg assumed command of the Officers Training Centre in Brockville, Ontario, where he proved an inspiring leader and brought more realism and difficulty to officer qualification training.[78]) By August 1943, NDHQ had decided to establish the new Canadian School of Infantry at Vernon, with Gregg as its commandant, in the rank of brigadier.

The institution absorbed the Canadian Battle Drill School and began running several types of advanced training. It also became NDHQ's agent for keeping infantry training in Canada up to date. Terms of reference specified that the school existed "to provide an authoritative source of inf[ormatio]n concerning details of technical and tactical developments in the Inf Corps."[79] This included furnishing NDHQ with the most current information on how best to train infantrymen and advice on how to refine programs in Canada, all in support of making reinforcement training as effective as possible. To meet its mandate, the school kept close contact with the British School of Infantry, the American Infantry School, and the Canadian Training School in Britain, which was the overseas army's main centralized training institution. To promote a common training doctrine, the new school also prepared training material and syllabuses for distribution to training centres and units across Canada, and it conducted various advanced courses on tactics and weapons handling.

The Canadian School of Infantry organized itself into wings that specialized in particular types of instruction. At first, the school had three wings.[80] Number 1 (Battle) Wing, also called the Senior Battle Wing, put company commanders through an intensive program in sub-unit tactics. Number 2 (Battle) Wing, also called the Junior Battle Wing, trained senior NCOs and junior officers to command platoons in battle. Number 3 (Carrier) Wing, for NCOs down to the rank of corporal and carrier platoon commanders, trained students to handle the carrier platoon as part of a battalion in battle. Soon, the school added other wings, including Number 4 (3-inch mortar) and Number 5 (Anti-tank), both of which trained NCOs down to the rank of corporal as well as officers.[81] More wings followed later. There was even one for the Veterans Guard. In late October 1943, the war diarist recorded how a Veterans Guard company, undergoing inspection by Gregg, added a colourful element to the school's diverse population:

> What a grand body of men they are and such glorious liars! One, with the South African ribbon, when asked his age said, without batting an eye, "48, Sir." Wearers of the Mons Star were 44 and 45. All turned out perfectly and what a March Past!

... No exaggerated arm-swinging but a mark of confidence which made the Canadians famous in the last war. The Brigadier in his talk afterwards, complemented them and said: "No wonder they wer[e] good soldiers, seeing that they had been at it, according to present ages, since they were six years of age."[82]

The School of Infantry may not have been able to do much with the aged Veterans Guard candidates, but it did a lot with students in the other wings and it helped elevate the quality of NCO training in Canada.

Because of the intensity of the training at Number 2 Wing, the school set a high standard for admission. NCOs had to hold the rank of sergeant or above, and all candidates had to be proficient in all platoon weapons.[83] The joining instructions cautioned that students had to possess sufficient experience to permit them to keep up in intensive tactical training. Students also had to report for the course capable of running across country "in battle order with rifle" for two miles in seventeen minutes. And they had to possess a medical profile deeming them fit for overseas duty. The school wanted energetic and eager students, noting that age and enthusiasm mattered: "Candidates should be young, keen and have an enthusiastic personality. Initiative is an essential quality." Candidates could not be older than thirty-five.

Each class of 108 troops, including 54 NCO candidates, concentrated almost entirely on fighting skills and fieldcraft. The syllabus followed the standard army training method: lectures, followed by demonstrations, followed by practice.[84] So, for example, students received a lecture on woods clearing, watched a demonstration, and then practised woods clearing themselves. The course used this format to teach tactics for obstacle crossings, flank attacks, assaults, patrolling, and house clearing, to name just a few subjects. Staff also conducted TEWTs to teach various platoon battle tasks (such as flank protection and village fighting) and company battle tasks (including defences, frontal attacks, consolidation, and night attacks). The commandant implored students to remember that because such battle tasks usually supported a larger unit plan, junior leaders had to "make sure that all ranks get the larger picture so that smooth team-work can be accomplished when most needed."[85] To practise particular battle drills, students participated in many short exercises, or "schemes." However, the school stressed that soldiers must not become "drill bound" – battle drill helped apply sound principles to real situations, but the actual drills ought "to be used, adapted, or discarded depending upon all the factors affecting your battle task."[86] Students also learned about the German and Japanese armies and how they fought at lower levels. Meanwhile, the course kept students fit with unarmed combat sessions and obstacle courses designed to replicate the physical challenges of battle. Such fitness periods were part of battle drill, the school emphasized, which aimed "to improve the standard of fitness for war" and could "only be done properly by practicing for war under as near as possible to war conditions."[87] Interestingly, the course contained none of the elementary material typically found in NCO courses elsewhere. There was no foot drill, barracks scrubbing, spit-and-polish, or NCO duties. The course focused almost entirely on fighting and included as much live-fire training, or "wet schemes," as staff could arrange.

Students found the training very demanding. The fit and enthusiastic Robert Sanderson, by now an Acting Sergeant confessed that the training was tough and that he looked forward to its conclusion. With good soldierly humour, he extolled Vernon's stunning countryside but complained that "running over the sides of mountains doesn't increase your love for them to any great extent" and that constantly crossing the same mountainside had shortened one of his legs. A letter home gave a good sense of what the training was like:

> Last Monday we went over the obstacle course ... and it certainly was quite an experience. Climbed up and down mountain sides, cliffs, up ropes, and down, over water by swinging ropes, through streams up to our necks in mud, water and ice, jumping out of the top windows of houses into mud holes (neck and waist height), climbing rope ladders, through tunnels and then through the crawl trench under live fire ... I thought I'd never get through it! The water was muddy and ice cold and had deep holes here and there. We were numb by the time we finished it (200 yds long) ... I was lucky with no after effects except my legs being a bit frost-bitten. They're ok. now. Practically everyone had that trouble ... We are into company tactics now. Yesterday I was platoon commander, so I was a busy boy in charge of flanking movements and then village clearing ... There's more brains needed for success in the infantry than civilians realize ... There's no end to the learning in battle procedure ... Have our final exam on Tuesday so guess I'd better study up a bit.[88]

Number 2 Wing encouraged the dissemination of the latest skills by issuing graduating students with a précis that summarized the course content.[89] Gregg advised graduates to use the précis when training their own troops. The following list depicts the contents of the précis, which distils the training that senior NCOs and junior officers underwent. NCO training in Canada had come a long way since September 1939. Compared to the courses the army ran for NCOs earlier in the war, S17 conducted the infantry equivalent of graduate-level studies.

Number 2 (Battle) Wing index to précis

Appreciations and Orders
Battle Drill Objectives
Carrier–Infantry Cooperation
Company Battle Tasks
    Consolidation
    Defence
    Flanking attack
    Frontal attack
    Vanguard operations
Explosives and Demolitions
Mine Clearing Using Prodders
Minefield Reconnaissance with Detector
Minelaying
Mortar–Infantry Cooperation
Platoon Battle Tasks
    Fire platoon
    Flank protection platoon
    Outposts
    Patrolling
    Vanguard
Village Fighting
Night Attack
Platoon Flanking Drill
Principles of Instruction: Demonstrations, TEWTs, and Exercises
Principles of Instruction: Lecturing
Pushing a Bangalore Torpedo Silently (Night)
Section Drill
Tactical Handling of Platoon Weapons
The Section in Three Groups
Thickness Required for Bullet Proofing[90]

The Canadian School of Infantry kept its training current with the latest developments overseas by gathering information from various Canadian and other Allied sources. For example, in late June 1944, the commandant passed to his instructors extracts from a letter he had received from Brigadier Eric Snow, commander of the 11th Canadian Infantry Brigade in Italy. Snow's letter contained all sorts of relevant information. He emphasized that training ought to stress mostly the basics – "strict discipline, high morale, full knowledge of one's wpns [weapons] and fieldcraft, battle drill and battle sense" – and just a few other points.[91] While the fighting in Italy had proven to be a platoon commander's battle throughout, Snow commented, in his experience Canadian platoon commanders did not use quite enough initiative and waited too long for direction. Soldiers needed greater proficiency in using and troubleshooting wireless radio sets. And because tanks had proven essential to infantry operations, personnel had to arrive in theatre with good knowledge of how to work with armour. Meanwhile, S17 sent personnel abroad to gather information. For instance, around the time Snow provided his views on training, the school dispatched a major to Britain to liaise with Canadian and British schools, and in mid-July he returned to S17 with fresh insights.[92] Furthermore, S17 had on its staff Canadian and British officers who had served overseas at the Canadian Training School and the British School of Infantry respectively.[93]

Despite these efforts, the training capacity of Number 2 Wing soon degraded because of the army's growing shortage of infantrymen reinforcements. In mid-October 1944, NDHQ started ordering the school's instructional personnel into the reinforcement system or to units in Canada, and the losses eroded 2 Wing's capacity to operate.[94] In late October, the commandant reported to DMT staff in Ottawa that he had found it more and more difficult to secure instructors because increasing numbers of staff were entering the reinforcement stream.[95] It got worse. Two weeks later, the school received orders warning that soldiers below the rank of warrant officer class 2 would be deployed overseas regardless of whether replacements existed, cutting "a big hole" in key parts of the staff, as the school's war diarist recorded.[96] In mid-November, orders arrived to send general service personnel who met age and medical requirements for overseas duty. Of course, by this time, the political crisis over the shortage of infantryman was cresting (even if the numbers in the field were improving), and the army overseas desperately needed all available infantrymen. Ottawa therefore refocused the S17 training centre, making it responsible for converting non-infantry officers to infantry.[97]

The school stopped running the high-end Number 2 Wing course for senior NCOs and junior officers in late November 1944, but several other programs kept running to help develop NCOs. Specialist training, such as mortar and anti-tank programs, continued operating into 1945.[98] In June 1945, with the fighting in Europe barely concluded, the Drill Wing began preparing a course for regimental sergeants major (RSMs).[99]

Overall, the Canadian School of Infantry proved a worthwhile investment. From the time it opened, the quality of low-level tactics training in Canada took a healthy stride forward and better-trained NCOs were part of it. The school provided NCOs and officers with high-quality, up-to-date instruction based on training regimes conducted at similar allied training centres and on lessons learned in battle. In fact, several months before 2 Wing closed, the army's inspector-general for Western Canada found that "the school is well supplied with summaries from troops on the active front, particularly Canadians in Italy."[100] Number 2 Wing in particular played an important role by training senior NCOs to be competent at handling a platoon in battle. These men then passed up-do-date tactical skills on to others, including soldiers who went overseas as reinforcements.

Controlling the Quality of NCOs Deploying Overseas

In the second half of 1944, the training system in Canada helped keep the army's backbone strong with a centralized program that lifted up the skills of hundreds of NCOs who were ordered into the reinforcement stream. In mid-July, NDHQ established the A34 Special Training Centre in Sussex, New Brunswick.[101] It was to run several programs, including one that ensured NCOs proceeding overseas were ready for duty in a theatre of war.[102] This served as an important quality-control function, not only honing NCOs about to deploy but also screening out of the reinforcement stream those who were unsuited for service in a combat zone.

The first serial of the NCO refresher course convinced authorities that they were right to implement such a program. The training started in late July 1944, with a focus on preparing support trade soldiers for deployment.[103] The eight-week course began with 409 men, for whom the training came as a shock. Most were not in good physical shape, and many had to cease training because they could not meet fitness standards. Many more, having spent most of their time in uniform as specialists, had much to learn about army life and garrison routines. The training whittled the group down considerably and, after the course ended on 19 September, only 281 left for Britain.[104] But the program did what it was supposed to do, and reports from the field suggested that the training had prepared the men well. NDHQ decided to continue the program.[105]

In late October, NDHQ ordered A34 to run training for another group allotted for overseas duty, this time infantry NCOs with long service in Canada. Authorities in Ottawa worried that their readiness for operations varied considerably because they had been employed in many different capacities, and some no doubt required a refresher.[106] Therefore, the A34 centre was to assess each candidate's basic skills and divide the men into smaller groups based on how much training they required. NDHQ also directed school staff to stress to the students the strict requirement to take the training seriously. Candidates unable to meet standards faced a reduction in rank.

As it turned out, this NCO refresher course went well compared to one run for non-infantry soldiers. Candidates consisted of corporals and sergeants, many of whom had served as instructors in various training centres. On 27 October, school staff began subjecting them to examinations and interviews, and then placed them into companies that would undergo three, five, or seven weeks of "basic refresher training."[107] Unsurprisingly these soldiers, numbering several hundred, proved more enthusiastic and hardier than those on the non-infantry course. At first, many even scoffed at the relatively easy physical demands. But morale soon improved. When staff ascertained that an adjustment of attitudes was needed, they ran the students through a demanding assault course at night.[108] As the men slinked their way across ropes suspended over a river, staff threw explosive charges into the water below. The explosions and plumes of icy water caused many to fall into the frigid current. Perhaps surprisingly, the candidates approved of this rigorous training – one lost his helmet, another his false teeth – and they began to accept that the course was pitched to their capabilities.

Despite the good start, events beyond the school's control conspired to undermine progress. On 17 November, with the infantry reinforcement crisis overseas preoccupying the senior leadership, the commanding officer received word that the training centre would expand to conduct advanced training for the large numbers of troops preparing to proceed overseas.[109] The school already had a serious shortage of instructors and some of those on staff desperately wanted to deploy overseas themselves, yet no plan existed to bring in replacements. Also, a few days after the government decision on 22 November to send conscripts abroad, 200 students had to cease training and proceed to Pacific Command for duty as instructors. After a flurry of administration the soldiers departed, and staff consolidated the remaining students into three groups.[110] The class size diminished further when others had to leave to help train reinforcements, while a few dozen more ceased training because their PULHEMS profiles did not meet overseas standards. On 15 January 1945, the second NCO refresher course finally finished. Even then, some graduates had to remain in Canada to instruct at A34 and other training centres, although seventy-six went to the Dufferin and Haldimand Rifles, which in early 1945 formed drafts for overseas deployment.

The program ceased in early 1945 when A34 refocused its efforts on training infantry reinforcements, including many conscripts, before they sailed for Britain.[111] By then, the NCO refresher program had provided much-needed training to about 700 NCOs and, in the process, screened out over 300 who could not meet standards. This clearly demonstrated the army's determination to ensure that only properly trained junior leaders entered the reinforcement stream. Later, more NCOs undoubtedly received refresher training at A34 as part of the larger reinforcement drafts that passed through the centre in 1945.

Conclusion

A network of BTCs, ATCs, and Schools of Instruction took shape in Canada by early 1941, and thereafter, this centralized training system played a major part in building the NCO corps. The Junior Leaders School in Mégantic and multipurpose training centres across the country produced a steady stream of non-commissioned leaders who, with up-to-date training under their belts, were ready to lead the rank and file in operational units or serve as instructors in the training system. Planners worked hard to ensure that NCO qualification programs stayed abreast of developments overseas, causing courses to grow longer and more sophisticated as the war progressed.

Meanwhile, instructional training featured prominently in NCO development programs. While teaching was an important skill for NCOs everywhere, it took on particular importance in Canada because of the requirement to turn hundreds of thousands of citizens into skilled soldiers. Clearly, their training had to be solid if the brand-new soldiers pouring out of the training system were to prove good enough in combat against Germany's battle-tested forces. At the same, the number of experienced NCOs available for the training system in Canada shrank as the army grew and as overseas requirements for regimental and reinforcement NCOs increased. Training centres had no choice but to take some of the best soldiers fresh out of basic training and turn them into instructors – hardly an ideal solution, but there was no other way. Consequently, in an effort to keep teaching standards high, NDHQ demanded that all instructors in Canada undergo standardized courses in methods of instruction and methods of coaching.

Eventually, the army's inability to furnish enough NCOs for all operational and training requirements meant that something had to give. By the fall of 1944, the infantry shortage in Europe had eroded the capacity to run certain programs in Canada as authorities diverted instructors into reinforcement drafts. A pressing requirement to send all available infantry NCOs overseas forced the S17 Canadian School of Infantry in Vernon, British Columbia, to cease operating Number 2 (Battle) Wing, which had provided high-end tactical training to senior NCOs, while the A34 Special Training Centre in Sussex, New Brunswick, had to shutter its NCO refresher program, which had ensured that soldiers proceeding overseas were ready for operational duty. Despite such challenges, over the course of the war the centralized training system in Canada churned out trained NCOs – ready to serve as leaders in field units, as regimental instructors for specialist skills, and as instructors for the army's training centres – in numbers that the decentralized programs could not possibly have produced on their own.

The Mass Army's Programs in the United Kingdom

The standard of knowledge of candidates arriving to attend courses is still far from satisfactory. Many units continue to send practically untrained, or otherwise unsuitable, personnel ... All courses at the Canadian Training School are designed for the purpose of training unit instructors ... Selected candidates must be potential instructors whose work on the courses concerned will be definitely handicapped if they do not possess a fairly complete pre-course knowledge ... It is requested that additional efforts be made to ensure that ... greater care be exercised in the selection of candidates to attend.

CANADIAN TRAINING SCHOOL MONTHLY TRAINING
REPORT, SEPTEMBER 1942

IN BRITAIN, AS IN CANADA, the senior leadership could not leave NCO training entirely to the field units. Even if commanding officers bore responsibility for developing and promoting their own non-commissioned leaders, and even if they wanted to train all of their own NCOs, units simply did not have the time or resources. Nor did their parent formations. Besides, someone had to look after NCO training and professional development for the reinforcement system. Canadian Military Headquarters (CMHQ) therefore oversaw a suite of centralized NCO programs that ran more or less continuously in Britain, just like what was going on in Canada. These included junior NCO qualification training, training for regimental instructors who specialized in particular subjects, and general instructor training for soldiers tasked to teach in the reinforcement system. Programs to ensure that reinforcement pool NCOs were ready for field unit duty were also put in place.

There were difficulties. The centralized programs in Britain were good, but the system itself was almost too large to maintain. Training staff complained that units frequently sent candidates who lacked the baseline knowledge needed for many courses, especially the regimental instructor programs. And sourcing high-performing instructors became problematic as well. The army had only so many good NCOs to spread around.

Training under Canadian Military Headquarters

The overseas army ran its own centralized leadership and skills training at the Canadian Training School (CTS), which authorities established in August 1940. Until then, the Canadians had been relying heavily on British schools for individual training that gave instruction in specialist and instructional skills.[1] But the British army, implementing its own aggressive expansion program, had to limit the vacancies allotted to the Canadians. The arrival of 2nd Canadian Division units in the summer of 1940 had only compounded Canada's instructor shortage and fuelled the army's need for its own dedicated training institution. So the new CTS, which became the primary agency for centralized NCO training in Britain, was designed to provide a range of individual training run by specialist wings. At first, a shortage of barracks meant that the school consisted of only a single wing that trained officer cadets. But in May 1941, the school acquired the use of Havannah Barracks in Bordon, Hampshire County, where it settled and formed additional training wings. Number 1 (Officer Candidate Training) Wing provided basic officer training, Number 2 (Technical) Wing ran driver and anti-gas training, and Number 3 (Weapons) Wing conducted various small arms courses and NCO training.[2] Other wings eventually followed, including Number 4 (Tactical) Wing for platoon and company commander courses, Number 5 (Battle) Wing for battle drill training, and Number 6 (Chemical Warfare) Wing for anti-gas and flame-thrower courses. Most important for this study, Number 3 Wing ran courses for potential NCOs, NCOs who needed to upgrade their skills, and NCOs who had to learn how to instruct.

In the spring of 1941, Number 3 Wing opened and started running CMHQ Course 804 (NCO Qualification).[3] Unlike the wing's other courses, which focused on producing specialist instructors, Course 804 taught leadership.[4] The program prepared soldiers to perform as section commanders and focused heavily on infantry skills, although soldiers from all arms attended.[5] Ideal candidates, according to the program's designers, were lance corporals or strong privates who had demonstrated leadership potential.[6]

The six-week course was fairly comprehensive.[7] Candidates gained a wider appreciation for how a unit worked and how NCOs figured in its functioning, especially in battle. They learned about the roles of the regimental sergeant major (RSM), the company sergeant major (CSM), and orderly NCOs. They learned how to navigate using map and compass; how to arrange trench systems and build defensive works using wire, booby traps, anti-tank mines, and obstacles; how to develop charges for disciplinary infractions and how to implement open and closed arrest arrangements, the basics of military law; how to instruct on the army's suite of platoon weapons – the rifle, 2-inch mortar, light

Figure 7.1 Centralized NCO training in Britain occurred at the Canadian Training School. These troops are undergoing battle drill training at the school's Number 5 (Battle) Wing, 8 June 1943. | Library and Archives Canada/Department of National Defence fonds/a132776.

machine gun, sub-machine gun, and anti-tank rifle; and how to conduct night operations. They practised their shooting skills and learned the theory of small arms fire. And they learned to give foot and rifle drill up to the company level. In short, Course 804 gave students the essential leadership and field skills they required as future NCOs in operational units. In contrast to the ad hoc unit-run courses described in Chapter 5, which took a *what can be done in the time available* approach, Course 804 introduced a *what needs to be done* approach to train new NCOs – similar to the centralized courses in Canada. Table 7.1 depicts the main subjects and the number of periods allotted to each.

Table 7.1

Syllabus for CMHQ Course 804 (NCO Qualification)

Subject	Periods	Subject	Periods
Airborne troops lecture	2	Small arms training: Anti-tank	
Anti-air recognition	5	rifle	3
Defence against gas	11	Small arms training: Bayonet	
Fieldcraft	71	fighting	12
Field engineering	15	Small arms training:	4
Hygiene and sanitation	3	Grenades	
Kit inspection	1	Small arms training: Light	33
Map reading	22	machine guns	32
Military law	6	Small arms training: Rifle	
NCO/warrant officer duties	3	Small arms training:	5
Organization and administration	6	Sub-machine gun	51
Practical camouflage	1	Squad drill	4
Principles of anti-air defence	1	Street and village fighting	4
Small arms training: 2-inch mortar	5	Tank hunting	
		Total periods	300

Source: Data from C.M.H.Q. Course No. 804 Six Weeks, No. 3 (Weapons) Wing C.T.S, LAC, RG24, vol. 9878, file 2/SYLLAB/2.

The first serial of Course 804 ran from 3 June to 12 July 1941 with fifty-seven candidates.[8] Thereafter, serials ran back to back, producing a steady stream of soldiers with formal junior NCO training. Soldiers attended from across the Canadian army in Britain, not just from field units but also from the reinforcement system and from specialist organizations such as the Forestry Corps. Each serial had room for sixty-four candidates, with CMHQ controlling allocations. The training proved useful even for some senior NCOs, as units sometimes sent sergeants and a few company sergeants major. While school records do not indicate why some higher-ranking soldiers took the training, units likely wanted to elevate the expertise of NCOs who had earned their stripes in the prewar army or shot up in rank on mobilization. These senior NCOs probably needed to update their skills in tandem with the army's modernization.

In the early fall of 1942, CTS began operating another important NCO course, one designed to refresh instructional skills for soldiers rotating through Canadian Reinforcement Units (CRU), the army's reinforcement-holding formation. At the time, the army cycled instructors from field units through CRU for four-month periods to bolster the quality of reinforcement training as part of a greater effort to distribute expertise across the whole NCO corps. Four months was just enough time for a field unit soldier to pass on the latest techniques without suffering too much skill fade in advance of returning to his unit.[9] But when reinforcement units complained that these soldiers had often "lost the knack of instruction," CTS inaugurated an instructor refresher course to redress the problem.[10] CMHQ Course 824 (CRU NCO Refresher) gave three weeks of training in methods of instruction to field unit NCOs destined for instructional tours of duty. Candidates from acting corporal up to warrant officer class 2 (CSM) attended, but most were corporals and sergeants.[11]

Those running Course 824 soon suspected that the problem of skill-deficient NCOs stemmed in part from the reluctance of field unit commanders to send strong people. The first serial of Course 824, which began on 20 September 1942, got off to a rocky start. The school returned eight of fifty-eight men to their units because they were "unlikely to become efficient instructors."[12] Furthermore, field units failed to fill all sixty-six available vacancies, which meant that too few soldiers would finish the training in time to relieve those whose instructional tours had ended. The matter troubled Major-General P.J. Montague, the senior officer at CMHQ, who complained to First Canadian Army that units had selected too many candidates lacking instructional aptitude. Montague wanted First Canadian Army to impress upon commanding officers the importance of sending the right candidates, for everyone's sake. Word soon started flowing down the chain of command. A week after Montague raised his complaint, Lieutenant-General H.D.G. Crerar addressed the matter in 1st Canadian Corps. He told his division commanders that the "qualifications and suitability of a considerable number of the NCOs who have been sent recently to [Course 824] have been far below the standard which is required," and that such a trend would ultimately harm field unit efficiency.[13] Reinforcements required the best possible training, and candidates nominated to attend Course 824 had to be "first-class NCOs." Crerar was right, but the message may have been a tough sell to unit commanders who naturally wanted to retain their best NCOs as they prepared to go into action.

In December 1942, CMHQ amended Course 824, maintaining the overall concept of a three-week program to train personnel in methods of instruction but having CRU choose the students from among soldiers posted to reinforcement units as instructors. Now, NCOs attended the course only after reporting to a reinforcement unit, and only if selected. Meanwhile, CRU worked with CTS to refine the syllabus as required, but the training still focused on practising instructional skills and increasing students' self-confidence. And CTS provided CRU with a report on each candidate once he had completed the course.[14]

Still, too many inadequate students continued to join the course. In late January 1943, the fifth serial of Course 824 finished with unimpressive results. Seventy candidates had reported for the training, most between the ranks of lance corporal and sergeant. During the first week, staff returned twelve to their units as "not likely to reach an efficient standard to instruct at the end of three weeks."[15] Of the fifty-seven students who finished the course, only thirty-one qualified as "fit to instruct." The next lot – actually selected by CRU unit commanders for the first time – showed no improvement. The course started with sixty-two candidates but staff returned fourteen after the first week, again because they were unlikely to reach the necessary standard, even after three weeks of training.[16] Of the forty-six who eventually completed the training, only thirty-three qualified as fit to instruct.

The problem of poor students had become chronic. Brigadier Frederick Phelan, the commander of CRU, admonished his commanding officers for not taking enough care to send good soldiers, insisting that they implement systems to ensure better results. But reinforcement unit commanding officers were not the only ones guilty of sending sub-par candidates for training. CTS staff complained that field units often sent poorly prepared candidates for all courses. For example, after Number 3 Wing had been operating for over a year, the officer commanding expressed disappointment that every course under his charge routinely received inadequate candidates, something he attributed to poor efforts to find the right individuals.[17] That may have been unfair.

The persistence of the problem suggests that units simply lacked enough sufficiently experienced soldiers to fill all the vacancies in all the specialist courses on offer. After all, units were even sending some senior NCOs to the junior NCO qualification program, CMHQ Course 804. The CTS commandant, Colonel Thomas Snow, offered an additional explanation. In mid-March 1943, he complained to CMHQ about the enduring issue of soldiers arriving at CTS to train as instructors in subjects for which they were utterly unqualified, attributing it to the school's practice of retaining the best graduates as instructors without concern for the impact on the losing units. On top of that, CTS periodically retained instructors for longer than the mandated four to eight months. This made commanding officers, raised in the Anglo-Canadian regimental system, reluctant to surrender their best people to the big-army machine.[18] In any event, the core of the difficulty was almost certainly related to the army's larger challenge: the NCO corps was still developing, many of its members were still new in rank, and only so many experienced and qualified junior leaders existed.

Shortfalls notwithstanding, the senior leadership considered Course 824 an essential program. In February 1943, CTS lost its capacity to conduct it because of a requirement to run additional programs, so CMHQ decided that CRU would run the course on its own. Course 824 had to continue because, despite the problems, it had "proved most beneficial in raising the standard of instruction" in the reinforcement units.[19] Each class, or serial, would accommodate 100 students, beginning in March. And 4 Canadian Infantry Reinforcement Unit (CIRU) would be responsible for the training.[20] Students did not always perform as well as authorities would have liked, but the course limped along, and it did sharpen the skills of CRU NCOs.

In fact, CRU instructors played an important role in developing the NCO corps by training soldiers awaiting transfer to field units. To determine just how much training each soldier posted to CRU required, staff subjected all new arrivals to tests of elementary training (TOETs) in fundamental subjects such as personal weapons handling, field engineering, map reading, first aid, and defence against gas.[21] Test results determined whether a soldier would join a two-, four-, or six-week refresher course that covered certain "basic common-to-arm" subjects, before proceeding to "basic special-to-arm" refresher training.[22] If a reinforcement soldier could pass these TOETs, he qualified as trained to a basic standard in subjects common to all arms.[23]

One set of TOETs verified NCO readiness.[24] Part 1 had eight questions on fire control and the conduct of range practices. For example, one question asked: "How many mag[azine]s per minute would your Bren use, when you give a normal fire control order?" ("1.") Another asked: "Your section is in action firing at a target 400x [yards, or 365 m] away. You see the bullets striking the ground about 50x short of the target. What order would you give?" ("Stop. Up 50. Go on.") Part 2 asked eight questions on general NCO duties in the field. One was: "What points would you look for in selecting a fire position for your section?" ("One that will give cover from view; protection from fire; a good field of fire; one that we could move from with as little exposure as possible, one that will give free use of the weapons.") Another asked: "You are in command of a section in action. You are given an arc of fire. What does that mean to you?" ("That my section is responsible for that arc and must engage all targets that appear in that area.") Part 3 asked nineteen questions on small arms instruction and military law. For example, a soldier could be asked: "When instructing a squad, what is the sequence of teaching?" ("Explanation – Instruction by the ear. Demonstration – Instruction by the eye. Execution – Imitation of the demonstration and correcting mistakes. Repetition – Further practice to improve.") Or: "While you are confining a man to the guard room for some serious offence, the man does a lot of talking or using threats. Would you answer the man in any way?" ("No. What the man said would be used in evidence against him.") Such tests allowed

CRU to gauge a reinforcement NCO's knowledge of basic subjects and give guidance on what his subsequent training should be.

In November 1943, field units saw their access to centralized NCO training programs curtailed when First Canadian Army strictly limited soldiers attending courses away from their units. With the campaign in Northwest Europe fast approaching, collective training for offensive operations took priority.[25] Training instructions stressed that all personnel in leadership positions were to remain at their posts unless there was a compelling reason:

> The time has now come when ... the number of offrs and NCOs away from their units on courses should be kept to a necessary minimum ... Offrs and NCOs should be detailed to attend courses only when it is essential to the unit as a whole in order to maintain the numbers of tradesmen and specialist personnel ... and to ensure an adequate cadre of trained instrs in any particular subject. Offrs and NCOs will NOT be detailed to attend courses merely for the purpose of filling available vacancies.[26]

The instructions initially empowered unit commanders to decide whether they required men to attend certain courses, but that discretionary authority did not last long.

Training instructions for January–March 1944 declared that NCOs and officers would attend courses only by rare exception.[27] Army headquarters wanted section, platoon, and company commanders to oversee the training of their subordinates. If a commanding officer believed he had a compelling reason to send one of these soldiers away for training, he had to submit an appeal to his brigade commander, the only person who could grant exemptions. The army commander clearly believed that, ready or not, his forces would soon launch into battle and should remain assembled as they would fight.[28]

With First Canadian Army freezing NCOs in their leadership positions, authorities refocused CTS on training non-commissioned leaders in the reinforcement system. The shift had actually started in early December 1943, when CMHQ ordered CTS to re-assume responsibility for conducting CMHQ Course 824 (CRU NCO Refresher), which still gave methods of instruction training to soldiers identified for instructional duty at CRU. The course took on a new name, CMHQ Course 1213, and in January 1944 began training candidates from various reinforcement units.[29] CTS then shifted its entire effort toward supporting the reinforcement system because First Canadian Army no longer needed its courses.[30] Over the next two months, CTS reorganized for its new and reduced mandate, dropping its large establishment from 1,240 all ranks to 735.[31] From February, the school had three main responsibilities: preparing reinforcement NCOs and junior officers for operations, running courses when the War Office could not meet Canadian requirements, and maintaining a cadre of instructors on weapons and vehicles unique to the Canadian forces.[32]

In the early spring of 1944, CTS staff rediscovered the old problem of NCOs arriving unprepared for refresher training and adjusted the curriculum of Course 1213 accordingly. In March, the school issued a scathing critique of the quality of student reporting for the course:

> The Weapons Trg Wing of CTS has found that the average N.C.O. on the Refresher Course lacks knowledge and ability to impart instruction. It is apparent that a large number of N.C.O.s have been promoted in the Field without previously having attended any type of course. The training of N.C.O.s is generally badly neglected. More effort should be made wherever there is a surplus of N.C.O.s to keep them under continual instruction until such times as they are required for field purposes. There is always room for improvement in the standard of weapons handling and map reading.[33]

Whether or not NCO proficiency was as bad as the school's instructors indicated, CTS overhauled Course 1213, making it longer and more demanding. It ceased being a refresher and instead became the NCO qualification course.[34] The new version took seven weeks rather than three, with the aim of improving both essential knowledge and the ability to teach.[35] (Around the same time, training authorities in Canada arrived at similar conclusions about how long it took to produce new junior NCOs. As described in Chapter 5, the NCO qualification program that ran at Mégantic until the end of 1943 grew to seven weeks, and when the assistant instructor course became the sole NCO qualification course in Canada in May 1944, it adopted a six-week curriculum. Slight differences in the curricula in Canada and Britain were to be expected, given that the former focused on the training system and home defence units and the latter on the reinforcement system.) Additionally, the school added a negative reinforcement: if a student failed to meet course standards, staff recommended a reduction in rank. The commandant believed the revised program had the desired effect: "This policy is proving very satisfactory and better results are being obtained. It has brought out a better effort by the individual and has made the average NCO realize that to retain his rank he has got to work, and not simply attend a course and see the instr[uctor] do all the work." Thus, the new Course 1213 became a more useful cog in the army's increasingly complex machinery for developing NCOs.

In the reinforcement units themselves, CRU introduced a new procedure for ensuring that all soldiers passing through demonstrated competence in essential military skills. As indicated above, in the preceding two years or so, soldiers reporting to a reinforcement unit had undergone a proficiency assessment, based on which they attended a two-, four-, or six-week refresher course in skills common to all arms.[36] In February 1944, CRU replaced this system with a scheme that put all new arrivals through a common two-week course, followed by further specialized training as required. The improved quality of reinforcements arriving from Canada permitted the change. As a CMHQ assessment indicated: "There is no doubt that the standard of trg of rfts arriving from Canada has improved."[37] The new two-week program assessed all reinforcements against up-to-date standards. It worked like this: troops fed into a reinforcement unit from many locations, especially the training system in Canada and field units in Britain.[38] Every man joining CRU, regardless of rank, underwent the two-week program, no exceptions, to refresh essential skills. For NCOs, the course exercised leadership skills. Staff ran them through the program in one of two ways.[39] Some joined platoons of rank-and-file candidates as section commanders. The remaining men formed NCO-only platoons. Either way, NCOs received additional instruction during the evenings in radio procedure, reports and messages, battle procedure, and map use. The program respected that everyone had already passed basic training elsewhere, and instructors therefore emphasized the practical aspects of each topic, providing comprehensive instruction only to correct obvious weaknesses. Table 7.2 depicts the main subjects and the number of periods allotted to each.[40] Staff used some of the spare periods for battle-experience lectures from recently returned personnel from Italy. Chief instructors could use the remaining spares for any worthwhile purpose, but all had to be used for training of some sort.

Even after completing the two-week refresher, reinforcements had several hoops to jump through before they could join a field unit. First, inspection teams conducted TOETs and examinations of all subjects covered on the course.[41] Only after passing those tests could soldiers who had already served with a field unit return to one, the same one wherever possible. Everyone else had to complete a few more steps. For NCOs and privates, a board examined each trainee's performance and assessed suitability for tradesman or specialist training. If the board found that a soldier had not met the standards of the two-week refresher, he repeated the course, more than once if necessary, to make up any deficiencies – although CMHQ expected such cases would be rare

Table 7.2

Syllabus for Canadian reinforcement units two-week refresher course

Subject	Periods	Subject	Periods
Anti-air rifle and light machine gun	2	Map reading	3
		Marching and field signals	8
Anti-gas	3	Mines and booby traps	6
Bayonet	2	Night training	12
Cooking in the field	1	Physical training	8
Drill	6	Projector, Infantry, Anti-Tank	
Field engineering	7	(PIAT)	2
Fieldcraft	10	Ranges	10
First aid and field hygiene	5	Rifle	7
Fundamental training	3	Security	4
Grenades (handling and throwing on ranges)	4	Spares	5
		Sten and Thompson sub-machine	
Light machine gun – Bren	6	guns	4
		Total periods	118

Source: Data from Canadian Reinforcement Units Block Syllabus Two-Week – Refresher Course, LAC, RG24-C-2, vol. 9804, file 2/Instrns CRU/1.

"in view of the improvement in [the] standard of drafts of personnel received from Canada."[42] NCOs and privates who had not come from field units but who met the standards went on to undergo "training special-to-the-arm" (for infantrymen, training based on the army's standardized advanced training syllabus), or received specialist or trades training (such as clerk or signals programs), depending on what the field units required. Eventually, all soldiers went to a reinforcement company to await posting to a field unit. Here, staff kept a close eye on the NCOs as collective training at the platoon and company level continued (see Figure 7.2).

This system of checks and remedial training seemed to improve the quality of reinforcements at all ranks, NCOs included, in subsequent months.[43] As far as CMHQ was concerned, the training level of reinforcements arriving from Canada had been rising steadily for about a year, an encouraging trend even if some troops still required a little "smartening up."[44] Efforts to raise the proficiency of all soldiers in the reinforcement system continued to pay dividends. And with the improving quality of the rank and file, the quality of the next generation of NCOs was improving as well.

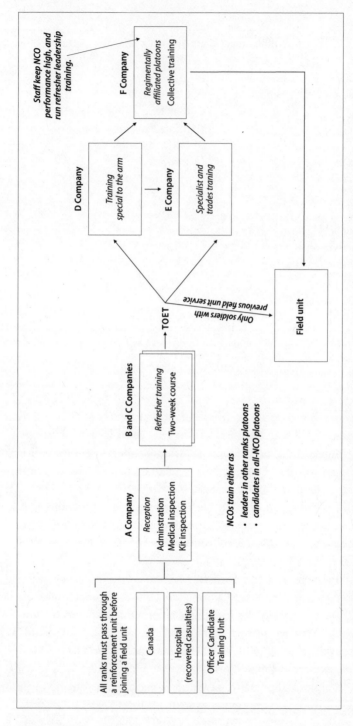

Figure 7.2 Canadian Reinforcement Units – Training Path for All Personnel Reporting to a Reinforcement Unit, as of March 1944. | Adapted from HQ Cdn Rft Units Trg Instr No. 6, 9 March 1944, LAC, RG24-C-2, vol. 9804, file 2/Instrns CRU/1.

Training Regimental Instructors

As in Canada, the centralized NCO training system in Britain included programs that produced regimental instructors. Building the overseas backbone of NCOs necessitated producing junior leaders with expertise in teaching specific skills. Some of these skills were new to the army, as new weapons systems and doctrines for their employment were adopted. Others were well established but remained essential to the process of turning Canada's new army into a force skilled enough to defeat the Germans.

For example, some NCOs took focused training in drill instruction, because, as described in Chapter 5, drill was fundamental to instilling discipline in the army's new citizen-soldiers. The rank and file probably did not always appreciate drilling for hours under the critical eye of an ornery sergeant major, but drill had always had its place as a means for instilling discipline, obedience, and, for NCOs and officers, command skills. The prewar manual *Infantry Training: Training and War, 1937,* a Canadian reprint of the War Office original, dedicated a whole chapter to the subject. Drill, the manual explained, "is the foundation of discipline and *esprit de corps* and forms part of the training of all infantry units."[45] Drill engendered instinctive obedience and habituated soldiers to carrying out a superior's exact intentions. And as the manual assured readers, drill stimulated a soldier's pride in himself and in his unit, and it restored morale in units that had become disorganized. Of course, in the wartime army, drill was important for helping transform masses of raw civilian material into disciplined soldiers who carried out difficult, often dangerous, orders without hesitation. But it had to be conducted properly. Lieutenant-General Bernard Montgomery explained its importance in a direction that reached the Canadians in 1941:

> I am a tremendous believer in the value of close order drill as an aid to operational and collective discipline, and to mental alertness ... Any drill done must be good drill; bad drill is worse than useless – it is definitely harmful ... It does the men of *any* unit a great deal of good to be "electrified" by a really good drill Sgt. or R.S.M.; the men are pulled together, made to hold themselves properly, and to work together in unison.[46]

Canadian commanders expressed similar sentiments. Formation training directives routinely mentioned the importance of drill. As late as the spring of 1943, with the beginning of sustained operations for part of the army just a few months away, First Canadian Army training instructions still ordered weekly periods of close order drill.[47]

With all this emphasis on drill, the army needed NCOs trained to conduct it. The overseas force used several centralized courses to teach drill instruction. NCO qualification and refresher courses almost always included some training in drill instruction. Furthermore, the Canadians received training support from the British, who ran courses that focused exclusively on teaching foot and arms drill. The sample group reviewed in this text shows that the Canadian Army Overseas trained NCOs as drill instructors by sending men on drill courses run by British guards units. In fact, about 7 percent of the senior NCOs in the sample attended a guards-run drill course – a fairly high proportion, given the dozens of different specialist courses for which the army needed instructors. Canadians who took this three- to four-week drill instructor training did so mostly in 1940 and 1941. The program produced drill instructors for units that faced the prospect of fighting soon and needed to tighten discipline among their newly mobilized citizen-soldiers, as Kenneth B. Smith of the Hastings and Prince Edward Regiment describes: "Although the Regiment was surviving [in early 1940], it was far from battle-ready and there was no time to lose ... Every phase of training was intensified. NCOs just back from a course with the Welsh Guards put rifle companies through their paces on the parade square."[48]

Small arms training in the overseas army was another step toward operational effectiveness, and a particularly important one. After all, the most disciplined, best-drilled soldiers in the world would have counted for little if they could not use their weapons effectively. The high command understood this well. First Canadian Army emphasized the point in its inaugural training directive of November 1942. Units were to make good use of their qualified weapons instructors, and commanding officers were to ensure their junior officers appreciated that weapons training demanded "closest supervision."[49] Several months later, a British General Headquarters (GHQ) monthly training letter, issued to all regional commands and the First Canadian Army, captured the essence of why weapons training mattered so much:

The object to be achieved in war is the complete destruction of the enemy. To be successful every operation, large or small, must have a weapon plan. Battle drills, minor tactics and the use of ground and cover are only the means of manoeuvring weapons to positions from which the weapon plan can be most effectively applied. Once the weapons are there, it is quick straight shooting that counts. The ultimate object of weapon training is the co-ordinated handling of weapons to gain superiority in the infantry fire fight, which begins at the moment when fire from supporting arms on the objective has to be lifted. Skill in manoeuvre and skill in firing are inter-dependent, and success can be achieved only by a combination of both.[50]

In essence, the entire national effort to deploy ground forces against the enemy – from recruiting to battle – would be utterly wasted if the troops could not employ their weapons properly once they made contact with Hitler's forces. Canadian success in the field depended on the army producing enough skilled weapons instructors to establish and maintain high weapons-handling standards across the force. Military authorities made the necessary investment.

The Canadian Army Overseas ran its main weapons instructor programs at CTS, in Number 3 (Weapons) Wing. In the summer of 1941, the wing began running several instructor courses.[51] Course 809 (Platoon Weapons), a five-week program, became a staple. It taught how to instruct on the light machine gun, the anti-tank rifle, the 2-inch mortar, the pistol, the bayonet, grenades, the Lewis machine gun, and the Thompson sub-machine gun. Authorities declared that Course 809 was "designed primarily for infantry platoon commanders and junior N.C.Os. to enable them to supervise efficiently weapons training, and act as junior regimental instructors respectively."[52] Over time, CTS adjusted the program to keep up with the maturing army's requirements and, by the time Canada committed forces to the Mediterranean theatre, Course 809 had a well-refined curriculum. The course had increased from five to six weeks as it integrated instruction on new weapons such as the Sten gun and the Projector, Infantry, Anti-Tank (PIAT), and a whole new section covered mines and booby traps.[53] Instructional staff provided demonstrations on the firepower of a platoon, observation of fire, and night firing. Students learned how to teach recognition of armoured fighting vehicles. And examinations assessed their instructional ability. Each candidate had to prepare ten lessons in accordance with the *Small Arms Training* series of weapons manuals and teach six of them to his classmates.

Number 3 Wing also ran courses to generate regimental instructors for other weapons. The six-week Course 810 (Medium Machine Gun) trained NCOs (mostly lance sergeants and sergeants) and junior officers how to teach the ins and outs of machine guns, including weapon mechanisms, fire control, and tactics. The four-week Course 808 (3-inch Mortar) covered how to teach other soldiers the finer points of maintaining, deploying, bedding in, and firing the 3-inch mortar. The three-week Course 812 (Snipers) taught prospective battalion intelligence (reconnaissance) officers and junior NCOs how to teach and make snipers at the unit level. These courses qualified regimental instructors to teach the material when they returned to field or reinforcement units. For example, one of the soldiers in the sample group, Corporal Edmond Derasp of the Royal 22nd Regiment, attended Course 808 (3-inch Mortar) in the late summer of 1941 while serving in 2 Canadian Infantry Holding Unit, where his new skills no doubt helped train mortarmen in the reinforcement stream.[54] Another in the sample group, Sergeant James Brown of the Saskatoon Light Infantry, a machine-gun battalion, attended Course 810 (Medium Machine Gun) in early 1942, a qualification that surely proved useful to him and his unit.[55] Army demand for small arms instructors was extremely high. For the platoon weapons qualification alone, Canadian authorities wanted every section of infantry to have one regimental instructor, although it is not clear whether this goal was reached.[56] Regardless, the courses at Number 3 (Weapons) Wing were of high quality. The only trouble was finding enough candidates from busy units that were engaged in other training and tasks. Occasionally, vacancies went unfilled.

Steeling the Reinforcements: Training after D-Day

After the Allied invasion of Normandy, CTS continued to operate its NCO qualification program, CMHQ Course 1213. Having noticed the previous spring that too many men reporting for the program had been promoted without proper training, CTS staff continued to coerce students to meet high standards by threatening poor performers with demotion. In fact, by June the policy had proven effective.[57] Nevertheless, CMHQ decided to reinforce success by tightening the screws further, authorizing CTS to return to unit any student who did not warrant further training, along with a recommendation for demotion. By this time, demotions could occur even before underperformers reported back to their units.[58] In essence, the course provided demanding catch-up training to not-yet-qualified junior NCOs and weeded out those who had been promoted above their ability or merit. All of this helped ensure that reinforcement NCOs were prepared and ready to join fighting units.

To run this training, CTS had to overcome a serious and familiar problem: finding enough suitable instructors. Ever since the army had dispatched forces to the Mediterranean theatre, the demand for instructors was outstripping supply. In June 1944, the situation became so critical that CMHQ authorized using 25 percent of course graduates as instructors for subsequent serials.[59] Those chosen remained at CTS for four to six months, but before they were allowed to teach, they received a one-week course in methods of instruction. In this regard, CTS was aligned with War Office efforts to improve the quality of instruction across Britain. A recent British survey of training establishments had revealed that too many instructors performed below expectations because they lacked formal training in how to instruct.[60] To redress the problem, British authorities had created mobile "methods of instruction" teams that travelled to training institutions and demonstrated proper teaching methods. Canadian officials took similar action by creating a CTS Methods of Instruction sub-wing that was in lockstep with the War Office program, and with what Canadian authorities were doing back home.[61] (As described in Chapter 6, training authorities in Canada had started providing instruction in "how to teach" in the summer of 1941, and by October 1944, developed a combined methods of instruction and methods of coaching course.) The instruction training at CTS proved worthwhile even for candidates with sound instructional experience.[62] Some started the program confident that they had little to learn, but after completing the training testified that it had been useful. None thought they had wasted their time.

Meanwhile, dramatic changes to the infantry reinforcement system helped boost the supply of NCOs for the reinforcement pool, starting with the June 1944 arrival from Canada of the 13th Canadian Infantry Brigade (13 CIB). The formation did not to deploy onward to Europe or the Mediterranean. Instead, it took on the task of training infantry reinforcements, independent of CRU, and soon assumed responsibility for converting several thousand soldiers into infantrymen as well.[63] The rush was now on to repair the growing shortage of infantry reinforcements. The brigade also produced infantry NCOs who would serve as instructors within 13 CIB, opening an NCO school for that purpose in September.[64] The school ran successive two-week courses that focused on the basic competencies. The brief program covered practical field skills such as weapons handling, fieldcraft, and patrolling.[65] A force-on-force exercise tested candidates in section discipline, night patrols, and the use of ground, and culminated with platoon deliberate attacks.[66] The NCO school ran until at least March 1945, by which time it had trained an estimated 650 NCOs.[67]

In the interest of efficiency, the overseas army soon reorganized its infantry reinforcement training system yet again. In the late fall of 1944, it merged 13 CIB with the Canadian Infantry Reinforcement Units (CIRUs) to form the 13th Canadian Infantry Training Brigade (13 CITB).[68] The new formation assumed responsibility for training *all* infantry reinforcements for the Northwest European and Mediterranean theatres. By mid-December, 13 CITB comprised a brigade headquarters and five Canadian Infantry Training Regiments (CITRs). Each regiment had a depot battalion – responsible for receiving, administering, and dispatching soldiers – and two training battalions, most of them commanded by veteran officers.[69] Under the new system, all infantrymen entering the reinforcement stream, regardless of where they came from – Canada, courses, the medical system, convalescence, or anywhere else – reported to a CITR. After administrative processing in a depot battalion, each man joined a training battalion for several weeks of refresher training.[70]

Table 7.3

Syllabus for two-week NCO conversion course (infantry)

Subject	Periods	Subject	Periods
Appreciations and orders	5	Mines and booby traps	3
Battle procedure	3	Organization and employment	4
Battle tactics	54	Physical training and	
Fundamental training (lectures		hardening	12
by veterans, etc.)	6	Spare	7
Map reading	2	Weapons training	6
Message writing	2	Wireless procedure	4
		Total periods	108

Source: Data from HQ Cdn Reinforcement Units Trg Instruction No. 13, Appendix E (Two Weeks NCO Conversion Course), 10 November 1944, LAC, RG24-C-2, vol. 9804, file 2/Instrns CRU/1/2.

Meanwhile, conversion of NCOs took place in the 10th Canadian Infantry Training Battalion (10 Trg Bn), which was part of 5 CITR, with an eight week NCO conversion program.[71] The first six weeks were a standard infantry conversion course for soldiers of most arms, regardless of rank.[72] Then, a two-week NCO conversion course prepared candidates to perform their leadership duties in battle (see Table 7.3). This short but intensive course included 108 training periods, conducted over five and a half days per week, with periods of night training conducted throughout. Staff designed the syllabus to flow logically from the six-week all-ranks conversion course that candidates had just completed. Fully half of the NCO conversion program covered tactics that these new infantry junior leaders needed to learn, and learn quickly: defensive operations (relief in the line, platoon and company defensive positions, siting platoon and section positions, and protective patrols), the attack (lines of advance, section and platoon fire and movement, the encounter battle, supporting arms, house clearing, cooperation with mortars and with tanks), and reorganization after a battle. The rest of the course dealt with essential skills such as battle procedure, the handling of platoon weapons, and administration (such as hygiene in the field), plus the organization of infantry battalions and armoured regiments and the evacuation of casualties.

Converting other-arms NCOs to infantry was not a straightforward, one-for-one exercise as far as rank was concerned. In the first two serials of 400-plus soldiers, nearly 60 percent were senior NCOs up to warrant officer class 2– experienced, just not infantry experienced. After the NCOs finished their conversion training, appraisal boards convened to confirm their suitability for employment at their higher ranks. A good number were not ready.[73] This should not have come as a surprise, given how much knowledge infantry NCOs required for modern warfare. Could a sergeant from, say, the signals or service corps really be ready to assume the duties of a platoon sergeant in battle after eight weeks of conversion training? Eight weeks was not much time for an NCO to make the mental shift to a new arm, let alone acquire all the skills of an infantry combat leader. That said, with the infantry reinforcement crisis in the late summer and autumn of 1944 causing serious problems in the field and a political crisis at home, the army had to increase the reinforcement pool as quickly as possible, and that included NCOs, so 10 Trg Bn infantry NCOs until the end of the war.[74] By then, the 13th Canadian Infantry Training Brigade (and its predecessor, 13 CIB) had converted an estimated 1,950 NCOs to infantry – no small feat.[75]

How many saw combat with field units is not entirely clear. Only 1.8 percent of senior NCOs in the sample group were remustered from other arms, although the number would be higher if the group included remustered junior NCOs killed in battle, which it does not. Still, this is a seemingly low proportion, given that the overseas army rushed to convert 12,638 other ranks to infantry. Why did so few converted NCOs make it to combat units, as the sample group suggests? While records offer little hard evidence, several contextual factors may have had an effect.

First, most of the conversion program occurred between August 1944 and January 1945.[76] By the time many of the remustered NCOs completed their training and moved through the reinforcement system into holding units in the operational theatres, the fighting formations had entered a period of reduced activity. After the Battle of the Scheldt wrapped up in early November, First Canadian Army experienced three relatively quiet months. Likewise, in Italy, the operational tempo of 1st Canadian Corps dropped to a low level after Christmas and stayed that way until the corps moved to Northwest Europe the following March. So the requirement for reinforcements overall slowed more than planners had expected.

Second, regimental tribalism might have resisted the flow of converted NCOs into field units. Battalions preferred filling NCO vacancies by promoting their own soldiers, men they knew and trusted, rather than accepting unknown reinforcements – and particularly those with little infantry experience. In other words, strong regimental cultures might have resisted the high command's solution for increasing infantry NCO numbers.

Finally, converting NCOs to infantry may simply not have worked well, especially for senior NCOs. The short weeks of training can hardly have been sufficient for transferring the depth of knowledge and experience one needed to lead troops in a fighting battalion, let alone take command of platoons, as sergeants so often did.

Conclusion

The army's centralized NCO training and development programs undoubtedly lightened the load for units that were too busy to run such training on their own. No unit commander could possibly have trained all his own NCOs, even if he had wanted to. Between guarding against a German invasion (at least until the threat dissipated by 1942), participating in collective training, and sending troops to all manner of individual qualification courses, field units had insufficient capacity to run enough NCO training and had to rely on centralized NCO training programs to help produce their NCO and instructor cadres. Centralized training also produced NCOs for the training and reinforcement systems, and brought a strong measure of standardization to a system in which unit commanders held responsibility for developing their own NCO cadres and took unique approaches to doing so.

In Britain, CMHQ established the Canadian Training School, which, as the heart of centralized training for the overseas army, ran NCO qualification and regimental instructor programs for both operational units and the reinforcement system. Meanwhile, CRU exercised an important quality-control function, ensuring that all soldiers in the reinforcement pool, NCOs included, were sufficiently trained to join operational units. And from late 1944, 13 CITB managed all infantry reinforcements, and it converted NCOs and other soldiers to infantry in an effort to alleviate the critical shortage.

While the network of centralized programs played a vital role in building and sustaining the NCO corps, the system required a large NCO establishment of its own. Tension existed between the requirement for NCOs at the sharp end and the need for them in the training system. There were not even enough good NCOs to attend all the programs CTS offered. Staff at CTS complained repeatedly that field units sent ill-prepared men for courses. The trainers were frustrated, partly because they wanted to turn out excellent graduates and partly because they needed to retain some for instructional duty. The message to the field units was "Send us your best," but the units either could not or would not. This was, perhaps, to be expected. After all, what unit commander preparing for battle and bearing the attendant burdens of command would risk losing strong NCOs to CTS training cadres? The army created an invaluable system of centralized NCO training, no doubt, but the field units it served were not always willing or able to play by its rules.

Ultimately, the persistent problem of not having enough strong NCOs to attend courses and to serve as instructors in the reinforcement system reflected the army's greater challenge. That is, the NCO corps was still developing and the army could not quite, in the time available, produce the quantity of experienced and qualified junior leaders needed.

8
Managing the Talent

My dear Harry ... Your Canadians have done magnificently ... My own view is that you ought to now get home to the U.K. a large number of experienced chaps and mix them into your Divisions.

GENERAL B.L. MONTGOMERY TO LIEUTENANT-GENERAL
H.D.G. CRERAR, SICILY, 25 AUGUST 1943

FROM THE TIME THE first Canadian troops landed in Britain, the overseas army grew fitter, more skilled, and better prepared for the task that lay ahead. Over time, the sharp end looked increasingly formidable, as units and formations built up their competence in the business of fighting. Everything behind the sharp end needed to be just as good to keep formations up to strength and operationally effective. As the military leadership well knew, the growing proficiency of the field force had to be matched by proficiency in the reinforcement holding units in Britain and in the training centres in Canada. The whole army needed to keep up with the latest innovations, so that a steady stream of properly trained reinforcements could replace casualties and keep units fighting. And from the outset, protecting the homeland meant that the units guarding Canada's coasts and skies had to keep up with the latest methods as well. Accordingly, authorities implemented several programs to distribute expertise across the force. NCOs played a key part, either as agents for transferring skills and knowledge or as recipients. In both cases, development of the NCO corps profited from projects to spread the latest know-how from the field force to the rest of the army. There were several.

The first project began in October 1940, when Major-General Harry Crerar, as chief of the general staff (CGS), and Lieutenant-General Andrew McNaughton, the senior Canadian officer in Britain, agreed to send field unit soldiers back to Canada as instructors. Designed to elevate the quality of training back home, the program ran for the rest of the war, and many hundreds of hand-picked NCOs went back to Canada for eight-month rotations in the army's training centres. Another program attached groups of Canada-based NCOs to British fighting formations to learn what was new and current in the field army. Yet another dispatched Canada-based NCOs to the Canadian Army Overseas for three-month attachments. Meanwhile, First Canadian Army orchestrated regular NCO rotations between field and reinforcement units. And in early 1943, authorities attached NCOs to British forces in North Africa to gain combat experience that could be shared across the entire Canadian army through written reports and briefings. Finally, after the army began sustained operations, programs transferred battle-experienced NCOs from Italy – and later, Northwest Europe – to the forces in Britain still awaiting deployment. Montgomery's proposal to Crerar to do just that was the start of only one of many initiatives to spread experience, which the army started doing after the so-called Phoney War ended in May 1940. All of these programs were about spreading hard-gained know-how across the NCO corps to stiffen the army's backbone along its whole length.

Sending Experienced NCOs Back to Canada

In the autumn of 1940, the overseas army began sending field unit soldiers to training centres in Canada for temporary instructional duty. At the time, the new system of training centres in Canada was expanding quickly to support the army's rapid growth, as described in Chapter 6. The army had just opened thirty-nine new centres to accommodate the conscripts raised under the National Resources Mobilization Act of 21 June 1940, in addition to fourteen raised earlier that year to train reinforcements. The program to send instructors back to Canada started after the Director of Military Training (DMT) at National Defence Headquarters (NDHQ) proposed bringing soldiers back from Britain in an effort to keep training as up to date as possible.[1] Planners had expected wounded soldiers to fulfill such a role, but the army had yet to begin operations. The immediate result, as Crerar informed McNaughton, was that the army in Canada had no instructors with experience in the latest training methods used in Britain.[2] The CGS proposed a steady rotation of soldiers from Britain to Canada, at least until a stream of returning casualties made the project unnecessary. He suggested starting with small numbers from infantry, artillery, signals, machine-gun, and service corps units. McNaughton agreed.[3] By November, small groups of NCOs and officers from overseas units were returning to teach in the army's training centres in Canada.

From the outset, authorities strove to ensure that only good instructors returned. McNaughton sent the first group to British training centres to absorb the latest teaching techniques, as there were no Canadian schools in Britain yet.[4] (The Canadian Training School had opened the previous August but only provided officer cadet training at this point.) By late October 1940 almost two dozen men, from sergeant to warrant officer class 1, were at British corps-of-arms schools for about ten days of training before making the journey across the Atlantic.[5] By late November, twenty-three NCOs and ten officers were on their way to Canadian training centres.[6]

Throughout 1941, the program took root as a small but increasing stream of carefully chosen soldiers returned to Canada for instructional duty, to good effect. In early February, McNaughton agreed to a request from Crerar for a group of NCOs to teach courses on universal carriers, 2-inch mortars, and the 2-pounder anti-tank gun.[7] As before, McNaughton arranged to give these men refresher training so that they would arrive in Canada with the latest skills. In late April, Crerar asked for another group of au courant instructors, this time seeking thirty-one for various training centres.[8] Again, the Canadian Corps complied.[9] Meanwhile, NDHQ refined the program's terms: soldiers sent for instructional duty could spend a maximum of eight months in Canada before returning overseas, and commandants had to provide NDHQ with written reports on each instructor after his second and seventh months.[10] The first reports painted a positive picture of the program. In mid-May, NDHQ informed Canadian Military Headquarters (CMHQ) that the instructors were rendering good service, and that personnel assessments indicated the individuals had been "very carefully selected and are doing satisfactory work."[11] In mid-October, NDHQ requested yet more instructors, this time about two dozen NCOs and two dozen officers, so that every training centre would have a pair of NCOs and officers with overseas experience.[12] The Canadian Corps turned to its units for nominations, emphasizing that the "object of this policy is to ensure that training methods are kept up-to-date and that full advantage is derived from experience gained by overseas units."[13] The corps complied yet again.[14] By this time, with the program's mechanics established and the concept validated, the flow of instructors back to Canada was set to increase in tandem with the next round of army growth.

In early 1942, the instructor program underwent enormous expansion in support of a training system that was working flat out to increase production. The war was not going well for the Allies, especially with Japanese forces now pushing across the Pacific. On 6 January, cabinet approved the program that would enlarge the overseas force to a two-corps army.[15] Later that month, the new CGS, Lieutenant-General Kenneth Stuart, informed Crerar, who had just taken acting command of the corps in Britain, that NDHQ planned to increase the number of reinforcement training facilities in Canada by 50 percent.[16] The trouble was, Stuart noted, that it would not be feasible to source all the necessary teaching staff in Canada. Could Crerar supply 50 percent of the new instructors?

This was a big request. Stuart needed 875 NCOs and 200 officers from the overseas army, over and above those already provided, to fill new positions in basic and advanced training centres. He also proposed continuing with eight-month tours, meaning that the overseas army would be burdened with supplying future groups of replacement instructors. McNaughton, in Canada at the time, supported rendering whatever help the corps could provide without jeopardizing operational efficiency.[17]

The Canadian Corps set to identifying suitable candidates. On 10 February, corps headquarters advised the formations of the requirement in Canada for hundreds of instructors.[18] Because reinforcement quality depended on good teaching, a large proportion of the instructional staff in Canada should include soldiers with field unit experience, and the corps therefore gave the divisions responsibility for providing the necessary soldiers.[19] In all cases, corps headquarters instructed, "only those who are thoroughly reliable and who have a satisfactory conduct sheet will be considered." As an expediency, corps staff would accept nominations of personnel one rank below any position to be filled, as such individuals could be granted acting rank. And, all other factors being equal, the nominating agencies were to give preference to soldiers who would soon be too old for field unit service.

Crerar even encouraged formations to use the program to shed their older NCOs. It was no coincidence that he did so while Lieutenant-General Bernard Montgomery was conducting visits to the Canadian battalions and finding too many NCOs past the appropriate age. Echoing Montgomery, Crerar told his subordinate commanders,

> It is ... dangerous to retain in a field unit N.C.O.s whose physical and mental energy is no longer sufficient to stand the heavy strain of battle. It is unfair to these men and doubly so to the rank and file of the unit ... Advantage should be taken of the opportunity now afforded to nominate for instructional duties in Canada as many as possible of those officers and N.C.O.s whose age has become a handicap to the performance of their duties under active service conditions.[20]

Days later, Crerar announced that units could nominate more soldiers than ordered, so as to clear out their older men.[21] While army records do not show the extent to which units followed Crerar's advice, several memoirs and regimental histories offer anecdotal evidence that units did post out those who were considered too old.[22] And army records do show that some of the soldiers who returned to Canada as instructors remained there because they no longer met age requirements for overseas service.[23]

Unfortunately for the training system, the Canadian Corps met only a fraction of the total instructor requirement. Shortly after NDHQ made its original request, demand exploded to 2,540 NCOs and 590 officers. Crerar simply did not have enough troops to meet such numbers. He informed Stuart that, while fully appreciating the need to lend as much assistance as possible, the corps could fill only a third of the positions.[24] Improving seasonal conditions increased the likelihood of operations, and supplying the numbers NDHQ requested would degrade operational effectiveness. Nevertheless, Crerar would attempt to provide the higher-ranking NCOs and officers requested, meaning NDHQ would only have to worry about the junior appointments. He made good on the commitment and provided 1,047 instructors, including 854 NCOs.[25] Shortfalls notwithstanding, this was still a significant investment on the part of the deployed army in the training of its future soldiers.

The field units supplying the instructors felt the loss of talent. Just as the demand for instructors in Canada began to climb, so too did demand for first-rate NCOs in units. In early March 1942, for example, the 48th Highlanders of Canada received orders to dispatch twenty-one NCOs and five officers for eight-month instructional tours of duty.[26] Thus, every company probably lost several of its good NCOs – at a time when Montgomery was telling Crerar that too many NCOs in the units he inspected were weak. Similarly, the Royal 22nd Regiment sent back twenty NCOs and four officers, the commanding officer reassuring them of the importance of their mission as they departed. They would "bring back to C[anada] the new ideas in training and the tactics that we have learned and developed ... over two years in E[ngland]."[27] The Royal Canadian Regiment (RCR) felt the heavy impact of losing nineteen NCOs and four officers, as the war diarist recorded: "The bn is slowly adjusting itself to the loss of so many officers and Senior NCO's to C[anada]."[28]

Corporal Burton Harper was one such NCO. An intelligent young soldier, he had done well enough on his M Test to earn an opportunity to apply for a commission, but the North Shore (New Brunswick) Regiment soldier went back to Canada instead, along with two more from his unit. He and a few other NCOs from overseas went to instruct at a basic training centre in Edmundston, New Brunswick, where they stood out as experienced NCOs: "There were three or four of ... us NCOs there who had come back and we were allowed to wear our patches ... as a badge of honour ... I had the Third Div French grey patch on and a couple of them First Div with a red patch. That set us aside, really from the other instructors."[29]

The sample group lends some insight into how the program affected the NCO corps overseas. About 4 percent of the group left field units and returned to

Canada temporarily for instructional duty, although the proportion of the overseas NCO corps who did so must have been higher, given that the sample does not include either men who stayed in Canada after shipping back or those who died at the rank of corporal. The personnel records in the sample also reveal that units lost these men for longer than eight months, partly because they often remained in Canada for longer than planned and partly because they entered the reinforcement stream on return to Britain and had to wait for vacancies to open up in their units. For example, in June 1943, Sergeant Viateur Paré of Le Régiment de la Chaudière returned to Canada and instructed at the Officers Training Centre in Trois-Rivières, Quebec, and the A12 Infantry Training Centre in Farnham.[30] Ten months later, he returned to Britain and joined a reinforcement unit. On 8 June 1944, Paré finally returned to Les Chaudières, a full year after having left the unit and two days after it stormed ashore at Normandy. In some cases, units never saw their men again. In March 1942, Corporal James Masterson of the RCR returned to Canada, where he instructed at the Number 12 Basic Training Centre in Chatham, Ontario, and at the A29 Advanced Infantry Training Centre in Listowel (later Ipperwash), until February 1943.[31] He landed back in Britain in March, a full year after having left the RCR, and went into a reinforcement unit. In November, he deployed to Italy through the reinforcement stream, and in late December, finally rejoined a field unit, the West Nova Scotia Regiment – not the RCR.

Over the spring of 1942, rapid army growth exacerbated the shortage of instructors in Canada. For the home defence force, NDHQ had recently authorized completing the establishment of the 7th Canadian Division and three new brigades for the 8th Canadian Division, and it wanted 161 sergeants and 75 officers from the overseas army to make it happen.[32] McNaughton replied that he simply could not meet the request.[33] In the previous four months, the corps had returned over 3,000 non-commissioned soldiers and almost 700 officers to fill instructional and organizational vacancies in Canada. Consequently, formations had lost a sizable portion of their talent, just as the new First Canadian Army headquarters and the 2nd Canadian Corps were standing up. Furthermore, the reinforcement units in Britain had recently taken on the added burden of training reinforcements who had not finished their basic training in Canada. And the problem worsened. By early August, training centres across Canada actually had a collective deficit of 1,020 NCOs and 420 officers, a gap that continued to widen as new training centres opened for battle drill and paratroops and as existing centres increased their establishments.[34] As Daniel Byers explains, when Ottawa expanded the home defence force to three divisions in 1942, finding enough qualified NCOs and officers proved so difficult that units in the 8th Division received authorization to recruit university students who had received incomplete training in the Canadian Officers' Training Corps and even to give direct commissions to civilian businessmen.[35] Stuart discussed the deteriorating situation with McNaughton, who acknowledged the importance of returning experienced instructors to Canada but stated plainly his inability to meet the demand.[36] He would try to meet 25 percent of the requirement over the next two months. That was the best that he could do.

Staff still worked hard to ensure that appropriate candidates went back. In fact, CMHQ implemented a new and more rigorous selection process. On 10 September CMHQ sent out a call for nominations, stating that units were to consider, above all, an individual's instructional ability and qualifications.[37] Nominees were also to be "thoroughly reliable" and have a good record of conduct. CMHQ would review all files, rejecting any unsuitable ones and demanding replacements from the affected units. Then, a board of officers convened by CMHQ would interview the candidates to confirm their suitability. Those who made the final cut would proceed to Canada for the standard eight-month period. They would depart in two drafts, half in October and half in November. That plan unfolded largely as CMHQ intended, as staff raised and dispatched the two groups.[38]

The always difficult task of finding quality candidates for instructional duty in Canada grew even harder after the Canadians joined the Allied war effort in the Mediterranean in the summer of 1943. In early August, for example, NDHQ sent CMHQ a fresh demand, this time for 143 NCOs, all sergeants and corporals, to replace Canada-based instructors due to return to Britain. As before, CMHQ set out to fill the demand.[39] It reiterated to units that nominees should be carefully selected but also cautioned units not to nominate too many older soldiers, because sending large numbers would produce in Canada a glut of instructors unable to return overseas and thereby staunch the westbound flow of those with recent experience. Meanwhile, CMHQ warned NDHQ that the difficulties in meeting demands for candidates had worsened because the pool of potential instructors in Britain had shrunk with the deployment of forces to Italy.[40] Nevertheless, by late September, CMHQ had assembled a list of suitable candidates, which it forwarded to NDHQ, along with a reminder that staff still had to interview each man to confirm suitability prior to dispatch.[41] As it turned out, this quality-control mechanism proved necessary.

Some units used the program to shed unwanted soldiers. While vetting nominations, CMHQ staff identified eight officers who clearly did not meet requirements yet had received commanding officer endorsement.[42] The unsuitable batch represented 17 percent of the officers returning to Canada. Would there

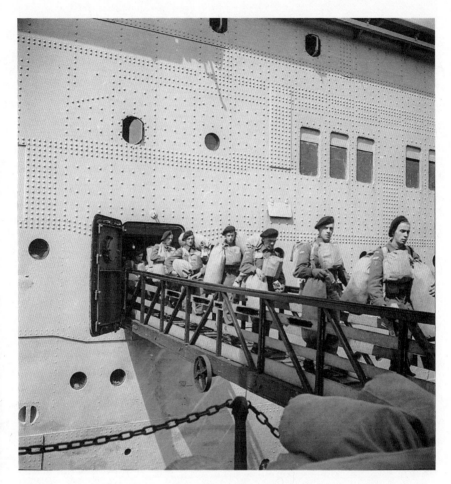

Figure 8.1 The Army strove to ensure that reinforcements like these soldiers arriving in England in June 1943 were well trained before they left Canada by some of the army's most experienced NCOs. | Library and Archives Canada/Department of National Defence fonds/a204806.

be a similar proportion of unacceptable NCOs? Following interviews, twenty-five had to be replaced.[43] CMHQ concluded that these cases constituted evident "unloading" by field units. While acknowledging that many of the army's best instructors had already gone back to Canada, staff feared that unloading would undermine efforts to give reinforcements proper training.

As might have been predicted, the supply of potential instructors for Canada continued to dwindle despite best efforts. In January 1944, Canadian Reinforcement Units (CRU), now the main source of instructors for Canada, experienced considerable difficulty finding the 303 instructors NDHQ had recently called for, with units submitting only 172 nominations.[44] Headquarters CRU ordered commanding officers to look again, reminding them that reinforcement quality depended on it. After scraping their barrels, they came up with just fifty-five more names.[45] Shortly after, CMHQ staff suggested that the program for rotating instructors through Canada was no longer practical because, with 1st Canadian Corps committed to Italy and the remainder of First Canadian Army preparing for pending operations in Northwest Europe, instructors had to come solely from CRU's limited resources. CRU needed instructors as much as Canada did, but the policy of sending the best back to Canada was causing teaching standards in CRU to slip.[46] Besides, fewer soldiers wanted to return to Canada, and CMHQ had even started to order soldiers to do so against their will.

Nonetheless, CMHQ decided to strengthen vetting procedures despite the risk it would diminish the number of approved NCOs.[47] Lieutenant-General Kenneth Stuart, now CMHQ chief of staff, ordered CRU to establish a selection board to conduct the final vetting of all nominations. Chaired by a lieutenant-colonel and filled with representatives of all arms and services, the board was to confirm or reject each nominated soldier, bearing in mind the requirement to provide Canada with the best instructors available. The board stood up as directed, and before long began screening out unsuitable candidates. In late April, the board interviewed 219 NCOs and 123 officers, and accepted only 116 and 47, respectively.[48] This fell far short of NDHQ's requirement for 183 NCOs and 88 officers. Explaining the high rejection rate to CMHQ, the board's president indicated that 58 percent of those disallowed had no instructional experience or were unsuitable, prompting suspicion that units were continuing their attempts to rid themselves of unwanted personnel. Another 32 percent lacked sufficient instructional experience, and the remaining 10 percent had various shortcomings, such as no field experience or inadequate time overseas. Much of this was short-sighted. A blanket demand for instructional experience meant casting aside soldiers, including some with combat experience, who could have made good teachers with a bit of training. Incredibly, the board rejected roughly half of all nominees recently returned from Italy.[49] The president blamed the resulting shortages on reinforcement units that "appeared to withhold desirable nominees until pressed to fill vacancies," which was probably an inaccurate assessment.[50]

CRU commander Major-General John Roberts was not buying it. Believing that selection standards were only making matters worse, he proposed corrective action.[51] The Canadian Army Overseas required a plan to *develop* more instructors because CRU simply could not keep up with demands. In the preceding six weeks alone, CRU had received requests for 514 instructors (NCOs and officers), while the reinforcement units themselves needed to maintain over 2,500. Furthermore, everyone employing instructors now wanted them to have battle experience, which resulted in high demand for soldiers returned from operations due to wounds, battle weariness, and other causes. Experience had shown, however, that battle experience alone did not necessarily turn a soldier into a good instructor. Roberts subscribed to the British belief that with proper training in methods of instruction, any competent NCO or officer could quickly be taught to instruct. Inspired by the War Office project that raised mobile "methods of instruction" teams, he argued that the Canadians needed a similar organization for raising the standard of teaching – focusing not on particular subject matter but on how well instructors imparted their knowledge.[52] His proposal that the Canadian Training School (CTS) establish a methods of instruction wing for such purposes eventually bore fruit. Shortly after D-Day, CTS established its wing that conformed to War Office policy for improving instructional skills.

Soon after, the dearth of soldiers with an aptitude for teaching compelled authorities on both sides of the Atlantic to settle on new terms for sending instructors to Canada. Future serials were to include just fifty to seventy-five NCOs and twenty-five to thirty-five officers. The NCO group, normally comprising corporals and sergeants, had to include some warrant officers class 2. New serials were to proceed every other month. The new CTS methods of instruction wing would select and vet nominations. And finally, successful soldiers would undergo the CTS methods of instruction course and additional specialized training if necessary. They would also receive the most current training syllabuses and précis.[53] These new terms went into effect in the late summer. Unfortunately, the reduced flow of instructors returning to Canada occurred just as demand was increasing.

In fact, the instructor shortage in Canada worsened after the invasion of Normandy. In July, senior NDHQ officials held a series of training conferences with local district and training centre authorities. In all locations, officers reported increasing difficulty in identifying potential instructors among the cohorts of trainees passing through the system.[54] Furthermore, many of the suitable candidates, eager to deploy overseas, had no desire to remain in Canada as instructors. Instructing raw recruits in basic training was particularly unpopular. With fewer soldiers returning to Canada to teach, the army looked for other ways to fill NCO billets in the training centres. In the late summer of 1944, NDHQ allowed schools to hold former students as instructors for longer than eight months.[55]

While the quantity of instructors returning from Britain was insufficient, at least the quality was good. In mid-July, NDHQ gave CMHQ positive feedback on the most recent batches, and CMHQ passed the good news to CRU: "The great majority of these reports [from Canada] are excellent, and disclose that instrs returned from UK are well qualified and enthusiastic. At the same time the reports show that these personnel are appreciated by Trg Centres in Canada, and are being used to good advantage."[56] Twenty-six NCOs, a relatively small number, had not worked out well, although this number included some who, despite positive attitudes, were hamstrung by age or medical conditions. Cases like these were to be expected, as the army had to find useful ways of employing those who were too old or medically unfit for combat duty, provided they had instructional ability.

From a purely quantitative perspective, the project to send instructors back to Canada had a discernible effect, even if it the numbers were fewer than authorities wanted. By the end of August 1944, all training centres in Canada had at least a modest cadre of instructors from overseas, including many with battle experience. And by late October, each training centre typically had between a handful and two dozen NCOs and up to nine officers on loan from the Canadian Army Overseas.[57]

Still, the army just barely managed to continue the program until the end of the war.[58] By April 1945, the scheme was almost untenable, as a staff officer in Britain warned NDHQ: "You cannot get blood out of a stone ... There soon will be no personnel available from which to cho[o]se instructors for Canada."[59] In late May, the last group, consisting of just sixty NCOs and thirty-seven officers, returned to Canada.[60] By then, the program had provided about 1,900 NCOs and 590 officers for instructional duty at home since its inception in 1940.

From the sample group, the case of Edward Cronk illustrates the program's importance. In April 1940, Cronk enlisted for active duty in the Edmonton Fusiliers from the Non-Permanent Active Militia (NPAM).[61] He rose to corporal in just five months, and to sergeant in just over fourteen. The army employed him in training centres until he deployed to Britain in February 1944, at the rank of sergeant. There, he joined an infantry reinforcement unit. On 23 June, Cronk went to France in the reinforcement stream and on 7 July, for the first time in his wartime career, he finally joined an active field unit, the Royal Winnipeg Rifles.[62] The reinforcement system produced many hundreds if not thousands of Edward Cronks, who served for long periods as NCOs nowhere near a field unit. The army correctly assessed that it had to give them as much up-to-date expertise as possible while they served in Canada, because there might not be much time after they deployed overseas to bring them up to field unit standards.

Sending Soldiers Overseas for Short Attachments

Spreading experience across the NCO corps also necessitated sending soldiers across the Atlantic in the other direction. In fact, the army started contemplating the first of several such projects just weeks before it initiated the program to cycle instructors from the overseas army through the training system at home. In mid-1940, concerned about the fast pace of developments in operating coastal defence systems, NDHQ staff decided that "troops in Canada should be kept up to date in all latest methods so that organization and training may conform in all respects to those followed by United Kingdom Forces."[63] In August, NDHQ therefore asked the War Office to accept a plan to send Canadian NCOs to Britain on short attachments for the purpose of updating these home defence soldiers' skills. NDHQ proposed a series of group attachments that would run for consecutive three-month periods. The first would be a modest one, for just thirteen NCOs. The War Office agreed, and before long NDHQ had selected suitable candidates and shipped them overseas. In mid-November, they joined their British units.[64] The first round lasted a bit longer than planned, and in mid-March 1941, the men returned home with four months of training in the latest methods.[65]

The War Office supported a slightly more ambitious scheme for the next group, made up of armoured corps soldiers. At the time, Canada's nascent armoured forces, the Canadian Army Tank Brigade and the Canadian Armoured Division, were forming in Canada, so NDHQ appealed for NCO attachments to British armoured units with a view to gaining "the latest information on Armoured Corps training."[66] Canada also wanted to attach soldiers to an armoured division's artillery, engineer, and service corps elements, which brought the Canadian request to forty-four NCO attachments. The War Office obliged. The troops – a mix of corporals and sergeants, plus several staff sergeants and squadron sergeants major – arrived in Britain in late April and joined their hosting units.[67] The attachments lasted three months, as planned, and at the end of July CMHQ ordered the freshly trained soldiers back to Canada.[68] The program proved so successful that it continued for another year.[69]

In the end, just over 100 Canadian NCOs from armoured, armoured reconnaissance, and armoured car regiments, plus some coastal defence and anti-air personnel, participated in the scheme. Though the numbers were small, these soldiers no doubt passed the knowledge they brought back to many more. The attachment program gave a shot in the arm to NCO proficiency by upgrading skills in several arms of service with the latest methods developed overseas.

Another program imported expertise into Canada by sending NCOs and officers from home defence units to the Canadian Army Overseas for three-month stints. The scheme, which the CGS stated would "afford officers and N.C.O.s of units in a Home Defence role an opportunity of service overseas," commenced in the autumn of 1941.[70] Home defence units of battalion or equivalent size each sent four soldiers – a junior NCO, a senior NCO, a junior officer, and a senior officer – while units of company or equivalent size sent only one NCO and one officer. As one tour ended another began, and the process repeated on a continuous cycle. The first of four rotations included soldiers from nineteen infantry battalions, among them units from W Force, the Canadian contingent securing Newfoundland. The program ran until July 1943. By then, more than 200 NCOs and a similar number of officers had spent time with overseas units, enough for all home defence units to have a group of NCOs with recent overseas experience.[71]

Yet another program drew on overseas expertise by sending unit instructional staff on short attachments to Canadian units in Britain, commencing in early 1943. The increasing proportion of conscripts in home defence units meant that the army in Canada required particularly strong instructors, but the best tended to find ways of proceeding overseas, some even reverting in rank if necessary. Consequently, the proficiency of unit instructional personnel remaining in Canada had become relatively low. To fix that, NDHQ wanted to send instructional staff from home defence units of all arms on attachment to units in Britain. CMHQ more than obliged, arranging courses and tailored instruction for the visiting NCOs.[72] During their time overseas, these instructors spent one month with a field unit, one month with a reinforcement unit, and one month attending British and Canadian training schools.[73] The program institutionalized a previously ad hoc arrangement – about 200 NCOs and officers had made similar visits to Britain before the program began – and it helped disseminate expertise to Canada without taking any personnel away from the field units in Britain.

The army kept sending instructors from home defence units to field units in Britain for short attachments until the initiation of Operation Overlord, and with good effect. Each group from Canada included about sixty NCOs and sixty officers. The periods of attachment continued to last three months, during which "both First Cdn Army and CRU as well as British Trg establishments did their best to make the visit[s] both profitable and enjoyable."[74] NDHQ certainly believed the program had merit. In late April 1944, staff had plans underway for a seventh serial and hoped to continue sending attachments for the foreseeable future.[75] But with Operation Overlord quickly approaching, the program ceased. Still, six serials had run between early 1943 and mid-1944, giving valuable experience to about 360 NCOs (and a similar number of officers) who carried it back to Canada.[76] Spread across the army at home, such numbers provided most major units of all arms with about six NCO instructors and six officers with some overseas experience, which they presumably spread further.

Sending Canada-based soldiers to Britain for short attachments constituted one of the smaller pieces of a larger mosaic of programs to develop the NCO corps across the army. Still, it played an important part in strengthening the home army's backbone at a time when much of the rank and file were serving involuntarily.

Posting Permanent Force NCOs to the Canadian Army Overseas

In late 1940 and early 1941, senior military officials on both sides of the Atlantic discussed posting Canada-based permanent force NCOs to the army overseas. The CGS had grown concerned that too many professional soldiers remained in Canada "engaged on instructional, technical or operational work" in support of raising forces.[77] This came as no surprise, given that the army's mobilization plans required at least 20 percent of the permanent force to run qualification courses and raise reinforcements at newly established training schools in Canada. Authorities counted about 460 NCOs from across several arms of service – artillery, engineers, infantry, medical, service, signals, and ordnance corps – who needed to update their expertise as they were likely to continue serving in the postwar army. NDHQ staff believed that the Canadian Corps should make room for them by sending other troops back to Canada.

By and large, the Canadian Corps division commanders and heads of supporting arms and services supported bringing these NCOs to Britain.[78] They were less inclined to engage in the other side of the equation: sending personnel back to Canada as part of the exchange. Many senior officers thought that the rapid expansion had already spread NCO talent too thinly across the overseas army. The corps senior artillery officer thought an overlap of two or three months should occur for any personnel exchanges. Others, including the chief engineer, the chief signal officer, and the director of supply and transport, thought the process should occur only gradually. The deputy director of medical services did not want to take anyone above the rank of staff sergeant because it was difficult to integrate higher-ranking NCOs who lacked recent experience. And the commander of 1st Canadian Division did not support returning men to Canada at all. Such reservations notwithstanding, Canadian Corps headquarters agreed to make room for these soldiers as long as the program occurred progressively and on a relatively small scale at first.[79] In early February 1941, NDHQ and CMHQ agreed to start with a trial party of twenty-five soldiers who would conduct a two-week handover.[80]

The program soon ran into problems. The first twenty-five, who came from several arms of service, set sail for Britain in April 1941.[81] Most were senior NCOs, from sergeant to warrant officer class 1. Staff in Ottawa soon realized that it would be awkward for formations to create vacancies for soldiers with senior non-commissioned rank by pushing aside trusted incumbents. The adjutant-general, Major-General B.W. Browne, attempted to resolve the problem. After all, Browne reminded senior Canadian officials in Ottawa and London, the army needed to provide these soldiers with overseas experience "to broaden their knowledge and to increase their value to the service in the postwar years."[82] Therefore, NDHQ introduced new rules designed to make things easier for the receiving units: personnel arriving from Canada would, if necessary, join their new units on a supernumerary basis until establishment positions opened up, and if no vacancy existed in a receiving unit's establishment for personnel holding acting rank, the soldier would revert to his confirmed rank.

Despite these allowances, over the next few months, NDHQ made only slight progress sending permanent force NCOs overseas. The first group of twenty-five did not even arrive safely in Britain. These men were aboard the SS *Nerissa*, the only Canadian troop-carrying vessel during the war to fall prey to the German U-boat menace. On 30 April, a submarine attacked and sank the ship northwest of Ireland. Most of the passengers perished, and only eight of the program's soldiers survived.[83] A second group had better luck. In early July, a group of twenty-one NCOs arrived, representing a variety of arms and services.[84] But shortly after, the program bogged down.

From the overseas army's perspective, the project provided little benefit and could not continue without major changes. In theory, absorbing the permanent force soldiers should have been easy because units would send back to Canada soldiers of equivalent rank, and because NDHQ had allowed more-senior personnel to remain with units on a supernumerary basis until vacancies opened.[85] In reality, units tended to use the supernumerary option without sending anyone back. CMHQ believed that this had "caused embarrassment" for the arriving professional soldiers who did not receive appointments commensurate to their ranks. Furthermore, CMHQ learned, in some cases the NCOs from Canada were unable to do the jobs that corresponded to their rank, with Canadian Corps headquarters complaining in mid-August that the program had "not proved entirely satisfactory."[86] Corps staff therefore made several suggestions for amending the terms: NDHQ should place permanent force soldiers who required overseas experience into units and formations in Canada that were preparing to join the overseas army; soldiers for whom no such vacancies existed should receive consideration for attachment to units in Britain only on receipt of a recommendation as "fully suitable for employment in their rank in a field unit"; NDHQ should supply Canadian Corps with a list of available warrant officers class 1 and 2, showing their qualifications, so that the corps could request particular individuals as required; and the corps should have authority to keep suitable NCOs as surplus to war establishment for up to six months while they awaited an appropriate vacancy. Furthermore, corps staff argued, no additional groups should come to Britain until NDHQ had reviewed these recommendations. CMHQ passed the proposals to NDHQ, concurring that they required attention before any further groups were dispatched.[87] But the only recommendation that NDHQ seemed to accept was the one about six-month supernumeraries, as no further groups followed.[88] McNaughton pronounced the program dead in April 1942.[89]

The failed program revealed an unanticipated cost of keeping permanent force troops in Canada. These career soldiers remained distant from the modernization occurring overseas, and their status as experts deteriorated. And although the unimpressive performance of some permanent force soldiers who made it overseas validated the need for the program, this meant little to units preparing for battle. In the grand scheme of things, the approximately 460 permanent force NCOs the program sought to develop represented only a small part of the growing army. Nevertheless, that a requirement for such a program existed raised old questions about the best way to employ permanent force NCOs during wartime. Were they primarily an instructional cadre, or were they also the skeleton of a mobilizing force? What was their role in developing the wartime NCO corps? As the program ground to a halt, these questions remained unanswered.

Rotating Soldiers between Field Units and the Reinforcement Pool

Keeping reinforcements trained to a sufficiently high standard and skilled in the latest methods was crucial to the army's capacity to continue fighting while taking casualties. The senior leadership therefore rotated field unit personnel with two distinct groups in the Canadian Reinforcement Units (CRU): NCOs serving as instructors in CRU training wings, and NCO reinforcements themselves. Authorities understood that taking experienced NCOs out of the field units, even temporarily, could undermine unit proficiency. But the cost was justifiable because constantly evolving field unit expertise had to be disseminated to the reinforcement system. The quality of soldiers who would move forward to replace casualties depended on it.

In the fall of 1942, CRU implemented a policy of temporarily exchanging instructors in its training wings with field unit personnel. CRU training instructions stipulated that the standard of its instructors must be constantly improved, and that keeping instructional skills sharp necessitated such rotation on a six-month basis.[90] The policy permitted no exceptions, even prohibiting training wings from retaining instructors of "exceptional ability" for longer than half a year. About 5 percent of the sample group in this text rotated from field to reinforcement units and back again – a fairly high number considering the nature of the sample. (That is, many individuals in this group did not receive NCO rank until they went into action, many did not arrive in Britain until later in the war, and many reported to a reinforcement unit in the first place.) The proportion of NCOs across the overseas army who rotated between field and reinforcement units as instructors must have been much larger. An example from the group demonstrates how the program typically worked on the field unit side. In June 1943, the Regina Rifle Regiment posted Lance Sergeant James Jacobs, who had been in a field unit since enlisting in July 1940, to a training company in 2 Canadian Infantry Reinforcement Unit (2 CIRU), as staff "on rotation."[91] Shortly after arriving, he rose in rank to sergeant. Jacobs surely had much to pass on to the reinforcements under his charge. He had been in Britain with his regiment since September 1941 and would have participated in the major training events the field units went through, including battle drill programs and the progressive, physically demanding collective training exercises of 1942. He had also picked up a qualification as a platoon weapons instructor (CMHQ Course 303) shortly before reporting to 2 CIRU. After completing a five-month tour there, he returned to the Regina Rifles, again on rotation, and continued to serve with the unit until he was killed in Normandy on 8 June 1944.

Before long, the chain of command decided that it had to expand the program to cross-pollinate expertise from the field units to the reinforcement system. In March 1943, First Canadian Army headquarters presented to CMHQ a plan to rotate reinforcements, not just their instructors, through the field units.[92] A growing number of new soldiers in the expanding reinforcement pool required posting into field units to give them experience and to keep morale high. First Canadian Army believed that monthly exchanges of up to 10 percent of each field unit's strength should occur. CMHQ concurred with the proposal, which quickly became policy. First Canadian Army headquarters notified its formations, stressing the policy's well-reasoned goals: to ensure that reinforcements gained field unit experience; to maintain morale in the reinforcement pool; to intensify the extant liaison between field and reinforcement units; to exercise field units in replacing battle casualties through the requirement to reorganize periodically and absorb reinforcements; and to support a future policy of sending on courses only soldiers in the reinforcement pool, allowing field units to focus on progressive collective training.[93] Rotations were to occur each month. These monthly turnovers, combined with other forms of wastage, would not exceed 12.5 percent of a unit's strength.

While it is not clear whether aspirations to rotate such large numbers each month became reality, the program certainly succeeded in moving many NCOs between field and reinforcement units. Almost 7 percent of the soldiers in the sample group, in addition to the instructors indicated above, rotated through the reinforcement units at least once, and sometimes twice.[94] The amount of time individuals spent in reinforcement units varied greatly, from as little as one month up to twenty-three months. Generally speaking, however, rotations lasted roughly six months. In June 1942, the Princess Patricia's Canadian Light Infantry (PPCLI) posted Corporal John Buck to 1 Division Infantry Reinforcement Unit (1 DIRU) as part of a rotation of NCOs.[95] Eight months later, he rotated back to the Patricias. Sometimes NCOs flowed in the other direction. Sergeant William Murray of the Queen's Own Rifles (QOR) went to a reinforcement unit on arriving in Britain in January 1943, and served in 3 and 4 CIRUs.[96] In May, he rotated to the QOR for a three-month stint, then returned to 4 CIRU as part of a routine rotation of NCOs. In late December 1943, he rotated back to the Queen's Own and remained with the unit until he was killed in action on 9 July 1944.

The policy helped ensure that skills and knowledge building up in the field units migrated to the reinforcement system. Rotations afforded reinforcement NCOs like Sergeant Murray the opportunity to serve in a field unit, and therefore to participate in collective training otherwise not available at CRU. And they allowed units to get to know their reinforcement NCOs. When Murray reported to the QOR in December 1943, the battalion already knew him from his previous rotation. The rotations also placed experienced field unit NCOs like Corporal Buck into the reinforcement pool for short periods. In essence, the policy helped prepare the army's reinforcement NCOs to step up when the time came to replace battle casualties. And when it did, units relied heavily on reinforcement NCOs. Company Sergeant Major (CSM) Charles Martin of the QOR describes just how high turnover was at the sub-unit level. By the time his company had finished its part in clearing the channel ports, only one officer and seventeen other ranks remained out of the 120 men who had landed at Normandy.[97] Reinforcements arrived but high turnover continued. To give but one example, after Operation Blockbuster in early March 1945, Martin states,

> we needed major reinforcement and the time to regroup. Our company had lost Dick Medland, our commander, all the platoon commanders and all our NCOs, except Jackie Bland (a sergeant), Bert Shepherd (a corporal) and myself ... Out of over 120 men, we had maybe 40 left. At least a dozen of us wore bandages on wounds considered minor, more or less.[98]

Attaching Soldiers to British Forces in a Theatre of War

No matter how hard soldiers trained, green and untested troops remained green and untested until they got battle experience. Appreciating this, in 1943, authorities ran a program to give Canadian soldiers much-needed exposure to combat operations by attaching NCOs and officers to the First British Army in North Africa. By the time the program finished in the early summer, hundreds of soldiers had acquired valuable operational experience, and CMHQ sprinkled that experience across the army when the soldiers returned to their Canadian units.

The program's genesis dated to late 1942. After more than three years of war, senior officers had grown concerned that Canadian troops still had little or no combat experience. So, a month after the 8 November Operation Torch landings in North Africa, Canadian officials made plans to send 140 NCOs and officers from the Canadian Army Overseas to the First British Army on attachment for three months.[99] The 1st Canadian Corps headquarters ordered formations to nominate soldiers from across the arms and services, so that the whole force would profit from the scheme. NCOs had to be sergeants or above, while officers could not be higher than major.[100] Carefully selected soldiers would join British units to perform duties, not merely observe. "The object of this," a 1st Canadian Corps instruction declared, "is to enable them to obtain first-hand information on actual battle conditions, which on their return ... they will pass on to the Cdn Army Overseas." On 3 January 1943, the first group, comprising sixty-three NCOs and seventy-eight officers, arrived in Algiers.[101] Thereafter, another fifty or so Canadians joined First British Army each month until May. Five groups eventually deployed, providing a total 147 NCOs and 201 officers with first-hand experience in combat operations.

The British treated the Canadians as though they were reinforcements, and this worked well as it ensured that they received appropriate employment. On arriving in Algiers, Canadian troops went to First Army's base depot, where each soldier received his operational assignment. Although the British posted these soldiers as "surplus to establishment," units often absorbed their Canadians into existing vacancies. And to the extent possible, the British gave each soldier employment suitable to his rank, trade, and experience. On the whole, the British treated the Canadians very well, offering every hospitality and useful employment opportunities.[102] The program proved a great success. One of the two most senior participants, Lieutenant-Colonel W.A. Bean of the Highland Light Infantry of Canada, reported after his tour that the Canadians had gained "invaluable" experience that would serve the army well when it began its own operations. Furthermore, Bean stated, the Canadians had made a favourable impression on the British, partly because participants had been carefully selected. In many cases, British officers had asked to keep their Canadians beyond the term of employment.[103] Other soldiers reported on the program's value as well. One junior infantry officer wrote that he had "learned as much in 5 days as one learns in 3 mths in England," remarking: "Our training in England since the introduction of battle drill has been pretty good but no scheme can approach the physical and mental discomfort of actual battle. If I am able to get across some ideas on my return it should make the initial impact of actual battle less severe on our troops."[104] The experience of combat also built the confidence of the Canadian participants.

Enough battle-experienced personnel came out of North Africa to ensure that every Canadian field unit had at least one soldier to assist in the final preparations for operations in 1943 and 1944.[105] The North Shore (New Brunswick) Regiment was lucky enough to have two unit members who had served in North Africa. In mid-April 1943, CSM F.E. Daley and Captain A.M. MacMillan provided lectures on their North African experiences to each of the unit's companies.[106] Elsewhere, the army even managed to send some of the knowledge back to Canada. Sergeant William MacLeod, for example, had served as a mortar detachment commander in North Africa, and rejoined his unit in Sicily after his tour.[107] After seeing a little action there, he received orders to return to Britain to pass on his battle knowledge to other soldiers still in training. Shortly after that, the army ordered him to Canada to pass on his experience to trainees, which he did at the A14 Infantry Training Centre in Aldershot, Nova Scotia.

Practical lessons were disseminated across the army by the soldiers who had learned them and in the reports those soldiers produced. Written reports described certain hard lessons of combat: "It will be found that during battle nearly everyone loses his appetite not through fear but from being 'keyed up' and ready for anything. However, this loss of appetite tends to lower resistance to fatigue. A bde order to the effect that all ranks must have a hot meal at night

Figure 8.2   At A14 Infantry Training Centre in Aldershot, Nova Scotia, Sergeant William MacLeod shows Sergeant Taylor a medal taken from a German prisoner of war when MacLeod was in action with British forces in North Africa. | Canadian War Museum, PER FOLIO UD A544, *Aldershot News* 1, 10 (December 1943).

was issued."[108] Elsewhere, tank crews learned bailing-out drills to be executed when an air threat existed: as soon as an enemy aircraft was detected, often by an alert air sentry, tank crews evacuated their vehicles, carrying haversacks with essential personal supplies. Crewmen had about thirty seconds to complete the drill before the first burst from the aircraft could tear into their vehicle. Failure to detect an aircraft or to bail out when one appeared had resulted in the death of crews on several occasions. One report even advised: "All ranks should know that it is suicidal to remain in the vehicle."[109] Removing heavy clothing in a tank could be fatal as well: "Many casualties were caused by serious burns, [and] in most cases where tank crews were wearing shorts or had taken off their jackets and shirts these proved fatal." [110] Crews needed to wear clothing that was tight-fitting around the ankles, wrists, and neck. Other reports discussed German tactics such as drawing fire at long distances to identify British positions, or leading assaults with heavy tanks and infiltrating with light armour supported by infantry.[111] Sergeant L.W. McCulloch of the Lord Strathcona's Horse, who had had some hair-raising close-combat experiences while serving as a troop sergeant with the 2nd Lothians and Border Horse, emphasized that tanks had to train closely with other arms, especially the infantry.[112] Various Canadian headquarters distributed all this valuable knowledge by circulating the reports widely. For example, headquarters 4th Canadian Armoured Division disseminated reports it had received from the field to CMHQ, First Canadian Army, 2nd Canadian Corps, and the army's three armoured corps reinforcement units at CRU. And CMHQ staff distilled important observations into a pamphlet called *Notes from Theatres of War*, which also received wide distribution.[113]

Not surprisingly, sending Canadian soldiers to acquire battle experience resulted in casualties. One of the soldiers in the sample group, Sergeant Arthur Lacroix of the Cameron Highlanders of Ottawa, for example, arrived in North Africa on 1 February 1943 to join the Lancashire Fusiliers.[114] While conducting reconnaissance in a Bren carrier and attempting to draw fire to determine the enemy's location, Lacroix struck a land mine. He initially survived the blast but lost both legs and was close to death. A party sent to retrieve Lacroix never found him, and authorities believed that the Germans had recovered and buried his remains without leaving any record of the location. Other soldiers became casualties, too. By the time the program wrapped up, eight soldiers had either been killed in action or died of wounds.[115] Another fifteen were wounded but survived, and two officers became prisoners of war, one dying in enemy captivity. These were the costs of this necessary mission to acquire battle experience for the Canadian army in the final months of its preparations for operations.

The North Africa scheme had a direct and indirect impact on the NCO corps. Some 147 NCOs received valuable battle experience, a small number relative to the army's size, but a much larger indirect impact was felt as the lessons they learned rippled through the field force through written reports and direct contact with their units.

Distributing NCO Battle Experience from Italy to the Forces in Britain

As the metallurgist adds tin to copper to make a hard bronze alloy, the senior Canadian military leadership fortified its green forces in Britain by adding battle-experienced soldiers fresh from the fighting in Italy. In late August 1943, with the Canadians in Sicily having just finished their first major campaign, Montgomery encouraged McNaughton in an enterprise that eventually sent about 1,000 battle-hardened NCOs and officers back to Britain.[116] Putting the plan into action took two months, as staffs worked out arrangements, but the final scheme operated on a head-for-head exchange basis, with parties dispatched from Britain each month and exchanges occurring only after the fresh troops arrived in theatre.[117] The first group, a roughly even mix of NCOs and officers from across the arms and services, left Britain in late October on Exercise Pooch, the codename for the project.[118] The NCOs ranged from corporal to regimental sergeant major (RSM), but most were corporals or sergeants. By the end of the year, 550 soldiers of all ranks from Britain had arrived in theatre and joined either the 1st Canadian Infantry Division or the 1st Canadian Armoured Brigade, and about 250 battle-experienced men were on their way back to Britain, with more to follow on a monthly basis.[119] The returning NCOs, about 130 of them, were mostly corporals and sergeants, but also included 7 RSMs and 25 company or squadron sergeants major (CSM/SSMs).

In mid-January 1944, CMHQ directed that 25 percent of the returning veterans go to field units, through the standard process of reporting first to CRU and awaiting call-up by a unit with a vacancy.[120] The rest were to instruct in reinforcement units until the next group arrived from Italy, after which time they would enter the reinforcement pool for posting to field units as soon as vacancies opened. The intention made sense, but the scheme did not unfold as planned.

The policy of apportioning the troops as ordered resulted in inefficient use of veterans, prompting CMHQ to implement a more practical plan. At the end of February, authorities in theatre complained to CMHQ about how the army employed soldiers who had returned from Italy.[121] They had learned through the grapevine that the soldiers carefully selected for their battle experience and ability to teach did not go to field units in Britain but rather to CRU or to the Canadian Training School and, in many cases, seemed to have become stuck in the reinforcement stream. Commanders in theatre felt put off that they had supported a plan to pass on battle experience, only to have their good men sitting idle. Brigadier A.W. Beament, the officer in command of the Canadian Section at General Headquarters (GHQ) 1st Echelon in Italy, asked CMHQ to determine if the reports had any truth, "in order that steps may be taken to prevent discouraging rumours circulating among formations in this theatre."[122] The accounts were accurate. When senior staff at CMHQ and headquarters First Canadian Army looked into the matter, they found that only 9 percent of the NCOs who returned from Italy had gone to field units.[123] Another 10 percent occupied instructional positions on the CRU permanent establishment, while a whopping 79 percent waited in the reinforcement stream.[124] CMHQ therefore decided that all soldiers returned from Italy (including those being held as reinforcements) would proceed to First Canadian Army field units, regardless of whether vacancies existed.[125]

Poor planning might not have been entirely responsible for the slow progress in sending the veteran soldiers to field units in Britain. The original decision to send only 25 percent stemmed from the intention of the First Canadian Army to freeze personnel in their positions and keep teams together during the final period before operations. In response, CMHQ decided not "to inject too much 'new blood' into field units" because the teams that would fight together had already become "more or less firm."[126] In any event, the scheme to return soldiers from Italy appears to have stopped by the end of March, probably because of the intense preparations for impending invasion.

In the end, the exchange scheme was a well-intentioned program that bumped up against another well-intentioned policy – keeping First Canadian Army's teams together. Although not all the benefits McNaughton had intended the plan to produce materialized, First Canadian Army probably derived some value. The project ultimately exchanged an estimated 1,000 troops, about half of them NCOs, most likely enough for every field unit in Britain to get several veterans.

Bringing hundreds of soldiers back from Italy to disseminate battle knowledge and experience constituted one more measure to strengthen the army's backbone. Even placing veterans in the reinforcement stream, where they rubbed shoulders with green troops awaiting posting to combat units, must have had some benefit. For example, Warrant Officer Class 1 Angus Duffy, who had been the RSM of the Hastings and Prince Edward Regiment since December 1939, returned from Italy in January 1944 and was posted to 4 CIRU. (He remained in the reinforcement system for some time, probably because no field unit wanted a new RSM just before going into battle.) Shortly before Operation Overlord, he gave some much-needed tactics training to a group of soldiers who were scheduled to go ashore as reinforcements on D-Day. Kenneth B. Smith, who had served with Duffy in Italy and later wrote about the RSM's military career, described Duffy's role in preparing these seventy fresh-faced troops for battle:

He spent the next couple of days putting them through the drills for sections and platoons in attack and defence. They seized this new knowledge with enthusiasm. Ten years or so later at a Militia camp Duffy met an officer of the Stormont, Dundas and Glengarry Highlanders who thanked him for this brief training session which, he said, had ensured his own survival and that of his platoon in the hours right after being committed to battle.[127]

Historian Daniel Dancocks views the program as part of the greater flow of Canadian experience from the Mediterranean theatre back to Britain, including the transfer of senior officers such as Harry Crerar, Guy Simonds, and George Kitching.[128] According to Dancocks the "Spaghetti Leaguers," as men who had served in Italy called themselves, unquestionably helped with preparations for operations in Northwest Europe. He cites one of the Exercise Pooch participants: "When we went in at Normandy, at least we'd been shot at. The plan was a good one, to take some people who had been out there and put them into the units that were going in to Northwest Europe."[129] In fact, based on several interviews Dancocks conducted, the veterans of Italy collectively made useful contributions to First Canadian Army's training before the Normandy invasion.

Mitigating the Infantry's High Wastage Rates

In the summer and fall of 1944, the Canadian Army Overseas experienced unexpectedly high infantry casualties as heavy fighting in Italy and Northwest Europe left many of the army's battalions understrength.[130] Army planners had bungled casualty estimates by relying on British analysis of wastage in North Africa, where German air activity had often caused casualties in rear areas. Relying on this pattern, Canadian staff had estimated that non-infantry personnel would take 52 percent of all casualties, but because no significant air threat existed in Italy or Northwest Europe, the infantry actually bore the brunt, accounting for 77 percent of all casualties incurred in 1943–44.

C.P. Stacey explains that the army saw the infantry reinforcement crisis coming in March 1944, when Headquarters 21st Army Group predicted that its invasion forces might suffer higher casualties than planned, and attempted to avert shortages by remustering soldiers from overstrength arms and services to infantry. Accordingly, CMHQ authorized a program to remuster 1,000 artillerymen, 500 engineers, and 500 armoured corps soldiers. Over the next few months, the remuster program grew and by January 1945, the Canadian army in Britain had converted 12,638 non-commissioned soldiers and 396 officers to infantry.[131] Even so, in September 1944, CMHQ discovered that the reinforcement pool had a surplus of 13,000 non-infantry soldiers but a deficit of 2,000 infantrymen, of whom about 340 were NCOs. Worse, CMHQ staff estimated, by the end of the year, the shortage would grow to 15,000 infantry troops, including an estimated 2,540 NCOs.[132] Authorities applied several measures to mitigate the impact on the NCO corps.

To preserve cadres of key personnel during major engagements, formation commanders imposed "left out of battle" (LOB) policies on their units. The concept had been around since the First World War, when British and Canadian forces implemented the practice so that units could reconstitute after taking heavy losses.[133] Ernest M.K. MacGregor, MC, who served as an officer with the Loyal Edmonton Regiment, describes how LOB policy worked in Italy:

> This was the process by which the Canadians always left out the second in command of a rifle company or the second in command of a platoon, a group of people [who] were left out of battle so that if the unit was badly damaged in battle or decimated they would have a nucleus on which to reorganize with reinforcements coming up.[134]

In the fall of 1944, Guy Simonds, the acting general officer commanding-in-chief (GOC-in-C) of First Canadian Army and by now a lieutenant-general, ordered all his Canadian formation commanders to implement an LOB policy whereby every infantry battalion and armoured regiment maintained a group of NCOs, officers, and men who remained out of harm's way during lengthy battles.[135] (These soldiers would not be idle. Simonds ordered units to use their LOBs to receive, test, and orient reinforcements.) The 4th Canadian Armoured Division's procedures exemplified the LOB policy in Northwest Europe in 1945. Each unit created an LOB that remained out of the fighting for days or weeks at a time, although the individuals within it rotated frequently.[136] For infantry companies and armoured squadrons, an LOB included one senior NCO, two or three junior NCOs, and two officers. Meanwhile, brigade commanders closely supervised the LOBs under their charge. In an infantry division, the LOB of an infantry company was larger, consisting of fifteen experienced soldiers: the second-in-command, one platoon commander, four NCOs (sergeants and corporals), plus nine privates.[137]

In any event, LOB policies were designed only to conserve a skeleton cadre of personnel. To replenish the "flesh" of the infantry battalions, the army had to increase the proportion of infantrymen in the reinforcement stream. That meant training more infantry NCOs. The army therefore established new training programs across the force. In Northwest Europe, where the three Canadian divisions had taken over 6,000 casualties during the month of October, divisional NCO schools opened in the field to repair the losses.[138] In Britain, CMHQ established new machinery for training infantry NCOs in the 13th Canadian Infantry Training Brigade, within which the 10th Canadian Infantry Training Battalion ran NCO training for soldiers converted to infantry.[139] Back in Canada, the army refocused an infantry training centre solely on converting and refreshing NCOs for infantry service overseas.[140]

While infantry NCO production ramped up across the army, battalions in the line often found shorter-term solutions by simply promoting proven men to fill vacancies. Service records show that some infantrymen suddenly rose in rank by several steps after the army started taking heavy casualties. A couple of examples from the sample group of NCOs illustrate how this happened. In March 1943, Ralph Brennan of Port Colborne, Ontario, volunteered for active duty as a signalman, after having served for fourteen months as a conscript.[141] The following August, the army re-allocated him to infantry. Private Brennan eventually proceeded to Britain, went into the reinforcement pool, and finally joined a field unit, the Argyll and Sutherland Highlanders, in January 1944. Brennan deployed with this battalion to France on 21 July, still a private. On 18 August, he became a lance corporal; on 5 September, a corporal; and on 1 November, a sergeant. In just over ten weeks, he had rocketed from private to sergeant, a rank normally reserved for those with long experience and proven leadership ability. In the Mediterranean theatre, Wilfred Goodburn, who had joined the army as an infantryman in April 1940 and went into the reinforcement system, was still a private when he finally joined the PPCLI in the field in August 1943.[142] He remained a private until mid-July 1944, when he suddenly shot up in rank. He rose to corporal on 18 July, lance sergeant on 1 September, and then sergeant on 30 September. Like Brennan, Goodburn went from private to sergeant in just over ten weeks after proving himself in action.[143] Such cases were not rare. In the sample group, roughly 7 percent rose dramatically in rank during the fall of 1944, when the NCO shortage was most acute.

While the infantry dealt with NCO shortages, the other arms and services faced the opposite problem up until the war's end. Despite the army's program to reallocate soldiers from overstrength arms and services to infantry, the reinforcement pool of non-infantrymen still held a surplus of NCOs in March 1945, including many with experience in a theatre of operations.[144] Headquarters First Canadian Army believed that these NCOs represented excellent but unused talent for their respective arms and services, and thought it wasteful to leave them in Britain just because no vacancies existed for their ranks in operational units. Therefore, NDHQ decided in April that CMHQ could reduce non-infantry NCOs to private to allow them to move forward, although the policy did not apply to soldiers who had earned confirmed rank in a theatre of operations. Any man thus demoted could continue drawing NCO pay for six months. Most of the soldiers affected were corporals and sergeants, although small numbers all the way up to warrant officer class 1 also faced demotion. By then, of course, Germany's collapse was just weeks away, so few probably moved to the combat zone as overly qualified privates before the shooting stopped.

Post-D-Day Projects to Distribute Battle Experience

After the Normandy invasion, spreading operational experience across the army remained as important as ever for the NCO corps' ongoing sustainment and development. Several programs distributed the latest hard-won expertise.

During the final five months of the war, CMHQ arranged for veteran soldiers from First Canadian Army to train infantry reinforcements in Britain. In late December 1944, preparing for the arrival of nearly 11,000 reinforcements above the normal flow from Canada (the conscripts were finally on their way), CMHQ senior administrative officer Major-General Ernest Weeks sent a request to headquarters First Canadian Army for CRU instructors: "The problem of providing experienced NCO Instrs to train these rfts properly is now acute, and we would much appreciate it if Sgts, Cpls or WOs Class II could be returned to the UK for this purpose."[145] He asked for 200 NCOs for three months, even if they came from among the "battle weary."[146] To fill the vacancies this would create, CMHQ staff prepared replacements to move forward. Encouraging such a scheme was nothing new, as a senior official told Weeks in early January: "We are always endeavouring to get the [deployed] units to absorb more confirmed NCOs without battle experience, and if they will accept up to 200, these could be provided."[147]

First Canadian Army satisfied CMHQ's requirements. In early January, the chosen soldiers moved back to Britain and joined various infantry training regiments in the 13th Canadian Infantry Training Brigade (CITB). Supporting the initiative entailed tangible costs for the losing units: battalions in Northwest Europe each furnished about nine soldiers, most of them corporals and sergeants but the occasional sergeant major, too.[148] Presumably, some of these men had already left their operational units and moved back temporarily into the reinforcement stream because of battle weariness, wounds, or illness – but not all, and units took some men out of the line.[149] Nonetheless, in all cases, these soldiers remained effective, if in need of a break, and the scheme involved returning them to the field after their three-month instructional tours in Britain. Therefore, the army once again demonstrated its commitment to investing valuable human resources in the training system. In early April, the time drew near for the instructors to return to Northwest Europe but the need for their services remained.[150] First Canadian Army agreed to rotate the men and later that month sent another 200 soldiers back to Britain.[151] Ultimately, the program benefited the green reinforcement NCOs undergoing training at 13 CITB by allowing them to learn directly from their veteran peers. Of course, the rank and file training under the veterans also benefited a great deal. Their morale increased, knowing that their instructors had come fresh from the fighting.

Many of these troops were conscripts, and they appreciated that the army would not deploy them to the theatre of operations until the veteran instructors considered them ready.[152]

Another program to distribute combat experience involved sending First Canadian Army formation and unit commanders back to Britain to lecture reinforcement NCOs and officers on the lessons of battle. As CMHQ acting chief of staff Major-General P.J. Montague reminded the First Canadian Army commander, Harry Crerar (by now a full general), the rotation of soldiers between field units and the reinforcement system before Operation Overlord had played an important role in finishing reinforcement training.[153] However, with all First Canadian Army formations now deployed, reinforcements had no opportunity to train in field units. Therefore, to ensure that reinforcement training remained as up to date as possible, the army needed to create a link with the deployed forces. Montague proposed that some of Crerar's formation and unit commanders visit the reinforcements in Britain to provide relevant lectures.

Crerar supported the plan and so did his boss, Field Marshal Bernard Montgomery, commander of 21st Army Group.[154] Crerar considered options with his chief of staff and with Lieutenant-General Guy Simonds, who was then the commander of 2nd Canadian Corps. The resulting plan consisted of weekly lectures, beginning on 2 December with a presentation by Simonds entitled "Leadership in Command and the Requirements Expected of a Junior Officer in Battle," followed the next week by two senior First Canadian Army staff officers with the lecture "The Military Situation and Problems Facing First Canadian Army." Thereafter, Crerar's program focused on tactical matters, with pairs of brigade commanders delivering tactics lectures for break-in and breakthrough battles, attacking and capturing enemy strong points, and assaulting enemy positions protected by water obstacles, all based on recent operations. Then, beginning in early January, the plan had unit commanders provide weekly lectures on unit and sub-unit operations, focusing on tactical and administrative problems and lessons.[155]

Staff executed the program in full, starting on 2 December with Simonds's presentation. Headquarters CRU arranged for the lectures to occur each Saturday morning at the Prince Consort's Library in Aldershot.[156] Reinforcement unit commanders received direction to fill their allotted vacancies, which totalled 500 seats. Soon after, staff at 2nd Canadian Corps headquarters arranged to supply the weekly unit commander lectures. Starting on 13 January, each week's presentations focused on a particular corps of arms, starting with infantry and working through artillery, engineers, armour, signals, the motorized and divisional machine-gun battalions, and finally, on 3 March, lectures on air support and on how morale affected a battalion in combat.[157] The presenters were for the most part unit commanders who flew in from Europe, and each week hundreds of NCOs and officers used a half day to learn about hard-won lessons of battle, straight from those doing the fighting.

Post-D-Day Reinforcement Quality

Clearly, a great deal of the effort to develop the NCO corps in the army's most active year of fighting focused on the reinforcement system. Authorities worked hard to ensure that it produced capable NCOs to replace casualties in the fighting units. Did they succeed? The question merits consideration, especially given perceptions then and later that reinforcements in general often arrived at field units poorly trained.[158] In fact, records suggest that the reinforcement system generally did a good job preparing soldiers for frontline service – at least after the Normandy invasion – producing reasonably well trained soldiers, including NCOs and the privates who were the next generation of junior leaders.

In the weeks following Operation Overlord, the reinforcement system appeared to be working fairly well. A CMHQ report on a draft of 300 soldiers that had arrived in Italy on 22 June painted a fairly good picture, and in general the soldiers "appeared to be good rft [reinforcement] material."[159] No concerns about NCOs were raised. Still, there was room for a little improvement overall before 1 Canadian Base Reinforcement Group (1 CBRG), which tested and held reinforcements arriving from Britain, could allow the soldiers to move forward and join their units. For example, some infantrymen required instruction in field engineering and mine warfare. But, as the report demonstrated, authorities in Britain and Italy monitored reinforcement quality closely, and NDHQ distributed their findings to the training centres in Canada with instructions to focus on correcting any weak areas. In late August, a senior CMHQ officer told CRU: "It is accepted that the standard of trg of rfts arriving from Canada is generally satisfactory but due to lack of eqpt and sometimes the necessity of despatching rfts prior to the completion of trg, Canada cannot be held responsible for bringing rft pers[onnel] up to f[iel]d standards."[160] Again, no NCO-specific concerns appeared. Overall, reinforcements arriving from Canada still needed some top-up training before joining field units, but for reasons that had nothing to do with the quality of instruction back home. Troops required hardening because they had done so little exercise during the journey across the Atlantic, and they usually required instruction in grenades, mines, and the Projector, Infantry, Anti-Tank (PIAT) because those items were not available in Canada.[161] Range work was also necessary to zero rifles – the process of

Figure 8.3 As acting commander of First Canadian Army in
the autumn of 1944, Lieutenant-General Guy Simonds, a most
exacting officer, was confident that the reinforcement training
system was operating effectively. Here, he speaks with NCOs
of the Royal Canadian Electrical and Mechanical Engineers
in Oldenburg, Germany, 2 June 1945. | Library and Archives
Canada/Department of National Defence fonds/a198014.

aligning the sight and the weapon to ensure accuracy. All of this meant that
infantry reinforcements flowing into Britain generally needed to spend about
three weeks training at CRU before proceeding to an operational theatre.

Later that fall, Lieutenant-General Guy Simonds, as acting commander of
First Canadian Army, believed that reinforcement quality remained good,
even though certain unit commanders had complained to him about training

standards. In late October 1944, he told all his Canadian formation commanders: "I am satisfied that most of the officers now responsible for training and testing remustered personnel, or drafts arriving from Canada, are officers who have had considerable infantry fighting experience in this war, know what is required and all are conscientious in their duty."[162] He thought the perceived inadequacies of new soldiers had more to do with how units absorbed their reinforcements. He understood that a reinforcement arriving at a unit was an outsider joining a close-knit group of veteran troops who often played up their experience. And no matter how thorough the new man's training, he might make mistakes in his first battle. Therefore, Simonds ordered that all unit LOBs form "reception schools" to integrate and evaluate new arrivals over the course of at least two days, five if possible. This would ensure that new soldiers became acquainted with leaders in their new units and the local situation before joining the units themselves. It was a form of forced team building that Simonds considered would enhance unit cohesion and reduce casualties.

He was not alone in believing that the reinforcement training system operated soundly. Reports continued to suggest that reinforcements required little refresher training, and none expressed concerns about NCOs. In mid-October, CMHQ reported that recent drafts of infantry reinforcements from Canada continued to show improvement, although the requirement remained for refresher training in mines and booby traps, the PIAT, and grenades, items that were still in short supply at home. Aside from these shortcomings, CMHQ reported no serious problems.[163] In Italy, 1 CBRG was happy with a draft that had arrived on 18 November.[164] Infantry reinforcements required a little improvement in a few subjects, such as the Thompson sub-machine gun, handling PIAT ammunition, and house clearing, but otherwise they were good. Authorities in Northwest Europe also seemed generally satisfied with reinforcement quality. During a late October visit to the theatre, Colonel J.G.K. Strathy, a staff duties and training officer at CMHQ, inquired about the quality of reinforcements arriving from Britain. The consensus of opinion, he discovered, held that most reinforcements were sufficiently trained except for physical hardening.[165]

Unit-level grumbling about reinforcement quality occasionally percolated up to senior officials, prompting authorities to have unit commanders see for themselves the soundness of reinforcement training. In early December, the newly promoted CMHQ chief of staff Lieutenant-General P.J. Montague and General Harry Crerar discussed complaints the latter had received from a couple of unit commanders about remustered soldiers who supposedly lacked sufficient training.[166] Montague did not put much stock in the two reports, which failed to provide any details about the drafts or training units the men had come from.

He remained certain that reinforcement training had improved considerably in recent months, especially with the establishment of 13 CITB, which had highly competent unit commanders and staffs. Admittedly, the occasional inadequately trained man slipped through, but Montague believed such cases had been an insignificant percentage for some time. He offered Crerar several possible explanations for the poor perceptions. Some soldiers who had transferred to the infantry against their wishes wanted to avoid frontline service, and the commander of 13 CITB had ascertained that some deliberately failed to hit targets on the range or failed tests of elementary training. Others, equally unhappy, falsely reported having not received proper training when they arrived at their new units. They seemed intent on capitalizing on rumours that the army rushed soldiers into combat without proper training: "The uproar produced in Canada by the Smythe–Drew charges has encouraged these types," Montague stated, and he believed that well-kept training records would set the record straight.[167]

Scholars have since ascertained from individual service records that infantry reinforcements were for the most part reasonably well trained by the fall of 1944.[168] Also, Robert Engen's survey of questionnaires completed by veteran infantry officers demonstrates that only a minority believed reinforcements were inadequately trained.[169] According to his research: "Reinforcement soldiers were generally considered to have been acceptably well trained, and data show that only a vocal minority voiced complaints about replacements."

In any case, Montague thought the army needed to demonstrate that the training system worked well, and therefore proposed that Crerar send commanding officers from Northwest Europe to CRU to see for themselves. This would establish confidence in the system while giving visitors the opportunity to offer suggestions for improvement. Crerar agreed and approved sending eight officers each week.[170] In turn, Montague directed that CRU show the visitors only genuine training in progress, nothing staged.

The field unit officers approved of what they saw. For example, the adjutants of the Loyal Edmonton Regiment and the Seaforth Highlanders of Canada both came away impressed with the training and the atmosphere at 1 Canadian Infantry Training Regiment (1 CITR).[171] While neither yet had experience receiving reinforcements in Northwest Europe, both reported satisfaction with the state of training of those they had received in Italy, regretting only that there had not been enough of them. Neither officer had any criticism or suggestions to offer. Shortly after, the second-in-command of the West Nova Scotia Regiment visited 5 CITR, and he too left with no complaints or substantive recommendations.[172] Then, the second-in-command of the Royal 22nd Regiment (R22R) visited 4

CITR, where he indicated his approval with both the training methods and the reinforcements themselves. In fact, since arriving in Northwest Europe, the R22R found that its reinforcements arrived in excellent condition and integrated easily with their companies.[173] While few visitors made comments on the quality of reinforcement NCOs and the training they received – a good sign in and of itself – those who did have something to say were generally positive, aside from a few minor criticisms about non-infantry NCOs.[174] Lieutenant-Colonel Ross Ellis of the Calgary Highlanders, who visited 2 CITR in early January, commented that reinforcement NCOs received good training but should receive fair warning that they could keep their rank only if they performed well on joining a field unit, and that "unsatisfactory NCOs will be broken immediately."[175] That was fair enough. He also proposed that reinforcement training emphasize to privates the need to think constantly about NCO responsibilities in preparation for moving up in rank.

On the whole, then, reinforcement quality, in general and among NCOs, seemed fairly good in the period after Operation Overlord. A mound of evidence suggests this, including the reports expressing general satisfaction with reinforcements who arrived in Italy in late June, Simonds's confidence in the autumn that the veteran officers in charge of training and assessing reinforcements in Britain had matters well in hand, reports from both Italy and Northwest Europe in late autumn indicating overall satisfaction with reinforcement quality, and the reactions of the field unit representatives when visiting CRU in early 1945 to see reinforcement training for themselves. Furthermore, the sample group shows that a high proportion of NCOs reporting to units as reinforcements – as much as 61 percent – were veterans returning after recovering from illness or injury, and that even many of the green NCOs had spent much time in the training or reinforcement systems. Robert Engen's finding that only a minority of veteran infantry officers believed reinforcements lacked enough training adds weight to this assessment of reinforcement quality after the Normandy invasion. Even official historian C.P. Stacey notes the "absence of serious complaints from the field in the final months of the campaign."[176] The army's investment in training reinforcement NCOs and the soldiers who would grow into NCOs paid off after Operation Overlord and constituted an important part of the greater effort to develop the NCO corps.

So what accounts for the enduring impression that infantry reinforcements lacked sufficient training? Why do some credible personal accounts report that reinforcements arrived at their units without certain fundamental skills? It is likely that, during the infantry reinforcement crisis in the late summer and fall of 1944, some soldiers the army had converted to infantry were prematurely rushed to battalions. During the Normandy campaign, the Canadian army experienced unexpectedly high infantry casualties and lower casualties for other arms, as did its British and American counterparts.[177] By August, the scarcity of infantry reinforcements had grown so acute that CMHQ redoubled efforts to convert soldiers from other corps.[178] It took several months to repair the shortage, which peaked at the end of August with battalions in Northwest Europe undersupplied by an average of 206 other ranks.[179] The situation gradually improved, notwithstanding a spike in early November as the Scheldt campaign finished. By mid-November, the average deficit was down to thirty-one and continued to decline until it hit zero by February 1945.[180] The crash program to convert soldiers to infantry helped rectify the problem, and by January 1945, 12,638 other ranks (and 396 officers) had been remustered to infantry.[181] As the army's official historian notes, however, some of these men may have proceeded to battalions without enough training.[182] One suspects this was especially so for some of the first soldiers rushed through the conversion scheme, when the crisis was at its worst and before 13 CITB established the six-week conversion program (eight weeks for NCOs) discussed above. The sample group for this book suggests this was the case. Four soldiers in the group converted to infantry between August and October 1944, and none went into action fully trained for infantry duty. They had just six, four, three, and zero weeks of conversion training, respectively. This finding reinforces the assessment that reports of poorly trained reinforcements reflect the rush to send converted soldiers to battalions in the late summer and fall of 1944, rather than problems with the reinforcement training system that extended back to Canada.

Conclusion

The army's senior leadership, understanding the need to disseminate field unit expertise and battle experience through training and reinforcement units in the United Kingdom and Canada, implemented measures to promote even development across the army's backbone of NCOs. General McNaughton referred to the importance of spreading expertise when ordering veterans in Sicily back to Britain, emphasizing that the effort was "essential for the proper training of the Canadian Army."[183] Collectively, programs that sent NCOs from Canada to Britain, from Britain to Canada, between field and reinforcement units, from the Canadian army in Britain to the British army in the desert, and from the forces in Italy and Northwest Europe to the training and reinforcement system helped distribute the latest knowledge and lessons of battle. For individual field units, some of the measures were an irritant because they involved sending away good NCOs, something no commanding officer concerned with winning battles relished. But, like all important investments, these programs entailed making difficult choices about how best to allocate valuable resources.

The choices grew more difficult once the whole of First Canadian Army was fighting and the infantry shortage peaked. In particular, the program to send some of the best instructors in Britain back to Canada contracted as it ground against the demand for more infantry reinforcements in the field. Nevertheless, all these expertise-sharing programs were essential for the effectiveness of the NCO corps in battle, so the army continued sending as many strong NCOs as possible from Northwest Europe to Britain, and from Britain to Canada, right up until the war ended. There was little choice. Allowing uneven development would have risked fighting efficiency, because the reinforcements going forward would be only as good as the training system that had prepared them.

Following the Normandy campaign, reinforcement quality was fairly good for both NCOs and the privates who would become NCOs, notwithstanding some converted soldiers who were probably sent into action prematurely when the infantry shortage was at its worst. From the outset, the senior military leadership worked hard to ensure that NCOs training in places such as Borden, Ontario, and Aldershot, England, learned the skills they needed to fight and win in places like Ortona, the Scheldt, and elsewhere. Investment in the training system paid off, even if the backbone in Canada was softening by the war's end, as instructional staff increasingly comprised men who had only recently been civilians.

Conclusion

Commanders and regimental and staff officers returning from theatres of operations are unanimous in their opinion that our soldiers have done their duty and done it well because they had been "shown how" properly.

YEAR-END MESSAGE FROM NDHQ DIRECTOR OF MILITARY
TRAINING, DECEMBER 1944

THE NOTION THAT NCOs form the backbone of any effective Western army has become axiomatic, with good reason. These soldiers fulfill indispensable roles: they lead and motivate troops in battle at the lowest level, they maintain discipline in combat and in garrison, and they form the instructional cadres that transform civilians into soldiers. They mentor both the young soldiers beneath them and the new, untested junior officers above them. They are the bridge between the officer corps and the soldiery, on the one hand ensuring the execution of orders and on the other advocating for the interests of the rank and file. An army simply cannot function without them. As the official historian C.P. Stacey so aptly puts it: "Without the [Corporal] Joneses there could be no Marlboroughs."[1] Understanding how Canada's Second World War army developed its NCO corps, then, contributes to our understanding of how the country created, almost from scratch, a powerful force that helped bring about the unconditional surrender of one of the world's most formidable armies.

In exploring how the Canadian army developed its wartime NCO corps, this book has tried to fill a conspicuous gap in the historiography. To that end, it builds on recent scholarship, especially that dealing with aspects of manpower.[2] It argues that military authorities used a two-track NCO development system of decentralized programs (run by units and formations) and centralized programs (overseen by the army), a hybrid of regimental- and mass-army approaches that was both practical and culturally comfortable. There was no single professional development model like those used in professional armies. Canada's wartime NCOs had no requirement to satisfy prescribed training and employment prerequisites or to serve minimum time at each rank to qualify for promotion. Instead, when war broke out, the army pushed responsibility down to the unit level, making commanding officers responsible for training, developing, and promoting their NCOs. Units therefore designed and conducted their own NCO training when circumstances allowed. However, they needed a great deal of outside assistance, because none had the capacity to run enough qualification courses and professional development programs to keep its NCO cadre trained and up to strength, especially when engaged in active operations. Thus, formations also ran NCO training, and eventually so did centralized schools controlled by NDHQ in Canada and CMHQ in Britain. The volume and standardization of NCO production probably could not have been addressed in any other way. Centralized establishments like the Junior Leaders School at Mégantic, Quebec, and the Canadian Training School in England could train NCOs to army norms, but even these schools could not produce enough non-commissioned officers for the rapidly expanding force. Instead, they seeded units and training centres both in Canada and overseas. This two-track approach took time to evolve because the centralized system did not even exist when the war started, and did not develop its final structure until around mid-1941, in response to decisions to form a large army.

The two-track approach, intended to create as many development opportunities as possible, made sense. From the outset, those concerned with NCO development knew only that it had to occur quickly. Few would have guessed that the army would not start sustained operations until July 1943. Canadian military authorities therefore acted logically in making commanding officers responsible for NCO training and promotions because doing so enabled units to keep vacancies filled with the best men they had. And while the system produced individual training profiles that differed from soldier to soldier, the army still managed to promote fairly even development across the NCO corps as a whole. To ensure that the expertise, and eventually the battle experience, building in the field units spread back to the reinforcements in England and to the training system at home, the army circulated NCOs between Canada, Britain, and the operational theatres.

The army had a monumental task in raising the NCO corps from raw material. The wartime force, which grew to almost half a million soldiers, needed an NCO corps of an estimated 110,660.[3] The prewar permanent force of 4,261 soldiers of all ranks and part-time Non-Permanent Active Militia (NPAM) of 51,400 could supply only so many, even if, as C.P. Stacey states, the prewar forces made invaluable contributions to the army's overall growth.[4] As demonstrated in Chapter 1, the army did indeed squeeze the prewar forces hard for NCO talent. This book's survey of nearly 400 records of infantry senior NCOs who died in service indicates that the permanent force provided about 4 percent of the wartime senior NCOs, a disproportionate contribution for a force about 0.85 percent of the wartime army's size. And the NPAM, about one-tenth the size of the wartime army, provided approximately a third of its senior NCOs. What is more, almost three-quarters of wartime infantry warrant officers had prewar military experience, including an astonishing 23 percent who had seen service in the permanent force. But even with this cohort of talent from the peacetime army, building up the wartime NCO corps took time. After all, the prewar force had given its soldiers no modern equipment and too little training, and its troops had a great deal to learn about modern weapons and tactics. Furthermore, the bulk of the wartime NCO corps had to be created out of raw civilian material. The sample group shows that it took on average thirty-five months to turn a civilian into a sergeant. For these reasons, the two-track system was sensible because it maximized opportunities for NCO training.

While this book investigates *how* the army developed the NCO corps, it does not assess *how well* individual programs worked. Doing so would have required establishing subjective assessment criteria and producing subjective conclusions. Instead, it assumes that the NCO corps ultimately performed well enough in battle, based on the army's sound performance, as historians have amply demonstrated in the last two decades or so. As Jack Granatstein argues, the army learned quickly after the invasion of Normandy and kept on learning, and by the time it reunited in Northwest Europe in the spring of 1945, it "was probably the best little army in the world."[5] Surely, a strong backbone of NCOs helped the army win its battles. Indeed, the army's record in combat contains few instances where substandard NCO performance might have affected unit performance. (One may have occurred during Operation Atlantic in Normandy, when two companies of the Essex Scottish Regiment withdrew in disorder, although one must recognize that the unit was under tremendous pressure from German panzers. Still, when the troops head for the rear under no control, NCOs have probably failed. Another possible instance occurred on 28 August 1944, when elements of the Queen's Own Cameron Highlanders withdrew in disorder at the Forêt de la Londe.[6])

What is more, the army's approach to developing NCOs was fundamentally about imparting skills, not granting formal qualifications. Few NCO production programs bothered to keep track of how many students passed or failed. To be sure, some courses held examinations and assigned grades, and staff removed weak or unsuitable candidates as necessary. But ultimately, the system was about giving as many skills as possible in the time available to as many soldiers as possible, so that unit NCO cadres could develop rapidly and replacements were ready to step in for NCOs who fell in battle.

The requirement to impart the latest skills meant that NCO training evolved considerably as the war progressed. As the army modernized, NCO training adjusted to accommodate more content. The various syllabuses presented in Chapters 5 to 7 demonstrate the ever-growing subject matter a prospective NCO had to master. Learning how to use, and provide instruction on, the latest weapons was a key aspect. (Things like the Sten gun, the PIAT, and the flame-throwers that the army eventually adopted did not exist in 1939.) Learning the latest tactics was another. The battle drill programs that swept across the army in 1942 taught soldiers sound tactical principles to consider in likely combat scenarios. In fact, this book reinforces Robert Engen's finding that battle drill training proved its worth for soldiers in combat.[7] It also shows just how important the army believed it to be, as the sample group reveals that more senior NCOs attended battle drill courses than any other specialist program; at least one in five graduated from a battle drill program.

In demonstrating how interarm training became important for imparting skills to NCOs, this study indicates that the army did not neglect it before commencing operations, as some scholars have suggested.[8] At various times from 1940 to June 1944, formation headquarters ordered interarm training that progressed up to live-fire formation exercises, and units and brigades carried it out. Repeated challenges with respect to interarm cooperation in combat may have occurred in part from factors other than too little training, a primary problem being the need to tailor tactics to the terrain and enemy situation.[9] In other words, it may have been all but impossible to conduct enough interarm training to account for all possible situations, especially when one considers the high personnel turnover in battle (including the NCOs who led teams at the lowest level), as well as the frequent regrouping of forces, which meant that units often had to work with unfamiliar counterparts of other arms.

Finally, this book probes the reinforcement training system. Developing the NCO corps entailed giving sound training to soldiers who would replace casualties in the field. The army kept the latest expertise flowing across the whole force by circulating NCOs between field units and the training and reinforcement systems. These efforts appear to have been successful. Despite impressions in the historiography that infantry reinforcements proved undertrained when they reported to units in action, a strong body of evidence suggests that the reinforcement system generally did a good job preparing soldiers, NCOs included, for frontline service – at least after June 1944. The sample group supports this, showing that more than 60 percent of NCO reinforcements were veterans returning after having recovered from injury or illness (some returning for a second or even third time). Even green NCO reinforcements were often well-trained men who had been rotated out of their field units for instructional duty. As a whole, the reinforcement system was not perfect and the occasional undertrained private slipped through, but by and large, the system was working. One important caveat applies: some of the soldiers who converted to infantry shortly after the reinforcement crisis peaked in late August 1944 might have been rushed forward without adequate training, including a handful of NCOs in the sample group.

The decentralized and centralized NCO development programs each played a major role in developing the NCO corps. In the sample group, the decentralized courses run by units and formations account for about 52 percent of the foundational NCO qualification and refresher courses that soldiers attended. Centralized courses, run at schools controlled by NDHQ and CMHQ, account for about 48 percent. However, the centralized system played the greater role in providing follow-on training. Whereas units and formations often had no time to run individual training of any type, schools in Canada and Britain ran serial after serial of specialist courses in small arms instruction, battle drill, urban combat, techniques of instruction, and many other subjects. NCOs received most of their specialist training at these centralized schools.

Plainly, the two-track system had certain flaws. With training distributed so widely across units, formations, and training establishments, the quality and thoroughness of instruction varied. The longer centralized courses, such as the detailed seven-week program at the Junior Leaders School in Mégantic, Quebec, looked nothing like the barebones two-week crash course tired and dirty troops received in Italy in early 1944, although there has to be some allowance for the fact that soldiers in the Italian theatre had already learned much by fighting. Commanding officers also differed in their approaches to NCO progression and development. As Montgomery discovered when he inspected Canada's infantry battalions in early 1942, some commanding officers did not yet fully appreciate the importance of training their NCOs and managing their promotions.[10] Even if matters improved after Montgomery's inspections, First Canadian Army eventually had thirty-nine infantry battalions, plus many more units of the other arms and services, and commanding officers were bound to vary in how they chose to develop their NCOs.

The army's approach to training and developing NCOs sometimes engendered tension between the regimental and "mass army" communities. Army culture still had one foot planted in the nineteenth century, with politically connected regiments championing their own interests, while the greater force came to grips with prosecuting twentieth-century industrial warfare.[11] Well-intentioned programs for the good of the whole NCO corps sometimes undermined regimental interests, and therefore did not enjoy regimental support. For instance, at the Canadian Training School in Britain, the heart of the overseas army's centralized training system, staff complained that units failed over and over to select high-quality NCOs to attend courses that produced regimental instructors, instead sending soldiers who were not ready for the training.[12] According to the school commandant, commanding officers resented how CTS retained strong graduates as instructors without even consulting the losing units. They also bristled when the school retained borrowed instructors for longer than the standard four to eight months. Their solution, according to the commandant, was to send candidates whom they could well do without, even if these men were seldom suitable.[13] To some extent, he was probably right. Because unit commanders controlled who left their lines, sometimes they kept their best soldiers, NCOs or otherwise, on a tight rein.[14] CMHQ even accused them of "unloading" unwanted men to instructional duty in Canada. Sending strong NCOs back to Canada to teach at centralized training centres was important for the NCO corps and for the army as a whole, but some units simply did not want to lose their good men indefinitely.[15] And when commanding officers in Italy willingly sent strong NCOs and officers back to Britain to help train the forces preparing for Normandy, frustrations mounted when the contributing units learned that most of their soldiers had ended up in the reinforcement stream.[16] As it turned out, CMHQ might have had good reason for sending only a small proportion of the Italy veterans into First Canadian Army field units – which had solidified into the teams that would fight together – but that probably did little to mollify units that had given up good leaders, only to learn that they were languishing as reinforcements.[17]

Some men in the sample group got by with very little in the way of formal NCO qualification training – a course at Mégantic or CTS, for example. In fact, only about one-third of the soldiers in the sample have such training listed in their service records, although this is not to say that the others were *unqualified*.[18] The great majority of soldiers in the sample underwent some sort of instructor training, for drill, battle drill, small arms, or many other specialties. These instructor courses included leadership training, in that they taught candidates to be teachers and supervisors, and about the tactical employment of certain weapons. Some even taught tactics as a subject unto itself, as with battle drill and town fighting courses. In Canada, where units had an easier time putting soldiers through NCO qualification courses than did formations in battle, a much higher ratio of NCOs had probably undergone qualification training.[19] In any event, NCOs did most of their learning in their regiments, which was very much in the tradition of the Anglo-Canadian armies of the late-nineteenth and early-twentieth centuries. Still, some NCOs slipped through the system without enough formal instruction in leadership. Charles Kipp provides an illustrative example, claiming that when he and three other properly trained corporals were posted to the Lincoln and Welland Regiment in England in October 1943, the battalion still "had many NCOs who, although they were good men, were not trained for the job."[20] He claims to have been lucky enough to fall under a good platoon sergeant, one of only a few in the unit with proper NCO training.

For better or for worse, much professional development occurred on the battlefield, for which no amount of training fully prepared a soldier. Combat taught NCOs many valuable lessons, and sometimes pointed up shortcomings in the training system. In the spring of 1944, an infantry brigade commander in Italy (records do not give his name) reported to CMHQ that senior NCOs and junior officers, in an abundance of aggressiveness, tended to demonstrate too much willingness to lead smaller teams from the front, when they should have remained back a bit where they could read and influence the battle. "In this division," he commented, "we have lost a great many officers and NCOs where more adequate training in this respect might have saved them."[21]

Some things had to be learned the hard way, as the testimony of those who fought suggests. Sergeant Fred Cederberg taught newly remustered soldiers in Italy that they had to learn to dig in very quickly – "You should know how to convert a tank rut into a slit [trench] in twenty seconds" – that a shovel was a soldier's most important piece of equipment for staying alive, and that using a ditch for cover was dangerous because of its open ends and the possibility that it was covered by fire.[22] Stanley Scislowski learned in Italy: "When you come under artillery fire, never move back to get out of it. Always move forward. You're more likely to survive moving through it than going the other way."[23] Regimental Sergeant Major Harry Fox and his men learned that they could detect German troops from their distinct smell, which came from a combination of the rations they ate, the tobacco they smoked, the soap they used, and the uniforms they wore.[24] Company Sergeant Major Charles Martin certainly believed that training took a soldier only so far: "Even the best training cannot prepare a man for the strange, the odd or the impossible that actually does take place under battle conditions."[25]

The two-track approach for developing NCOs also had some notable advantages. For one thing, it allowed units and formations to tailor training to particular or immediate requirements. The 2nd Canadian Infantry Brigade's two-week NCO school in Ortona included instruction in urban combat and capturing a prisoner, both subjects of considerable importance at that time and place.[26] Similarly, the 2nd Canadian Infantry Division's NCO course in Cuijk emphasized training on German tactics, house clearing, village and woods clearing, and attacking a pillbox, all things that combat leaders in the Netherlands had to master.[27] Conversely, for all their close attention to carefully crafted syllabuses, centralized courses were far removed from the action and probably slower to collect and integrate into training the latest expertise developed in battle. Indeed, syllabuses for the programs in Canada did not include the latest methods for capturing prisoners or assaulting pillboxes.

Furthermore, the two-track approach provided catch-up training to NCOs who had been promoted before receiving formal NCO training or who needed a good refresher. This was important for a system in which commanding officers promoted from within to fill vacancies. For example, CTS Course 804 (NCO Qualification) conveyed just the basic knowledge that junior NCOs required. The Canadian Army Routine Order advertising the course indicated that "candidates should be Junior N.C.O.s or privates who show promise of becoming good N.C.O. material."[28] Yet course records show that units frequently sent sergeants and even the occasional company sergeant major to receive this foundational training. In 1942, the North Shore (New Brunswick) Regiment ran a pair of six-week courses that provided elementary NCO training for about forty soldiers who had already been promoted to lance corporal or corporal.[29] And once the army started fighting, catch-up training became important for soldiers who were promoted in battle without having had any leadership training. In Italy, when the 1st Canadian Infantry Division's school at Riccione ran sergeants through an eight-day refresher, it became clear that many students required more training than the program provided. Even extending the course to two weeks proved insufficient because so many of the students were recently appointed lance sergeants who had no previous NCO training. Some needed even more instruction before they could assume their responsibilities in their units.[30]

By the end of the war, the NCO corps had developed from a small cadre in 1939 to well over a hundred thousand non-commissioned leaders for the wartime force of nearly half a million. To be sure, the system for developing the NCO corps had flaws, especially the lack of a common standard of qualification training. Few NCOs followed the same path to professional development, and each man's training and development profile was about as distinctive as his fingerprints. Further, the system depended heavily on commanding officers tending properly to NCO development.

While imperfect, the ad hoc approach suited the difficult conditions facing army planners. Building a force of that size on only a ramshackle foundation, arming it with modern weapons, training it to orchestrate the combat power needed to defeat entrenched German forces, and ensuring a steady supply of properly trained reinforcements was an enormous task. And no one was certain just how much time was available to do it – not in 1939, nor even in 1941. It made sense to put unit commanders at the centre of NCO development, where they could focus on unit needs. It also made sense to pack around them training support from formations and centralized schools. This approach worked, although Canada was fortunate to have had the years it needed to build the army's backbone. When it came time to fight, the army performed respectably, and it could not have done so without solid NCOs to drive the fighting at the lowest levels, which was where most battles were decided. Junior leader training and development may have been uneven across the army, but there were enough good NCOs to keep units pushing forward and winning.

Notes

Introduction

Epigraph: C.P. Stacey, "Canadian Leaders of the Second World War," *Canadian Historical Review* 66 (March 1985): 64.

1 Until November 1940, Canada's ground forces were officially called the Active Militia. That was changed to the Canadian Army by an order-in-council on 19 November 1940. The order designated continuous service units as active and all others, including non-permanent active militia units, as reserve. C.P. Stacey, *Six Years of War: The Army in Canada, Britain and the Pacific*, vol. 1 of *Official History of the Canadian Army in the Second World War* (Ottawa: Department of National Defence and the Queen's Printer, 1955), 89.

2 Ibid., 34.

3 C.P. Stacey, *Arms, Men and Governments: The War Policies of Canada, 1939–1945* (Ottawa: Queen's Printer, 1970), 4–5. See also David Bercuson, *Our Finest Hour: Canada Fights the Second World War* (Toronto: HarperCollins, 2015), 25.

4 Stacey, *Arms, Men and Governments*, 48. The army maintained three divisions for home defence, plus units assigned to the military districts and the Atlantic and Pacific Commands.

5 For example, excellent accounts appear in the very detailed *Official History of the Canadian Army in the Second World War*, which includes C.P. Stacey's *Six Years of War* (1955) and *The Victory Campaign: The Operations in North-West Europe, 1944–1945* (1960), and G.W.L. Nicholson's *The Canadians in Italy, 1943–1945* (1956). Jack Granatstein's *Canada's Army: Waging War and Keeping the Peace* (2002) is also outstanding. E.L.M. Burns assesses how the army allocated its human resources in *Manpower in the Canadian Army, 1939–1945* (1956). As for how the historiography has shifted regarding the army's performance in battle, see n30.

6 Stacey, *Six Years of War*, 138. The Officers Training Centres (OTCs) were at Brockville, Ontario, and Gordon Head, British Columbia. In 1942, the army established a third and temporary OTC at Trois-Rivières, Quebec, but in August 1943, by which time the army had produced a surplus of reinforcement officers, closed both it and the one at Gordon Head. Ibid., 139.

7 Geoffrey Hayes, *Crerar's Lieutenants: Inventing the Canadian Junior Army Officer, 1939–45* (Vancouver: UBC Press, 2017).

8 Robert Engen, *Strangers in Arms: Combat Motivation in the Canadian Army, 1943–1945* (Montreal and Kingston: McGill-Queen's University Press, 2016), 40 and 200–7.

9 Caroline D'Amours, "Canadian Military Culture and Tactical Training, 1940–1944: The Making of Infantry Junior NCOs," *Journal of Military History* 82, 4 (October 2018): 1175–98. D'Amours argues that infantry junior NCO training up to 1944 was not as good as it should have been. This article, and her doctoral dissertation, provide valuable insight into an important aspect of NCO development, opening the way for a wider examination of how

the army developed the NCO corps. See "'Notre tâche est de rendre les hommes prêts au combat': La formation des sous-officiers de renfort d'infanterie du Canada pendant la Seconde Guerre mondiale" (PhD diss., University of Ottawa, 2015).

10 John A. English, *The Canadian Army and the Normandy Campaign: A Study of Failure in High Command* (New York: Praeger, 1991), 129.

11 A battalion is a *unit* in the infantry. It comprises *sub-units* called companies, which are further broken down into platoons. In the armoured and engineer corps, a unit is called a regiment. A regiment is broken down into sub-units called squadrons, which are further broken down into troops. In the artillery, a unit is also called a regiment. Artillery regiments are broken down into batteries, which are further broken down into troops.

12 For the composition of sections and platoons, see War Office (DND reprint), *Infantry Training Part VIII – Fieldcraft, Battle Drill, Section and Platoon Tactics, 1944* (Ottawa: King's Printer, 1944), 39. While the official "establishment" (or composition and size) of an infantry battalion changed several times during the war, in July 1943 a battalion had 741 other ranks, including the regimental sergeant major. Perth Regiment War Diary, Field Return of Other Ranks 30 Jul 43, appended to war diary for July 1943, Library and Archives Canada (LAC), Record Group (RG) 24-C-3, vol. 15135.

13 A staff sergeant, as company quartermaster, had only a handful of subordinates to assist him in running the company stores.

14 Canada, Department of National Defence, *The King's Regulations and Orders for the Canadian Militia, 1939* (Ottawa: Edmond Cloutier, Printer to the King's Most Excellent Majesty, 1941), 50, para. 310.

15 Canada, Department of National Defence, *Report of the Department of National Defence for the Fiscal Year Ending March 31, 1942* (Ottawa: King's Printer, 1942), 11.

16 Canada, Department of National Defence, *Report of the Department of National Defence for the Fiscal Year Ending March 31, 1943* (Ottawa: King's Printer, 1943), 11.

17 Canada, Department of National Defence, *Mobilization Instructions for the Canadian Militia, 1937* (Ottawa: King's Printer, 1937), 15–16. Also, Canada, Department of National Defence, General Staff, Canadian Active Service Force Routine Orders (CASF RO), Volume 1, 14 September 1939–30 June 1940, Routine Order No. 22, 27 September 1939 (Ottawa: King's Printer, 1939–40).

18 A *formation* is an element comprising two or more units grouped under a single commander. The term *formation* usually refers to brigades, divisions, and corps.

19 Stacey, *Six Years of War*, 35.

20 Ibid., 50.

21 Ibid., 51–52.

22 Just before the war, the permanent force and NPAM combined numbered 55,661 soldiers. By the end of 1941, the NCO corps numbered approximately 63,000. See Table I.2.

23 For analysis of how the army managed conscription, see Jack Granatstein and J.M. Hitsman's *Broken Promises: A History of Conscription in Canada* (Toronto: Oxford University Press, 1977). For assessments of the so-called Terrace Mutiny, when conscripts in Terrace, British Columbia, took up arms to resist the government's decision in November 1944 to send conscripts overseas, see Reginald H. Roy, "Mutiny in the Mountains: The Terrace 'Incident,'" in *Men at War: Politics, Technology and Innovation in the Twentieth Century*, ed. Timothy Travers and Christon Archer (Chicago: Precedent, 1982), 49–67, and Peter A. Russell, "BC's 1944 'Zombie' Protests against Overseas Conscription," *BC Studies* 122 (1999): 49–76.

24 Daniel Byers, *Zombie Army: The Canadian Army and Conscription in the Second World War* (Vancouver: UBC Press, 2016).
25 Ibid., 55.
26 Ibid., 199.
27 Stacey, *Arms, Men and Governments*, 602.
28 Stacey, *Six Years of War*, 524.
29 Granatstein, *Canada's Army*, 292.
30 Burns, *Manpower in the Canadian Army*, 79.
31 Robert Engen, *Canadians under Fire: Infantry Effectiveness in the Second World War* (Montreal and Kingston: McGill-Queen's University Press, 2009), 101.
32 Several historians have demonstrated that previous work criticizing Canadian performance, particularly during the Normandy campaign, failed to recognize the achievements. For example, Terry Copp argues in *Fields of Fire: The Canadians in Normandy* (2003) and *Cinderella Army: The Canadians in Northwest Europe, 1944–1945* (2006) that historical criticism of the army in Northwest Europe fails to appreciate how well Canadian formations actually performed. *Fields of Fire* shows that the Canadian contribution to the Normandy campaign was disproportionate to the army's relatively small size. This book counters previous unfavourable assessments – especially those of John English, who contends that supposedly mediocre Canadian performance resulted in high casualties – by demonstrating that Canadian divisions spent more days engaged in close combat than practically any British formation, and thus suffered a higher proportion of casualties. Furthermore, in *Cinderella Army*, Copp demonstrates that, after the breakout from Normandy, Canadian divisions proved remarkably effective, given that they were some of the most heavily committed formations in all the Allied armies in Northwest Europe. Gregory Liedtke further contributes to reassessments of the Canadian Army's performance during the Normandy campaign, showing that German forces were larger and more powerful than critics of the Canadians had appreciated, in "Canadian Offensive Operations in Normandy Revisited," *Canadian Military Journal* 8, 2 (Summer 2007): 60–68. Robert Engen, in *Canadians under Fire* (2009), establishes that Canadian infantry demonstrated combat effectiveness in all the army's campaigns. Most recently, Marc Milner makes a significant contribution with *Stopping the Panzers: The Untold Story of D-Day* (2014), in which he dismantles the argument that the 3rd Canadian Division failed to seize Caen because of hesitancy and tactical incompetence. He shows that the division fought exactly according to the Overlord plan and prevented the Germans from seizing the only ground they could have used to stage a counter-attack powerful enough to defeat the invasion. Milner argues that 3rd Division's successful and costly actions should probably count as the greatest Canadian contribution to the Normandy landings. Jack Granatstein argues that the First Canadian Army had become "probably the best little army in the world" by the spring of 1945. *The Best Little Army in the World: The Canadians in Northwest Europe, 1944–1945* (Toronto: HarperCollins, 2015), 279.
33 From his study of factors that contributed to unit-level cohesion, Robert Engen shows that NCO and junior officer leadership and experience proved "central to continued effectiveness and cohesion" at the battalion level. *Strangers in Arms*, 206.

Chapter 1: Profile of the Infantry Senior NCOs
Epigraph: Charles Cromwell Martin, *Battle Diary: From D-Day and Normandy to the Zuider Zee and VE* (Toronto: Dundurn Press, 1994), 70.

1 Alexander Connolly service file, Library and Archives Canada (LAC), Record Group (RG) 24, vol. 25626.

2 Producing generalizations about soldiers' educational backgrounds proves tricky, given the lack of detail in many personnel files and the different educational standards between provinces. For example, attestation forms might indicate that an individual completed two years of high school in Saskatchewan, public school in Nova Scotia, Grade 8 in Alberta, or junior matriculation in Ontario.

3 Canada, Dominion Bureau of Statistics, *Eighth Census of Canada, 1941*, vol. 2, *Population – Local Subdivisions* (Ottawa: King's Printer, 1944).

4 Canada, Dominion Bureau of Statistics, *Eighth Census of Canada*, vol. 1, *General Review and Summary Tables* (Ottawa: King's Printer, 1950), 289, Table 1. In Ontario, Anglicans constituted 21.6 percent of the population, behind Roman Catholics (22.5 percent) and the United Church (28.4 percent). See *Eighth Census*, vol. 1, 295, Table 5.

5 For the Anglican Church's support for the First World War, see Melissa Davidson, "Preaching the Great War: Canadian Anglicans and the War Sermon, 1914–1918" (MA thesis, McGill University, 2012), 25, 27, 37, 125. Mark McGowan shows that in the First World War, Anglicans made up the greatest number of volunteers for the Canadian Expeditionary Force, at least up to June 1917. See *The Imperial Irish: Canada's Irish Catholics Fight the Great War, 1914–1918* (Montreal and Kingston: McGill-Queen's University Press, 2017), 108. He also explains that the Roman Catholic community was not homogeneous in its support for the First World War. But Irish-Canadian Roman Catholics volunteered for the army in large numbers, and Irish-Canadian Roman Catholic bishops vigorously supported the war effort (110 and 288).

6 Robert Engen, *Strangers in Arms: Combat Motivation in the Canadian Army, 1943–1945* (Montreal and Kingston: McGill-Queen's University Press, 2016), 23–24.

7 Attestation forms asked individuals to declare their "trade or calling" but not their employment status, so unemployed individuals may or may not have declared themselves as such. Some files, but unfortunately not all, include an occupational history form that indicates whether a soldier was unemployed or working when he enlisted.

8 According to the 1941 census, Ontario had an estimated 830,000 males between the ages of eighteen and forty-five. Quebec had the second-highest number, with 699,000. Saskatchewan came in at a distant third, with 191,000. C.P. Stacey, *Arms, Men and Governments: The War Policies of Canada, 1939–1945* (Ottawa: Queen's Printer, 1970), Appendix R, 590.

9 *Eighth Census, 1941*, vol 1, 318, Table 8. This document shows that citizens of Ontario between the ages of twenty and twenty-four had the second-highest median number of years in school, at ten (meaning half of the population had more than ten and half had fewer). British Columbians had the highest median education, at 10.2 years. The national median was 9.1.

10 Stacey, *Arms, Men and Governments*, Appendix R, 590. Quebec had by far the lowest proportion of its military-age males in the armed forces, at 25.69 percent. Alberta had the second-lowest, at 42.38 percent. British Columbia had the highest, at 50.47 percent.

11 This book considers as rural areas those that lie outside the commuting zone of centres with populations of over 10,000, similar to a definition Statistics Canada used previously. The 1941 census was used to check the population levels of towns listed on the attestation forms.

12 NPAM soldiers with less than six months of part-time service, who did not have much training, are counted in this calculation as not having military experience.

13 Interview with Major Burton Harper, FCWM Oral History Project, CWM 20020121-022, George Metcalf Archival Collection, Canadian War Museum — Military History Research Centre.

14 For example, NPAM training centres could appoint 4 percent of students under their instruction to lance corporal to help maintain discipline. Canada, Department of National Defence, *General Orders, 1940* (Ottawa: King's Printer, 1941), G.O. 61. A soldier appointed to lance corporal held the *rank* of private, and a soldier appointed to lance sergeant held the *rank* of corporal. Therefore, a private who earned an appointment to lance sergeant received the rank of corporal. Similarly, a private appointed to acting lance sergeant received the rank of acting corporal. Canada, Department of National Defence, *Canadian Army Routine Orders*, vol. 9, January to June 1944, CARO 4366 (Ottawa: King's Printer, 1944).

15 Canada, Department of National Defence, *Canadian Army Routine Orders*, vol. 4, 2 July 1941 to 31 December 1941, CARO 1340 (Ottawa: King's Printer, 1941).

16 Edward George Evans service file, LAC, RG24, vol. 25835. Evans made sergeant again ten days after jumping into Normandy.

17 For the regulations governing reductions in rank, see Canada, Department of National Defence, *General Orders, 1939* (Ottawa: King's Printer, 1940), G.O. 246 and 247 and *General Orders, 1940*, G.O. 217. These orders should be read in conjunction with *KR&O, 1939*, 54–55, articles 327–30.

18 Paul Eugene Dugas service file, LAC, RG24, vol. 26360. His rise back to sergeant took some time because of further disciplinary infractions – as a private he told a corporal to "mange de la merde," and he absented himself without leave twice, once for a whole week. An army examiner wrote that Dugas "could probably be a good NCO if he could learn to obey an order." Evidently, he did. Dugas went to France as a private with Le Régiment de la Chaudière, then quickly climbed back to sergeant.

19 Canada, Department of National Defence, *Mobilization Instructions for the Canadian Militia, 1937* (Ottawa: King's Printer, 1937), 15.

20 Canada, Department of National Defence, *Extracts from Canadian Army (Overseas) Routine Orders* (London: Canadian Military Headquarters, 1943), appendix to Routine Order No. 431.

21 Canada, Department of National Defence, *Canadian Army Routine Orders*, vol. 7, January to June 1943, CARO 2987 (Ottawa: King's Printer, 1943).

22 Joseph P. Downey service file, LAC, RG24, vol. 25770.

23 William Steven Steele service file, LAC, RG24, vol. 27113.

24 Glen E. Miller service file, LAC, RG24, vol. 26616.

25 John William Gray service file, LAC, RG24, vol. 26002.

26 Robert Arthur Joyes service file, LAC, RG24, vol. 26224.

27 William R. Johnston service file, LAC, RG24, vol. 26214.

28 Aubrey Cosens service file, LAC, RG24, vol. 25645. Cosens was killed in action during this battle, a platoon attack on the hamlet of Mooshof, Germany.

29 Brigadier M.H.S. Penhale to Commander CRU [Canadian Reinforcement Units], 25 August 1944, LAC, RG24-C-2, vol. 9777.

30 E.L.M. Burns, *Manpower in the Canadian Army, 1939–1945* (Toronto: Clarke, Irwin, 1956), 99.

31 For example, according to Denis Whitaker and Shelagh Whitaker, the First Canadian Army received poorly trained reinforcements, including NCOs, during the Scheldt campaign, when the army rushed remustered soldiers to battle without giving them proper conversion training. *Tug of War: The Allied Victory That Opened Antwerp*, 2nd ed. (Toronto: Stoddart, 2000), 213–36. For a reference to NCOs, see p. 221.

32 The army set high age limits for recruiting. In the war's first four years, regulations permitted men to enlist between the ages of eighteen and forty-five. In 1943, updated regulations established new standards that varied by corps of arms and unit type (operational, line of communication, base in a theatre of war, or static establishments), but even then allowed older men to enlist. For instance, general duty infantry had to be forty or younger to serve in an operational capacity, or a maximum of forty-five to serve in line of communications units or at a base in a theatre of war. Canada, Department of National Defence, *Physical Standards and Instructions for the Medical Examination of Recruits for the Naval, Military and Air Services, 1938* (Ottawa: J.O. Patenaude, Printer to the King's Most Excellent Majesty, 1938), 8; see also the 1940 version, p. 9; and Canada, Department of National Defence, *Physical Standards and Instructions for the Medical Examination of Serving Soldiers and Recruits for the Canadian Army, 1943* (Ottawa: King's Printer, 1943), section 4 part 3.

33 In October 1943, the Edmonton Regiment became the Loyal Edmonton Regiment, based on its association with the Loyal Regiment (North Lancashire). G.W.L. Nicholson, *The Canadians in Italy 1943–1945*, vol. 2 of *Official History of the Canadian Army in the Second World War* (Ottawa: Queen's Printer, 1956), 246.

34 Arthur McIlvena service file, LAC, RG24, vol. 26469. McIlvena died of heart disease on 2 March 1946, after he had been released from the army. Officials deemed that his death was related to military service, which is why the file is publicly available.

35 Charles P.R. Nelson service file, LAC, RG24, vol. 26699. Nelson was killed in action on 8 June 1944.

36 John Dixon Elliott service file, LAC, RG24, vol. 25819.

37 William Ross Howard service file, LAC, RG24, vol. 26146. Howard was killed in action on 4 January 1945.

38 Private (Acting Corporal) William Ross Howard Military Medal recommendation, approved by Field Marshal H.R. Alexander, October 1944, Directorate of History and Heritage (DHH), Canadian Army Overseas Honours and Awards, Citation Details, accessed 9 July 2018, http://www.cmp-cpm.forces.gc.ca/dhh-dhp/gal/cao-aco/doc/D1_HEAP-HYN_075.pdf.

39 Albert Lionel Laprade service file, LAC, RG24, vol. 26313.

40 Corporal (Acting Sergeant) Albert Lionel Laprade Military Medal recommendation, approved by Field Marshal B.L. Montgomery, June 1945, DHH, Canadian Army Overseas Honours and Awards, Citation Details, accessed 9 July 2018, http://www.cmp-cpm.forces.gc.ca/dhh-dhp/gal/cao-aco/doc/D1_KEN-LEC_077.pdf.

41 Ibid., 34.

42 C.P. Stacey, *Six Years of War: The Army in Canada, Britain and the Pacific*, vol. 1 of *Official History of the Canadian Army in the Second World War* (Ottawa: Department of National Defence and the Queen's Printer, 1955), 51.

43 The initial phase of recruiting for the Canadian Active Service Force (CASF) lasted until October 1939, during which time the two-division force grew to about 60,000, using the Mobile Force concept of Defence Scheme No. 3. For details on the initial mobilization, see Stacey, *Six Years of War*, 43–55.

44 Sixty-two percent of the permanent force men in the sample group came to the active army as privates. The remaining 38 percent were senior NCOs between the ranks of sergeant and warrant officer class 2 (CSM).

45 Wendell Clark service file, LAC, RG24, vol. 28204.

46 Lewis H. Pengelley service file, LAC, RG24, vol. 28209. Pengelley was a member of the Instructional Cadre, which is described in Chapter 2.

47 Victor E. Cahill service file, LAC, RG24, vol. 25515.

48 Cahill was still on active service when he died of pneumonia on 10 December 1946, which is why his file is publicly available.

49 On mobilization, the government called out 106 NPAM units, or elements thereof, for home defence duties, especially guarding vulnerable points and defending coastal areas. The affected soldiers either attested voluntarily into the CASF or had to be released from the service. Stacey, *Six Years of War,* 41 and 43.

50 Or in the Reserve Army, the new name for the NPAM as of 19 November 1940.

51 Andrew Burns Currie service file, LAC, RG24, vol. 28203. Sadly, Currie committed suicide in January 1941.

52 John Roderick Daly service file, LAC, RG24, vol. 30808.

53 Austin George Murray service file, LAC, RG24, vol. 26682.

54 RSM (WO Class 1) Austin George Murray Military Cross recommendation, November 1944, DHH, Canadian Army Overseas Honours and Awards, Citation Details, accessed 11 July 2018, http://www.cmp-cpm.forces.gc.ca/dhh-dhp/gal/cao-aco/doc/D1_MIN-NIC_073.pdf.

55 In May 1940, when the German offensive in Northwest Europe sparked a sense of crisis in Canada, the government's plans to expand the army included raising a Veterans Home Guard, comprising companies of First World War veterans. Later taking the name the Veterans Guard of Canada, this organization raised 250-man companies across the country. In June 1943, the Veterans Guard reached its peak strength of 41 officers and 9,806 other ranks. These men formed thirty-seven companies in Canada, seventeen internment camp guards, plus a company each in the Bahamas, British Guiana, Newfoundland, and at CMHQ in Britain. Stacey, *Six Years of War,* 79 and 151.

56 Daniel Byers describes how the army in Canada allowed NRMA troops to become NCOs, and indicates that by early 1944, most of the NCOs in 13 Canadian Infantry Brigade (CIB) were conscripts. *Zombie Army: the Canadian Army and Conscription in the Second World War* (Vancouver: UBC Press, 2016), 168–69 and 199. Also, the commander of 13 CIB, Brigadier W.H.S. Macklin, wrote in May 1944 that the Régiment de Hull had two NRMA acting warrant officers, and that most of the unit's sergeants were conscripts, too. He also stated that other units had NRMA sergeants, corporals, and lance corporals. Brigadier W.H.S. Macklin's Report on the Mobilization of the 13th Infantry Brigade on an Active Basis, 2 May 1944, Appendix S to C.P. Stacey, *Arms, Men and Governments: The War Policies of Canada, 1939–1945* (Ottawa: Queen's Printer, 1970), 595, para. 51.

57 Many proved good instructors and leaders, one volunteered to be a paratrooper, and two won the Military Medal.

Chapter 2: NCO Development before the War

Epigraph: Craig B. Cameron, *Born Lucky: RSM Harry Fox, MBE, One D-Day Dodger's Story* (St. Catharines, ON: Vanwell, 2005), 14–16.

1 Department of National Defence, *The King's Regulations and Orders for the Canadian Militia, 1939* (Ottawa: Edmond Cloutier, Printer to the King's Most Excellent Majesty, 1941), 1. *KR&O, 1939* explains the Instructional Cadre's roles at 56–57, paras. 334–45.

2 Department of National Defence, *Physical Standards and Instructions for the Medical Examination of Recruits for the Naval, Military and Air Services, 1938* (Ottawa: J.O. Patenaude, Printer to the King's Most Excellent Majesty, 1938), 3–9.

3 DND, *KR&O*, *1939*, Appendix 1 (*The Militia Act*), 285.
4 Ibid., 292.
5 Major-General W.D. Otter to the Secretary of the Militia Council, 21 February 1911, Library and Archives Canada (LAC), Record Group (RG) 24-C-1-a, vol. 6503, file HQ 313-9-12.
6 CGS to Commandants of Schools of Instruction, 2 March 1911, LAC, RG24-C-1-a, vol. 6503, file HQ 313-9-12. The Militia used the term Schools of Instruction in reference to the infantry, artillery, cavalry, and engineer schools.
7 Canada, Department of National Defence, *The King's Regulations and Orders for the Canadian Militia, 1917* (Ottawa: King's Printer, 1917), 65, para. 334 and Appendix 6, 311.
8 The next version did not appear until April 1939, and even then, the requirements for promotion did not change much.
9 Canada, Department of National Defence, *The King's Regulations and Orders for the Canadian Militia, 1926* (Ottawa: King's Printer, 1926), 66. A few exceptions existed. Soldiers who had served as NCOs for at least one year in the British regular forces, the Canadian Expeditionary Force, or the permanent force did not require a certificate.
10 Canada, Department of National Defence, *How to Qualify: Instructions on the Qualification of Officers and Other Ranks for Promotion – Non-Permanent Active Militia, 1938* (Ottawa: King's Printer, 1938), 4, 8–10.
11 DND, *KR&O*, *1926*, 170 and Annex 7, 348–49.
12 Ibid., 170.
13 Ibid., 62–63.
14 Ibid., 64.
15 Ibid., 165.
16 DND, *How to Qualify, 1938*, 9.
17 DND, *KR&O*, *1926*, 156–57. The school had three wings that prepared students to instruct in certain skill sets: A Wing taught the rifle, bayonet, revolver, light automatic weapons, and grenades; B Wing taught the Vickers machine gun; and C Wing taught other small arms and protection against gas.
18 Ibid., 67–68.
19 Ibid., 165–66.
20 John Clifford Cave, interview by Chris D. Main, 14 August 1978, University of Victoria, Military History Oral Collection, accessed 29 January 2019, http://contentdm.library. uvic.ca/cdm/compoundobject/collection/collection13/id/433/rec/1.
21 The one exception to this rule was for quartermasters sergeant, who after three years became merely *eligible* for appointment to sergeant major instructor (warrant officer class 1). See DND, *KR&O*, *1926*, 69.
22 *Individual training* imparts skills to individual soldiers, whereas *collective training* prepares soldiers to work in groups.
23 Colonel H.H. Mathews to CGS [Chief of the General Staff], 23 January 1930, LAC, RG24-C-1-a, vol. 2643, file HQS-3498-vol. 1.
24 Defence Scheme No. 1 concerned defending Canada from the United States, and No. 2 dealt with defending Canada from Japan. Lieutenant-Colonel H.D.G. Crerar to DMO and I [Directorate of Military Operations and Intelligence], 15 May 1931, LAC, RG24-C-1-a, vol. 2643, file HQS-3498-vol. 1.
25 CGS to Adjutant General, 13 September 1932, LAC, RG24-C-1-a, vol. 2643, file HQS-3498-vol. 2.

26 CGS Memorandum, Policy As to Organization and Employment of Permanent Force under Conditions Visualized in Defence Scheme No. 3, 24 June 1940, LAC, RG24-C-1-a, vol. 2643, file HQS-3498-vol. 1.

27 See examples of District returns in LAC, RG24-C-1-a, vol. 2644, file HQS-3498-vol. 5; and vol. 2645, file HQS-3498-vol. 4.

28 Lieutenant-Colonel H.D.G. Crerar (A/DMO&I) to all District Officers Commanding, 6 December 1933, LAC, RG24-C-1-a, vol. 2645, file HQS-3498-vol. 4.

29 Defence Scheme No. 3 (draft version, approved by MND on 17 March 1937), ch. 5, p. 19, LAC, RG24-C-1-a, vol. 2648, file HQS-3498-vol. 22.

30 CGS to MND [Minister of National Defence], Defence Scheme No. 3, 15 March 1937, LAC, RG24-C-1-a, vol. 2648, file HQS-3498-vol. 22. Ashton made no reference to other potential obligations under the Versailles or Locarno treaties, or to mutual assistance under imperial defence.

31 Ibid.

32 MND to CGS, 17 March 1937, LAC, RG24-C-1-a, vol. 2648, file HQS-3498-vol. 22.

33 Military planners knew that an expeditionary task was much more likely than a home defence mission but probably emphasized the latter for political purposes. See C.P. Stacey, *Six Years of War: The Army in Canada, Britain and the Pacific*, vol. 1 of *Official History of the Canadian Army in the Second World War* (Ottawa: Department of National Defence and the Queen's Printer, 1955), 30–31; C.P. Stacey, *Arms, Men and Governments: The War Policies of Canada, 1939–1945* (Ottawa: Queen's Printer, 1970), 9–10; and Stephen Harris, *Canadian Brass: The Making of a Professional Army, 1860–1939* (Toronto: University of Toronto Press, 1988), 183.

34 Defence Scheme No. 3 (draft version), chapter 1, page 2, para. 2(c), LAC, RG24-C-1-a, vol. 2648, file HQS-3498-vol. 22.

35 Some of these instructors could be posted to their designated Mobile Force units for active service.

36 Canada, Department of National Defence, *Mobilization Instructions for the Canadian Militia, 1937* (Ottawa: King's Printer, 1937).

37 CGS to MND, 12 June 1939, LAC, RG24, vol. 2648, file HQS-3498-vol. 22.

38 DND, *Mobilization Instructions, 1937.*

39 Defence Scheme No. 3 (draft version), chapter 5, page 20, para. 23.

40 DND, *Mobilization Instructions, 1937.*

41 Ibid. The Field Force included the Mobile Force and the units raised for local defence and internal security.

42 CGS to MND, 12 June 1939. The minister approved this document with a handwritten minute. Also, the CGS indicated that the plan to concentrate the Mobile Force in a single location, in two successive waves, for collective training should be abandoned. The militia had no camp with the necessary infrastructure, so Anderson recommended that units concentrate at several camps across Canada, based on arm of service.

43 Canada, Department of National Defence, *Report of the Department of National Defence for the Fiscal Year Ending March 31, 1938* (Ottawa: King's Printer, 1938), Statement No. 3 — Comparative Statement of Expenditure, Militia, Naval, Air, and Other Services for Ten Years from 1928–29 to 1937–38, 12–13.

44 Canada, Department of National Defence, *Report of the Department of National Defence for the Fiscal Year Ending March 31, 1933* (Ottawa: King's Printer, 1934), 51.

45   Canada, Department of National Defence, *Report of the Department of National Defence for the Fiscal Year Ending March 31, 1936* (Ottawa: King's Printer, 1936), 27–28.

46   Canada, Department of National Defence, *Report of the Department of National Defence for the Fiscal Year Ending March 31, 1939* (Ottawa: King's Printer, 1939), 31–32, 40.

47   Canada, Department of National Defence, *Report of the Department of National Defence for the Fiscal Year Ending March 31, 1941* (Ottawa: King's Printer: 1941), Statement No. 3 — Comparative Statement of Expenditure, Militia, Naval, Air and Other Services for Ten Years from 1931–32 to 1940–41, 36–37.

48   Harris, *Canadian Brass*, 197–98.

49   Chief of Staff Committee Memorandum, Canada's National Effort (Armed Forces) in the Early Stages of a Major War, 29 August 1939, LAC, RG24, vol. 2648, file HQS-3498-vol 22.

50   Ibid.

51   CGS Memorandum, 1 September 1939, LAC, RG24, vol. 2647, file HQS-3498-vol 14.

52   CGS Memorandum, 1212 hrs, 1 September 1939, LAC, RG24, vol. 2647, file HQS-3498-vol 14. C.P. Stacey attributes the name change to the government's desire to avoid perceptions of having decided on the force composition in advance of the crisis. *Six Years of War*, 43.

53   DND, *Fiscal Year Ending March 31, 1939*, 69, 70, 73.

54   In fact, 730,625 Canadians served in the army over the course of the war, including 25,251 women and 100,573 conscripts, more than thirteen times the number of personnel in uniform just before mobilization. C.P. Stacey, *The Canadian Army 1939–1945: An Official Historical Summary* (Ottawa: King's Printer, 1948), 324. The estimated number of NCOs is shown in Table 1.2 on p. 22.

Chapter 3: The Wartime Army's Expectations of Its NCOs

Epigraph: W. Denis Whitaker and Shelagh Whitaker, *Tug of War: The Allied Victory That Opened Antwerp*, 2nd ed. (Toronto: Stoddart, 2000), 221.

1   Bernd Horn describes these immutable roles in "A Timeless Strength: The Army's Senior NCO Corps," *Canadian Military Journal* (Spring 2002): 41–45.

2   For examples, see Tim Cook, *The Necessary War: Canadians Fighting the Second World War 1939–1943* (Toronto: Allen Lane, 2014), 334; and Gordon Brown and Terry Copp, *Look to Your Front – Regina Rifles: A Regiment at War* (Waterloo, ON: Laurier Centre for Military, Strategic and Disarmament Studies, 2001), 7.

3   Today, operations that involve more than one arm of service (such as infantry, armour, artillery, and engineers) are known as combined arms operations. Operations involving more than one service (army, navy, air force, or special operations forces) are known today as joint operations.

4   2 Cdn Div Training Instruction No. 2, 21 December 1940, Library and Archives Canada (LAC), Record Group (RG) 24-C-2, vol. 9805, file 2/Instrns 2 Div/1.

5   Major-General V.W. Odlum to Cdn Corps, Report on Training, 21 February 1941, LAC, RG24-C-2, vol. 9805, file 2/Instrns 2 Div/1.

6   Colonel J.K. Lawson memorandum, TRAINING, 30 May 1941, appended to Directorate of Military Training (DMT) War Diary (WD) for May 1941, LAC, RG24-C-3, vol. 13239.

7   Department of National Defence, Directorate of History and Heritage (DHH), Canadian Military Headquarters (CMHQ) Reports, Historical Officer Report No. 73, South Eastern Command Exercise "Tiger," 19–30 May 1942, dated 24 June 1942, 1, 2, 9, 10.

8   Major-General C.B. Price to 1 Cdn Corps (A), Exercise "Tiger" – Fitness of Troops, 6 July 1942, LAC, RG24-G-3-1-a, vol. 10771, file 222C1 (D282).

9 Gordon Alexander service file, LAC, RG24, vol. 29219. Alexander died of a stroke in September 1943 while serving in a reinforcement unit in Britain. Craig Cameron describes how the unit posted Alexander out because of his age, in *Born Lucky: RSM Harry Fox, MBE, One D-Day Dodger's Story* (St. Catharines, ON: Vanwell, 2005), 46.

10 Fred Cederberg, *The Long Road Home: The Autobiography of a Canadian Soldier in Italy in World War II* (Don Mills, ON: General, 1984), 26–27.

11 Appendix 10 to RCR WD for July 1942, Record of Marching Time etc. of Platoons from Field Firing Range to Arundel Camp, 11/12 July 42, LAC, RG24-C-3, vol. 15208.

12 R22R WD, 15 September 1942, LAC, RG24-C-3, vol. 15237.

13 Lieutenant-General H.D.G. Crerar, cover letter for First Canadian Army Training Directive No. 1, 31 October 1942, LAC, RG24-G-3-1-a, vol. 10770, file 222C1 (D236).

14 In November 1944, NDHQ recommended that airborne reinforcement soldiers in Canada preparing to proceed overseas undergo a series of tests that culminated in marching 50 miles (over 80 kilometres) in twenty-four hours, in battle order and carrying platoon weapons. These men needed to reach this standard to be suitable for service in 1st Canadian Parachute Battalion, where the training only became harder. Appendix 9 to DMT WD for November 1944, Lieutenant-Colonel F.L. Nichols to DOC MD No. 10, Paratrp Trg In U.K., 9 November 1944, LAC, RG24-C-3, vol. 13243.

15 Appendix 87 to DMT WD for May 1944, DMT Circular Letter No. 1354, dated 20 May 1944, LAC, RG24-C-3, vol. 13241. The British had implemented the tests, and informed Canada of them, with Army Council Instruction No. 577 – Physical Efficiency Tests.

16 The three tests can be found at Physical Efficiency Tests, 20 May 1944, LAC, RG24-C-3, vol. 13241, Appendix 87 to DMT WD for April 1944. The Battle Physical Efficiency Test given here is derived from LAC, RG24-C-3, vol. 13241, Appendix 87 to Directorate of Military Training WD for April 1944.

17 Lieutenant-General B.L. Montgomery, Notes on Inf. Bdes of Canadian Corps, written between 3 February and 4 March 1942, LAC, General H.D.G. Crerar Papers, Manuscript Group (MG) 30-E157, vol. 2, file 958C.009 (D182).

18 Crerar memorandum, untitled, 24 February 1942, LAC, RG24-G-3-1-a, vol. 10771, file 222C1 (D292).

19 War diaries show that units sent groups of soldiers back to Canada to instruct others, but do not indicate how many of these individuals were selected for their age.

20 The men in the sample group who had to leave their units due to age or physical condition died later, in most cases of natural causes, while still in service, which is why their files are available to the public.

21 William Beattie service file, LAC, RG24, vol. 25406. The army discharged Beattie in May 1942 because he no longer met military physical standards.

22 William Davidson service file, LAC, RG24, vol. 29215.

23 John A. English, *The Canadian Army and the Normandy Campaign: A Study of Failure in High Command* (New York: Praeger, 1991), xiv and 312–13.

24 C.P. Stacey, *The Victory Campaign: The Operations in North-West Europe, 1944–1945*, vol. 3 of *Official History of the Canadian Army in the Second World War* (Ottawa: Department of National Defence and the Queen's Printer, 1960), 275–77.

25 Carlo D'Este, *Decision in Normandy* (New York: Konecky and Konecky, c. 1994), 291–97.

26 Timothy Harrison Place, *Military Training in the British Army, 1940–1944: From Dunkirk to D-Day* (London and Portland, OR: Frank Cass, 2000), 153–67.

27   1 Canadian Division Training Instruction No. 2, 9 March 1940, LAC, RG24-C-2, vol. 9886, file 2/Trng. Instrns/1.

28   1 Canadian Division Training Instruction No. 3, 27 April 1940, LAC, RG24-C-2, vol. 9886, file 2/Trng. Instrns/1.

29   Seaforth Highlanders WD, 2 May and 22–24 May 1940, LAC, RG24-C-3, vol. 15254.

30   HQ 2 CIB [Canadian Infantry Brigade] WD, 29 May 1940, LAC, RG24-C-3, vol. 14063 (reel T-11063); HQ 3 CIB WD, 20 June 1940, LAC RG24-C-3, vol. 14082 (reel T-11078); West Nova Scotia Regiment WD, final entry for June 1940, LAC, RG24-C-3, vol. 15285.

31   On 9 May 1940, 1st Canadian Infantry Brigade held a demonstration infantry-cum-tank attack, with all battalions in attendance. On 20 May, a brigade-run exercise had the 48th Highlanders attack the RCR, in conjunction with a squadron of medium tanks. 1 CIB WD, 9, 19, and 20 May 1940, LAC, RG24-C-3, vol. 14063 (reel T-11056).

32   John Clifford Cave, interview by Chris D. Main, 14 August 1978, University of Victoria, Military History Oral Collection, accessed 29 January 2019, http://contentdm.library.uvic.ca/cdm/compoundobject/collection/collection13/id/433/rec/1.

33   The Canadian Corps formed on 25 December 1940 and included the 1st Canadian and 2nd Canadian Divisions. (The 1st Division had previously been part of the British 7th Corps, commanded by Lieutenant-General McNaughton.) The Canadian Corps became 1st Canadian Corps on 6 April 1942, the same day that Headquarters First Canadian Army stood up. C.P. Stacey, *Six Years of War: The Army in Canada, Britain and the Pacific*, vol. 1 of *Official History of the Canadian Army in the Second World War* (Ottawa: Department of National Defence and the Queen's Printer, 1955), 86 and 99.

34   Major-General V.W. Odlum, Report on Training, 21 February 1941, LAC, RG24-C-2, vol. 9805, file 2/Instrns 2 Div/1.

35   1st Canadian Corps Training Instruction, No. 5, 25 November 1941, LAC, RG24-G-3-1-a, vol. 10770, file 222C1 (D235).

36   First Canadian Army Training Instruction No. 1, November 1942, LAC, RG24-G-3-1-a, vol. 10437, file 212C1 (D44).

37   Address by Lieutenant-General H.D.G. Crerar to Senior Officers, First Canadian Army, 14 May 1944, LAC, RG24-G-3-1-a, vol. 10586, file 215C1 (D286).

38   Canadian Corps Training Directive, 16 January 1942, LAC, RG24-G-3-1-a, vol. 10770, file 222C1 (D235).

39   War diaries of the 1st, 2nd, and 3rd Canadian Infantry Brigades, January to March 1942. LAC, RG24-C-3, vols 14066 and 14067 (reel T-11061) (for 1 CIB); vol 14072 (reels T-11067 and T-11068) (for 2 CIB); and vol. 14083 (reel T-11136) (for 3 CIB). Just prior to Exercise Mickey, Brigadier G.G. Simonds, the 1st Canadian Corps Brigadier General Staff, lectured all 3 CIB officers on cooperation between infantry and tanks. Carleton and York Regiment WD, 24 March 1942, LAC, RG-24-C-3, vol. 15049. Similarly, to study all-arms cooperation in the counter-attack, 2 CIB held a cloth model exercise and a TEWT of all unit officers down to company commanders, plus representatives from artillery, armour, and machine gun units. Exercise Mickey instructions, dated 7 March 1942, LAC, RG24-C-3, vol. 15255, Appendix 13 to Seaforth Highlanders WD for March 1942.

40   HQ 1 CIB WD, 4–9 July 1942, LAC, RG24-C-3, vol. 14075 (reel T-11071); HQ 2 CIB WD, 9 and 20–21 July 1942, LAC, RG24-C-3, vol. 14073 (reel T-11069); and HQ 3 CIB WD, 1–3 August 1942, LAC, RG24-C-3, vol. 14161 (reel T-12396).

41   Stacey, *Six Years of War*, 245.

42   For example, on 2–3 September, 1 CIB conducted Exercise Breaststroke, a live-fire, all-arms brigade group attack. 1 CIB WD, LAC, RG24-C-3, vol. 14075 (reel-T11071). Or see

48th Highlanders WD, 2–3 September 1942, LAC, RG24-C-3, vol. 15296. 2 CIB and 3 CIB each practised a brigade-group amphibious assault with Exercise Viking, on 17–18 September and 14–15 September, respectively. See WD entries on LAC reels T-11069 and T-12396.

43 Brigadier C.C. Mann memorandum, Training in Co-operation – Army Tk Regts and Infantry, 10 November 1942, LAC, RG24-G-3-1-a, vol. 10769, file 222C1 (D207). 2 CIB and 3 CIB units conducted the training in December 1942. See WD entries at LAC, RG24-C-3, vol. 14073 (reel T-11069) and vol. 14161 (reel T-12396), respectively. 1 CIB's units conducted the training in January 1943, after the brigade returned from combined arms training in Scotland. The 1 CIB direction for this training refers to the Corps training directive of 10 November 1942. See Infantry Cum Tank Trg (undated), appended to WD for January 1943, LAC, RG24-C-3, vol. 14075 (reel T-11072). The West Nova Scotia Regiment WD shows that the training included one day of familiarization training, one day of platoon-troop training, and one day of company-squadron training, just as the Corps had ordered. WD, 20–22 December 1942, LAC, RG24-C-3, vol. 15288.

44 In early May 1943, First Canadian Army and its formations received a copy of a monthly training letter that contained lessons from the campaign. It included lessons that the British had learned about using armoured forces in support of infantry at El Alamein. Major A.L. Saunders memorandum, GHQ Monthly Trg letter – April 1943, 12 May 1943 and Appendix C to GHQ Monthly Training Letter – April 1943, dated 1 May 1943. Both documents are at LAC, RG24-G-3-1-a, vol. 10770, file 222C1 (D236).

45 Notes on a Common Doctrine for the Emp of Inf and Tks, undated; and Brigadier C. Foulkes memorandum, Notes on Common Doctrine, 23 June 1943, LAC, RG24-C-2, vol. 9804, file 2/Instrns Army/1.

46 A First Canadian Army's training directive dated June 1943 ordered 1st Canadian Corps to practise interarm attacks on defended positions, using the drills described in the document. First Cdn Army Trg Directive Number 15, 22 June 1943, LAC, RG24-C-2, vol. 9804, file 2/Instrns Army/1. Early the next month, the commander of the 5th Canadian Armoured Brigade held a conference for all the 5th Canadian Armoured Division's manoeuvre unit commanders (infantry battalions and armoured regiments), to discuss the British doctrine, just as the division started a six-week series of short tactical exercises. 5th Canadian Armoured Brigade WD, 5 July 1943, LAC, RG24-C-3, vol. 14107 (reel T-10662). Days later, units practised the doctrine in the field, with infantry battalions paired with armoured regiments. For instance, the Perth Regiment and the 2nd Canadian Armoured Regiment (Lord Strathcona's Horse) conducted several days of infantry-cum-tank exercises to practise the doctrine discussed at the conference. Perth Regiment WD, 8–10 and 12 July 1943, and Syllabus of Trg for July 1943, dated 8 July 1943, appended to WD, LAC, RG24-C-3, vol. 15135. Similarly, all battalions in the 11th Canadian Infantry Brigade practised infantry-cum-tank attacks with armoured regiments, again, explicitly to practise the techniques discussed at the 5 July conference. Headquarters 11th CIB WD, Appendix 7 to WD for July 1943, Trg Program, dated 6 July 1943, LAC, RG24-C-3, vol. 14158 (reel T-12393).

47 Robert Engen, *Strangers in Arms: Combat Motivation in the Canadian Army, 1943–1945* (Montreal and Kingston: McGill-Queen's University Press, 2016), 203.

48 Ibid., 140 and 168.

49 DHH, CMHQ Historical Officer Report No. 135, Canadian Operations in Sicily, July–August 1943, 105–9. I am grateful to Timothy Carroll for bringing this source to my attention.

50 Ibid., 107.

51   G.W.L. Nicholson, *The Canadians in Italy, 1943–1945,* vol. 2 of *Official History of the Canadian Army in the Second World War* (Ottawa: Queen's Printer, 1956), 578, 600, 630–31.

52   Ibid., 124, 236, 260, 378–79, 423, 467–68, 550.

53   Robert L. McDougall, *A Narrative of War: From the Beaches of Sicily to the Hitler Line with the Seaforth Highlanders of Canada, 10 July 1943–8 June 1944* (Ottawa: The Golden Dog Press, 1996), 171.

54   Ibid., 178.

55   Memorandum to Brigadier General Staff (BGS), 16 March 1942, LAC, RG24-G-3-1-a, vol. 10769, file 222C1 (D207).

56   Canadian Corps Training Instruction no. 7, 16 March 1942, LAC, RG24-G-3-1-a, vol. 10770, file 222C1 (D235).

57   Wilfred Grimshaw service file, LAC, RG24, vol. 26015, and William Moore service file, vol. 26647. In fact, thirteen soldiers in the sample group underwent ALC training in 1942, a fairly high number compared to attendance rates for courses in general.

58   Canadian Corps Training Instruction no. 8, 30 April 1942, LAC, RG24-G-3-1-a, vol. 10770, file 222C1 (D235).

59   Stacey, *Six Years of War,* 247–48.

60   1st Canadian Corps Training Instruction no. 20, 24 December 1942, LAC, RG24-G-3-1-a, vol. 10770, file 222C1 (D235).

61   1 Cdn Corps BGS memorandum, Town Fighting, 18 September 1942, LAC, RG24-G-3-1-a, vol. 10769, file 222C1 (D208).

62   Draft War Office Military Training Pamphlet on Town Fighting, undated, LAC, RG24-G-3-1-a, vol. 10769, file 222C1 (D208).

63   Ibid.

64   From "Extracts from an Interview with Brigadier S.W. Thomson, dated 15 July 1960, at Victoria, B.C.," in McDougall, *A Narrative of War,* 157.

65   For a good overview of the army's adoption of battle drill training, see DHH, CMHQ Historical Officer Report No. 123, Battle Drill Training, 31 August 1944.

66   Brigadier M.F. Gregg, Battle Drill – School of Infantry (Eng), 18 July 1943, LAC, RG24-C-3, vol. 16910, Appendix 10 to S17 Canadian School of Infantry WD.

67   DHH, CMHQ Historical Officer Report No. 123, 5.

68   The unit's war diary for the last two months of 1941 contains numerous enthusiastic endorsements of battle drill. Calgary Highlanders WD, LAC, RG24-C-3, vol. 15016.

69   DHH, CMHQ Historical Officer Report No. 123, 5.

70   Ibid., 6–8.

71   Major-General P.J. Montague memorandum, CMHQ, 18 November 1942, LAC, RG24, vol. 9779, file 2/CTS SA/1/3.

72   No. 3 Wing (CTS) Monthly Training Report for January 1942, LAC, RG24, vol. 9841, file 2/Reports/4.

73   S17 Canadian School of Infantry WD opening statement, October 1943, LAC, RG24-C-3, vol. 16910.

74   CTS 1 Wing Battle Drill précis, appended to #1 Wing Monthly Training Report for January 1942, LAC, RG24-C-2, vol. 9841, file 2/Reports/4.

75   Ernest Morgan Keith MacGregor, interview by Rick Aylward, 22 July 1986, University of Victoria, Military History Oral Collection, accessed 30 January 2019, http://contentdm. library.uvic.ca/cdm/compoundobject/collection/collection13/id/215/rec/1. MacGregor became a career soldier in the PPCLI and retired in 1977 as a brigadier-general.

76 DMT WD, 22 April 1942, LAC, RG24-C-3, vol. 13240.

77 Appendix 1 to DMT WD for December 1942, DMT memorandum, Military Training in Canada 1942, dated 2 December 1942, LAC, RG24-C-3, vol. 13240.

78 Appendix B to GHQ Monthly Training Letter – April 1943, dated 1 May 1943, LAC, RG24-G-3-1-a, vol. 10770.

79 Engen, *Strangers in Arms*, 60.

80 Colonel R.H. Keefler memorandum, Battle Drill Training Policy, 20 January 1943, appended to DMT WD for January 1943, LAC, RG24-C-3, vol. 13240.

81 For example, the fifteenth battle drill course began on 1 August 1943 for thirty-eight officers and seventy NCOs. The sixteenth course began on 29 August for thirty-two officers and fifty-one NCOs. DMT WD, 9 July and 6 August 1943, LAC, RG24-C-3, vol. 13240.

82 Kenneth B. Smith, *"Duffy's Regiment": A History of the Hastings and Prince Edward Regiment* (Toronto: Dundurn Press, 1987), xiii–xiv.

83 Brown and Copp, *Look to Your Front*, 189.

84 War Office, *Infantry Section Leading, 1938* (Ottawa: King's Printer, 1941), 64–67.

85 War Office, *Infantry Training Part I: The Infantry Battalion, 1944* (Ottawa: King's Printer, 1944), 27.

86 War Office, *Infantry Training Part VIII – Fieldcraft, Battle Drill, Section and Platoon Tactics, 1944* (Ottawa: King's Printer, 1944), 24.

87 Jean Portugal provides a brief description of the battle in *We Were There: A Record for Canada*, vol. 2 (Shelburne, ON: Royal Canadian Military Institute Heritage Society, 1998), 968; CSM George William Green DCM recommendation, approved by Field Marshal B.L. Montgomery, April 1945, DHH, Canadian Army Overseas Honours and Awards, Citation Details, accessed 30 May 2019, http://www.cmp-cpm.forces.gc.ca/dhh-dhp/gal/cao-aco/doc/D1_GRAY-HEAD_011.pdf.

88 Portugal, *We Were There*, 2: 968–69; CSM John McKay Kemp DCM recommendation, approved by Field Marshal B.L. Montgomery, April 1945, DHH, Canadian Army Overseas Honours and Awards, Citation Details, accessed 30 May 2019, http://www.cmp-cpm.forces.gc.ca/dhh-dhp/gal/cao-aco/doc/D1_HYS-KEM_104.pdf.

89 R.W. Queen-Hughes, *Whatever Men Dare: A History of the Queen's Own Cameron Highlanders of Canada, 1935–1960* (Winnipeg: Bulman Brothers, 1960), 107.

90 Ibid., 112–13.

Chapter 4: Wartime Drivers of NCO Development

Epigraph: Lieutenant-General Crerar memorandum, 18 June 1943, Library and Archives Canada (LAC), Record Group (RG) 24-G-3-1-a, vol. 10767, file 222C1 (D172).

1 Canada, Department of National Defence, *Mobilization Instructions for the Canadian Militia, 1937* (Ottawa: King's Printer, 1937), 15–16. For promotions to warrant officer class 1, commanding officers submitted recommendations up the chain of command, but only NDHQ authorized.

2 Canada, Department of National Defence, General Staff, *CASF Routine Orders (CASF RO)* (Ottawa: King's Printer, 1939/1940), Routine Order No. 22, 27 September 1939. Also, Canada, Department of National Defence, *How to Qualify: Instructions on the Qualification of Officers and Other Ranks for Promotion – Non-Permanent Active Militia, 1939* (Ottawa: King's Printer, 1940).

3 CASF RO No. 22 implicitly acknowledged that the peacetime practice of conducting promotion examinations would be overly burdensome. It announced that CASF officer

promotions above lieutenant required only the recommendation of a unit commander – no examinations required. Although the order did not say so explicitly, the same applied to NCOs.

4 For the granting of acting ranks for non-commissioned soldiers, see Army Order 139, 31 August 1939, The National Archives, WO 123/81 Army Orders, 1939, plus *Straits Times*, 22 October 1939, 9. For the suspension of officer promotion exams, see Army Order 204, 10 October 1939, The National Archives, WO 123/81 Army Orders, 1939.

5 As before, promotions were to be "acting" first, and after three months, a soldier either received confirmation or reverted to his former rank. The same applied to lance appointments. However, overseas formation commanders at division level and higher, and the Senior Officer CMHQ for units under his command, authorized promotion to, and confirmation of, warrant officer class 1, instead of NDHQ. Canada, Department of National Defence, *Extracts from Canadian Army (Overseas) Routine Orders* (London: Canadian Military Headquarters, 1943), appendix to Routine Order No. 431.

6 Sergeant George Caya, interview by Gary Francis McCauley, 7 July 1997, Canadian War Museum — Military History Research Centre CWM 20100129-004, George Metcalf Archival Collection.

7 Canada, Department of National Defence, *Canadian Army Training Pamphlet No. 8: How to Qualify, 1941* (Ottawa: J.O. Patenaude, Printer to the King's Most Excellent Majesty, 1941), 4.

8 These requirements did not apply to soldiers of the medical, dental, and pay corps. Ibid., 14.

9 Ibid., 16, emphasis added. NCO promotion policies for the Reserve Army remained much like those of the prewar army.

10 Jonathan Fennell, *Combat and Morale in the North African Campaign: The Eighth Army and the Path to El Alamein* (Cambridge: Cambridge University Press, 2011), 98–109. See also Jonathan Fennell, *Fighting the People's War: The British and Commonwealth Armies and the Second World War* (Cambridge: Cambridge University Press, 2019), 276–84.

11 David French, *Raising Churchill's Army: The British Army and the War against Germany, 1919–1945* (Oxford: Oxford University Press, 2000), 68.

12 Fennell, *Combat and Morale*, 109.

13 Fennell, *Fighting the People's War*, 442.

14 Canada, Department of National Defence, *Report of the Department of National Defence for the Fiscal Year Ending March 31, 1942* (Ottawa: King's Printer, 1942), 14.

15 Canada, Department of National Defence, *Second Edition Physical Standards and Instructions for the Medical Examination of Serving Soldiers and Recruits for the Canadian Army, Active and Reserve 1943* (Ottawa: King's Printer, 1943), 99–100.

16 Geoffrey Hayes, *Crerar's Lieutenants: Inventing the Canadian Junior Army Officer, 1939–45* (Vancouver: UBC Press, 2017), 58–76.

17 DND, *Second Edition Physical Standards and Instructions for the Medical Examination of Serving Soldiers and Recruits, 1943*, 100–01.

18 Canada, Department of National Defence, *Report of the Department of National Defence for the Fiscal Year Ending March 31, 1944* (Ottawa: King's Printer, 1944), 30.

19 DND, *Second Edition Physical Standards and Instructions for the Medical Examination of Serving Soldiers and Recruits, 1943*, 4–5.

20 Ibid., Section 4.

21 Ibid., 8.

22 Terry Copp and William J. McAndrew, *Battle Exhaustion: Soldiers and Psychiatrists in the Canadian Army, 1939–1945* (Montreal and Kingston: McGill-Queen's University Press, 1990), 33–35, 38–39.
23 This formation included British, Canadian, and New Zealand forces. It had an anti-invasion role.
24 7 Corps Training Instruction No. 2, 5 October 1940, LAC, RG24-C-2, vol. 9804, file 2/Instrns 1 Corps/1.
25 BGS [Brigadier General Staff] 7 Corps to CMHQ, 1 December 1940, LAC, RG24-C-2, vol. 9943, file 5/JL SCHOOL/1.
26 2 Cdn Div Training Instruction No. 2, 21 December 1940, LAC, RG24-C-2, vol. 9805, file 2/Instrns 2 Div/1.
27 Crerar memorandum, Organization of Training, 26 February 1942, LAC, RG24-G-3-1-A, vol. 10769, file 222C1 (D208).
28 Lieutenant-General B.L. Montgomery, Notes on Inf. Bdes of Canadian Corps, 3 February 1942, LAC, General H.D.G. Crerar Papers, Manuscript Group (MG) 30-E157, vol. 2, file 958C.009 (D182).
29 The information in this paragraph and the next comes from the notes that Montgomery provided to Crerar, ibid. These reports, numbered 1 through 7 and written between 3 February and 4 March 1942, are in LAC, MG30-E157, vol. 2, file 958C.009 (D182).
30 Attendance at the army's many NCO courses – including both centralized and decentralized programs – frequently included many junior NCOs and a few privates.
31 Crerar memorandum, untitled, 24 February 1942, and Crerar memorandum, untitled, 26 February 1942, LAC, RG24-G-3-1-a, vol. 10771, file 222C1 (D292). Several soldiers' memoirs and regimental histories describe how certain field units posted out some of their older soldiers in 1942, demonstrating that the Canadians acted on Montgomery's advice to clear out the dead wood. For examples, see Fred Cederberg, *The Long Road Home: The Autobiography of a Canadian Soldier in Italy in World War II* (Don Mills, ON: General, 1984), 26–27; Craig B. Cameron, *Born Lucky: RSM Harry Fox, MBE, One D-Day Dodger's Story* (St Catharines, ON: Vanwell, 2005), 46; and Gordon Brown and Terry Copp, *Look to Your Front – Regina Rifles: A Regiment at War* (Waterloo, ON: Laurier Centre for Military, Strategic and Disarmament Studies, 2001), 7.
32 Montgomery to Crerar, 6 March 1942, and Montgomery, Some General Notes on What to Look for When Visiting a Unit, undated, LAC, MG30-E157, vol. 2, file 958C.009 (D182).
33 Montgomery, Some General Notes on What to Look for When Visiting a Unit, undated.
34 Ibid.
35 Canadian Corps Order No. 132, 6 March 1942, reprinted in Carleton and York Regiment War Diary (WD), Part 1 Orders, 11 March 1942, appended to WD for March 1942, LAC, RG24-C-3, vol. 15049.
36 Crerar to All Commanders and Commanding Officers, 16 March 1942, LAC, RG24-G-3-1-a, vol. 10767, file 222C1 (D172).
37 Brigadier A.E. Walford memorandum, Damages by Canadian Troops, 24 May 1942, LAC, RG24-G-3-1-a, vol. 10771, file 222C1 (D270).
38 Crerar to Major-General C.B. Price, 29 May 1942, ibid.
39 Lieutenant-Colonel E.B. Wilson to Major-General G.R. Pearkes, 3 June 1942, ibid.
40 Crerar to G.O.C., 1 Cdn Division, 4 June 1942, ibid.
41 Pearkes to Crerar, 9 June 1942, ibid.

42   Brooke to Crerar, 3 June 1942, and McNaughton to Brooke, 15 June 1942, ibid.
43   R.P. Wilson to DPM South-Eastern Command, 23 June 1942, ibid.
44   Montgomery to Crerar, 26 June 1942, ibid.
45   Montgomery to Crerar, 28 June 1942, ibid.
46   Crerar memorandum, Petty Crimes, 9 July 1942, ibid.
47   1st Canadian Corps Training Instruction No. 12, 27 June 1942, LAC, RG24-C-2, vol. 9804, file 2/Instrns 1 Corps/1.
48   1st Canadian Corps Order No. 440, published 28 September 1942, LAC, RG24-G-3-1-a, vol. 10767, file 222C1 (D172).
49   1st Canadian Corps Order No. 442, published 28 September 1942, ibid.
50   Crerar to All Commanders and Commanding Officers, 16 October 1942, LAC, RG24-C-2, vol. 9804, file 2/Instrns 1 Corps/1.
51   1st Canadian Corps Training Instruction No. 17, 20 October 1942, LAC, RG24-G-3-1-a, vol. 10770, file 222C1 (D235). A month later, corps training instructions demanded that unit training plans pay particular attention to developing junior leaders. 1st Canadian Corps Training Instruction No. 19, 27 November 1942, ibid.
52   Crerar to GOCs [General Officers Commanding] 1,2,3 Cdn Divs and Comd 1 Cdn Army Tank Bde, 28 December 1942, LAC, RG24-G-3-1-a, vol. 10767, file 222C1 (D172).
53   Crerar to GOCs 1,2,3 Cdn Divs and Comd 1 Cdn Army Tank Bde, 18 January 1943, LAC, RG24-G-3-1-a, vol. 10769, file 222C1 (D207).
54   Major-General H.L.N. Salmon memorandum, Training of NCOs, 22 January 1943, ibid.
55   Major-General J.H. Roberts to Comd 1 Cdn Corps, 21 January 1943, ibid.
56   Major-General J.H. Roberts to All Commanding Officers, 2 January 1943, ibid.
57   Major-General R.F.L. Keller to GOC 1 Cdn Corps, 22 January 1943, ibid.
58   Brigadier R.A. Wyman to GOC 1 Cdn Corps, 20 January 1943, ibid.
59   Crerar to GOCs 1, 2, and 3 Div, Comd 1 Cdn Army Tk Bde and OC 1 Cdn Armd Regt, 22 March 1943, LAC, RG24-G-3-1-a, vol. 10767, file 222C1 (D172).
60   Crerar to GOC 2 and 3 Cdn Divs, Comd 1 Cdn Army Tk Bde and OC 1 Cdn Armd C Regt (RCD), 28 March 1943, ibid.
61   First Cdn Army Trg Directive Number 14 – Period 1 May–30 Jun 43, dated 17 April 1943, LAC, RG24-C-2, vol. 9804, file 2/Instrns Army/1.
62   For example, see 1st Canadian Corps training instructions for May and June 1943 (Training Instruction No. 22, dated 18 April 1943), LAC, RG24-G-3-1-a, vol. 10770, file 222C1 (D235). Also see 2nd Canadian Infantry Division commander's direction in Major-General E.L.M. Burns memorandum, Trg of the NCO, 2 June 1943, LAC, RG24-G-3-1-a, vol. 10769, file 222C1 (D207).
63   For instance, in the West Nova Scotia Regiment (WNSR), the unit ran a one-week refresher course for twenty-two sergeants in late October 1942. The same week, all unit NCOs attended a lecture by their brigade commander on the prospects for future operations and the associated training requirements. And in late December, the unit's NCOs and officers attended a demonstration of a combat team attack from the approach march. See WNSR WD, 26 and 28 October and 31 December, LAC, RG24-C-3, vol. 15288.
64   As discussed in Chapter 1, about 4 percent of the sample group had prior service in the permanent force, 32 percent had served in the NPAM, and 4 percent had fought in the First World War. Some of these individuals had mixed forms of previous military experience (for example, First World War, and NPAM service). Thus, over 60 percent of the sample group had no prior service.

65 French, *Raising Churchill's Army,* 275.
66 Ibid., 277.
67 Ibid., 282.
68 C.P. Stacey, *Six Years of War: The Army in Canada, Britain and the Pacific,* vol. 1 of *Official History of the Canadian Army in the Second World War* (Ottawa: Department of National Defence and the Queen's Printer, 1955), 544.
69 Ibid.
70 French, *Raising Churchill's Army,* 86.
71 Stacey, *Six Years of War,* 544.
72 French, *Raising Churchill's Army,* 88.
73 Ibid., 89.
74 Stacey, *Six Years of War,* 544.

Chapter 5: Unit and Formation Programs

Epigraph: Calgary Highlanders war diary (WD), 29 November 1941, Library and Archives Canada (LAC), Record Group (RG) 24-C-3, vol. 15016.

1 Various PPCLI [Princess Patricia's Canadian Light Infantry] WD entries and Unit Part 1 Orders, September–December 1939, LAC, RG24-C-3, vol. 15154.
2 RCR [Royal Canadian Regiment] WD, 30 October 1939, LAC, RG24-C-3, vol. 15206. The course ran in London, Ontario.
3 R22R [Royal 22nd Regiment] WD, 18 September and 23 October 1939, LAC, RG24-C-3, vol. 15235.
4 Seaforth Highlanders WD, 30 September and 4 October 1939, LAC, RG-24-C-3, vol. 15253.
5 48th Highlanders WD, 24 September 1939, LAC, RG24-C-3, vol. 15295.
6 Edmonton Regiment WD, 20 November 1939, LAC, RG 24-C-3, vol. 15107.
7 QOR [Queen's Own Rifles] (CASF [Canadian Active Service Force]) WD, first entry for June 1940, PRE-MOBILIZATION, LAC, RG24-C-3, vol. 15166.
8 Training Instructions Q.O.R. of C., 3 September 1940, Appendix C to QOR WD for September 1940, ibid.
9 Appendix G2 to QOR WD for October 1940, ibid.
10 Appendix to QOR WD for November 1940, Syllabus "C" Coy Individual Training, 4–11 Nov, dated 31 October 1940, ibid. Company officers underwent the daily refresher training, too.
11 Appendix to QOR WD for March 1941, N.C.O.s Course – "C" Coy, 24–29 Mar, ibid.
12 Raymond Skelton Gray, interview by Tom Torrie, 8 August 1987, University of Victoria, Military History Oral Collection, accessed 29 January 2019, http://contentdm.library.uvic.ca/cdm/compoundobject/collection/collection13/id/301/rec/1. Gray went on to serve as a captain in Northwest Europe.
13 QOR WD, 13 January 1941 and Unit Part 1 Orders No. 6, dated 8 January 1941, appended to WD for January 1941, LAC, RG24-C-3, vol. 15166.
14 N.C.O. Class – Q.O.R. of C., syllabus for weeks 1 and 2, appended to QOC WD for January 1941, ibid.
15 Lieutenant-Colonel H.C. MacKendrick, Training Progress Report, 19 January 1941, appended to QOC WD for February 1941, ibid. Unfortunately, only a partial syllabus survives in the unit war diary.
16 Leslie John McMurray service file, LAC, RG24, vol. 26518. However, he did not become a sergeant until September 1944.

17   C.P. Stacey, *Six Years of War: The Army in Canada, Britain and the Pacific*, vol. 1 of *Official History of the Canadian Army in the Second World War* (Ottawa: Department of National Defence and the Queen's Printer, 1955), 243–44.

18   R22R WD, 2 March and 11 May 1942, LAC RG24-C-3, vol. 15237.

19   Regina Rifles, Unit Part 1 Orders Nos. 73 and 74, appended to Regina Rifles WD for March 1942; and WD, 6 April 1942, LAC, RG24-C-3, vol. 15195.

20   RCR WD, 9 February 1942 and 21 March 1942, LAC, RG24-C-3, vol. 15207.

21   Appendix 29 to PPCLI WD for January 1942, PPCLI Regimental Refresher Course Junior N.C.O.'s – Syllabus of Training, LAC RG24-C-3, vol. 15155.

22   Russell Hugh "Smitty" Smith, interview for The Memory Project, Veteran Stories, Historica Canada, Military History Oral Collection, accessed 30 January 2019, http://www.the memoryproject.com/stories/189:russell-hugh-smitty-smith.

23   Appendix 16 to PPCLI WD for March 1942, P.P.C.L.I. Regimental Course for Junior N.C.O.s – Syllabus of Training, LAC RG24-C-3, vol. 15155. The WD mentions these two courses at 30 March 1942, and the PPCLI syllabus of unit training for the week ending 14 March 1942, appended to WD for March 1942.

24   NCO Course Syllabus, Appendix 4 to WNSR [West Nova Scotia Regiment] WD for August 1942, LAC, RG24-C-3, vol. 15287; Training Report week ending 31 Oct 42, appended to WNSR WD for October 1942, LAC, RG24-C-3, vol. 15288; Captain J.R. Cameron memorandum, NCO School – 2 Nov 42, dated 30 October 1942, appended to WNSR WD for November 1942; and Syllabus – West N.S.R. – NCOs School, 1 Nov–28 Nov 42, Appendix to WD for November 1942.

25   Appendix 4 to NS(NB)R [North Shore (New Brunswick) Regiment] WD for October 1942, Training Syllabus; Appendix 6 to WD for December 1942, syllabus for Regimental N.C.Os School No. 2; Appendix 5 to WD for January 1943, Regimental N.C.Os. School Syllabus; and Appendix 1 to WD for December 1942, Regimental Part 1 Orders, dated 6 December 1942, all at LAC, RG24-C-3, vol. 15126.

26   Edward Joseph Rigley service file, LAC, RG24, vol. 26900. Rigley performed well, as the only student on his serial who earned a grade of *distinguished*. One month after the course, he received a promotion to acting sergeant.

27   WNSR WD, 26 October 1942, LAC, RG24-C-3, vol. 15288.

28   Appendix 4 to WNSR WD for October 1942, Syllabus of Training for Sergeants Refresher Course (26–31 Oct 42), ibid.

29   WNSR WD, 31 October 1942, ibid.

30   War Office Urgent Postal Telegram, 23 September 1940, LAC, RG24-C-2, vol. 9943, file 5/JL SCHOOL/1.

31   BGS [Brigadier General Staff] 7 Corps to CMHQ, 1 December 1940, ibid. Also Canadian Corps Junior Leaders School – War Establishment, undated, ibid.

32   General Report by Commandant, Cdn Corps Jr Leaders School [for serial 9], undated, LAC, RG24-C-2, vol. 9782, file 2/D JUN L/1.

33   Lieutenant-Colonel I.C. Campbell, untitled memorandum on school's war establishment, 1 May 1941, LAC, RG24-C-2, vol. 9943, file 5/JL SCHOOL/1.

34   General Report by Commandant, Cdn Corps Jr Leaders School [for serial 9], undated, LAC, RG24-C-2, vol. 9782, file 2/D JUN L/1.

35   Ibid.

36   Charles Cromwell Martin, *Battle Diary: From D-Day and Normandy to the Zuider Zee and VE* (Toronto: Dundurn Press, 1994), 127–28.

37 The 4th Canadian Infantry Division converted into the 4th Canadian Armoured Division in 1942.

38 Colonel J.K. Lawson memorandum, Training – 4th Division, 14 May 1941, appended to 4th Divisional Instructional School WD for June 1941, LAC, RG24-C-3, vol. 13239.

39 Colonel J.K. Lawson memorandum, Training – 4th Canadian Division, 21 May 1941, LAC, RG24-C-3, vol. 16873, file MD No. 4.

40 Appendix 3 – sheet 1, appended to 4th Division Instructional School WD for June 1941, ibid.

41 Appendix 7 – sheet 1, appended to 4th Division Instructional School WD for June 1941, ibid.

42 Appendix 6 to 4th Divisional Instructional School WD for July 1941, ibid.

43 Lieutenant R.W. Pilot, Report on Training Carried Out, undated, LAC, RG24-C-3, vol. 16873, file MD No. 4. As discussed in Chapter 1, the personnel files reviewed show that, on rare occasions, units fast-tracked brand new but promising recruits to NCO rank almost immediately.

44 Appendix 6 to 4th Divisional Instructional School WD for July 1941, list of personnel attached for training, LAC, RG24-C-3, vol. 16873, file MD No. 4.

45 Block Standard Syllabus, appended to 4th Divisional Instructional School WD for July 1941, ibid.

46 The sequence was as follows: naming the drill (such as "slope arms"), demonstrating, practising individual movements of the drill, taking questions, practising the complete drill for precision, testing the class, and ending the class with praise.

47 Various syllabuses appended to 4th Divisional Instructional School WDs for July and August 1941, LAC, RG24-C-3, vol. 16873, file MD No. 4.

48 4th Canadian Division WD, 8 September 1941, ibid.

49 2 CIB [Canadian Infantry Brigade] WD for August 1942, Appendix 11, 2 Cdn Inf Bde N.C.O.'s School – Joining and Admn Instructions, 13 August 1942, LAC, RG24-C-3, vol. 14073 (reel T-11069).

50 2 CIB WD for August 1942, Appendix 18, 2 Cdn Inf Bde Training Report for the Week Ending 22 August 1942, ibid.

51 2 CIB WD for August 1942, unnumbered appendix, 2 Cdn Inf Bde Training Report for the Week Ending 29 August 1942, ibid.

52 Appendix 16 to 2 CIB WD for September 1942, Training Report for the Week Ending 5 September 1942, ibid.

53 2 CIB WD, 12 September 1942, ibid.

54 Appendix 14 to 2 CIB WD for September 1942, Training Instructions No. 3, 19 September 1942, ibid.

55 2 CIB WD, 21 November 1942, ibid. The third serial graduation was a rather high-profile event in the 1st Canadian Division, attended by the GOC, Major-General Harry Salmon, Vokes, senior brigade staff, the 2 CIB unit commanders, and all available unit officers.

56 Appendix 18 to 2 CIB WD for November 1942, 2 CIB N.C.O.'s School Joining and Administrative Instructions (Course No. 4), ibid.

57 In 1942, an infantry battalion typically had twenty-eight sergeants and sixty-one corporals. Carleton and York Regiment WD, Field Return of Other Ranks, 6 March 1942, appended to WD for March 1942, LAC, RG24-C-3, vol. 15049.

58 The 1st Canadian Corps headquarters even took advantage of the transit time during the voyage to the Mediterranean theatre to conduct NCO refresher training. In late October

1944, shortly after embarking for Exercise Timberwolf – the code name for moving the corps headquarters and the 5th Canadian Armoured Division to Italy – staff distributed training instructions to all units, sub-units, and detachments, ordering a polishing of NCO skills. Sub-unit commanders were to concern themselves with training their NCOs in field duties, while unit adjutants and RSMs received direction to instruct in administrative matters and to cultivate "a high sense of responsibility." That the corps headquarters ordered its forces to hone NCO cadres demonstrates that the leadership remained conscientious about keeping junior leader skills sharp as the force slipped across the ocean and made final preparations for battle. In fact, the instructions directed: "Full advantage will be taken of every opportunity to carry on with the education of the Warrant and Non Commissioned Officer Cadre." Unfortunately, records do not show the extent to which training actually occurred.

59 Kenneth B. Smith, *"Duffy's Regiment": A History of the Hastings and Prince Edward Regiment* (Toronto: Dundurn Press, 1987), 122–23.

60 1 CIB WD, 11 November 1943, LAC, RG24-C-3, vol. 14076.

61 G.W.L. Nicholson, *The Canadians in Italy 1943–1945*, vol. 2 of *Official History of the Canadian Army in the Second World War* (Ottawa: Queen's Printer, 1956), 338–39.

62 Ibid.

63 Ibid., 380–81.

64 Colin McDougall, DSO, later became registrar of McGill University and an acclaimed writer. His novel *Execution*, set in the Canadian campaign in Italy, won the 1958 Governor General's Award for English-language fiction.

65 2 CIB WD, 15 February 1944; and Appendix 22 to 2 CIB WD for February 1944, 2 CIB NCOs School Joining Instructions, undated, LAC, RG24-C-3, vol. 14077 (reel T-11074).

66 2 CIB WD, 16, 18, and 21 February 1944, ibid.

67 Syllabus of Training – 2 Cdn Inf Bde N.C.O.'s School 15–25 February 1944, Appendix 26 to 2 CIB WD for February 1944, ibid.

68 2 CIB WD, 3, 9, and 11 March 1944, LAC, RG24-C-3, vol. 14078 (reel T-11074).

69 Leslie John McMurray service file, LAC, RG24, vol. 26518. McMurray was killed in action fifteen days after becoming a sergeant.

70 Nicholson, *The Canadians in Italy*, 384–86.

71 2 CIB WD, 14 and 20 April 1944, LAC, RG24-C-3, vol. 14078 (reel T-11074).

72 Syllabus of Training 2 Cdn Inf Bde Junior N.C.O.s School, undated, Appendix 26 to 2 CIB WD for April 1944, ibid.

73 2 CIB WD, 16 May 1944, LAC, RG24-C-3, vol. 14078 (reel T-11075).

74 Department of National Defence, Directorate of History and Heritage (DHH), Canadian Military Headquarters (CMHQ) Reports, Historical Officer Report No. 121, Canadian Operations in the Liri Valley May–June 1944, 8 August 1944, Annex E.

75 2 CIB WD, 28 May, 15 June, and 15 July 1944, LAC, RG24-C-3, vol. 14078 (reel T-11075).

76 Felix Carriere, interview by Tom Torrie, 4 June 1987, University of Victoria, Military History Oral Collection, accessed 29 January 2019, http://contentdm.library.uvic.ca/cdm/compoundobject/collection/collection13/id/244/rec/1.

77 First Canadian Army Training Policy – Winter 1944/45 (draft), 25 November 1944, LAC, RG24-G-3-1-a, vol. 10585, file 215C1 (D278).

78 Lieutenant-General C. Foulkes to 1 Corps formation commanders, 12 March 1945, LAC, RG24-G-3-1-a, vol. 10586, file 215C1 (D279).

79 Lieutenant-Colonel W.A.B. Anderson (for GOC-in-C) to 21 Army Gp Main (G Ops (Trg and Inf)), 16 January 1945, LAC, RG24-G-3-1-a, vol. 10585, file 215C1 (D278).

80 Joining Instructions, 1 Cdn Inf Div Trg School, 31 December 1944, appended to 1st Canadian Infantry Division Training [1 Cdn Inf Div Trg] School WD for January 1945, LAC, RG24-C-3, vol. 16864.

81 Timetable for 1st Course, undated, Appendix 2 to 1 Cdn Inf Div Trg School WD for January 1945, ibid.

82 Timetable for 2nd Course, undated, Appendix 6 to 1 Cdn Inf Div Trg School WD for February 1945, ibid.

83 Report on 2nd Course, undated, appended to 1 Cdn Inf Div Trg School WD for January 1945, ibid.

84 Ibid., and Report on 1st Course.

85 Lieutenant-Colonel J.W. Ritchie to GOC 1 Cdn Inf Div, 14 February 1945, Appendix 4 to 1 Cdn Inf Div Trg School WD for February 1945, ibid.

86 1 Cdn Inf Div Trg School WD, 17 February 1945, ibid.

87 Nominal Roles for NCOs Wing Course No. 3, undated, Appendix 1 to 2 Canadian Infantry Division (CID) Trg School WD for December 1944, ibid.

88 Syllabus NCO Wing – Course No. 4, appended to 2 CID Trg Sch WD for January 1945, ibid.

89 7 CIB Wing – Syllabus for Week Ending 13 Feb 45, appended to 3 CID Trg School WD for February 1945, LAC, RG24-C-3, vol. 16865. For the last serial before Germany surrendered, the school added a fourth week to provide classes in directing fire and street and village fighting, plus a TEWT to practise defensive operations. 9th Bde Wing – Syllabus for Week Ending 5 May 1945, appended to 3 CID Trg School WD for May 1945.

90 The curriculum included instruction on section tactics, signals, explosives (mines and booby traps), weapons handling, and discipline (drill and inspections). 5 Cdn Armd Div Trg School (NCO's Wing), Appendix 2 to 5 Cdn Armd Div Trg School WD for January 1945, LAC, RG24-C-3, vol. 16865. However, aside from a single serial in early 1945, constant requirements for the school to move thwarted repeated attempts to run NCO training. Just as the war ended, the school finally ran three courses in succession. Training Instruction, 1 May 1945, Appendix 7 to 5 Cdn Armd Div Trg School WD for April 1945; Amendment No. 1 to Adm Instr No. 5, 9 May 1945, appended to WD for May 1945; and WD, 7–10 May, 15 May, 1 June, and 21 June 1945.

91 Joining Instructions (amended 4 Jan 1945), appended to 4 Cdn Armd Div Trg School WD for December 1944, LAC, RG24-C-3, vol. 16865.

92 Syllabus, appendix 6 to 4 Cdn Armd Div Trg School WD for December 1944, LAC, RG24-C-3, vol. 16865. The school amended the syllabus from time to time. See Training Directive for Week Ending 23 December 1944, appended to WD for December 1944; Advanced Class Syllabus — Week ending 30 Dec 1944, appended to WD for December 1944; various weekly syllabuses appended to WD for February 1945; and syllabus appended to WD for March 1945, ibid.

93 2 CID Trg School WD, 22 January 1945, LAC RG24-C-3, vol. 16864.

94 2 CID Trg School WD, 12, 15–18, and 28 February, and 16, 17, and 21 April 1945, ibid.

95 R.W. Queen-Hughes, *Whatever Men Dare: A History of the Queen's Own Cameron Highlanders of Canada, 1935–1960* (Winnipeg: Bulman Brothers, 1960), 151.

96 3 CID Trg School WD for January to May 1945, *passim*, LAC, RG24-C-3, vol. 16865.

97 For example, see 2 CID WD, 3, 21, and 30 December 1944, and 31 January 1945, LAC, RG24-C-3, vol. 16864.

98 2 CID Trg Sch WD, 21 December 1944, ibid.

99 2 CID Trg Sch WD, 16 December 1944, ibid.

100 2 CID Trg Sch WD, 12 and 23 December 1944, ibid.
101 3 CID Trg School WD for January and February 1945, *passim,* LAC, RG24-C-3, vol. 16865.
102 Training Instruction, 1 May 1945, Appendix 7 to 5 Cdn Armd Div Trg School WD for April 1945; Amendment No. 1 to Adm Instr No. 5, 9 May 1945, appended to WD for May 1945; and WD, 1 June 1945, LAC, RG24-C-3, vol. 16865.
103 2 CID Trg Sch WD December 1944–May 1945, *passim,* LAC, RG24-C-3, vol. 16864. Each serial took twelve soldiers from each battalion, plus a handful from the brigade field companies.
104 Results – NCOs Course No. 2, 20 December 1944, Appendix 5 to 2 CID Trg Sch WD for December 1944, ibid.
105 For the dates each training centre in Canada was placed on active service, see Stacey, *Six Years of War,* Appendix D, 528–35.
106 About 56 percent of the NCO qualification and refresher courses attended were unit or formation run. Forty-four percent were at the centralized institutions in Canada and Britain. Given the incomplete nature of personnel records, however, these figures are not precise.

Chapter 6: The Mass Army's Programs in Canada
Epigraph: A14 Canadian Army Infantry Training Centre, Aldershot, War Diary (WD), 29 and 30 April 1946, Library and Archives Canada (LAC), Record Group (RG) 24-C-3, vol. 17047.
1 For a list of the operational units in the North American zone, see C.P. Stacey, *Six Years of War: The Army in Canada, Britain and the Pacific,* vol. 1 of *Official History of the Canadian Army in the Second World War* (Ottawa: Queen's Printer, 1955), Appendix E, 536–39.
2 Ibid., Appendix D, 528–35.
3 Calculated by subtracting the size of the overseas army on 30 June 1944 from the size of the total army on 21 June 1944, as listed in Stacey, *Six Years of War,* 191 and 522, respectively.
4 Calculated using the formulae indicated in Table I.2, i.e., based on the estimation that other ranks constituted 94 percent of all ranks and, in Canada, 27 percent of the other ranks were NCOs.
5 Stacey explains that the home defence army reached its peak strength in the spring of 1943, and that the Canadian Army Overseas completed building its structures that summer. *Six Years of War,* 174–75 and 108, respectively. He also shows the Canadian Army Overseas' growth rate on p. 191.
6 Ibid., 121, 133–34, 138, and Appendix D, 527–35.
7 Ibid., 79–80.
8 Ibid., 169–72.
9 Appendix D to Army Junior Leaders School WD for September 1941, LAC, RG24-C-3, vol. 16892. Also see Syllabus – Junior Leaders School, Appendix D to WD for August 1941.
10 Comparison between detailed syllabuses for Course Number 3, appended to Army Junior Leaders School WD for November 1941, and Course Number 5, appended to WD for February 1942, both LAC, RG24-C-3, vol. 16892.
11 Detailed Syllabus for Course Number 6 Regular, 15 June to 11 July 1942, Appendix to Army Junior Leaders School WD for June 1942, LAC, RG24-C-3, vol. 16893.
12 Standard Syllabus for S52 J.L.S., revised on 18 July 1942, Appendix D to Army Junior Leaders School WD for July 1942, ibid.

13 Instructions for Night Patrol Exercise, Appendix F to Army Junior Leaders School WD for July 1942, ibid. Three platoons each conducted a standing patrol, employing strong all-round defence to protect an assigned position. Each platoon then sent a reconnaissance patrol to gather information on one of the other platoons and, once the information had been gathered and used for planning, dispatched a fighting patrol to destroy the other platoon's standing patrol and take prisoners. Staff designed the patrol routes so that every reconnaissance team crossed paths with an enemy fighting patrol. And before the patrols set out, student patrol leaders led their men through mission preparations. Each patrol commander received a warning order that prompted him to select a second-in-command for the mission and to direct his men to initiate preparations. Then, after receiving formal orders, he devised a plan, prepared his own orders, and issued them to his men.

14 DMT [Directorate of Military Training] Memorandum, Military Training in Canada, 1942 (undated), Appendix 1 to DMT WD for December 1942, LAC, RG24-C-3, vol. 13240. This report states that the school ran seven courses in English or French, producing 1,400 graduates, whereas the school's war diary indicates that ten courses ran, with about 1,680 students.

15 Syllabus – NCO No. 1 Course, Appendix D to S6 Canadian Army Junior Leaders School WD for September 1942, LAC, RG24-C-3, vol. 16893.

16 Block Syllabus N.C.O. Course 1943, Appendix E to S6 Canadian Army Junior Leaders School WD for March 1943, LAC, RG24-C-3, vol. 16894. Emphasis added.

17 The National Defence Headquarters (NDHQ) ordered the name change in January 1943. S-6 Canadian Junior Leaders School WD [hereafter S6 WD], cover page for December 1942, LAC, RG24-C-3, vol. 16893.

18 Compiled from various DMT WD entries, LAC, RG24-C-3, vol. 13240.

19 In July 1943, an infantry battalion had forty-five corporals and fifty sergeants. Perth Regiment, Field Return of Other Ranks for the Week Ending 31 July 1943, appended to WD for July 1943, LAC, RG24-C-3, vol. 15135.

20 For the composition of First Canadian Army, see C.P. Stacey, *The Canadian Army 1939–1945: An Official Historical Summary* (Ottawa: King's Printer, 1948), Appendix B, 335–39; for the operational units of the North American Zone, see Stacey, *Six Years of War*, Appendix E, 536–39.

21 S6 WD, 31 July 1943, and list of appendices for August 1943, LAC, RG24-C-3, vol. 16894.

22 Course No. 9 Syllabus, Appendix D to S6 WD for October 1943, ibid.

23 C.P. Stacey states that the school trained 1,566 francophone soldiers during this period. *Arms, Men and Governments: The War Policies of Canada, 1939–1945* (Ottawa: Queen's Printer, 1970), 422. However, according to attendance figures for each course listed in S6 WD, 1,483 students passed through the training centre during the period of francophone-only instruction. Also, using the war diary's figures for each course, about 3,170 soldiers in total passed through this junior leaders school throughout its operation.

24 French-speaking soldiers now constituted 80 percent of all instructors at training centres across Quebec. Stacey, *Arms, Men and Governments*, 422. And, by then, the active army was very close to reaching peak strength.

25 Ibid.

26 Entries in soldiers' training records are not always clear. Nine of the soldiers in the sample group attended an unspecified NCO school, NCO course, or junior leaders course.

27 Ottawa did not permit training centres to amend standardized syllabuses, or introduce new courses, without approval. In October 1943, NDHQ learned that some corps training centres had done so. The office of the Chief of the General Staff (CGS) issued direction

that such practices must cease, although training centres could submit to NDHQ recommendations to amend syllabuses. Col. J.G.K. Strathy memorandum, Syllabi of Training, 30 October 1943, Appendix 26 to DMT WD for October 1943, LAC, RG24-C-3, vol. 13240.

28　A15 Infantry (Rifle) Training Centre M.D. 10 WD [hereafter A15 WD], entries for January 1940, LAC, RG24-C-3, vol. 17048. The school initially took the name Infantry Training Centre M.D. 10.

29　A15 WD, 1 January 1940, and Unit Part 2 Orders Nos. 10 and 11, appended to WD for January 1940, ibid.

30　A15 Unit Part 1 Orders No. 23, 25 January 1940, appended to WD for January 1943, ibid.

31　A15 Unit Part 1 Orders No. 8, appended to WD for January 1941, LAC, RG24-C-3, vol. 17049.

32　This calculation is based on the summary of the course that ended on 28 March 1942: N.C.O.'s Qualifying Course – Course S.I. 74 (see "SUMMARY FOR SIX WEEKS"), appended to A15 WD for March 1942, LAC, RG24-C-3, vol. 17052.

33'　For example, a course in February 1942 had twenty-five candidates. The next month, the course had forty candidates.

34　Schedule for Course No. S.I. 58, appended to A15 WD for October 1941, LAC, RG24-C-3, vol. 17051.

35　Schedule for Course No. S.I. 61, appended to A15 WD for October 1941, ibid.

36　Schedule for Course No. S.I. 66, appended to A15 WD for December 1941, ibid.

37　Schedule for Course No. S.I. 63, appended to A15 WD for December 1941, and 5th week schedule, appended to A15 WD for January 1942, ibid.

38　A29 Advanced Infantry Training Centre WD [hereafter A29 WD], 23–27 April 1942, LAC, RG24-C-3, vol. 17127.

39　Syllabus of Training – 5 Weeks Instructors Course, appended to A29 WD for April 1942, ibid.

40　Stacey, *Six Years of War,* Appendix A, 522.

41　A29 WD for October 1942, LAC, RG24-C-3, vol. 17127.

42　A29 WD for November 1942, LAC, RG24-C-3, vol. 17128.

43　Robert Miles Sanderson and Marie Sanderson, *Letters from a Soldier: The Wartime Experiences of a Canadian Infantryman, 1943–1945* (Waterloo, ON: Ecart Press, c. 1993), 37, letter dated 11 July 1943.

44　Ibid., 38–39, letter dated 11 August 1943.

45　Before Operation Overlord, A29 had run twelve serials of the course. The thirteenth course graduated on 10 June 1944. Private C.J.S. "Syl" Apps, who had led the Toronto Maple Leafs to win the Stanley Cup in 1942 and who had recently taken leave from the National Hockey League to join the army, completed the course as the only candidate with a *distinguished* grading. A29 WD, 10 June 1944, LAC, RG24-C-3, vol. 17129. Apps returned to the Leafs after the war, going on to lead the team to two more Stanley Cup wins, and later had a career in Ontario politics.

46　Ibid., 4 September 1944.

47　Ibid., 5 September 1944.

48　Ibid., 6 and 7 September 1944.

49　Ibid., 2 October 1944.

50　In November 1944, cabinet had committed to contributing armed forces to the war against Japan after Germany's defeat. Canada's contribution was to include a 30,000-strong ground contingent, based on an infantry division with ancillary troops and reinforcements, to operate under American command. Summary of Cabinet Decisions Regarding Canadian Pacific Force, undated, Directorate of Heritage and History (DHH), 112.3M2009 (D79).

51 A29 WD, 8 and 9 May 1944, LAC, RG24-C-3, vol. 17130.
52 Ibid., 29 May and 13 June 1944.
53 Colonel J.K. Lawson memorandum, Courses – Assistant Instructors A.F. and R.F. and unit N.C.Os., 11 May 1941, RG24-C-3, vol. 13239.
54 DMT Circular Letter No. 1327 – Extension of AIs Course, dated 22 March 1944, Appendix 62 to DMT WD for March 1944, LAC, RG24-C-3, vol. 13241.
55 DMT Circular Letter No. 1355 – Training-Assistant Instructors, dated 23 May 1944, appended to DMT WD for May 1944, ibid.
56 Ibid.
57 Appendix J to DMT Circular Letter No. 1355 – Sequence of Trg & Employment of AIs – Inf, ibid. Appendices for corps other than infantry, such as engineers or signals, show the same requirements for keeping basic and leadership skills sharp. See also Appendix 93 to DMT WD for May 1944, Amendment No 1 to all appendices to DMT Circular Letter No. 1355.
58 DMT Circular Letter No. 1355 – Training-Assistant Instructors, dated 23 May 1944, appended to DMT WD for May 1944, LAC, RG24-C-3, vol. 13241.
59 Ibid., and Appendix J – Sequence of Trg & Employment of AIs – Inf, DMT WD for May 1944, LAC, RG24-C-3, vol. 13241. In fact, for some time now, NCOs who passed the course were liable for eight-month instructional tours of duty. DMT Circular Letter No. 1327 – Extension of AIs Course, 22 March 1944, Appendix 62 to DMT WD for March 1944, LAC, RG24-C-3, vol. 13241.
60 DCGS(B) [Deputy Chief of the General Staff] to CGS [Chief of the General Staff], 30 June 1944, Appendix 191 to DMT WD for June 1944, LAC, RG24-C-3, vol. 13241.
61 For example, see Company Commanders Conference, 15 November 1943, appended to A30 WD for November 1943, and Company Commanders Conference 9 November 1944, appended to A30 WD for November 1944, both LAC, RG24, vol. 17131.
62 Stacey, *Six Years of War*, 134. In May 1940, authorities raised two CASF Small Arms Training Centres, one at Connaught Camp in Ottawa and another at Sarcee Camp in Alberta, both locations of the prewar Canadian Small Arms Schools. Two other schools appeared a short time later. In March 1941, authorities established the A25 Canadian Small Arms Training Centre (CSATC) in Long Branch, a suburb of Toronto. To support units and formations in Western Canada, the army established a similar school, the A26 Canadian Small Arms School, in Nanaimo, British Columbia.
63 Raymond Skelton Gray, interview by Tom Torrie, 8 August 1987, University of Victoria, Military History Oral Collection, accessed 29 January 2019, http://contentdm.library.uvic.ca/cdm/compoundobject/collection/collection13/id/301/rec/1. Gray went on to commission and served as a captain in Northwest Europe.
64 Robert Engen, *Canadians under Fire: Infantry Effectiveness in the Second World War* (Montreal and Kingston: McGill-Queen's University Press, 2009), 123 and 124. Engen surveyed 161 battle experience questionnaires, completed by Canadian infantry captains, majors, and lieutenants-colonel. One of the War Office's objectives with the questionnaires was to "determine the battlefield use and usefulness of infantry small arms employed by the Commonwealth armies." Engen's analysis reveals that several weapons had proven particularly effective, including the Projector, Infantry, Anti-Tank (PIAT), the Bren light machine gun, the 3-inch mortar, and the number 36 grenade. Of course, such weapons effectiveness was possible only with operator skill. Ibid., 121–22.
65 Lieutenant-Colonel S. Ball memorandum, Courses for Instructors, 12 June 1941, LAC, RG24-C-3, vol. 13239.

66   Syllabus for Methods of Instruction Course no. 502, Appendix 10 to A25 CSATC WD for April 1942; and Syllabus for Methods of Instruction Course #505, Appendix 6 to A25 CSATC WD for July 1942, both at LAC, RG24-C-3, vol. 16878.

67   DMT Circular Letter No. 1438, 23 October 1944, Appendix 73 to DMT WD for October 1944, LAC, RG24-C-3, vol. 13242.

68   *A15 Link* 2, 2 (15 December 1944). A15 CITC periodical, available at the Canadian War Museum – Military History Research Centre.

69   A25 CSATC WD, 3 January 1945, LAC, RG24-C-3, vol. 16881.

70   Techniques of Instruction syllabus, appended to A25 CSATC WD for January 1945, ibid.

71   Drill and Duties syllabus, Appendix E to A25 WD for January 1945, ibid.

72   This is based on war diary entries listing each serial. About thirty-nine serials ran, including six serials of the three-part course that started in January 1945, and serials typically trained about thirty soldiers each.

73   Major A.A. Bell memorandum, Courses at School of Instruction – Unit W.Os. and N.C.O.s, 11 June 1941, Appendix 10 to DMT WD, LAC, RG24, vol. 13239.

74   Major A.A. Bell memorandum, Courses at School of Instruction – Unit W.Os. and N.C.O.s, 24 June 1941, Appendix 31 to DMT WD for June 1941, ibid.

75   About a third of the periods focused students on teaching drill. Another third concentrated on small arms training. The remainder of the periods covered various topics, such as map reading, military law, and protection against gas. Tests took up nine periods. Unit W.O.'s and N.C.O.'s Course No. S.I. 73, Appendix to A15 WD for February 1942, LAC, RG24-C-3, vol. 17052.

76   DMT WD, 14 June 1943, LAC, RG24-C-3, vol. 13240. Various DMT WD entries show that a new serial ran about once per month, with roughly 150 students or more in attendance.

77   S17 Canadian School of Infantry WD [hereafter S17 WD], opening statement for October 1943, LAC, RG24-C-3, vol. 16910.

78   Geoffrey Hayes, *Crerar's Lieutenants: Inventing the Canadian Junior Army Officer, 1939–45* (Vancouver: UBC Press, 2017), 80–86.

79   Extract from Terms of Reference, Appendix 2 to S17 WD for October 1943, undated, LAC, RG24-C-3, vol. 16910.

80   Ibid.

81   Syllabus (5 Wings), Appendix 1 to S17 WD for October 1943, LAC, RG24-C-3, vol. 16910.

82   S17 WD, 29 October 1943, LAC, RG24-C-3, vol. 16910.

83   Joining Instructions for Canadian School of Infantry, undated, appended to DMT WD for October 1943, LAC, RG24-C-3, vol. 13240.

84   Syllabus for No 2 (Pl Comds) Wing Course No 2, appended to S17 WD for October 1943, LAC, RG24-C-3, vol. 16910.

85   Canadian School of Infantry Precis, Appendix D to S17 WD for October 1943, ibid.

86   Ibid.

87   Ibid., Precis – The Battle Drill Objectives, para. 7.

88   Sanderson and Sanderson, *Letters from a Soldier,* 53–54, letter dated 7 January 1944.

89   Canadian School of Infantry Precis, Appendix D to S17 WD for October 1943, LAC, RG24-C-3, vol. 16910.

90   Data from Appendix D to S17 WD for October 1943, Canadian School of Infantry Precis, LAC, RG24-C-3, vol. 16910.

91   Gregg to Chief Instructor, 26 June 1944, Appendix G to S17 WD for June 1944, ibid. Snow became commandant of S17 in early September 1944. S17 WD, 4 September 1944.

92   Ibid., 13 July 1944.

93 Gregg, Forward – Canadian School of Infantry Precis, Appendix D to S17 WD for October 1943, ibid.

94 S17 WD, 16 October 1944, ibid.

95 Snow to DMT/NDHQ (Monthly Training Liaison Letter No. 7), 30 October 1944, Appendix D to S17 WD for October 1944, LAC, RG24-C-3, vol. 16910.

96 S17 WD, 11 and 15 November 1944, Ibid.

97 Ibid., 18 November 1994. On 22 December, the school received word from Ottawa to expect a first group of 250 officers. A month later, another 188 officers, most from the artillery and armoured corps, reported for conversion training at the new Number 1 (Officer Conversion) Battle Wing. S17 WD, 22 December 1944 and 19–24 January 1945, LAC, RG24-C-3, vol. 16910.

98 In late January, the Number 4 (Mortar) and Number 5 (Anti-tank) wings merged into a support wing.

99 S17 WD, 8 March and 2 June 1945, LAC, RG24-C-3, vol. 16910.

100 Major-General J.P. Mackenzie, Inspector-General Report on S.17 Canadian School of Infantry, 7–10 April 1944, LAC, RG24-C-1, file 8328-1299 (reel C-4994).

101 A34 Special Training Centre WD [hereafter A34 WD], 3 August 1944, LAC, RG24-C-3, vol. 17136. Prior to mid-June 1944, A34 had been a Special Officers Training Centre that trained officers chosen for "on loan" service with the British army. A34 WD, 17 June 1944.

102 Another program refreshed basic training for undertrained reinforcements of all trades, and in early 1945, yet another assessed and sharpened the skills of conscripts selected for overseas duty.

103 A34 WD, 7 July and 21 August 1944, LAC, RG24-C-3, vol. 17136. Early that month, NDHQ decided that a group of NCOs selected for overseas service required two months of general refresher training. These troops came from the ordnance, electrical mechanical engineer, and service corps, and included mostly tradesmen and clerks who had little tactical experience. In fact, most had obtained NCO rank only by virtue of their trade qualifications.

104 A34 WD, 24 and 31 August, and 7, 19, and 29 September 1944, LAC, RG24-C-3, vol. 17136.

105 Ibid., 12 October 1944 and 8 December 1944.

106 Lieutenant-Colonel F.L. Nichols to DOC [District Officer Commanding] MD No. 7, 23 October 1944, Appendix 76 to DMT WD for October 1944, LAC, RG24-C-3, vol. 13242.

107 A34 WD, 14 and 27 October 1944, LAC, RG24-C-3, vol. 17136.

108 Ibid., 31 October, and 4 and 10 November 1944.

109 Ibid., 16, 17, and 20 November 1944.

110 Ibid., November 1944 to February 1945, *passim.*

111 Ibid., February 1945, *passim.*

Chapter 7: The Mass Army's Programs in the United Kingdom

Epigraph: Monthly Training Report – Canadian Training School [CTS], for the Month of August 1942, dated 24 September 1942, Library and Archives Canada (LAC), Record Group (RG) 24, vol. 9841, file 2/Reports/4.

1 C.P. Stacey, *Six Years of War: The Army in Canada, Britain and the Pacific,* vol. 1 of *Official History of the Canadian Army in the Second World War* (Ottawa: Department of National Defence and the Queen's Printer, 1955), 231–32 and 236–37.

2 Ibid., 240.

3 Canadian Military Headquarters (CMHQ) controlled the distribution of seats, as it did for a very wide variety of so-called CMHQ courses.

4 Training Resume – C.T.S. (July/40–October/41), 11 November 1941, LAC, RG24-C-2, vol. 9841, file 2/Reports/2.

5 No. 3 (Weapons) Wing First Report on Training, 12 November 1941, ibid.

6 Lieutenant-Colonel M.F. Gregg to General Staff-CMHQ, 4 August 1941, LAC, RG24-C-2, vol. 9878, file 2/SYLLAB/2.

7 The information on course content in this paragraph comes from the course syllabus: C.M.H.Q. Course No. 804, ibid.

8 First Report on Training, No. 3 (Weapons) Wing, 12 November 1941, LAC, RG24-C-2, vol. 9888, file 2/TRG SCH MISC/1.

9 Brigadier N.E. Rodger to C.R.U., 24 November 1942, ibid.

10 Brigadier N.E. Rodger to D.A.G., [Deputy Adjutant General] 18 November 1942, ibid.

11 Course nomination rolls for serials 2 and 5, ibid.

12 Major-General P.J. Montague memorandum, C.R.U. Instructors' Refresher Course, 7 October 1942, ibid.

13 Lieutenant-General H.D.G. Crerar memorandum, CRU Instructors' Refresher Course, 16 October 1942, LAC, RG24-C-2, vol. 9779, file 2/CTS Inf/1.

14 Brigadier N.E. Rodger memorandum, C.R.U. Instructors Refresher Course at C.T.S., 10 December 1942, LAC, RG24-C-2, vol. 9888, file 2/TRG SCH MISC/1.

15 One student dropped out for medical reasons. Major J.T. Harper to Commandant CTS, 23 January 1943, LAC, RG24-C-2, vol. 9779, file 2/CTS Inf/1.

16 One student dropped out for medical reasons and another was kicked off the course for disciplinary reasons. Brigadier F.R. Phelan memorandum, CMHQ Course 824 Serial 6, 26 February 1943, LAC, RG24-C-2, vol. 9888, file 2/TRG SCH MISC/1.

17 Major J.T. Harper to Commandant CTS, 30 September 1942, ibid.

18 Colonel T.E. Snow to "Trg" CMHQ, 15 March 1943, ibid.

19 Brigadier N.E. Rodger to D.A.G., 10 February 1943, LAC, RG24-C-2, vol. 9777, file 2/CRU/3.

20 Brigadier F.R. Phelan to Senior Officer CMHQ, 9 February 1943, ibid.

21 Lieutenant-Colonel I.L. Ibbotson, minutes for Conference Held at "G" Branch C.R.U. 20 Jan 43, undated, LAC, RG24-C-2, vol. 9804, file 2/Instrns CRU/1. See also Lieutenant-Colonel I.L. Ibbotson, Canadian Reinforcement Units Training Instruction No. 1, 18 October 1942, ibid.

22 Various Canadian Reinforcement Unit tests of elementary training (CRU TOETs) are located in LAC, RG24-C-2, vol. 9804, file 2/Instrns CRU/1.

23 Major-General P.J. Montague to HQ First Cdn Army, 16 September 1943, ibid.

24 CRU Standard TOETs – NCOs Only, ibid.

25 First Cdn Army Trg Directive Number 17, 17 October 1943, LAC, RG24-C-2, vol. 9804, file 2/Instrns/1/2.

26 Ibid.

27 Collective training at platoon, company, and unit level was to occur in January, February, and March respectively. First Cdn Army Trg Directive Number 18, 15 December 1943, LAC, RG24-C-2, vol. 9804, file 2/Instrns/1/2.

28 At the time, Lieutenant-General Kenneth Stuart was the acting commander of First Canadian Army. Crerar did not take command until 20 March 1944. C.P. Stacey, *The Victory Campaign: the Operations in North-West Europe, 1944–1945*, vol. 3 of *Official History of the Canadian Army in the Second World War* (Ottawa: Department of National Defence and the Queen's Printer, 1960), 32.

29 Colonel T.W. Snow memorandum, No 3 (Weapons) Wing – Courses, 19 January 1944, LAC, RG24-C-2, vol. 9888, file 2/TRG SCHOOL/1-4.

30 Brigadier M.H.S. Penhale to Commandant CTS, 10 January 1944, ibid.
31 Brigadier M.H.S. Penhale to Commandant CTS, 18 February 1944, ibid. In the new establishment, only 219 would be permanent staff. The remainder would be incremental staff, drawn as necessary to run courses.
32 CMHQ Monthly Training Letter No. 5 – February 1944, Directorate of History and Heritage (DHH), 312.032 (D1). Several organizational changes occurred. Number 1 (OCTU) Wing ceased operations in March, Number 2 (Technical) Wing reduced in size by training officers and NCOs at the same time, Number 3 (Weapons) Wing absorbed Number 4 (Tactics) Wing – while continuing to run its most important program, the NCO Refresher Course – and Number 7 (Educational) Wing closed at the end of February.
33 CMHQ Monthly Trg Liaison Letter No. 6 – Mar 44, DHH, 312.032 (D1).
34 Colonel F. Barber, CMHQ Monthly Training Letter No 7, 4 April 1944, LAC, RG24-C-2, vol. 9888, file 2/TRG SCHOOL/1-4.
35 Brigadier N.N. Rodger memorandum, C.R.U. Instructors Refresher Course at C.T.S., 10 December 1942, RG24-C-2, vol. 9888, file 2/Trng Sch Misc/1.
36 Lieutenant-Colonel B.B. King memorandum, CRU Trg Instrn No. 6 – 1 Mar 44, 3 March 1944, LAC, RG24-C-2, vol. 9804, file 2/Instrns CRU/1.
37 Ibid.
38 Some officers arrived from officer candidate training units. Two Week Refresher Syllabus, 9 February 1944, ibid.
39 Ibid. Similar arrangements existed for officers.
40 Table 7.2 demonstrates that the course covered many elemental subjects that each received only a few periods. That CRU staff had ascertained reinforcements now required only such a simplified refresher program suggests reinforcement quality really was improving in early 1944.
41 HQ Cdn Rft Units Trg Instr No. 6, 1 March 1944, LAC, RG24-C-2, vol. 9804, file 2/Instrns CRU/1. For CMHQ's authority to use this process, see Brigadier M.H.S. Penhale memorandum, CRU Trg Instrn No. 6 – 1 Mar 44, dated 4 March 1944, ibid.
42 HQ Cdn Rft Units Trg Instr No. 6, 1 March 1944, ibid.
43 CMHQ Monthly Trg Liaison Letter No, 7 – April 1944, DHH, 312.032 (D1).
44 In June, CMHQ told National Defence Headquarters (NDHQ) again that infantry reinforcements – which meant all infantrymen, including NCOs – continued to arrive from Canada with improved states of training. CMHQ Monthly Trg Liaison Letter No. 9 – June 1944, DHH, 312.032 (D1).
45 Great Britain, War Office, *Infantry Training: Training and War, 1937* (Ottawa: King's Printer, 1939), 31.
46 Lieutenant-General B.L. Montgomery, Corps Commander's Personal Memoranda for Commanders, 1 June 1941, LAC, General H.D.G. Crerar Papers, Manuscript Group (MG) 30-E157, vol. 23, file 958C.009 (D233).
47 First Cdn Army Trg Directive Number 14, 17 April 1943, LAC, RG24-C-2, vol. 9804, file 2/Instrns Army/1.
48 Kenneth B. Smith, *"Duffy's Regiment": A History of the Hastings and Prince Edward Regiment* (Toronto: Dundurn Press, 1987), 46.
49 First Canadian Army Training Instruction No. 1, November 1942, LAC, RG24-G-3-1-a, vol. 10437, file 212C1 (D44).
50 GHQ Monthly Training Letter – April 1943, dated 1 May 1943, LAC, RG24-G-3-1-a, vol. 10770, file 222C1 (D236). The letter stressed that all soldiers, not just infantry, "must be trained to the highest degree."

51 No. 3 (Weapons) Wing First Report on Training, 12 November 1941, LAC, RG24-C-2, vol. 9841, file 2/Reports/4.
52 CA(O) Routine Order No. 1412, LAC, RG24-C-2, vol. 9888, file 2/TRG SCH MISC/1.
53 Block Syllabus for CMHQ Course #809 Platoon Weapons as of 5 Jul 43, undated, LAC, RG24-C-2, vol. 9779, file 2/CTS SA/1/4.
54 Edmond Derasp service file, LAC, RG24, vol. 25729.
55 James Cameron Brown service file, LAC, RG24, vol. 25259.
56 Stacey, *Six Years of War*, 236.
57 Colonel J.G.K. Strathy, TL Report No. 1, June 1944, LAC, RG24-C-2, vol. 9880, file 2/TL Rep I/1.
58 Commander CRU now had authority to demote poor performers. Brigadier M.H.S. Penhale memorandum, CMHQ Course No 1213 – NCO CIC (Qualifying), 7 June 1944, ibid.
59 Brigadier M.H.S. Penhale to Comd CTS, 16 June 1944, LAC, RG24-C-2, vol. 9888, file 2/ TRG SCHOOL/1-5.
60 CMHQ Monthly Trg Liaison Letter No 9 – June 1944, DHH, 312.032 (D1).
61 The sub-wing had two roles: to teach proper teaching methods to CRU instructors, and to provide a board of assessment to assist with selecting instructors for duty in Canada. (As described in Chapter 6, training authorities in Canada had started providing instruction in "how to teach" in the summer of 1941, and by October 1944, developed a combined methods of instruction and methods of coaching course.)
62 CMHQ Monthly Trg Liaison Letter No 10, 15 July 1944, DHH, 312.032 (D1).
63 On 2 August, the brigade learned that it would convert several thousand soldiers from the service, ordnance, artillery, and engineer corps. Ten days later, the first draft of soldiers from various reinforcement units arrived for conversion training, and within about a month approximately 4,100 men reported to 13 CIB [Canadian Infantry Brigade] to be trained as infantry. 13 CIB WD, 2 and 25 August, and 2, 9, and 16 September 1944, LAC, RG24-C-3, vol. 14166 (reel T-12401).
64 Ibid., 20 September 1944.
65 Syllabus for 13 Cdn Inf Bde NCO School First Week Course #3, Appendix 42 to 13 CIB WD for October 1944, LAC, RG24-C-3, vol. 14166 (reel T-12401).
66 13 CIB WD, 20 October 1944; and Appendix 21 to WD for October 1944, Exercise Rosedale instruction, 18 October 1944, both LAC, RG24-C-3, vol. 14166 (reel T-12401).
67 War diary entries for 13 CIB, and its 13 Canadian Infantry Training Brigade (CITB) successor, show that the course ran twice per month, with about fifty students per serial, and that serials ran until at least mid-March 1945.
68 CMHQ Training Liaison Letter No. 15, 15 December 1944, DHH, 312.032 (D1). See also 13 CITB WD, 18 November 1944, LAC, RG24-C-3, vol. 14167 (reel T-12401).
69 13 CITB WD, 20 November 1944, LAC, RG24-C-3, vol. 14167 (reel T-12401).
70 Here, soldiers underwent CRU's standard two-week program that all reinforcements attended, regardless of corps or experience, followed by at least one week of infantry training. After completing these three weeks of instruction, each soldier underwent continuation training while awaiting dispatch to a field unit. HQ Cdn Reinforcement Units Trg Instruction No. 13, 10 November 1944, LAC, RG24-C-2, vol. 9804, file 2/Instrns CRU/1/2.
71 5 CITR [Canadian Infantry Training Regiment] WD, 18 December 1944, LAC, RG24-C-3, vol. 16767. For the month before, the 8th battalion of 4 CITR fulfilled this role. The 8th battalion reverted to a standard battalion for training infantry reinforcements but focused

exclusively on French-speaking soldiers. CMHQ Monthly Trg Liaison Letter No. 16, 15 January 1945, DHH, 312.032 (D1).

72 The six-week program was for soldiers from the armoured, artillery, engineer, signals, service, and provost corps. Men from other trades had to undergo a program based on the standard basic training for infantry. HQ Cdn Reinforcement Units Trg Instruction No. 13, Appendix E (Two Weeks NCO Conversion Course), 10 November 1944, RG24-C-2, vol. 9804, file 2/Instrns CRU/1/2.

73 5 CITR WD, 7 March 1945, LAC, RG24-C-3, vol. 16767. On 9 March 1945, the brigade commander met with his unit commanders to discuss the situation. Perhaps, the attendees allowed, the conversion training had not been long enough. The brigade commander decided that affected individuals would receive another three weeks of training, after which they would revert in rank if they did not meet standards. Unfortunately, records do not show how well the subsequent training went. 5 CITR WD, 9 March 1945.

74 C Coy Training Time Table Week Ending 30 June 1945, Appendix 5 to 5 CITR WD for June 1945; and 5 CITR WD, 22 July 1945, both LAC, RG24-C-3, vol. 1677.

75 The army's remuster program in Britain ultimately shifted 12,638 other ranks to infantry. Of these, about 10,830, perhaps slightly more, underwent remuster training in Britain starting in August 1944. Stacy, *Arms, Men and Governments*, 437–38. NCOs probably constituted 18 percent of this number, bringing the number of NCOs to about 1,950.

76 Stacy, *Arms, Men and Governments*, 438.

Chapter 8: Managing the Talent

Epigraph: Montgomery to Crerar, 25 August 1943, Library and Archives Canada (LAC), General H.D.G. Crerar Papers, Manuscript Group (MG) 30-E157, vol. 7, file 958C.009 (D172).

1 Directorate of Military Training (DMT) War Diary (WD), 25 September 1940, LAC, Record Group (RG) 24-C-3, vol. 13239.

2 DEFENSOR to CANMILITRY (GS 2206), 5 October 1940, LAC, RG24-C-2, vol. 12235, file 1/Instructors/1 (reel T-17836).

3 CANMILITRY to DEFENSOR (GS 2139), 10 October 1940, ibid.

4 Major-General P.J. Montague to the Under-Secretary of State, War Office (DDMT), 15 October 1940, ibid.

5 Lieutenant-Colonel C.S. Booth to CMHQ/A.A.G. [Canadian Military Headquarters/ Assistant Adjutant General], 20 October 1940, ibid. RSM Paul Triquet of the Royal 22nd Regiment (R22R), who later won the Victoria Cross as an officer in Italy, made the list.

6 DMT WD, 20 November 1940, LAC, RG24-C-3, vol. 13239.

7 CANMILITRY to DEFENSOR (GS 179), 3 February 1941, LAC, RG24-C-2, vol. 12235, file 1/Instructors/1 (reel T-17836).

8 DEFENSOR to CANMILITRY (GST 621), 23 April 1941, ibid.

9 Major N.B. Rodger to the Senior Officer CMHQ, 1 June 1941, and Major M.S. Dunn to Headquarters Cdn Corps, 1 July 1941, ibid. These soldiers did not deploy until early July, and the group included some officers.

10 DMT to CGS [Chief of the General Staff], 1 April 1941, Directorate of History and Heritage (DHH), 112.3S200 (D263). The army later published the eight-month limit in Canadian Army Routine Order (CARO) 1288. Canada, Department of National Defence, *Canadian Army Routine Orders*, vol. 4 (Ottawa: King's Printer, 1941), 2 July 1941 to 31 December 1941, CARO 1288.

11   VCGS [Vice Chief of the General Staff] to Senior Officer CMHQ, 15 May 1941, LAC, RG24-C-2, vol. 12235, file 1/Instructors/1 (reel T-17836). In fact, only two NCOs had demonstrated weak instructional skills.

12   DEFENSOR to CANMILITRY (GDS 1552), 15 October 1941, DHH, 112.3S200 (D263).

13   Major N.E. Rodger memorandum, Instructors for Training Centres in Canada, 23 October 1941, LAC, RG24-C-2, vol. 12235, file 1/Instructors/1 (reel T-17836).

14   Major N.E. Roger to Senior Officer CMHQ, 23 November 1941, ibid.

15   C.P. Stacey, *Six Years of War: The Army in Canada, Britain, and the Pacific*, vol. 1 of *Official History of the Canadian Army in the Second World War* (Ottawa: Department of National Defence and the Queen's Printer, 1955), 97.

16   DEFENSOR to CANMILITRY (GST 126), 31 January 1942, LAC, RG24-C-2, vol. 12235, file 1/Instructors/1 (reel T-17836).

17   CANMILITRY to DEFENSOR (GST 191), 11 February 1942, ibid.

18   Brigadier G.G. Simonds memorandum, Instructors for Training in Canada, 10 February 1942, LAC, RG24-G-3-1-a, vol. 10771, file 222C1 (D292).

19   Each division received orders to supply a number of infantry and armoured soldiers. The heads of the other arms – artillery, engineers, signals, and service corps – were ordered to fill allotted numbers, too.

20   Crerar memorandum, untitled, 24 February 1942, LAC, RG24-G-3-1-a, vol. 10771, file 222C1 (D292).

21   Crerar memorandum, untitled, 26 February 1942, ibid.

22   For examples, see Fred Cederberg, *The Long Road Home: The Autobiography of a Canadian Soldier in Italy in World War II* (Don Mills, ON: General, 1984), 26–27; Craig B. Cameron, *Born Lucky: RSM Harry Fox, MBE, One D-Day Dodger's Story* (St. Catharines, ON: Vanwell, 2005), 46; and, Gordon Brown and Terry Copp, *Look to Your Front – Regina Rifles: A Regiment at War* (Waterloo, ON: Laurier Centre for Military, Strategic and Disarmament Studies, 2001), 7.

23   Major-General P.J. Montague memorandum, Provision of Instructors for Canada, 8 December 1942, LAC, RG24-C-2, vol. 12235, file 1/Instructors/1/2 (reel T-17836).

24   CANMILITRY to DEFENSOR (GS 665), 23 February 1942, LAC, RG24-C-2, vol. 12235, file 1/Instructors/1 (reel T-17836).

25   Major-General P.J. Montague memorandum, Instructors for Canada, 21 March 1942, LAC, RG24-G-3-1-a, vol. 10771, file 222C1 (D292).

26   48th Highlanders WD, 2 and 4 March 1942, LAC, RG24-C-3, vol. 15296.

27   R22R WD, 4 March 1942, LAC, RG24-C-3, vol. 15237.

28   RCR [Royal Canadian Regiment] WD, 3 and 5 March 1942, LAC, RG24-C-3, vol. 15207.

29   Major Burton Harper, interview for FCWM Oral History Project, CWM 20020121-022, George Metcalf Archival Collection, Canadian War Museum — Military History Research Centre.

30   Viateur Brund Paré service file, LAC, RG24, vol. 26754.

31   James Craig Masterson service file, LAC, RG24, vol. 26853.

32   DEFENSOR to CANMILITRY (AG253), 16 May 1942, LAC, RG24-C-2, vol. 12235, file 1/Instructors/1 (reel T-17836).

33   Lieutenant-Colonel N.E. Rodger to Senior Officer CMHQ, 22 May 1942, ibid.

34   DEFENSOR to CANMILITRY (GS330), 5 August 1942, LAC, RG24-C-2, vol. 12235, file 1/Instructors/1/2 (reel T-17836).

35 Daniel Byers, *Zombie Army: The Canadian Army and Conscription in the Second World War* (Vancouver: UBC Press, 2016), 112.

36 CANMILITRY to DEFENSOR (GS2844), 13 August 1942, LAC, RG24-C-2, vol. 12235, file 1/Instructors/1/2 (reel T-17836).

37 Major-General P.J. Montague memorandum, Provision of Instructors for Canada, 10 September 1942, ibid.

38 Major-General P.J. Montague memorandum, Instructors Selected for Appointment in Canadian Training Centres, 13 November 1942, ibid. CMHQ did not quite meet the 25 percent commitment because the screening process removed thirty-five NCOs and eleven officers.

39 Lieutenant D.G. Robertson memorandum, Provision of Instructors for Canada, 10 August 1943, LAC, RG24-C-2, vol. 12235, file 1/Instructors/1/4 (reel T-17837).

40 CANMILITRY to DEFENSOR (GS1919), 11 August 1943, ibid.

41 Major-General P.J. Montague memorandum, Instructors Selected for Duty at Canadian Training Establishments, 24 September 1943, ibid.

42 Major F.J. Fleury memorandum, Instructors for Training Centres in Canada, 15 September 1943, LAC, RG24-C-2, vol. 9809, file 2/Instructors/1/2. The Stormont, Dundas and Glengarry Highlanders nominated an officer who had recently been fired from the Canadian Training School as "unsuitable as an instructor." The Régiment de la Chaudière submitted an officer who had arrived in Britain five months earlier in such weak shape that his reinforcement unit initiated a confidential report on his state of training and considerable flaws: "This officer has a very poor background and his physical condition is far from satisfactory. In addition, this officer's conduct since arrival in this country has been questionable." The armoured corps nominated an officer whose course report from previous training suggested that he might not thrive in the instructional environment: "Tries hard. A pleasant personality. He seems to find it hard to pick up new ideas. A very slow thinker. Short of general military knowledge."

43 Major J.A. Northey memorandum, Instrs for Training Centres in Canada, 16 September 1943, ibid.

44 Lieutenant-Colonel F. Nichols memorandum, Provision of Instrs for Canada, 12 January 1944, LAC, RG24-C-2, vol. 9809, file 2/Instructors/1/3.

45 Lieutenant-Colonel J.E.C. Pangman memorandum, Provision of Instrs for Canada, 1 February 1944, ibid. CRU proposed that First Canadian Army make up the deficiency. Records do not show the army's response.

46 Lieutenant-Colonel M.P. Johnston to SD&T, 9 February 1944, ibid.

47 Lieutenant-General K. Stuart memorandum, Selection of Instrs for Canada, 22 March 1944, LAC, RG24-C-2, vol. 12235, file 1/Instructors/1/5 (reel T-17837).

48 Lieutenant-Colonel H.C. Griffith to Lieutenant-Colonel J.E.C. Pangman, 27 April 1944, LAC, RG24-C-2, vol. 9809, file 2/Instructors/1/4.

49 Major-General J.H. Roberts to CMHQ (G Trg), 11 May 1944, ibid.

50 Lieutenant-Colonel H.C. Griffith to Lieutenant-Colonel J.E.C. Pangman, 27 April 1944, ibid.

51 Major-General J.H. Roberts to CMHQ (G Trg), 11 May 1944, ibid.

52 Ibid.

53 Lieutenant-General K. Stuart to DND (DMT), 6 June 1944, LAC, RG24-C-2, vol. 9809, file 2/Instructors/1/4; and Lieutenant-Colonel D.D. Stewart to SD&T [Staff Duties and Training], 30 August 1944, file 2/Instructors/1/5.

54 The officials included Brigadier H.D. Graham, the Deputy Chief of the General Staff (B), and Colonel A.J. Creighton, the Director of Military Training. Minutes of Training Conference for Central Canada held 12 July 1944, Appendix 54 to DMT WD for July 1944, and Minutes of Training Conference for Western Canada held on 26 July 1944, Appendix 26 to DMT WD for August 1944, both LAC, RG24-C-3, vol. 13242.

55 Minutes of Training Conference for Western Canada held on 26 July 1944, Appendix 26 to DMT WD for August 1944, LAC, RG24-C-3, vol. 13242.

56 Brigadier M.H.S. Penhale to HQ CRU [Canadian Reinforcement Units] (G Trg), 19 July 1944, LAC, RG24-C-2, vol. 9809, file 2/Instructors/1/5.

57 Survey of Instructional Personnel Currently on Duty in Canada, 30 October 1944, Appendix 97 to DMT WD for October 1944, LAC, RG24-C-3, vol. 13242.

58 The infantry shortage took a toll. See DEFENSOR to CANMILITRY (TRG 4113), 28 November 1944, LAC, RG24-C-2, vol. 9809, file 2/Instructors/1/5.

59 Lieutenant-Colonel F.S. Wilder to Colonel J.G.K. Strathy, 10 April 1945, LAC, RG24-C-2, vol. 9809, file 2/Instructors/1/6.

60 Brigadier B. Mathews to OIC Records, 28 May 1945, LAC, RG24-C-2, vol. 9808, file 2/Instrs CDA/16/1.

61 Edward Ernest Cronk service file, LAC, RG24, vol. 25761.

62 Sergeant Cronk was killed in action on 15 August 1944.

63 DEFENSOR to CANMILITRY (GS953), 2 August 1940, LAC, RG24-C-2, vol. 12236, file 1/INTERCHANGE/2. The plan also included a proposal to exchange small groups of officers, which the War Office accepted. Until the program ended, officer exchanges occurred parallel to the NCO attachments but in smaller numbers.

64 Major M.S. Dunn to Chief Paymaster CASF [Canadian Active Service Force], 2 December 1940, ibid.

65 Major M.S. Dunn to HQ Canadian Base Units, 10 March 1941, ibid. The Canadians also managed to secure additional attachments for another forty-one NCOs and fifteen officers (some from Canada but most from units in Britain) who received attachments to an armoured division of the 7th Corps.

66 Major-General P.J. Montague to War Office (DMT Branch), 20 February 1941, ibid. NDHQ also wanted to attach a few more soldiers to coastal defence units.

67 Major M.S. Dunn to HQ Cdn Base Units, 21 April 1941, ibid.

68 Major M.S. Dunn to HQ Cdn Base Units, 28 July 1941, LAC, RG24-C-2, vol. 12236, file 1/INTERCHANGE/2/2.

69 Major-General P.J. Montague to HQ RAC, 15 July 1941, and, Major-General P.J. Montague to War Office, 15 September 1941, ibid. A third round comprised an officer-only exchange of about twenty men from each country.

70 CGS memorandum to AG [Adjutant General], 6 October 1941, DHH, 112.3S2009 (D263).

71 DEFENSOR to CANMILITRY (TRG3109), 10 March 1943, LAC, RG24-C-2, vol. 9809, file 2/Instructors/1. This document shows that a fourth group departed shortly after 26 March and included fifty-three NCOs and fifty-two officers.

72 CANMILITRY to DEFENSOR (GS222), 2 February 1943, ibid.

73 Lieutenant-Colonel DD. Stewart memorandum to SD&T, Liaison and Interchange of Officers, 30 August 1944, LAC, RG24, vol. 9809, file 2/Instructors/1/5. The program eventually ran six serials, each with about sixty NCOs and sixty officers.

74 Lieutenant-Colonel D.D. Stewart memorandum to CMHQ SD&T, Liaison and Interchange of Officers, 30 August 1940, ibid.

75 CGS memorandum, 7th Series of Attachments Overseas, 19 April 1944, Appendix 41 to DMT WD for April 1944, LAC, RG24-C-3, vol. 13241.
76 Lieutenant-Colonel D.D. Stewart memorandum to CMHQ SD&T, Liaison and Interchange of Officers, 30 August 1940, LAC, RG24-C-2, vol. 9809, file 2/Instructors/1/5.
77 Defensor Ottawa to Canmilitry London (AG1885), 13 December 1940, LAC, RG24-C-2, vol. 12236, file 1/Interchange/3 (reel T-17838).
78 HQ Cdn Corps memorandum, Interchange of P.F. Other Ranks (1/147(G), 13 December 1940, ibid.
79 BGS [Brigadier General Staff] Cdn Corps to Senior Officer CMHQ, 31 December 1940, ibid. CMHQ relayed these terms to NDHQ five days later. See CANMILITRY to DEFENSOR (A21), 4 January 1941, ibid.
80 Major M.S. Dunn to DAG, Summary of Cables, 14 July 1941, ibid.
81 Major-General B.W. Browne memorandum, Interchange of P.F. Personnel for Overseas Service, 18 March 1941, ibid.
82 Major-General B.W. Browne memorandum, Service in a Theatre of Operations: Other Ranks – Permanent Force, 10 April 1941, ibid.
83 Captain M.J. Griffin note to file, Personnel from Canada, 10 May 1941, and Lieutenant-Colonel N.B. MacDonald to A.G.2, 9 June 1941, ibid. The former document lists by name seven survivors who reported for duty. However, a later CMHQ document states that eight soldiers arrived in Britain. See Major M.S. Dunn to HQ Cdn Corps (Liaison) and CMHQ (A.G.2a), 14 July 1941, ibid.
84 Captain M.J. Griffin to DAG, 12 June 1941, ibid.
85 Major M.S. Dunn to D.A.G., 14 July 1941, ibid.
86 Major N.E. Rodger to Senior Officer CMHQ, 22 August 1941, ibid.
87 Colonel A.W. Beament, Bomber Mail letter to the Secretary DND, 26 August 1941, ibid.
88 For example, in February 1942, CMHQ reminded the corps that no further exchanges had occurred after the first two, and that staff had seen no reason to publish a new administrative order to amend the program's terms. See Major-General P.J. Montague to Cmdr Cdn Corps, 4 February 1942,LAC, RG24-C-2, vol. 12236, file 1/Interchange/3/2 (reel T-17838).
89 Lieutenant-Colonel N.E. Rodger to Senior Officer CMHQ, 14 April 1942, ibid.
90 Canadian Reinforcement Units Training Instruction No. 1, 18 October 1942, LAC, RG24-C-2, vol. 9804, file 2/Instrns\CRU/1. All officers in the training wings rotated every six months, too.
91 James Jacobs service file, LAC, RG24, vol. 26183. Jacobs enlisted into the Princess Patricia's Canadian Light Infantry (PPCLI) but transferred to the Regina Rifles in August 1941 to proceed overseas. During his time in Britain, he also spent two very short stints in 2 Canadian Infantry Reinforcement Unit (CIRU), once to attend a platoon weapons course and once for a brief hospitalization.
92 BGS [Brigadier General Staff] First Canadian Army to BGS CMHQ, 20 March 1943, LAC, RG24-G-3-1-a, vol. 10437, file 212C1 (D44). The plan indicated that the six-month rotations for instructors should continue but, First Canadian Army proposed, all CRU instructors should be fit for field duty. Those not suitable should be moved to administrative jobs or returned to Canada.
93 Brigadier C. Foulkes memorandum, Rotation of Personnel Fd and Rft Units, 21 April 1943, LAC, RG24-G-3-1-a, vol. 10437, file 212C1 (D44).

94   This number does not include those who rotated through the reinforcement system before they were NCOs, nor those who moved from field to reinforcement units because of injury or illness.

95   John Buck service file, LAC, RG24, vol. 25273.

96   William George Murray service file, LAC, RG24, vol. 26687.

97   Charles Cromwell Martin, *Battle Diary: From D-Day and Normandy to the Zuider Zee and VE* (Toronto: Dundurn Press, 1994), 85–86.

98   Ibid., 129.

99   Department of National Defence, DHH, CMHQ Reports, Historical Officer Report No. 95, Attachment of Canadian Officers and Soldiers to First British Army in Tunisia, 1942–1943, 12 May 1943, 1. The author, Major C.P. Stacey, states that the Eighth Army's previous operations had not afforded a realistic opportunity because of the lengthy line of communication that stretched around the southern tip of Africa.

100 Brigadier C.C. Mann memorandum, Attachments – British Army, 6 December 1942, LAC, RG24-G-3-1-a, vol. 10771, file 222C1 (D286).

101 DHH, Historical Officer Report No. 95, 1, and Amendment No. 1 to the report.

102 Major J.W. Atkinson, Report on Attachment 1 Br. Army, 9 October 1943, and Report on Attachment of Captain T. Statten, to First British Army, BNAF [British North Africa Forces], Mar 5 to Jul 31 1943, undated, LAC, RG24-G-3-1-a, vol. 10438, file 212C1 (D52). Also DHH, Historical Officer Report No. 95, 2 and 7.

103 Lieutenant-Colonel W.A. Bean to Senior Officer CMHQ, attachment – First British Army, North Africa, 10 April 1943, DHH, 112.3M3009 (D180). Also DHH, Historical Officer Report No. 95, 4.

104 Captain G.M. MacLachlan, Royal Regiment of Canada, quoted in DHH, Historical Officer Report No. 95.

105 Stacey, *Six Years of War*, 248–49.

106 North Shore (New Brunswick) Regiment NS(NB)R WD, 14, 16, and 19 April 1943, LAC, RG24-C-3, vol. 15126.

107 *Aldershot News* [A14 camp periodical] 1, 10 (December 1943), appended to A14 Canadian Army Infantry Training Centre (CAITC) WD for December 1943, LAC, RG24-C-3, vol. 17046.

108 Active Service Notes from Experiences of Lt TG Bowie, 3 September 1943, DHH, 159.7009.

109 Joint report on Reconnaissance Regiments by Major A.A. Ballachey, Lieutenant N.A. McLean, and Sergeant Stevenson, undated, DHH, 159.7009.

110 Major F.E. White, Captain A.S. Christian, Captain T. Johnston, Sergeant J.J. Jenner, Sergeant R.W. Pitt, and Sergeant K.W. Waugh, Report by C.A.C. [Canadian Armoured Corps] Personnel B.N.A.F., undated, DHH, 159.7009.

111 Sergeant E.F. Hill, Report of Attachment, 3 May 1943, DHH, 159.7009.

112 Sergeant, L.W. McCulloch, Report on Attachment to 1st Army (Br), undated, DHH, 159.7009.

113 Captain J.D. Hilton memorandum, Reports of Officers – North Africa, 14 July 1943, DHH, 159.7009.

114 Sergeant A. Lacroix service file, LAC, RG24, vol. 26290.

115 DHH, Historical Officer Report No. 95, Amendment No. 1.

116 In fact, Montgomery believed that up to 25 percent of the deployed Canadian force should rotate back to Britain. McNaughton concurred with the aim of such a program but thought that securing shipping for so many soldiers would prove difficult, and that 5 or 10 percent

was more realistic. Extracts from Minutes of a Conference Held at CND [sic] Sec GHQ 1 Ech 15 Army Group Sicily 0900 hrs 26 Aug 43, undated, LAC, RG24-C-2, vol. 9770, file 2/CMF&U.K./1.

117 Brigadier E.G. Weeks Most Secret Memorandum, 19 October 1943, ibid.

118 CMHQ Officer I/C Records, Nominal Role of Personnel Embarking in U.K., dated 1 November 1943, LAC, RG24-C-2, vol. 9349, file 8/A.A.I.&UK/1. The first group included 243 NCOs and 247 officers. See LCol E.C. Brown (AAG(Org)) to SD&T, 13 December 1943, ibid.

119 Major-General P.J. Montague memorandum, Interchange of Personnel – CMF [Central Mediterranean Force] and UK, 22 December 1943, ibid. For the soldiers returning to Britain, see Brig A.W. Beament, Officer i/c Cdn Sec GHQ 1 Ech, to Senior Officer CMHQ, 10 December 43, ibid.

120 Brigadier M.H.S. Penhale memorandum, Exchange CMF and UK, 13 January 1944, ibid.

121 Brigadier A.W. Beament to Chief of Staff CMHQ, 29 February 1944, ibid.

122 Ibid.

123 Major A.B. MacLaren memorandum, Personnel Returning from C.M.F. on Interchange, 24 March 1944, ibid.

124 A handful of returned NCOs was designated for return to Canada. The situation for officers was only slightly better. Of 164 officers, twenty-nine (18 percent) went to field units, twenty-six (16 percent) went to instructional positions, ninety-two (56 percent) sat in the reinforcement pool, and seventeen (10 percent) would return to Canada. Brigadier C.S. Booth to BGS, Postings of Officers and NCO's Returned from C.M.F. on Interchange, 29 March 1944, ibid.

125 Lieutenant-Colonel C.J. Lauren memorandum (signed over Crerar's name), Rft Personnel returned from CMF, 24 March 1944, LAC, ibid.

126 Major-General P.J. Montague memorandum, Interchange of Personnel, C.M.F. & U.K., 7 March 1944, and Major-General P.J. Montague to HQ First Cdn Army (Attn: S.D.), Interchange of Personnel – CMF and UK, 27 December 1943, ibid.

127 Kenneth B. Smith, "Duffy's Regiment": A History of the Hastings and Prince Edward Regiment (Toronto: Dundurn Press, 1987), 144–45. Duffy was disappointed that the reinforcement system did not use him as an instructor as much as it could have. He eventually returned to France with the Canadian Section – General Headquarters 2nd Echelon, a rear-area administrative organization that sorely needed an experienced RSM to maintain discipline and order. RSM Harry Fox, who had been RSM of the Queen's Own Rifles (QOR), replaced Duffy in Italy. Cameron, Born Lucky, 65.

128 Daniel G. Dancocks, The D-Day Dodgers: The Canadians in Italy, 1943–1945 (Toronto: McClelland and Stewart, 1991), 220–22.

129 Ibid., 222.

130 J.L. Granatstein, Canada's Army: Waging War and Keeping the Peace (Toronto: University of Toronto Press, 2002), 291–92.

131 C.P. Stacey, Arms, Men and Governments: The War Policies of Canada, 1939–1945 (Ottawa: Queen's Printer, 1970), 427, 428, 438.

132 Granatstein, Canada's Army, 292. The estimated number of NCOs is based on the proportion of NCOs to overall numbers in the overseas army, listed beneath Table I.2.

133 Tod Strickland, "Creating Combat Leaders in the Canadian Corps: The Experiences of Lieutenant-Colonel Agar Adamson," in Great War Commands: Historical Perspectives on Canadian Army Leadership 1914–1918, ed. Andrew B. Godefroy (Kingston, ON: Canadian Defence Academy Press, 2010), 216.

134 Ernest Morgan Keith MacGregor, interview by Rick Aylward, 22 July 1986, University of Victoria, Military History Oral Collection, accessed 30 January 2019, http://contentdm. library.uvic.ca/cdm/compoundobject/collection/collection13/id/215/rec/1.

135 Lieutenant-General G.G. Simonds to All Commanders – Canadian Formations, 28 October 1944, LAC, RG24-C-2, vol. 9880, file 2/TL Rep 12/1.

136 Major-General C. Vokes to All Commanding Officers [4 Canadian Armoured Division], 3 February 1945, LAC, RG24-G-3-1-a, vol. 10939, file 245C4.006 (D3).

137 DHH, Army Headquarters (AHQ) Report No. 63, Manpower Problems of the Canadian Army in the Second World War, vol. 2, Appendix L, 35, para. 6, 17 August 1953.

138 GOC-in-C [General Officer Commanding-in-Chief] First Cdn Army to Commander-in-Chief 21 Army Group, 17 November 1944, LAC, MG30-E157, vol. 2, file 958C.009 (D93). Casualty figures are for the period 1 October–7 November 1944.

139 CMHQ Monthly Training Liaison Letter No. 15, 15 December 1944, Appendix 24 to DMT WD for January 1945, LAC, RG24-C-3, vol. 13243.

140 Canada, Department of National Defence, *Report of the Department of National Defence for the Fiscal Year Ending March 31, 1945* (Ottawa: King's Printer, 1945), 39. This source does not indicate which training centre changed focus but probably refers to the camp at Sussex, New Brunswick, where the A34 Special Training Centre began training NCOs in October 1944.

141 Ralph D. Brennan service file, LAC, RG24, vol. 25239.

142 Wilfred Goodburn service file, LAC, RG24, vol. 25977.

143 Goodburn died of wounds on 15 February 1945. He rendered a great service to his nation, soldiering nearly continuously with the PPCLI in the field from August 1943 until his death in February 1945.

144 Lieutenant-Colonel H.M. Cathcart memorandum, NCOs – Rft Policy, 6 April 1945, LAC, RG24-G-3-1-a, vol. 10836, file 229C2 (D26).

145 Major-General E.G. Weeks to HQ First Cdn Army, 30 December 1944, LAC, RG24-C-2, vol. 9777, file 2/CRU/2.

146 Weeks wanted ten warrant officers class 2, sixty-five sergeants, and 125 corporals. He also asked for five officers to command infantry training battalions, plus another twenty-five to command training companies. CMHQ did not bother asking 1st Canadian Corps in Italy to provide any of the required instructors because the transit time would not allow them to arrive in Britain quickly enough, and because the contingent in Italy already employed "battle weary" soldiers as instructors for in-theatre training at 1 Canadian Base Reinforcement Group (CBRG). But First Canadian Army had no such arrangement for employing the exhausted troops, so CMHQ hoped to acquire some in exchange for green NCOs in Britain.

147 Brigadier W.N. Bostock to MGA, 3 January 1945, LAC, RG24-C-2, vol. 9777, file 2/CRU/2. Also, Bostock to OIC [Officer in Charge] Cdn Sec GHQ 1 Ech, 4 January 1945, ibid.

148 Some regiments also provided a captain or a major. Nominal Roll Draft Exag 50, undated, LAC, RG24-C-2, vol. 9809, file 2/Instructors/1/6.

149 For example, the Queen's Own Rifles dispatched, from their companies in the field, four corporals, two sergeants, and one company quartermaster sergeant. Part 1 Orders 9 Jan 1945, appended to QOR WD for January 1945, LAC, RG24-C-3, vol. 15169.

150 Major-General E.G. Weeks to GO i/c Cdn Sec 1 Ech HQ 21 A Gp, 7 April 1945, LAC, RG24-C-2, vol. 9809, file 2/Instructors/1/6.

151 Brigadier W.H.S. Macklin to D.A.G., handwritten minute II to ADAG(A), 24 April 1945, ibid.

152 DHH, AHQ Report No. 63, vol. 1, 276, para. 647, 17 August 1953.
153 Major-General P.J. Montague to GOC-in-C First Cdn Army, 11 November 1944, LAC, RG24-C-2, vol. 9777, file 2/CRU/2.
154 Crerar to A/C of S CMHQ, 20 November 1944, ibid.
155 Colonel G.F. Beament memorandum, Lecture to Rft Offrs – Cdn Experiences in European Theatre, 25 November 1944, ibid.
156 Lieutenant-Colonel J.C. Anderson memorandum, Lectures – By Comds and Staff Offrs from France, 25 November 1944, ibid.
157 Brigadier N.E. Rodger memorandum, Lectures to Rft Offrs – Cdn Experiences in European Theatre, 5 January 1945, ibid.
158 For a discussion of such perceptions, and of historians' uncertainty about the matter, see Andrew Brown, "New Men in the Line: An Assessment of Reinforcements to the 48th Highlanders in Italy, January–October 1944," *Canadian Military History* 21, 3 (2012): 35, especially n 7.
159 Colonel A.J. Creighton memorandum, Report from AAI – State of Trg-Rfts, 13 September 1944, Appendix 16 to DMT WD for September 1944, LAC, RG24-C-3, vol. 13242.
160 Brigadier M.H.S. Penhale to Comd CRU, 25 August 1944, LAC, RG24-C-2, vol. 9777, file 2/CRU/2.
161 Colonel J.G.K. Strathy to DCGS, 5 August 1944, ibid.
162 Lieutenant-General G.G. Simonds to All Commanders Canadian Formations, 28 October 1944, LAC, RG24-C-2, vol. 9880, file 2/TL REP 12/1.
163 CMHQ Monthly Training Liaison Letter No. 13, 15 October 1944, DHH, file 312.032 (D1). For non-infantry reinforcements, staff had some concerns about clerk training, provost corps troops who required two weeks of refresher drill to meet the local provost standards, and drivers who had little training in night convoys.
164 Brigadier H.D. Graham (for CGS) memorandum, State of Trg of Rfts – Report from CBRG AAI, 22 January 1945, Appendix 58 to DMT WD for January 1945, LAC, RG24-C-3, vol. 13243.
165 Colonel J.G.K. Strathy memorandum, Trg Liaison – Visit by SD&T to NW European Theatre, 10 November 1944, LAC, RG24-C-2, vol. 9889, file 2/TL Rep 12/1.
166 Lieutenant-General P.J. Montague to GOC-in-C First Canadian Army, 1 December 1944, LAC, RG24-C-2, vol. 9812, file 2/LIAIS THEATRE/1.
167 In September 1944, the well-known Toronto sports entrepreneur Conn Smythe, who had been injured the previous July in France as a major in command of an anti-aircraft battery, complained to the media that reinforcements badly lacked training and suffered many needless casualties. His claim, widely republished, generated much public concern. Smythe may have had a motive, as his statement concluded with a call for citizens to insist that the government send the army's conscripts overseas. Ontario premier George Drew used Smythe's allegations to attack the federal government. Stacey, *Arms, Men and Governments*, 440 and 442.
168 Caroline D'Amours, "Reassessment of a Crisis: Canadian Infantry Reinforcements during the Second World War," *Canadian Army Journal* 14, 2 (Summer 2012): 72–89; Brown, *New Men in the Line*, 35–47.
169 Robert Engen, *Strangers in Arms: Combat Motivation in the Canadian Army, 1943–1945* (Montreal and Kingston: McGill-Queen's University Press, 2016), 203. See also 121–22, 159–60, and 192–93.
170 Brigadier W.H.S. Macklin to Comd CRU, 12 December 1944, LAC, RG24-C-2, vol. 9812, file 2/LIAIS THEATRE/1.

171   Lieutenant-Colonel Bruce B. King to SD&T, 18 April 1945, ibid.
172   Major F.N. Rutherford to SD&T, dated 21 April 1945, ibid.
173   Lieutenant-Colonel Bruce B. King to SD&T, 27 April 1945, ibid. Reports from other arms of service generally expressed satisfaction, too. For example, in January and February 1945, representatives from the engineers, artillery, signals, ordnance, service, and medical corps visited reinforcement units and provided good feedback for the most part. Field ambulance unit commanders were the exception, indicating that medical corps reinforcements needed more basic and corps training. LAC, RG24-C-2, vol. 9812, file 2/LIAIS THEATRE/1, *passim*. For the medical corps, see Lieutenant-Colonel Bruce B. King to SD&T, 16 February 1945.
174   A service corps officer from 48 Company, 2nd Armoured Brigade, stated that NCOs arriving as reinforcements had proven acceptable with only a few exceptions. An engineer officer from 31 Field Company indicated that his unit had to break in its NCO reinforcements, who could learn their role only by leading real troops. Lieutenant-Colonel Bruce B. King to SD&T, 2 February 1945, and Memorandum, Visit of Maj R.J. Carson, RCE, 24 January 1945, both LAC, RG24-C-2, vol. 9812, file 2/LIAIS THEATRE/1.
175   Colonel J.G.K. Strathy memorandum, Comments on trg by COs fd [field] units – First Cdn Army, 6 January 1945, ibid.
176   C.P. Stacey, *The Victory Campaign: the Operations in North-West Europe, 1944–1945*, vol. 3 of *Official History of the Canadian Army in the Second World War* (Ottawa: Department of National Defence and the Queen's Printer, 1960), 633.
177   Ibid., 284.
178   Stacey, *Arms, Men and Governments*, 437–38. See also Stacey, *Victory Campaign*, 632.
179   Stacey, *Victory Campaign*, 632.
180   Ibid., 633.
181   Stacey, *Arms, Men and Governments*, 438.
182   Ibid., 440.
183   Extracts from Minutes of a Conference Held at CND [sic] Sec GHQ 1 Ech 15 Army Group Sicily, 26 August 1943, LAC, RG24-C-2, vol. 9770, file 2/CMF&U.K./1.

Conclusion

Epigraph: A30 Cdn Inf Trg Centre Daily Orders Part 1, 30 December 44, appended to War Diary (WD) for December 1944, Library and Archives (LAC), Record Group (RG) 24, vol. 17131.

1   C.P. Stacey, "Canadian Leaders of the Second World War," *Canadian Historical Review* 66 (March 1985): 64.
2   Good examples are Geoffrey Hayes's structural and cultural study of the army's junior officers, Robert Engen's study on the Canadian soldier's combat motivation, and Caroline D'Amours's evaluation of how the army trained infantry junior NCOs for the reinforcement system. Geoffrey Hayes, *Crerar's Lieutenants: Inventing the Canadian Junior Army Officer, 1939–45* (Vancouver: UBC Press, 2017); Robert Engen, *Strangers in Arms: Combat Motivation in the Canadian Army, 1943–1945* (Montreal and Kingston: McGill-Queen's University Press, 2016); and Caroline D'Amours, "Canadian Military Culture and Tactical Training, 1940–1944: The Making of Infantry Junior NCOs," *Journal of Military History* 82, 4 (October 2018): 1175–98. See also her doctoral dissertation, "'Notre tâche est de rendre les hommes prêts au combat': La formation des sous-officiers de renfort d'infanterie du Canada pendant la Seconde Guerre mondiale" (University of Ottawa, 2015).
3   See analysis at Table I.2, p. 10.

4 C.P. Stacey, *Six Years of War: The Army in Canada, Britain and the Pacific*, vol. 1 of *Official History of the Canadian Army in the Second World War* (Ottawa: Department of National Defence and the Queen's Printer, 1955), 51.

5 Jack Granatstein, *The Best Little Army in the World: The Canadians in Northwest Europe, 1944–1945* (Toronto: HarperCollins, 2015), 279.

6 See Terry Copp, *Fields of Fire: The Canadians in Normandy*, 2nd ed. (Toronto: University of Toronto Press, 2014), 150–51, and *Cinderella Army: The Canadians in Northwest Europe 1944–1945* (Toronto: University of Toronto Press, 2006), 31. For an examination of the Essex Scottish Regiment's performance, which finds that Brigadier Hugh Young's poor planning and mismanagement of the battle caused the defeat, see John Maker, "The Essex Scottish Regiment in Operation Atlantic: What Went Wrong?," *Canadian Military History* 18, 1 (Winter 2000): 7–19. Also, Kevin R. Connolly suggests in his MA thesis that these two incidents might have had roots in the losses of junior leadership the 2nd Canadian Division had suffered at Dieppe. "Soldiering On: The Long-Term Effects of the Dieppe Raid on the 2nd Canadian Division" (MA thesis, Royal Military College of Canada, 2016), 67–68.

7 Engen, *Strangers in Arms*, 60.

8 For a discussion of historians' perceptions that the Canadians neglected interim training during their years in England, see p. 64–70.

9 Engen, *Strangers in Arms*, 140, 168, 203.

10 Lieutenant-General B.L. Montgomery, Notes on Inf. Bdes of Canadian Corps – No. 6, 2nd March 1942, dated 3 March 1942, LAC, General H.D.G. Crerar Papers, Manuscript Group (MG) 30-E157, vol. 2, file 958C.009 (D182).

11 For example, as Douglas Delaney explains, the Seaforth Highlanders enjoyed the patronage of John Arthur Clark, who served as honorary lieutenant-colonel from 1924 to 1957. A prominent Vancouver lawyer and, from 1921 to 1930, a Conservative member of parliament, Clark was the "regimental godfather." He used his political influence to support the unit, as when he arranged for funding for a new armoury in 1934 or convinced the government to waive import duties on kilts for the unit in 1938. As chair of the regiment's officer selection committee, he populated the officership of the Seaforths with the elite of Vancouver society. *The Soldier's General: Bert Hoffmeister at War* (Vancouver: UBC Press, 2005), 17–18.

12 Major J.T. Harper to Commandant CTS [Canadian Training School], 30 September 1942, LAC, RG24-C-2, vol. 9888, file 2/TRG SCH MISC/1.

13 Colonel T.E. Snow to "Trg" CMHQ [Canadian Military Headquarters], 15 March 1943, ibid.

14 For instance, in 1940, Lieutenant-Colonel J.B. Stevenson of the Seaforth Highlanders barred his company commanders from attending any training outside his unit, out of fear that someone might assign his best officers to other duty. Delaney, *The Soldiers' General*, 22.

15 Major J.A. Northey memorandum, Instrs for Training Centres in Canada, 16 September 1943, LAC, RG24-C-2, vol. 9809, file 2/Instructors/1/2.

16 Brigadier A.W. Beament to Chief of Staff CMHQ, 29 February 1944, LAC, RG24-C-2, vol. 9349, file 8/A.A.I.&UK/1.

17 Major-General P.J. Montague memorandum, Interchange of Personnel, C.M.F. [Central Mediterranean Force] & U.K., 7 March 1944, ibid.

18 Some 103 of the 388 files (27 percent) have NCO qualification or refresher courses listed. Thirteen soldiers have two courses listed, and one has three. The incomplete nature of

many records makes it all but certain, however, that more than 27 percent of all NCOs underwent formal qualification or refresher courses.

19 The A15 school of instruction in Shilo ultimately trained 4,009 NCOs and officers. One can safely estimate that at least half of these were junior NCOs. Similarly, the A14 school of instruction in Aldershot had trained 1,481 NCOs by May 1943. By the end of the war, A14 had very likely trained over 2,000 junior NCOs as well. If every infantry training centre in Canada trained about 2,000 junior NCOs, all ten schools would have produced about 20,000 qualified soldiers. Of course, NCO training occurred at other corps-of-arms schools in Canada too, all for about half of the total wartime force that remained in Canada. *A15 Link* 2, 11/12 (September 1943) and *A14 Aldershot News* 1, 3 (May 1943), both available at the Canadian War Museum — Military History Research Centre.

20 Charles D. Kipp, *Because We Are Canadians: A Battlefield Memoir* (Toronto and Vancouver: Douglas and McIntyre, 2003), 27–29.

21 CMHQ Monthly Trg Liaison Letter No. 7 – Apr 44, dated 8 May 1944, Directorate of History and Heritage (DHH), file 312.032 (D1).

22 Fred Cederberg, *The Long Road Home: The Autobiography of a Canadian Soldier in Italy in World War II* (Don Mills, ON: General), 145.

23 Stanley Scislowski, *Not All of Us Were Brave* (Toronto: Dundurn Press, 1997), 203.

24 Craig B. Cameron, *Born Lucky: RSM Harry Fox, MBE, One D-Day Dodger's Story* (St. Catharines, ON: Vanwell, 2005), 78–79.

25 Charles Cromwell Martin, *Battle Diary: From D-Day and Normandy to the Zuider Zee and VE* (Toronto: Dundurn Press, 1994), 77.

26 2 CIB [Canadian Infantry Brigade] WD, 16, 18, and 21 February 1944, LAC, RG24-C-3, vol. 14077 (reel T-11074).

27 Syllabus NCO Wing – Course No. 4, appended to 2 CID Trg Sch WD for January 1945, LAC, RG24-C-3, vol. 16864.

28 Canadian Army (Overseas) routine order no. 1412, LAC, RG24-C-3, vol. 9888, file 2/TRG SCH MISC/1.

29 Appendix 4 to North Shore (New Brunswick) Regiment [NS(NB)R] WD for October 1942, Training Syllabus; Appendix 6 to WD for December 1942, Syllabus for Regimental N.C.O.s School No. 2; Appendix 5 to WD for January 1943, Regimental N.C.O.s School Syllabus; and Appendix 1 to WD for December 1942, Regimental Part 1 Orders, dated 6 December 1942, all in LAC, RG24-C-3, vol. 15126.

30 Report on 1st Course, undated, Appendix 3 to 1 Cdn Inf Div Trg School WD for January 1945, and Lieutenant-Colonel J.W. Ritchie to GOC 1 Cdn Inf Div, 14 February 1945, Appendix 4 to 1 Cdn Inf Div Trg School WD for February 1945, both LAC, RG24-C-3, vol. 16864.

Bibliography

Archival Sources

Canadian War Museum—Military History Research Centre, Ottawa
George Metcalf Archival Collection

Department of National Defence, Directorate of History and Heritage
Army Headquarters Reports
Canadian Army Overseas Honours and Awards
Canadian Military Headquarters Reports
Kardex files

Historica Canada
Military History Oral Collection

Library and Archives Canada, Ottawa
Department of National Defence Records, Second World War, Record Group 24 series
General H.D.G. Crerar Papers, Manuscript Group 30-E157

The National Archives, Kew, UK
War Office Files
Army Orders (WO 123/81)

University of Victoria, British Columbia
Military History Oral Collection

Books and Articles

Bercuson, David. *Our Finest Hour: Canada Fights the Second World War.* Toronto: HarperCollins, 2015.
Brown, Andrew. "New Men in the Line: An Assessment of Reinforcements to the 48th Highlanders in Italy, January–October 1944." *Canadian Military History* 21, 3 (2012): 35–47.
Brown, Gordon, and Terry Copp. *Look to Your Front – Regina Rifles: A Regiment at War.* Waterloo, ON: Laurier Centre for Military, Strategic and Disarmament Studies, 2001.
Burns, E.L.M. "How to Train the Militia." *Canadian Defence Quarterly* 16, 2 (1939): 148–56.
–. *Manpower in the Canadian Army, 1939–1945.* Toronto: Clarke, Irwin, 1956.
Byers, Daniel. "Canada's Zombies: A Portrait of Canadian Conscripts and Their Experiences during the Second World War." In *Forging a Nation: Perspectives on the*

Canadian Military Experience, edited by Bernd Horn, 155–76. St. Catharines, ON: Vanwell, 2002.

–. *Zombie Army: The Canadian Army and Conscription in the Second World War*. Vancouver: UBC Press, 2016.

Cameron, Craig B. *Born Lucky: RSM Harry Fox, MBE, One D-Day Dodger's Story*. St. Catharines, ON: Vanwell, 2005.

Canada. Department of Militia and Defence. *The King's Regulations and Orders for the Canadian Militia, 1917.* Ottawa: Department of Militia and Defence, 1917.

Canada. Department of National Defence. *Canadian Active Service Force/Canadian Army Routine Orders*. September 1939–June 1945. Volumes 1–12. Ottawa: King's Printer, 1939–45.

–. *Canadian Army Training Pamphlet No. 8: How to Qualify, 1941*. Ottawa: King's Printer, 1941.

–. *Canadian Army Training Pamphlet No. 13: Map Using, 1942*. Ottawa: King's Printer, 1942.

–. *General Orders, 1937.* Ottawa: King's Printer, 1937.

–. *General Orders, 1939*. Ottawa: King's Printer, 1940.

–. *General Orders, 1940*. Ottawa: King's Printer, 1941.

–. *How to Qualify: Instructions on the Qualification of Officers and Other Ranks for Promotion – Non-Permanent Active Militia, 1938*. Ottawa: King's Printer, 1938.

–. *How to Qualify: Instructions on the Qualification of Officers and Other Ranks for Promotion – Non-Permanent Active Militia, 1939*. Ottawa: King's Printer, 1940.

–. *Infantry Section Leading, 1938*. Ottawa: King's Printer, 1940.

–. *Infantry Training: Training and War, 1937*. Ottawa: King's Printer, 1939.

–. *Infantry Training Part I – The Infantry Battalion, 1944*. Ottawa: King's Printer, 1944.

–. *Infantry Training Part VIII – Fieldcraft, Battle Drill, Section and Platoon Tactics, 1944*. Ottawa: King's Printer, 1944.

–. *The King's Regulations and Orders for the Canadian Militia, 1917*. Ottawa: King's Printer, 1917.

–. *The King's Regulations and Orders for the Canadian Militia, 1926*. Ottawa: King's Printer, 1926.

–. *The King's Regulations and Orders for the Canadian Militia, 1939*. Ottawa: King's Printer, 1941.

–. *Mobilization Instructions for the Canadian Militia, 1937*. Ottawa: King's Printer, 1937.

–. *Physical Standards and Instructions for the Medical Examination of Recruits for the Canadian Active Service Force and for the Non-Permanent Active Militia, 1940*. Ottawa: J.O. Patenaude, Printer to the King's Most Excellent Majesty, 1940.

–. *Physical Standards and Instructions for the Medical Examination of Recruits for the Naval, Military and Air Services, 1938*. Ottawa: J.O. Patenaude, Printer to the King's Most Excellent Majesty, 1938.

–. *Physical Standards and Instructions for the Medical Examination of Serving Soldiers and Recruits for the Canadian Army, Active and Reserve 1943 (Second Edition)*. Ottawa: King's Printer, 1943.

–. *Programme of Work for Section Leaders' Course*. Ottawa: J.O. Patenaude, Printer to the King's Most Excellent Majesty, 1940.

–. *Report of the Department of National Defence for the Fiscal Year Ending March 31 ...* Multiple vols. Ottawa: King's Printer, 1936–45.

Canada. Dominion Bureau of Statistics. *General Review and Summary Tables*. Vol. 1 of *Eighth Census of Canada, 1941*. Ottawa: King's Printer, 1950. http://publications.gc.ca/collections/collection_2017/statcan/CS98-1941-1.pdf.

–. *Population – Local Subdivisions*. Vol. 2 of *Eighth Census of Canada, 1941*. Ottawa: King's Printer, 1950. http://publications.gc.ca/collections/collection_2017/statcan/CS98-1941-2.pdf.

Cederberg, Fred. *The Long Road Home: The Autobiography of a Canadian Soldier in Italy in World War II*. Don Mills, ON: General, 1984.

Connolly, Kevin. "Soldiering On: The Long-Term Effects of the Dieppe Raid on the 2nd Canadian Division." MA thesis, Royal Military College of Canada, 2016.

–. *The Necessary War: Canadians Fighting the Second World War 1939–1943*. Toronto: Allen Lane, 2014.

Copp, Terry. *Cinderella Army: The Canadians in Northwest Europe, 1944–1945*. Toronto: University of Toronto Press, 2006.

–. *Fields of Fire: The Canadians in Normandy*. Toronto: University of Toronto Press, 2014.

Copp, Terry, and William J. McAndrew. *Battle Exhaustion: Soldiers and Psychiatrists in the Canadian Army, 1939–1945*. Montreal and Kingston: McGill-Queen's University Press, 1990.

D'Amours, Caroline. "Canadian Military Culture and Tactical Training, 1940–1944: The Making of Infantry Junior NCOs." *Journal of Military History* 82, 4 (October 2018): 1175–98.

–. "'Notre tâche est de rendre les hommes prêts au combat': La formation des sous-officiers de renfort d'infanterie du Canada pendant la Seconde Guerre mondiale." PhD diss., University of Ottawa, 2015. https://ruor.uottawa.ca/handle/10393/31958.

–. "Reassessment of a Crisis: Canadian Infantry Reinforcements during the Second World War." *Canadian Army Journal* 14, 2 (Summer 2012): 72–89.

Dancocks, Daniel G. *The D-Day Dodgers: The Canadians in Italy, 1943–1945*. Toronto: McClelland and Stewart, 1991.

Davidson, Melissa. "Preaching the Great War: Canadian Anglicans and the War Sermon, 1914–1918." MA thesis, McGill University, 2012.

Delaney, Douglas. *The Imperial Army Project: Britain and the Land Forces of the Dominions and India, 1902–1945*. Oxford: Oxford University Press, 2017.

–. *The Soldiers' General: Bert Hoffmeister at War*. Vancouver, UBC Press, 2005.

D'Este, Carlo. *Decision in Normandy*. New York: Konecky and Konecky, 1994.

Dickson, Paul Douglas. *A Thoroughly Canadian General: A Biography of General H.D.G. Crerar*. Toronto: University of Toronto Press, 2007.

Engen, Robert. *Canadians under Fire: Infantry Effectiveness in the Second World War*. Montreal and Kingston: McGill-Queen's University Press, 2009.

–. *Strangers in Arms: Combat Motivation in the Canadian Army, 1943–1945*. Montreal and Kingston: McGill-Queen's University Press, 2016.

English, John A. *The Canadian Army and the Normandy Campaign: A Study of Failure in High Command*. New York: Praeger, 1991.

–. *On Infantry*. Rev. ed. Westport, CT: Praeger, 1994.

Fennell, Jonathan. *Combat and Morale in the North African Campaign: The Eighth Army and the Path to El Alamein*. Cambridge: Cambridge University Press, 2011.

–. *Fighting the People's War: The British and Commonwealth Armies and the Second World War*. Cambridge: Cambridge University Press, 2019.

French, David. *Military Identities: The Regimental System, the British Army, and the British People c. 1870–2000.* Oxford: Oxford University Press, 2005.

–. *Raising Churchill's Army: The British Army and the War against Germany, 1919–1945.* Oxford: Oxford University Press, 2000.

Graham, Dominick. *The Price of Command: A Biography of General Guy Simonds.* Toronto: Stoddart, 1993.

Granatstein, J.L. *The Best Little Army in the World: The Canadians in Northwest Europe, 1944–1945.* Toronto: HarperCollins, 2015.

–. *Canada's Army: Waging War and Keeping the Peace.* Toronto: University of Toronto Press, 2002.

–. *The Generals: The Canadian Army's Senior Commanders in the Second World War.* Toronto: Stoddart, 1993.

Granatstein, Jack, and J. Mackay Hitsman. *Broken Promises: A History of Conscription in Canada.* Toronto: Oxford University Press, 1977.

Great Britain. War Office. *Extracts from Manual of Military Law 1929, Reprinted for Use in the Canadian Army.* Ottawa: King's Printer, 1941.

–. *Infantry Section Leading, 1938.* Ottawa: King's Printer, 1941.

–. *Infantry Training Part I – The Infantry Battalion, 1944.* Ottawa: King's Printer, 1944.

–. *Infantry Training Part VIII – Fieldcraft, Battle Drill, Section and Platoon Tactics, 1944.* Ottawa: King's Printer, 1944.

–. *Infantry Training: Training and War, 1937.* Ottawa: King's Printer, 1939.

–. *Manual of Elementary Drill (All Arms), 1935.* Ottawa: King's Printer, 1940.

–. *Operations: Military Training Pamphlet No 23, Part 1-General Principles, Fighting Troops and their Characteristics.* Ottawa: King's Printer, 1942.

Hart, Russell A. *Clash of Arms: How the Allies Won in Normandy.* Boulder, CO: Lynne Rienner, 2001.

Harris, Stephen. *Canadian Brass: The Making of a Professional Army, 1860–1939.* Toronto: University of Toronto Press, 1988.

Haycock, Ronald G. "'The Stuff of Armies': The NCO throughout History." In *Backbone of the Army: Non-Commissioned Officers in the Future Army,* edited by Douglas L. Bland, 9–23. Montreal and Kingston: McGill-Queen's University Press, 2000.

Hayes, Geoffrey W. *Crerar's Lieutenants: Inventing the Canadian Junior Army Officer, 1939–45.* Vancouver: UBC Press, 2017.

Horn, Bernd. "A Timeless Strength: The Army's Senior NCO Corps." *Canadian Military Journal* (Spring 2002): 39–48.

Kipp, Charles D. *Because We Are Canadians: A Battlefield Memoir.* Toronto and Vancouver: Douglas and McIntyre, 2003.

Liedtke, Gregory. "Canadian Offensive Operations in Normandy Revisited." *Canadian Military Journal* 8, 2 (Summer 2007): 60–68.

Maker, John. "The Essex Scottish Regiment in Operation Atlantic: What Went Wrong?" *Canadian Military History* 18, 1 (Winter 2009): 7–19.

Martin, Charles Cromwell. *Battle Diary: From D-Day and Normandy to the Zuider Zee and VE.* Toronto: Dundurn Press, 1994.

McDougall, Robert L. *A Narrative of War: From the Beaches of Sicily to the Hitler Line with the Seaforth Highlanders of Canada, 10 July 1943–8 June 1944.* Ottawa: The Golden Dog Press, 1996.

McGowan, Mark. *The Imperial Irish: Canada's Irish Catholics Fight the Great War, 1914–1918.* Montreal and Kingston: McGill-Queen's University Press, 2017.

Milner, Marc. *Stopping the Panzers: The Untold Story of D-Day*. Lawrence: University Press of Kansas, 2014.

Nicholson, G.W.L. *The Canadians in Italy, 1943–1945*. Vol. 2 of *Official History of the Canadian Army in the Second World War*. Ottawa: Queen's Printer, 1956.

Pellerin, R. Daniel. "Battle Drill Comes to Canada, 1942–1945." *Canadian Army Journal* 16, 1 (2015): 49–69.

Place, Timothy Harrison. *Military Training in the British Army, 1940–1944: From Dunkirk to D-Day*. London and Portland, OR: Frank Cass, 2000.

Portugal, Jean. *We Were There: A Record for Canada*. Vol. 2. Shelburne, ON: Royal Canadian Military Institute Heritage Society, 1998.

Queen-Hughes, R.W. *Whatever Men Dare: A History of the Queen's Own Cameron Highlanders of Canada, 1935–1960*. Winnipeg: Bulman Brothers, 1960.

Rice, Gary Harold. *Paratrooper: The Story of the 1st Canadian Parachute Battalion's First Regimental Sergeant Major, Warrant Officer Class 1, Wendell James (Knobby) Clark*. Carleton Place, ON: GEHR, 1999.

Rickard, John Nelson. *The Politics of Command: Lieutenant-General A.G.L. McNaughton and the Canadian Army, 1939–1943*. Toronto: University of Toronto Press, 2010.

Roy, Reginald H. "Mutiny in the Mountains: The Terrace 'Incident'." In *Men at War: Politics, Technology and Innovation in the Twentieth Century*, edited by Timothy Travers and Christon Archer, 49–67 (Chicago: Precedent, 1982).

Russell, Peter A. "BC's 1944 'Zombie' Protests against Overseas Conscription." *BC Studies* 122 (1999): 49–76.

Sanderson, Robert Miles, and Marie Sanderson. *Letters from a Soldier: The Wartime Experiences of a Canadian Infantryman, 1943–1945*. Waterloo, ON: Ecart Press, c. 1993.

Scislowski, Stanley. *Not All of Us Were Brave*. Toronto: Dundurn Press, 1997.

Smith, Kenneth B. *"Duffy's Regiment": A History of the Hastings and Prince Edward Regiment*. Toronto: Dundurn Press, 1987.

Stacey, C.P. *Arms, Men and Governments: The War Policies of Canada, 1939–1945*. Ottawa: Queen's Printer, 1970.

–. *The Canadian Army 1939–1945: An Official Historical Summary*. Ottawa: King's Printer, 1948.

–. "Canadian Leaders of the Second World War." *Canadian Historical Review* 66 (March 1985): 64–72.

–. *Six Years of War: The Army in Canada, Britain and the Pacific*. Vol. 1 of *Official History of the Canadian Army in the Second World War*. Ottawa: Department of National Defence and the Queen's Printer, 1955.

–. *The Victory Campaign: The Operations in North-West Europe, 1944–1945*. Vol. 3 of *Official History of the Canadian Army in the Second World War*. Ottawa: Department of National Defence and the Queen's Printer, 1960.

Strickland, Tod. "Creating Combat Leaders in the Canadian Corps: The Experiences of Lieutenant-Colonel Agar Adamson." In *Great War Commands: Historical Perspectives on Canadian Army Leadership 1914–1918*, edited by Andrew B. Godefroy, 201–38 (Kingston, ON: Canadian Defence Academy Press, 2010).

Whitaker, W. Denis, and Shelagh Whitaker. *Tug of War: The Allied Victory That Opened Antwerp*. 2nd ed. Toronto: Stoddart, 2000.

Index

Note: "(i)" after a page number indicates an illustration or figure; "(t)" after a page number indicates a table. For abbreviations in entries and subentries, please see the Abbreviations list on pp. xiii–xiv. Numbered units are indexed first in a separate group, followed by training centres and schools A11 to S17 in a second separate group; all other units are indexed alphabetically.

1 Canadian Base Reinforcement Group (1 CBRG), 201, 256*n*146
1 Canadian Infantry Training Regiment (1 CITR), 204
1st Canadian Armoured Brigade, 194
1st Canadian Army. *See* First Canadian Army
1st Canadian Corps. *See* Canadian Corps (later 1st Canadian Corps)
1st Canadian Division, 85, 112, 185, 228*n*33; discipline/professionalism in, 91–92, 94; fitness standards of, 60; heavy casualties of, 110–11; Infantry Reinforcement Unit of (1 CIRU), 29(t), 189; interarm training by, 65, 69
1st Canadian Infantry Brigade (1 CIB), 65, 110, 228*n*31
1st Canadian Infantry Division, 15, 67, 69, 92, 194; NCO training by, 114–15, 215
1st Canadian Parachute Battalion, 15, 27, 38, 77, 227*n*14
1st Canadian Tank Brigade, 92
2 Canadian Infantry Holding Unit, 165–66
2nd Canadian Armoured Regiment, 229*n*46
2nd Canadian Corps, 114, 177, 193, 200–1
2nd Canadian Division, 73, 92, 152, 228*n*33; at Dieppe, 61, 259*n*6; fitness standards of, 60; Infantry Reinforcement Unit of (2 CIRU), 188, 253*n*91; interarm training by, 66; NCO refresher training in, 85
2nd Canadian Infantry Brigade (2 CIB), 87, 237*n*55; interarm training by, 65;

marching exercise of, 60; NCO training by, before July 1943, 108–10; NCO training by, in theatre of operations, 110–13, 214–15
2nd Canadian Infantry Division: NCO training by, 115, 116–17, 118, 215
2nd Lothians and Border Horse (UK), 193
2nd/10th Dragoons (Ontario militia unit), 40
3rd Canadian Division, 61, 92, 115–16, 219*n*32
3rd Canadian Infantry Brigade (3 CIB), 61–62, 67, 87
3rd Canadian Infantry Division, 15; D-Day experiences of, 219*n*32; NCO training by, 117
4th Canadian Armoured Division, 15, 36, 237*n*37; field reports disseminated by, 193; and LOB policy, 197; NCO training by, 116, 117–18
4th Canadian Division, 29(t)
4th Canadian Infantry Division, 107, 237*n*37
5th Canadian Armoured Division: interarm training by, 68, 229*n*46; NCO training by, 116, 117, 118
5th Canadian Division, 112
6th Canadian Division, 8, 124
7th Canadian Division, 8, 124, 177
7th Canadian Infantry Brigade, 86
7th Corps (later Canadian Corps), 85, 228*n*33, 252*n*65; Junior Leaders School of, UK, 29(t), 85, 106–7, 108

8th Canadian Division, 8, 124, 177–78
10th Canadian Infantry Training Battalion (10 Trg Bn), 168, 169, 197; NCO conversion course run by, 168(t), 168
11th Canadian Infantry Brigade (11 CIB), 145–46, 229*n*46
12th Canadian Tank Regiment (Three Rivers Regiment), 69
13th Canadian Infantry Brigade (13 CIB), 13, 29(t), 167, 169
13th Canadian Infantry Training Brigade (13 CITB), 29(t), 167, 169, 197, 199
14th Army Tank Battalion, 67
21st Army Group (UK), 114, 196, 200
48th Highlanders of Canada, 35, 71, 100, 176, 228*n*31

A11 Advanced Infantry Training Centre (Borden, ON), 123(i)
A12 Infantry Training Centre (Farnham, QC), 177
A14 Infantry Training Centre (Aldershot, NS), 121, 191, 192(i), 260*n*19
A15 Advanced Infantry Training Centre (Shilo, MB), 128–29, 244*n*75, 260*n*19; Methods of Coaching course at, 139–40; parachute instructors at, 134(i); School of Instruction at, 129; syllabus for assistant instructor course at, 133–35, 137, 137(t)
A25 Canadian Small Arms Training Centre (Long Branch, ON), 137, 140–41, 243*n*62
A26 Small Arms School (Nanaimo, BC), 137, 243*n*62
A29 Advanced Infantry Training Centre (southwestern Ontario), 129–33, 177; army pamphlets used at, 131; locations of, 130, 131; syllabus for instructor/NCO course at, 130(t), 130–31; updated curriculum at, 132–33, 137, 242*n*45
A34 Special Training Centre (Sussex, NB), 29(t), 147–49, 245*n*101, 256*n*140

absent without leave (AWL) charges, 35, 36
acting ranks, 27–28, 175, 186, 221*n*14, 232*n*5; Instructional Cadre and, 50; at mobilization, 55, 81, 99

Advanced Infantry Training Centres (AITCs). *See* A11, A15, *and* A29
Alexander, Gordon, 61, 227*n*9
Alexander, Harold, 73
Algonquin Regiment, 32, 40–41, 82
American Infantry School (Fort Benning, GA), 141, 142
amphibious assault training. *See* assault landing craft (ALC) training
Anderson, Thomas, 55, 225*n*42
anti-tank guns: (2-pound), 30, 174; (6-pound), 30, 133, 138
anti-tank rifles, 56, 65, 96–97; and interarm training, 66, 68, 69; training in use of, 30, 109, 129, 142, 146, 153, 165. *See also* Projector, Infantry, Anti-Tank (PIAT)
Apps, C.J.S. (Syl), 242*n*45
Arbour, Abram, 77
Argyll and Sutherland Highlanders of Canada, 33, 198
armoured corps, 15, 123, 196, 200, 250*n*19, 251*n*42; brigades of, 4, 9, 183, 194; conversion training for, 245*n*97, 249*n*72; divisions of, 8, 9, 10, 17; interarm training with, 60, 64–70, 112, 146, 193, 211, 226*n*3; regiments of, 65–66, 168, 183, 197, 218*n*11, 229*n*46; soldiers from, as attached to British units, 183–84; training drills for, 192–93. *See also* 4th Canadian Armoured Division; 5th Canadian Armoured Division
armoured vehicles: German, 96–97; training in recognition of, 95, 137, 165
artillery corps, 15, 123, 250*n*19; conversion training for, 245*n*97, 248*n*63, 249*n*72; interarm training with, 60, 64–70, 112, 226*n*3; physical requirements for, 46, 62; promotion in, 48, 49; and redistribution of members, 173, 183, 185, 196, 200; regiments of, 218*n*11; training for, 108, 141
Ashton, Ernest, 51–52, 225*n*30
assault landing craft (ALC) training, 60, 62, 70–71, 109
awards, military: Distinguished Conduct Medal (DCM), 70, 77; Military Cross, 41, 77; Military Medal, 36, 37, 78(i), 223*n*57; Victoria Cross, 33, 141, 249*n*5

battalions: battle drill by, 73–75; definition of, 218n11; interarm training by, 65, 67–68, 228n31, 229n46; and LOB policy, 197; Montgomery's visits to/comments on, 86–88, 175, 212; and NCO conversion, 168–70, 197, 206; NCO ranks within, 6–8, 7(t), 218n12, 237n57, 241n19; and NCO rotation, 184; NCO training in, 91, 100–5, 119; number of, 126, 212; promotions in, 169, 198

battle drill, 30, 31(t), 72–75, 78, 177, 188; at Canadian School of Infantry, 74, 75, 141–42, 143–44, 145; at Canadian Training School (UK), 31(t), 73–74, 75, 152, 153(i); handbooks on, 75, 131; at Junior Leaders School, 124, 125, 127(t); at School of Instruction, 132; success of, 211

bayonets, 63, 106–7; training in instruction on, 165; training in use of, 116, 129, 224n17

Beament, A.W., 194

Bean, W.A., 191

Beattie, William, 64

Black Watch (Royal Highland Regiment of Canada), 86, 118

Borden, ON: NCO training at, 39, 123(i), 207

Boys anti-tank rifle, 96–97

Bren light machine gun, 75, 76, 96, 243n64; carrier for, 31, 129, 131, 193; training in, 157

Brennan, Ralph, 198

brigades: armoured/tank, 92, 194; battle drill by, 74; interarm training by, 65, 66–68, 211, 228n31, 228n39, 228–29nn42–43, 229n46; Montgomery's assessments of, 86–87; and NCO conversion, 248n63, 249n73; NCO training by, 4, 9, 29(t), 30, 99, 108–10, 111–13, 167, 214–15; number of, 8, 177. *See also* brigades, training; *specific numbered brigades and entries starting with* formations, NCO training by

brigades, training: 10th Canadian (10 CITB), 168, 168(t), 169, 197; 13th Canadian (13 CITB), 29(t), 167, 169, 197, 199

British Columbia: conscription in, 218n23; education in, 22, 220n9; and

Japan's entry into war, 124; Officers Training Centre in, 217n6; small arms school in, 137, 243n62. *See also* Canadian School of Infantry (Vernon, BC)

British School of Infantry (Barnard Castle), 141, 142, 146

Brooke, Alan, 89

Brown, James, 166

Browne, B.W., 186

Buck, John, 189

built-up areas, fighting in, 60, 71–72

Burns, E.L.M., 34

Cahill, Victor, 39

Calgary Highlanders, 99, 205; as battle drill advocates, 73, 230n68; NCO training by, 102–3

Cameron Highlanders of Ottawa, 39–40, 193

Canadian Active Service Force (CASF), 57; Routine Order No. 22 on regimental courses, 81, 82

Canadian Corps (later 1st Canadian Corps), 34, 61, 169, 180, 228n33; Crerar's training regimen for, 62; interarm training by, 66–68, 70–71; and NCO refresher training, 155; NCO training by, before July 1943, 103–10; NCO training by, in theatre of operations, 112–14; and sending of NCOs back to Canada, 174–77; and sending of NCOs to North Africa, 190; and sending of permanent force NCOs overseas, 185–87; and senior leadership's role in NCO training/development, 85–94

Canadian Corps, Junior Leaders School of. *See* Junior Leaders School of Canadian Corps (formerly 7th Corps), UK

Canadian Field Force (later Canadian Active Service Force), 55, 57

Canadian Infantry Reinforcement Units (CIRUs), 157, 188, 189, 195, 253n91

Canadian Infantry Training Regiments (CITRs), 167–68, 204–5, 248n71, 249n73

Canadian Military Headquarters, UK, courses run by. *See* centralized NCO training programs (UK); *entries starting with* Canadian Training School (CTS), UK

Canadian Military Headquarters (CMHQ), UK, 34, 69, 214; centralized NCO training run by, 4–5, 151–71, 209, 212; continuing management of NCO corps by, 172–207, 213; fitness complaints by, 62

Canadian Officers' Training Corps, 178

Canadian Reinforcement Units (CRUs), 11, 34, 167, 179(i), 184, 193, 194–95; difficulties in finding instructors for, 155–56, 158, 170, 179–82, 213; NCO conversion course for, 168, 168(t); post-D-Day redistribution/quality of, 199–206, 207; rotation of field units with, 187–90. *See also* Canadian Reinforcement Units (CRUs), training for NCOs in; reinforcements

Canadian Reinforcement Units (CRUs), training for NCOs in, 154–61, 170; Course 824 (refresher), 154–57, 158; Course 1213 (refresher), 158–60; CTS Methods of Instruction sub-wing for instructors in, 166–67, 248n61; flow chart diagram of, 162(i); tests of elemental training (TOETs), 157–58, 160; two-week refresher course, 160–61, 161(t), 247n40; weekly lectures by field unit commanders, 200–1

Canadian School of Infantry, Number 2 (Battle Wing) of, 142, 143–46, 147; battle drill training at, 142, 143–44; demise of, as caused by personnel deployments, 145; as kept updated by overseas reports, 145–46; précis of course content issued by, 144–45

Canadian School of Infantry (Vernon, BC), 29(t), 141–47, 149; battle drill training at, 74, 75, 141–42, 143–44, 145; wings of, 142–43. *See also* Canadian School of Infantry, Number 2 (Battle Wing) of

Canadian Scottish Regiment, 35–36, 102, 137–38

Canadian Small Arms School, 49, 50, 243n62

Canadian Small Arms Training Centres (CSATCs), 29(t), 82, 137–41, 243n62

Canadian Training School, CRU training run by. *See* Canadian Reinforcement Units (CRUs), training for NCOs in

Canadian Training School, Methods of Instruction sub-wing of, 166–67, 248n61

Canadian Training School, Number 3 (Weapons) Wing of, 152–54, 165–66, 247n32; Course 804 (NCO qualification), 152–54, 154(t), 215

Canadian Training School, Number 3 (Weapons) Wing of, regimental instructors' courses at, 165–66; Course 808 (3-inch Mortar), 165–66; Course 809 (Platoon Weapons), 165; Course 810 (Medium Machine Gun), 165, 166; Course 812 (Snipers), 165

Canadian Training School, Number 5 (Battle) Wing of, 152, 153(i)

Canadian Training School (CTS), UK, 9, 29, 29(t), 142, 146, 151–71, 173, 209; battle drill training at, 31(t), 73–74, 75, 152, 153(i); instructional skills training at, 166–67, 181, 194, 213; wings of, 152. *See also entries starting with* Canadian Training School

Cape Breton Highlanders, 61

Carleton and York Regiment, 86–87

Carriere, Felix, 113

Cave, John Clifford, 50, 65–66

Caya, George, 82

Cederberg, Fred, 214

centralized NCO training programs (Canada), 4–5, 121–50, 209, 212; for advanced tactical training, 141–47; at dedicated training centres, 122–33; and NDHQ control of syllabuses, 9, 18, 128, 139, 215, 241n27; refresher courses at, 147–49; for training instructors, 133–41. *See also entries* A11–A34; Junior Leaders School, Canada (Mégantic, QC); *entries starting with* Canadian School of Infantry

centralized NCO training programs (UK), 151–71; CMHQ qualification and refresher courses in, 152–61; after D-Day, 166–70; for training regimental instructors, 163–66. *See also* Canadian Reinforcement Units (CRUs), training for NCOs in; *entries starting with* Canadian Training School

Churchill, Winston, 133

Clark, John Arthur, 259*n*11

Clark, Wendell, 37–38, 38(i)

combined army-navy operations, 64, 70–71; assault landing craft training, 60, 62, 70–71, 109

commanders. *See* division commanders; platoon commanders; unit commanders

company sergeants major (CSMs; warrant officers class 2), 7(t), 87, 128, 194; as CMHQ course attendees, 154, 155, 215; with NPAM/reserve experience, 40(t); roles of, 7, 140, 152; stories of, 19–20, 33, 35, 38, 39, 40, 77, 78(i), 106, 189–90, 191, 214

Connolly, Alexander, 19–20

conscripts: as NCOs, 12–13, 43, 198, 223*n*56; as serving in home defence, 13, 42, 121, 123, 184; and Terrace Mutiny, 218*n*33; training of, 123, 131, 148, 173, 199–200, 245*n*102

Copp, Terry, 219*n*32; and William J. McAndrew, 84

corporal, rank of, 7(t), 7–8, 221*n*14; and progression to rank of sergeant, 24–27, 99, 102–3, 198; promotion to, 20, 26, 28, 33, 49, 81, 86; qualification certificate for, 47–48; reversion to, 27, 32; training for promotion to, 102, 112. *See also* corporals; *entries starting with* lance corporal

corporals, 3, 7–8, 208; as casualties, 113, 177; fitness of, 62; as instructors, 50, 51, 70–71, 176, 177, 178, 199; leadership roles of, 7, 62, 72, 75, 113; with NPAM experience, 40(t); as reinforcements, 34; rotation of, 189–90; as sent from Canada to UK, 183–84; as sent from Italy to UK, 194; stories of, 32–33, 35–36, 112, 118, 176, 214; training for, 104–5, 108, 111, 124, 142, 148, 155, 165–66, 215

Cosens, Aubrey, 33

Crerar, H.D.G. (Harry), 62, 67, 71, 80, 93(i), 97, 155, 196, 200, 203–4; and Montgomery's inspection/assessment of Canadian NCOs, 63–64, 85–89, 175,

176; and NCO training/discipline, 85–92; and sending of NCOs back to Canada, 172–76

Crocker, John, 117

Cronk, Edward, 182–83

Currie, Andrew, 39–40

Daley, F.E., 191

Daly, John, 40

D'Amours, Caroline, 6, 12, 217*n*9, 258*n*2

Dancocks, Daniel, 196

Davidson, William, 64

D-Day, 19, 195; casualties of, 35, 38; NCO training after, 166–70; NCO training of reinforcements in UK after, 199–201; quality of reinforcements trained after, 201–6, 207; 3rd Canadian Division and, 219*n*32

decentralized NCO training programs, as run by units and formations, 4, 9, 19, 31, 99–120, 208–15; in battle drill, 73, 74–75; before July 1943, 99–110, 118–19; in interarm cooperation, 64–71; overview of, 29, 29(t); in theatre of operations, 110–18, 119–20. *See also* units, NCO training by; *entries starting with* formations, NCO training by

Defence Scheme No. 3, 51–53, 57, 222*n*43

Derasp, Edmond, 166–67

D'Este, Carlo, 64–65

Dieppe Raid (1942), 59, 61, 259*n*6

discipline: problems of, as overcome by NCOs, 35–37, 44; and professionalism, 80, 85–94; in sub-units, 76–77

division commanders: and heavy casualties, 110–11; and interarm training, 69; and NCO training/development, 91–92, 155; promotions by, 28; and sending of NCOs to UK, 185

divisions: battle drill by, 74; heavy casualties of, 110–11, 197, 219*n*32; interarm training by, 65–71, 229*n*46; NCO training by, 9, 29(t), 30, 99, 107–8, 114–18, 197; number of, 4, 8–9, 10(t), 85, 121, 122–24, 177–78; prewar mobilization plans for, 51, 52, 55, 56–57. *See also specific numbered divisions; entries starting with* formations, NCO training by

Downey, Joseph, 31–32
Duddle, Joseph McPhee, 70
Duffy, Angus, 110, 195, 255*n*127
Dugas, Paul Eugene, 27, 221*n*18

Edmonton Regiment, 222*n*33; and Exercise Tiger booing incident, 89–90; instructors from, 109; Montgomery's assessment of, 87; stories of NCOs in, 34–35; Warrant Officers School of Qualification run by, 100. *See also* Loyal Edmonton Regiment
Elgin Regiment, 40
Elliott, John, 35, 37
Ellis, Ross, 205
Engen, Robert, 6, 21, 68, 75, 138, 204, 205, 211, 243*n*64
engineers, corps of, 15, 108, 141, 185, 196, 200, 202(i), 245*n*10, 250*n*19, 258*n*173; conversion training for, 248*n*63, 249*n*72; instructors in, 50; interarm training with, 60, 64–70, 146, 193, 211, 226*n*3; regiments of, 218*n*11; soldiers from, as attached to British units, 183. *See also* field engineering, training in
English, John, 6, 64, 219*n*32
Essex Scottish Regiment, 33, 118, 210, 259*n*6
Evans, Edward George, 27
Exercise Pooch, 193–96
Exercise Tiger, 61, 89–90

Fennell, Jonathan, 82–83
field engineering, training in, 30, 104, 117, 125, 157, 201
First Canadian Army, 75, 114, 163, 169, 213, 219*n*32, 221*n*31; under Crerar, 67, 246*n*28; full complement of, 9, 126, 212; and interarm training, 66, 67, 229*n*44, 229*n*46; and management of NCO corps, 173, 177, 180, 188–89, 193, 194–200, 207; and NCO discipline/professionalism, 93–94; and NCO rotations, 173, 188–89; and reinforcement training, 155, 158; under Simonds, 197, 202(i), 202–3; and small arms training, 164–65
First World War, 21, 57, 141; LOB concept and, 196–97; NCOs as veterans of, 20,

35, 39, 42–43, 43(t), 128, 142–43, 223*n*55, 234*n*64; weapons/equipment from, 3, 45, 95, 96. *See also* Veterans Guard
fitness and skills. *See* fitness standards, for NCOs; skills, as required of NCOs
fitness standards, for NCOs, 59–64, 79, 83–84, 227*n*14; as adopted by NDHQ, 62–64; and culling of older men, 60, 61, 63–64, 79; Exercise Tiger as test of, 61; and marching capacity, 59–62; physical efficiency test of, 62–63
flame-throwers, 30, 97
formation: definition of, 218*n*18
formations, NCO training by, 29, 29(t), 31, 99, 105–18, 119–20, 209. *See also* decentralized NCO training programs, as run by units and formations; units, NCO training by; *entries starting with* formations, NCO training by
formations, NCO training by, before July 1943, 105–10; commanders' interest in, 109, 237*n*55; at instructional cadre courses, 107–8; at junior leaders schools, 106–7, 108; as run by 2 CIB, 108–10
formations, NCO training by, in theatre of operations, 110–18, 119–20; commanders' interest in, 111, 111(i), 117; and feedback to units, 118; and local fighting conditions, 114–16, 119; in platoon commander duties, 111–12; and proximity of enemy, 116–17; and replacement of casualties, 110–14, 116, 117–18, 119; as run by divisions, 9, 29(t), 30, 99, 107–8, 114–18, 197; as run by 2 CIB, 110–13, 214–15. *See also specific numbered divisions*
Fort Osborne Barracks (Winnipeg): NDHQ training school at, 128; PPCLI training at, 99–100
Foulkes, Charles, 114
Fox, Harry, 45, 214
French, David, 82, 94–95
Fusiliers de St-Laurent, 27
Fusiliers Mont-Royal, 86

German forces, 59, 95, 98, 140, 149, 163, 216, 219*n*32; Canadian NCOs' heroism vs, 35–36, 77, 78(i); identification of, 214; interarm cooperation by, 65; methods/ tactics of, as studied by NCOs, 112, 114, 115, 117, 124, 131, 143, 192–93, 215; in North Africa, 95, 193, 196; and sinking of Canadian troop ship, 186; threat of invasion by, 64, 65, 119, 121, 170; weapons/ tanks of, 68, 96–97, 112, 116–17, 210

Germany, 52, 95, 116, 122; army of, 6, 83, 95; Canadian forces in, 116–17, 202(i), 221*n*28; defeat of, 117, 118, 133, 198, 242*n*50

Gibson, Thomas, 113

Goodburn, Wilfred, 198, 256*n*143

Graham, Howard D., 111(i)

Granatstein, Jack, 210

Gray, John, 32–33

Gray, Raymond, 102, 137–38

Green, George, 77

Gregg, Milton F., 141–43, 144

grenades, 243*n*64; training in instruction on, 165, training in use of, 109, 201, 203, 224*n*17

Grimshaw, Wilfred, 71

Harper, Burton, 26, 176

Hastings and Prince Edward Regiment, 76, 110, 164, 195

Hawkes, G.W., Sergeant's Qualification Certificate of, 48(i)

Hayes, Geoffrey, 6, 83, 141–42, 258*n*2

Highland Light Infantry of Canada, 96(i), 191

Hitler Line (Italy), 69–70, 76, 113

Hoffmeister, Bert, 111, 117

How to Qualify (army pamphlet on training/examinations), 81, 82

Howard, William, 35–36, 37

Hudson, Ralph, 101

Infantry Section Leading (training pamphlet), 76

infantry senior NCOs. *See entries starting with* NCOs, senior infantry

Infantry Training Centres. *See entries* A12 *and* A14

Instructional Cadre (Permanent Active Militia), 38, 45, 46, 49–51, 57, 100, 129

instructional cadres, training/development of, 14, 71, 136; at Borden, ON, 123(i); at Saint-Hyacinthe, QC, 107–8

Instructors' Handbook on Fieldcraft and Battle Drill, 75

interarm (infantry/artillery/armour/ engineers) cooperation, 60, 64–70, 211, 226*n*3; and British experience in North Africa, 68, 95, 229*n*44; challenges of, 70; as crucial, 193; division-/formation-level training in, 65–68; historians' views of, 64–65; in Italy, 69–70, 146; at Normandy, 68; in Sicily, 69

Italy, 52; Canadian campaigns in, 10(t), 17, 69–70, 72, 145–46, 169, 237*n*58; Hitler Line assault in, 69–70, 76, 113; LOB policy in, 197; NCO training in, 9, 69, 110–15, 118, 119, 212, 214, 215, 256*n*146; NCOs sent back to Canada from, 11, 177, 180; NCOs sent to UK from, 160, 173, 193–96, 213; reinforcements in, 34, 201, 203, 204, 205; stories of NCOs in, 32–33, 35, 76, 214. *See also* Operation Husky (Allied invasion of Sicily, 1943)

Jacobs, James, 188, 253*n*91

Japan, 52, 242*n*50; army/forces of, 143, 174; entry into war by, 8, 123–24; surrender of, 133, 137

Johnston, William, 33

Joyes, Robert, 33

Junior Leaders School, Canada (Mégantic, QC), 9, 20, 28–30, 29(t), 124, 125–27, 129–30, 149, 159, 209, 212, 213; six-week syllabus at, 126, 127(t); three-week syllabus at, 126, 126(t)

Junior Leaders School of Canadian Corps (formerly 7th Corps), UK, 29(t), 85, 106–7, 108

Keith, Walter, 76

Keller, Rodney, 92

Kemp, John, 77

King's Regulations and Orders for the Canadian Militia (KR&Os), 47

Kipp, Charles, 214

Kitching, George, 196

Lacroix, Arthur, 193
Lake Superior Regiment, 36
lance corporal, rank of: as appointment, 7(t), 8, 221*n*14; and progression to sergeant, 24(t), 102–3, 198; promotion to, 26, 35, 36, 37–38, 81, 112; as skipped, 25, 26(t), 27. *See also* lance corporals
lance corporals, 88, 103, 124; with NPAM experience, 40(t); training for, 102, 104, 105, 106, 152, 156, 215; stories of, 26, 32, 35, 36, 37–38, 102–3, 118. *See also* lance corporal, rank of
lance sergeant, rank of: as appointment, 7(t), 8, 221*n*14; and progression to sergeant, 24(t), 32, 198; as skipped, 20, 25, 26(t), 27. *See also* lance sergeants
lance sergeants: culling of, 64; with NPAM experience, 40(t); rotation of, 188; training for, 102, 114, 115, 215; as training to be instructors, 165
Laprade, Albert, 36, 37
Lee-Enfield rifles, 15, 95
"left out of battle" (LOB) policies, 196–97, 203
Lewis machine guns, 96, 165
Lincoln and Welland Regiment, 20, 214
Lord Strathcona's Horse (Royal Canadians), 93(i), 193, 229*n*46
Loyal Edmonton Regiment, 204, 222*n*33; and battle drill, 74; and LOB policy, 197; stories of NCOs in, 32, 33, 112. *See also* Edmonton Regiment

M test (aptitude), 83, 84, 176
MacBrien, James, 51
MacGregor, Ernest M.K., 74, 197
machine gun. *See* Bren light machine gun
machine-gun units/companies, 49, 65, 116, 118, 122, 166, 173, 200
MacKendrick, Harry, 100–1
Mackenzie, Colin, 47
Mackenzie, Ian, 52, 55, 225*n*42
MacLeod, William, 191, 192(i)
MacMillan, A.M., 191
management of NCO training/development, 172–207; mitigating high casualty rates, 196–98; posting perma-

nent force NCOs to overseas army, 185–87; rotating NCOs between field units and reinforcement pool, 187–90; sending experienced NCOs back to Canada, 173–83, 207; sending experienced NCOs to UK from Italy, 193–96, 206; sending experienced NCOs to UK to train post-D-Day reinforcements, 199–201, 207; sending NCOs to British Army in North Africa, 190–93; sending NCOs overseas for short attachments, 183–85; and success of post-D-Day reinforcement training, 201–6, 207
Martin, Charles Cromwell, 19, 106–7, 189–90, 214
Masterson, James, 177
Matthews, A. Bruce, 117
McCulloch, L.W., 193
McDougall, C.M., 111, 238*n*64
McDougall, Robert, 69–70
McIlvena, Arthur, 34–35
McManus, J.E.E., 77
McMullen, F.D., 70
McMurray, L.J., 102, 112
McNaughton, Andrew, 85, 90, 93, 195; and sending of Canadian NCOs to UK, 193–94, 206, 254*n*116; and sending of NCOs back to Canada, 172, 173–74, 175, 177–78, 187
Mégantic, QC, Junior Leaders School in. *See* Junior Leaders School, Canada (Mégantic, QC)
Militia Act, 53
Miller, Glen, 32
Mobilization Instructions for the Canadian Militia, 1937, 53–55, 81
Montague, P.J., 155, 200, 203–4
Montgomery, Bernard, 86–90, 92, 110, 172; and Exercise Tiger, 61, 89–90; on importance of drill, 163; inspection/assessment of Canadian NCOs by, 63, 86–89, 97, 175, 176, 212, 233*n*31; and sending of Canadian NCOs to UK, 173, 193–94, 200, 254*n*116
Moore, William, 71
mortars, 71, 191; and mortar–infantry cooperation, 145, 168. *See also* mortars, training in use of

mortars, training in use of, 73, 117, 123, 129, 131, 138, 146; (2-inch), 97, 152, 165, 174; (3-inch), 31, 97, 142, 165–66, 243*n*64; (4.2-inch), 31, 97
Murray, Austin, 40–41
Murray, T.D., 116
Murray, William, 189

National Defence Headquarters (NDHQ), Canada, 8, 208; and battle drill, 74–75; centralized NCO training run by, 4–5, 9, 121–50, 209, 212; continuing management of NCO corps by, 172–207; control of training syllabuses by, 9, 18, 128, 139, 215, 241*n*27; fitness standards adopted by, 62–64; and instructional cadre training, 107–8; military districts of, 46; and prewar army, 45, 46, 49–55; and wartime NCO training/development, 81–85. *See also* centralized NCO training programs (Canada)
National Resources Mobilization Act (NRMA), 12–13, 123, 173, 223*n*56
navy, army cooperation with. *See* combined army–navy operations
NCO corps, Canadian, 3–18; milestones in growth of, 9, 10(t), 16(i), 18; prewar status of, 46–47; problems of developing, 3–4, 8–11; rank structure/terminology of, 6–8, 7(t); scholarship on, 6, 11–17; senior members of, 19–44; terminology of, 8. *See also entries starting with* NCO; *entries for specific ranks*
NCO corps, Canadian, training/development of, 3–18; army's continuing management of, 172–207; and army's fitness/skill expectations, 59–79; centralized programs of, in Canada, 121–50; centralized programs of, in UK, 151–71; decentralized programs of, at unit/formation level, 99–120; in prewar period, 3–4, 45–58; two-track system for, 4–6, 9–11, 17–18, 28–29, 29(t), 208–16; wartime drivers of, 80–98. *See also specific topics*
NCOs, senior infantry, 19–44; centralized training for, 28–31, 29(t); demographics of, 19–24; as instructors, 32–33, 38–39;

as overcoming disciplinary issues, 35–37, 44; with prior military experience, 37–43, 44; and progression to rank of sergeant, 19, 24–26, 24(t), 25(t), 44; recognition of qualities/skills in, 34–37, 44; as reinforcements, 31–34; as reverting backward in rank, 27–28, 28(t); as skipping ranks to advance, 26(t), 26–27, 31–32; specialist training courses for, 30–31; as warrant officers, 43(t), 43–44. *See also entries starting with* NCOs, senior infantry
NCOs, senior infantry, demographics of, 19–24; age, 20, 34–35, 44; education, 20–21, 21(t), 22; pre-service employment/trade, 22, 23(t); province/jurisdiction of origin, 22, 23(t), 24; religion, 21, 22(t)
NCOs, senior infantry, with prior military experience, 37–44; as conscripts, 43; as First World War veterans, 42–43; from NPAM/reserve force, 39–42, 40(t)–42(t), 43, 44; from permanent force, 37–39, 43–44
NCOs and Warrant Officers Course (Canada), 141
Nelson, Charles, 35
Nerissa, SS (Canadian troop ship), 186
Netherlands: Laprade's heroism in, 36; NCO training in, 68, 116–17, 215
New Brunswick. *See* A34 Special Training Centre (Sussex, NB); North Shore (New Brunswick) Regiment
Nicholson, G.W.L., 69
non-commissioned officers, Canadian. *See entries starting with* NCO corps, Canadian
Non-Permanent Active Militia (NPAM; later Reserve Army), members of, 19, 39–44, 53–58, 209–10, 223*n*49, 234*n*64; certificates of qualification for, 47–48; continuous service limits for, 46–47, 53; defence budget shortfalls and, 41, 56; depots for, 54; as First World War veterans, 42–43; length of service by, 41, 41(t); with previous military experience, 8, 11–14, 20, 37, 39–44, 40(t), 43(t), 45, 210; promotion of, 39–41, 45, 47–48,

49, 100, 182, 221*n*14; retention of ranks by 24, 27, 27(t), 39, 40(t), 55; time period served by, 41–42, 42(t); training of, 46, 49–50, 51, 57

North Africa: British forces in, 68, 95, 97, 190, 229*n*44; Canadian NCOs sent to, 190–93, 192(i); German forces in, 95, 193, 196

North Shore (New Brunswick) Regiment, 26–27, 64; instructors from, 176; NCO training by, 104–5, 215; North Africa veterans in, 191

Northney, HMS (UK shore establishment): assault landing craft training at, 70–71

Nova Scotia, 46; AITC in, 121, 191, 192(i), 260*n*19. *See also* West Nova Scotia Regiment

Nova Scotia Highlanders, 87

Odlum, Victor, 66

Officer Cadet Training Unit (OCTU), UK, 5, 152, 173

Officers Training Centres (OTCs), Canada, 5–6; in Brockville, ON, 33, 142, 217*n*6; in Gordon Head, BC, 217*n*6; in Trois-Rivières, QC, 177, 217*n*6

Ontario, 22, 40, 46, 128; basic training centre in, 177; Infantry Training Centre in, 123(i); NCOs from, 19–20, 22, 23(t), 198, 242*n*45; OTC in, 33, 142, 217*n*6. *See also* A25 Canadian Small Arms Training Centre; A29 Advanced Infantry Training Centre

Operation Atlantic (Battle of Normandy, 1944), 210, 259*n*6

Operation Blockbuster (Allied invasion of Germany, 1945), 190

Operation Chesterfield (Canadian assault on Hitler Line, 1944), 69–70

Operation Crusader (North Africa), 97

Operation Husky (Allied invasion of Sicily, 1943), 40, 62, 80, 85, 93, 105, 126

Operation Overlord (Battle of Normandy, 1944), 38, 62, 184–85, 195, 200, 201, 205

Operation Torch (North Africa), 190

Operation Varsity (Allied airborne support mission, 1945), 77

Ortona, Italy, 72, 207; NCO school in, 110, 112, 214. *See also* Italy

parachute instruction: at Shilo, MB, 134(i)

paratroopers: 1st Canadian battalion of, 15, 27, 38, 77, 227*n*14

Paré, Viateur, 177

Pengelley, Lewis, 38–39

Permanent Active Militia (PAM), members of, 3, 8, 11–12, 14, 46–47; mobilization of, 51–55; as prewar instructors/ Instructional Cadre members, 38, 45, 46, 48, 49–51, 53–54, 57, 100, 129; qualification examinations for, 47–49, 48(i); as senior infantry NCOs, 20, 24, 27, 37–39, 43–44

Phelan, Frederick, 156

Place, Timothy Harrison, 65

platoon commanders, 7, 26, 72, 89, 101; as casualties, 113, 190; in Italy, 146; and LOB policy, 197; and sub-unit leadership/discipline, 76–77; training for, 85, 115, 142, 152, 165; training of NCOs in duties of, 111–12

platoon sergeants, 7, 25, 89–90, 111, 169, 214; help given to commanders by, 76; training for, 85, 106, 108, 109, 115, 125

platoon sergeants major (PSMs; warrant officers class 3), 7(t)

platoon weapons, 129, 152–53; training in instruction on, 122, 129, 152–53, 165, 166, 188; training in use of, 31, 104, 105, 115, 143, 145, 168; in urban combat, 71

platoon(s), 7, 218*n*11; battle drill by, 73, 74, 75; and Exercise Tiger booing incident, 89–90; as headed by NCOs, 19, 35–36, 75, 77–78, 95, 170; interarm training by, 67, 68; marching by, 61; training relevant to, 104, 105–7, 113, 114–16, 132–33, 143, 160, 161, 167, 168, 195, 229*n*43, 241*n*13

prewar period, Canadian army in, 3–4, 45–58; certification/promotion policies for, 47–49; entrance requirements/ physical standards for, 46; instructors/ Instructional Cadre of, 38, 45, 46, 48, 49–51, 53–54, 57; mobilization plans for, 51–57; NCO corps of, 46–47; NDHQ

and, 45, 46, 49–55; and training/
development of NCOs, 47–51. *See also*
prewar period, mobilization plans in
prewar period, mobilization plans in,
51–57; as affected by years of budget
austerity, 56; and Defence Scheme No.
3, 51–53, 57, 222*n*43; and *Mobilization
Instructions*, 53–55, 81; and need for
qualified NCOs, 54–55, 57–58
Princess Patricia's Canadian Light
Infantry (PPCLI): at A29 AITC, 128–
29; instructors from, 109, 111, 128;
Montgomery's assessment of, 87; NCO
rotation in, 189; NCO training by, 99–
100, 103–4; stories of NCOs in, 35–36,
39, 50, 64, 71, 113, 198, 256*n*143
private, rank of, 7(t); and appointment
to lance corporal, 27, 32, 36, 37–38, 112,
221*n*14; demotion to, for reallocation
purposes, 198; reversion to, 27, 33, 36,
40. *See also* privates
privates: as First World War veterans, 42;
with NPAM experience, 39, 40(t); promotion of, 13, 20, 27, 31–32, 37–38, 86;
as reinforcements, 160–61, 205, 207, 212;
stories of, 26, 90, 118, 132, 198, 242*n*45;
training for, 70, 96(i), 99–100, 108, 112–
13, 115, 119, 132, 135, 152, 201, 215, 233*n*30
Projector, Infantry, Anti-Tank (PIAT), 97,
211, 243*n*64; training in use of, 96(i),
165, 201, 203
promotions, prewar, 9, 13–14; qualification exams/certificates for, 42, 47–48,
48(i), 50–51, 54, 57; standards for, 45,
47, 50–51, 81. *See also entries starting
with* promotions, wartime
promotions, wartime, 14, 15, 54–55, 80–82;
as commanders' decisions, 28, 49, 55,
80–82, 97, 151, 231*n*3; as conditional
on performance, 28, 81, 232*n*5; of conscripts, 13, 198; disciplinary problems
and, 35–37; and discontinuation of
qualification exams, 54, 81, 97, 231*n*3;
and M Test, 83; Montgomery on, 86–
88, 212; NCO selection boards and, 88–
89; of NPAM members, 39–41, 45; of
older men, 34–35; of permanent force
members, 37–39; to rank of sergeant,

24–27, 24(t), 25(t), 44; as rapid, 13, 24,
26–27, 31–32, 54, 64; of reinforcements,
32–34; and reversion in rank, 27–28,
28(t); skipping ranks in, 26(t), 26–27;
from within units, 31–32, 215
promotions, wartime, and NCO training,
208–9, 215; at AITCs, 128; by battalions,
169, 198; and catch-up/refresher courses,
99, 102–3, 119, 166, 215; before July 1943,
99, 100, 102–5; post-D-Day, 166; in
theatre of operations, 110, 114, 115, 118,
119; in UK, 151, 159
PULHEMS profile (physical/medical
assessment), 83–84, 148

quartermasters sergeant, 7(t), 218*n*13; as
instructors, 50, 109, 224*n*21; stories of,
32, 34; training for, 30, 48
Quebec: Infantry Training Centre in, 177;
instructional cadre course in, 107–8;
NCOs from, 22, 23(t); Officers' Training
Centre in, 177, 217*n*6. *See also* Junior
Leaders School, Canada (Mégantic,
QC); Royal 22nd Regiment
Queen's Own Cameron Highlanders, 77,
129, 210
Queen's Own Rifles: NCO rotation in,
189–90, 256*n*149; NCO training in, 100–
2; and older NCOs, 61; stories of NCOs
in, 19, 33, 45, 106–7

Ralston, James, 131
ranks. *See* acting ranks; *entries for specific
ranks*
Régiment de la Chaudière, 61, 177, 221*n*18,
251*n*42
regimental sergeants major (RSMs;
warrant officers class 1), 7(t), 194; as
instructors, 104; Montgomery's respect
for, 88; with NPAM experience, 40(t);
roles of, 7, 140, 152; School of Infantry
course for, 146; stories of, 38, 38(i), 39,
214
Regina Rifle Regiment, 35, 76, 103, 188
reinforcements, 4, 5, 11, 13, 14, 31–34;
infantry crisis of, 114, 146, 148, 169, 196,
205–6, 212; post-D-Day training of, 199–
201, 207; promotion of, 13, 32–34; qual-

ity of, 20, 32–34, 201–6, 207; rotation of field units with, 187–90; as veterans, 33–34; warrant officers as, 34, 195. *See also* Canadian Infantry Reinforcement Units (CIRUs); *entries starting with* Canadian Reinforcement Units (CRUs)

Reserve Army. *See* Non-Permanent Active Militia

Rhodes, J.K., 105

rifles, 63, 73, 129, 152; importance of training in use of, 140; Lee-Enfield, 15, 95; in urban combat, 71; "zeroing" of, 201–2

Rigley, Edward Joseph, 105

Roberts, John, 92, 180–81

Ronson and Wasp flame-throwers, 97

Royal Air Force (RAF), 95

Royal Canadian Regiment, 61, 111(i), 141, 228*n*31; instructors from, 32–33, 38–39, 176, 177; NCO training by, 100, 103; stories of NCOs in, 32–33, 37–39, 40

Royal Highland Regiment of Canada (Black Watch), 86, 118

Royal Navy, 95

Royal Regiment of Canada, 87

Royal 22nd Regiment: disciplinary problems of, 90; marching exercise by, 61–62; Montgomery's assessment of, 87; NCO rotation in, 176; NCO training by, 100, 103; quality of reinforcements from, 204–5; at regimental instructor training, 165–66

S17 Canadian School of Infantry. *See* Canadian School of Infantry (Vernon, BC); Canadian School of Infantry, Number 2 (Battle Wing)

Salmon, Harry, 91–92, 237*n*55

Sanderson, Robert, 132, 144

Scheldt, Battle of the (1944), 169, 206, 207, 221*n*31

Scislowski, Stanley, 214

Scott, J.F., 73,

Seaforth Highlanders of Canada, 204, 259*n*11, 259*n*14; instructors from, 108–9; interarm training by, 65, 69–70; Montgomery's assessment of, 87; NCO training by, 100; and urban combat, 72

sergeant, rank of, 7(t), 7–8; progression to, 19, 24–27, 24(t), 25(t), 28, 34–40, 44, 99, 102–3, 198, 210; and promotion to higher rank, 28, 32; qualification certificate for, 47–48, 48(i); and reversion to lower rank, 27, 32, 33. *See also* lance sergeant, rank of; lance sergeants; platoon sergeants; quartermasters sergeant; sergeants

sergeants, 7–8; fitness of, 62; as instructors, 38–39, 49–51, 96(i), 109, 177, 178, 199; leadership roles of, 7, 62, 68, 76–78, 103–4, 105, 169–70; in North Africa, 190–93; with NPAM experience, 40(t); as reinforcements, 20, 34, 182; rotation of, 188–89; as sent from Canada to UK, 183–84; as sent from Italy to UK, 194; stories of, 20, 32–40, 82, 188, 189, 214; training for, 99–120, 140–41, 143, 144, 148, 154–56, 165–66, 215

sergeants major. *See* company sergeants major; platoon sergeants major; regimental sergeants major

Sherbrooke Fusiliers (27th Armoured Regiment), 65–66

Sicily, Allied invasion of. *See* Operation Husky (Allied invasion of Sicily, 1943)

Simonds, Guy, 69, 196, 197, 200, 202(i), 202–3, 205

skills, as required of NCOs, 59–60, 64–79; battle drill, 72–75; combined operations expertise, 60, 62, 64, 70–71, 79, 109; fighting in built-up areas, 60, 71–72; interarm cooperation expertise, 64–70, 95, 211; leadership within sub-units, 76–78. *See also* fitness standards, for NCOs

small arms training, for NCOs/instructors, 95–97, 109; at AITCs, 129–30, 137–38; at CMHQ course, 152–53, 154(t); at CRU refresher course, 161(t); at CTS Weapons Wing, 165–66. *See also* Canadian Small Arms School; Canadian Small Arms Training Centres; platoon weapons; *specific weapons*

Smith, James A., 78(i)

Smith, Kenneth B., 76, 164, 195

Smith, Russell, 103

Smythe, Conn, 204, 257*n*167
Snow, Eric, 145–46
Snow, Thomas, 156
South Saskatchewan Highlanders: James A. Smith of, 78(i)
South Saskatchewan Regiment, 129
Spry, Daniel, 117
Stacey, C.P., 3, 6, 11–12, 37, 64, 196, 205, 208, 209
Steele, William, 32
Sten sub-machine gun, 96, 211; training in, 109, 165
Stormont, Dundas and Glengarry Highlanders, 195, 251*n*42
Strathy, J.G.K., 203
Stuart, Kenneth, 141, 174–75, 176, 178, 180, 246*n*28
sub-machine guns. *See* Sten sub-machine gun; Thompson sub-machine gun
sub-units: battle drill training of, 73, 142; definition of, 218*n*11; high turnover in, 189–90; interarm training by, 65, 70; leadership in, 76–78; leadership training in, 90–91, 101–2; promotion in, 48, 49–50, 88; refresher training for, 237*n*58; terminology/definitions of, 218*n*11
syllabuses, of NCO training programs, 47, 81; at A15 AITC, 129, 137, 137(t); at A29 AITC, 130(t), 130–31; for assistant instructor course, 133–35, 137, 137(t); at brigade level, 109; at Canadian School of Infantry, 142; for CMHQ Course 804, 153, 154(t); for CRU refresher course, 160, 161(t); at division level, 115–16; for instructional cadre course, 107, 108; at Junior Leaders School, 124, 125–27, 126(t), 127(t); for NCO conversion course, 168, 168(t); NDHQ control of, 9, 18, 128, 139, 215, 241*n*27; at unit level, 105

tactical exercises without troops (TEWTs): at Canadian training centres, 140, 143, 145; in interarm training, 66, 67, 228*n*39; as led by commanding officers, 92; in theatre of operations, 114–15, 116, 239*n*89

tanks, 64–70, 112, 114–15, 116, 146, 168, 192–93; Churchill, 65–66; German, 96–97, 210; identification of, 137; learning to bail out of, 192; in urban combat, 71–72. *See also* anti-tank guns; anti-tank rifles; armoured corps; *numbered armoured units*
tests of elementary training (TOETs), 157–58, 160
Thompson sub-machine gun, 95–96; training in, 109, 165, 203
Thomson, Sydney W., 72
Tomlinson, Tommy, 76
training/development of Canadian NCOs. *See* NCO corps, Canadian, training/development of

unit: terminology/definition of, 218*n*11. *See also* sub-units
unit commanders: and battle drill, 75; and NCO discipline/professionalism, 80, 89–94; and NCO training/development, 86, 88–89, 94, 97, 102, 117, 170, 202–4, 216; and older NCOs, 63–64; physical training run by, 59–60; promotions by, 28, 49, 55, 80–82, 97, 151, 231*n*3; and sending of NCOs out for instructional training, 11, 155–56, 158, 170, 213; as sent to UK for lectures to reinforcements, 200–1
units, NCO training by, 29, 29(t), 31, 99–105, 119–20; in battle drill, 73, 74–75; before July 1943, 99–105; in interarm cooperation, 64–71; in theatre of operations, 110, 114. *See also* decentralized NCO training programs, as run by units and formations; *entries starting with* formations, NCO training by; *specific units*
urban combat, 60, 71–72

Veterans Guard, 42–43, 128, 223*n*55; School of Infantry wing for, 142–43
Vokes, Chris, 69, 109, 110–11, 117, 237*n*55

warrant officers, 146, 155, 186, 187, 198; classes of, and corresponding infantry ranks, 7(t), 8; conversion of, 168–69; as CTS instructors, 181; as having previous military experience, 12, 40(t), 43(t), 43–44, 210; NCOs and Warrant Officers Course for, 141; as older men, 86; promotions to rank of, 20, 28, 35, 38–39, 40, 45, 48–50, 55, 64, 81, 103, 232n5; as reinforcements, 34, 195; School of Qualification for, 100. *See also* company sergeants major; regimental sergeants major

wartime training/development of NCOs, 80–98; aptitude testing and, 83, 84, 176; evolving nature of, 94–97; NDHQ and, 81–85; physical/mental assessments and, 82–85; promotion policy and, 81–82; PULHEMS profile used in, 83–84, 148; senior leadership's role in, 80–81, 85–94, 97–98; in tactical procedures, 95; in use of new weapons, 95–97, 96(i).

See also wartime training/development of NCOs, senior leadership's role in

wartime training/development of NCOs, senior leadership's role in, 80–81, 85–94, 97–98; in aftermath of Montgomery's inspection, 63, 86–89, 97, 175, 176, 212, 233n31; Crerar's emphasis on, 85–92, 93(i); disciplinary problems and, 89–91, 92

weapons training. *See* platoon weapons; small arms training, for NCOs/instructors; *specific weapons*

Weeks, Ernest, 199, 256n146

West Nova Scotia Regiment, 177, 204, 229n43; NCO training by, 104, 105, 234n63

Whitaker, Denis, 59, 221n31

Wilson, Sgt. D., PIAT instruction by, 96(i)

Wyman, Robert, 92

STUDIES IN CANADIAN MILITARY HISTORY

John Griffith Armstrong, *The Halifax Explosion and the Royal Canadian Navy: Inquiry and Intrigue*

Andrew Richter, *Avoiding Armageddon: Canadian Military Strategy and Nuclear Weapons, 1950–63*

William Johnston, *A War of Patrols: Canadian Army Operations in Korea*

Julian Gwyn, *Frigates and Foremasts: The North American Squadron in Nova Scotia Waters, 1745–1815*

Jeffrey A. Keshen, *Saints, Sinners, and Soldiers: Canada's Second World War*

Desmond Morton, *Fight or Pay: Soldiers' Families in the Great War*

Douglas E. Delaney, *The Soldiers' General: Bert Hoffmeister at War*

Michael Whitby, ed., *Commanding Canadians: The Second World War Diaries of A.F.C. Layard*

Martin F. Auger, *Prisoners of the Home Front: German POWs and "Enemy Aliens" in Southern Quebec, 1940–46*

Tim Cook, *Clio's Warriors: Canadian Historians and the Writing of the World Wars*

Serge Marc Durflinger, *Fighting from Home: The Second World War in Verdun, Quebec*

Richard O. Mayne, *Betrayed: Scandal, Politics, and Canadian Naval Leadership*

P. Whitney Lackenbauer, *Battle Grounds: The Canadian Military and Aboriginal Lands*

Cynthia Toman, *An Officer and a Lady: Canadian Military Nursing and the Second World War*

Michael Petrou, *Renegades: Canadians in the Spanish Civil War*

Amy J. Shaw, *Crisis of Conscience: Conscientious Objection in Canada during the First World War*

Serge Marc Durflinger, *Veterans with a Vision: Canada's War Blinded in Peace and War*

James G. Fergusson, *Canada and Ballistic Missile Defence, 1954–2009: Déjà Vu All Over Again*

Benjamin Isitt, *From Victoria to Vladivostok: Canada's Siberian Expedition, 1917–19*

James Wood, *Militia Myths: Ideas of the Canadian Citizen Soldier, 1896–1921*

Timothy Balzer, *The Information Front: The Canadian Army and News Management during the Second World War*

Andrew B. Godefroy, *Defence and Discovery: Canada's Military Space Program, 1945–74*

Douglas E. Delaney, *Corps Commanders: Five British and Canadian Generals at War, 1939–45*

Timothy Wilford, *Canada's Road to the Pacific War: Intelligence, Strategy, and the Far East Crisis*

Randall Wakelam, *Cold War Fighters: Canadian Aircraft Procurement, 1945–54*

Andrew Burtch, *Give Me Shelter: The Failure of Canada's Cold War Civil Defence*

Wendy Cuthbertson, *Labour Goes to War: The CIO and the Construction of a New Social Order, 1939–45*

P. Whitney Lackenbauer, *The Canadian Rangers: A Living History*

Teresa Iacobelli, *Death or Deliverance: Canadian Courts Martial in the Great War*

Graham Broad, *A Small Price to Pay: Consumer Culture on the Canadian Home Front, 1939–45*

Peter Kasurak, *A National Force: The Evolution of Canada's Army, 1950–2000*

Isabel Campbell, *Unlikely Diplomats: The Canadian Brigade in Germany, 1951–64*

Richard M. Reid, *African Canadians in Union Blue: Volunteering for the Cause in the Civil War*

Andrew B. Godefroy, *In Peace Prepared: Innovation and Adaptation in Canada's Cold War Army*

Nic Clarke, *Unwanted Warriors: The Rejected Volunteers of the Canadian Expeditionary Force*

David Zimmerman, *Maritime Command Pacific: The Royal Canadian Navy's West Coast Fleet in the Early Cold War*

Cynthia Toman, *Sister Soldiers of the Great War: The Nurses of the Canadian Army Medical Corps*

Daniel Byers, *Zombie Army: The Canadian Army and Conscription in the Second World War*

J.L. Granatstein, *The Weight of Command: Voices of Canada's Second World War Generals and Those Who Knew Them*

Colin McCullough, *Creating Canada's Peacekeeping Past*

Douglas E. Delaney and Serge Marc Durflinger, eds., *Capturing Hill 70: Canada's Forgotten Battle of the First World War*

Brandon R. Dimmel, *Engaging the Line: How the Great War Shaped the Canada–US Border*

Meghan Fitzpatrick, *Invisible Scars: Mental Trauma and the Korean War*

Patrick M. Dennis, *Reluctant Warriors: Canadian Conscripts and the Great War*

Frank Maas, *The Price of Alliance: The Politics and Procurement of Leopard Tanks for Canada's NATO Brigade*

Geoffrey Hayes, *Crerar's Lieutenants: Inventing the Canadian Junior Army Officer, 1939–45*

Richard Goette, *Sovereignty and Command in Canada–US Continental Air Defence, 1940–57*

Geoff Jackson, *The Empire on the Western Front: The British 62nd and Canadian 4th Divisions in Battle*

Steve Marti and William John Pratt, eds., *Fighting with the Empire: Canada, Britain, and Global Conflict, 1867–1947*

Steve Marti, *For Home and Empire: Voluntary Mobilization in Australia, Canada, and New Zealand during the First World War*

Douglas E. Delaney and Serge Marc Durflinger, *Capturing Hill 70: Canada's Forgotten Battle of the First World War*

Peter Kasurak, *Canada's Mechanized Infantry: The Evolution of a Combat Arm, 1920–2012*

Sarah Glassford and Amy Shaw, eds., *Making the Best of It: Women and Girls of Canada and Newfoundland during the Second World War*

Alex Souchen, *War Junk: Munitions Disposal and Postwar Reconstruction in Canada*

George Belliveau and Graham W. Lea, eds., *Contact! Unload: Military Veterans, Trauma, and Research-Based Theatre*

Tim Cook and Jack J.L. Granatstein, eds., *Canada 1919: A Nation Shaped by War*

Arthur W. Gullachsen, *An Army of Never-Ending Strength: Reinforcing the Canadians in Northwest Europe, 1944–45*

Peter Farrugia and Evan J. Habkirk, *Portraits of Battle: Courage, Grief, and Strength in Canada's Great War*

Studies in Canadian Military History
Published by UBC Press in association with the Canadian War Museum